New York hustlers

ENCOUNTERS cultural histories

Series editors:
Roger Cooter
Harriet Ritvo
Carolyn Steedman
Bertrand Taithe

Over the past few decades cultural history has become the discipline of encounters. The issues raised by new 'turnings' – linguistic, pictorial, and spatial – through theorists such as Bourdieu, Foucault, Derrida, Deleuze, and Spivak have contributed to the emergence of cultural history as a forum for bold and creative exchange. This series places encounters – human, intellectual, and disciplinary – at the heart of historical thinking. *Encounters* provides an arena for exploring new and reassembled historical subjects, for stimulating perceptions and re-perceptions of the past, and for methodological challenges and innovations. It invites short, innovative and theoretically informed books from all fields of history.

Already published

Benjamin's Arcades: *An unGuided tour* Peter Buse, Ken Hirschkop, Scott McCracken and Bertrand Taithe

Poison, detection and the Victorian imagination Ian Burney

Plants, patients and the historian Paolo Palladino

Mourning becomes . . . : Post/memory, commemoration and the concentration camps of the South African War Liz Stanley

Dust Carolyn Steedman

Resisting history: Religious transcendence and the invention of the unconscious Rhodri Hayward

New York hustlers

Masculinity and sex in modern America

BARRY REAY

Manchester University Press

Copyright © Barry Reay 2010

The right of Barry Reay to be identified as the author of this work has been asserted by him in accordance with the Copyright, Designs and Patents Act 1988.

Published by Manchester University Press
Altrincham Street, Manchester, M1 7JA
www.manchesteruniversitypress.co.uk

British Library Cataloguing-in-Publication Data
A catalogue record for this book is available from the British Library

ISBN 978 0 7190 8007 4 *hardback*

ISBN 978 0 7190 8008 1 *paperback*

First published 2010

The publisher has no responsibility for the persistence or accuracy of URLs for any external or third-party internet websites referred to in this book, and does not guarantee that any content on such websites is, or will remain, accurate or appropriate.

Typeset in Sabon
by Servis Filmsetting Ltd, Stockport, Cheshire
Printed in Great Britain by Lightning Source

For Athina, far more than an old Greek goddess

Contents

	List of figures	*page* ix
	Acknowledgements	xi
	Prologue	1
1	Introduction	5
2	Contexts	34
3	Hustlers and trade	77
4	Sexualities	111
5	Effeminacy	147
6	Hustler hustled	188
7	Conclusion	234
	Epilogue	262
	Index	275

Figures

1	The Moss (Ross) Bar	page 2
2	Moss (Ross) Bar hustler	3
3	Map of New York City, circa 1940–60	6
4	Thomas Painter and 'buddy' at Coney Island	18
5	Thomas Painter and model	19
6	Transvestite prostitutes	24
7	Times Square hustlers and Johns (clients)	25
8	Times Square fairies or queens	26
9	Two New York hustlers	46
10	Groups of cross-dressed and effeminate men in police custody	48
11	Irish-American hustler	52
12	A sailor/hustler	53
13	Bowery hustler	54
14	Peg house owner in drag	56
15	Paul Cadmus, *Shore Leave*	57
16	Paul Cadmus, *Sailors and Floosies*	58
17	Jon Voight in *Midnight Cowboy*	78
18	Times Square 'undesirables'	81
19	Hustlers at the beach	83
20	42nd Street hustler	84
21	Times Square	86
22	Italian-American boxer/hustler	88
23	Coney Island trade	90
24	Bronx teenage gang member	91
25	Puerto Rican 'hustler'	93
26	Sailor trade in Kenneth Anger's film *Fireworks*	95
27	Sailors in Times Square	95
28	Henry Faulkner and two sailors	96
29	Times Square hustler and 'clip artist'	99
30	The hustler 'Biceps'	100
31	Hustler with jail tattoos	101
32	Puerto Rican gang members	116

List of figures

33	Puerto Rican 'hustler'	117
34	Hustler	119
35	Hustler	120
36	Times Square hustler	126
37	Italian-American hustler	127
38	Fairies and sailors	152
39	Fairies and pansies	153
40	William Haines	154
41	Homosexual drawings	162
42	Cliff Gorman in *Boys in the Band*	166
43	Marlon Brando as Stanley Kowalski	193
44	Edward Melcarth, Sculpture of hustler head	195
45	Italian-American hustler	196
46	Hustler	197
47	Edward Melcarth, *Last Supper*	198
48	*Blow Job*	199
49	*Thirteen Most Wanted Men*	200
50	*Rebel Without a Cause*	201
51	*Scorpio Rising*	202
52	Paul America in *My Hustler*	205
53	Jackie Curtis and Joe Dallesandro in *Flesh*	207
54	New York hustler	208
55	Male hustler	210
56	Hustler masculinity	211
57	Pornographic pose	212
58	'Flirtation' by Art-Bob	214
59	Dallesandro in a mirror	215
60	Jon Voight in *Midnight Cowboy*	216
61	Paul America in *My Hustler*	217
62	Hustler/hoodlum	218
63	Hustler	220
64	Wounded hustler	221
65	Hustler as Michelangelo's Adam	222
66	Paul Cadmus, *Playground*	223
67	*Forty Deuce*	241
68	Hustlers in Gus Van Sant's *My Own Private Idaho*	243
69	Gay hustler in Gregg Araki's *Mysterious Skin*	244
70	Hustler in Bruce LaBruce and Rick Castro's *Hustler White*	245
71	New York hustler	247
72	New York hustler	248
73	New York hustler	249
74	Herbert Huncke	264
75	Herbert Huncke	265

Acknowledgements

Although, given its subject matter, this book may well be classified as a history of homosexuality or gay culture when its cataloguing occurs, it actually is intended as an early instalment in a longer history of heterosexuality; as readers will see, I am interested in challenging some assumptions about the histories of both and will dwell on the many instabilities of sexual categories that are supposedly firmly established by the mid-twentieth century. Whether I, or those around me, will be able to sustain my interest in things historically sexual is another matter entirely.

I have many debts to acknowledge but would like to start with the just-mentioned those around me. Athina Tsoulis and our daughters, Alexa and Kristina Tsoulis-Reay, have been very patient. Whenever Alexa and Kristina visit us from overseas one of them has to sleep in a temporary bed, surrounded by bookcases groaning with literature relating to things hustler. (They probably negotiate the loser on the flight to New Zealand.) My parents too have always been supportive. Sadly, my mother died in 2008, mercifully really given the content of my book and her constant urging that I write about 'beautiful things': she did not have male prostitution in mind and would have been rather shocked by what awaits the reader. My father, however, is less easily scandalized.

I am grateful also to current and former colleagues. The History 102 (*Sexual Histories*) gang, Kim Phillips, Nina Attwood, and Claire Gooder, have been marvellous to teach with. And Nina and Claire also made teaching History 206/306 (*Making Sex*) a lot of fun. Moreover, Dr Attwood has acted latterly as a research assistant on this book, offering her disconcerting blend of enthusiastic encouragement and no-nonsense critique, while also hammering out inconsistencies in my footnoting. I owe much to people in the Department of History at Auckland and in the Faculty of Arts and University more widely, who have made institutional life easier and/or more entertaining and have facilitated the completion of this project in various ways. I am particularly indebted to Barbara Batt, James Belich, Charlotte Burgess, Malcolm Campbell, Jennifer Curtin, Raewyn Dalziel, Laurel Flinn, Erin Griffey, John Morrow, Nisha Saheed, Jennie Taylor, and Joe Zizek. The staff of the University Library, as always, has been unfailingly helpful. Igor Drecki very kindly produced the map.

Friends have helped to keep me on track (if I can use a railway metaphor that will have resonance shortly). In Auckland, Robyn Sutherland and Jennifer Curtin and Craig Symes are always good company, while Lauren Gunn has shown an interest in my hustlers project from its first inception. Overseas, Laura Accinelli is such a great host that I always visit her in Oakland, CA, upon entering and leaving the USA, even though I can no longer beat her son Nicholas at table tennis (ping pong) now that he is a teenager. Marta Vicente and Luis Corteguera, both historians at the University of Kansas, have invited me to Lawrence as well as meeting up with me in New York; they too have provided that winning combination of intellectual stimulus and merriment.

I have two special acknowledgments. In 2006 the Marsden Fund of the Royal Society of New Zealand awarded the three-year funding (Contract UOA0614) that made this book possible, my strand in a collaborative project with Annamarie Jagose and Lee Wallace called 'Acts and Identities: Towards a New Cultural History of Sex'. It proved to be a controversial awarding for reasons that I may discuss more deeply at a later date, though I will disclose that there were murmurs that the money involved could have been better spent on New Zealand's railway infrastructure and that the issue was raised both in Parliament and on talk-back radio! Amusingly (for two of us) the focus fell not on Reay and Wallace but on Jagose's project on the orgasm. Orgasms – fake, simultaneous – and their researcher bore the brunt of the attention, while the hustlers (and Lee's sexual life of apartments) slipped under the radar. Anyway, we are grateful to those who championed academic freedom and research support for the humanities during those rather bleak, anti-intellectual moments, including the Chairs of the Marsden Committee, the Vice Chancellor and Deputy Vice Chancellor of Auckland University, the Minister for Research, Science, and Technology, who was also Minister of Education (Tertiary), if I recall correctly, and the then president of our professional union. Annamarie and Lee, the combined second of my special debts, have been wonderful collaborators, providing critique, wit, and (non-Marsden-funded) cocktails, almost in equal measure – although it has felt like much of our teamwork has consisted of trying to get the funding initially, defending the decision (or rather refusing to justify ourselves) when we did get it, and then writing various reports on its progress.

Acknowledgements

I have been constantly impressed with the friendliness and efficiency of the various Libraries and Archives that I have consulted in my quest for hustler-related material. The Library of the Kinsey Institute for Research in Sex, Gender, and Reproduction, at Indiana University, has been absolutely crucial to my research. The Head of Library, Liana Zhou, and the Public Services Manager, Shawn Wilson, must have despaired of ever getting rid of the demanding visitor who kept returning: short visits to Bloomington were my preferred strategy for research in a town that, outside the archives, is a little less exciting than, say, New York. Thomas Albright, the Institute's System Analyst and Programmer very kindly reworked the Kinsey data used in Chapter 4. I am most grateful for their help.

I am also deeply appreciative of the assistance of the staff at Harry Ransom Center, University of Texas, Austin; National Archives and Records Administration, Washington, DC; University of Chicago Library Special Collections Research Center; Archives of American Art, Smithsonian Institution, Washington, DC; New York Public Library Manuscripts and Archives Division; State Library of Victoria, Melbourne, Australia; University of Delaware Library, Newark, Delaware; Rare Book, Manuscript, and Special Collections Library, Duke University, Durham, North Carolina; Manuscript Division, Moorland Spingarn Research Center, Howard University, Washington, DC; Fales Library Special Collections, Elmer Holmes Bobst Library, New York University; GLBT Historical Society Archives, San Francisco; Department of Special Collections, Stanford University Libraries, Stanford, California; and The Forbes Collection, New York. The artist Robert Morgan kindly wrote to me from Venice, providing information about Edward Melcarth.

I would like to express my thanks to the following for their permission to use illustrative material reproduced in this book: The Kinsey Institute for Research in Sex, Gender, and Reproduction; I. C. Rapoport; Tranz International Image Library/CORBIS; Whitney Museum of American Art; The Paul Cadmus Estate; Associated Press; Archives of American Art, Smithsonian Institution; Photofest; Viscopy Limited, Australia; Duke University Rare Book, Manuscript, and Special Collections Library; Georgia Museum of Art, The University of Georgia; The Forbes Collection, New York; and Bruce LaBruce. Fuller citation is made in the figure captions. Every effort has been made to trace the copyright owners of the images used in this book and anyone claiming copyright should get in touch with this author. I am exceptionally grateful to the New York artist Richard Taddei for his generosity with his personal photographic archive and fine collection of Edward Melcarth's photography of hustlers and trade.

I am excited that this book is appearing in the Manchester University

Acknowledgements

Press series, *Encounters: Cultural Histories*, and am appreciative of the early enthusiasm and encouragement of the Series Editors, Carolyn Steedman, Bertrand Taithe, and Roger Cooter. The Press's Emma Brennan, my Commissioning Editor, has been a delight to work with, as I had been counselled she would be. A few paragraphs from my Introduction (dealing with theoretical and historiographical matters) have been recycled from my 'Writing the modern histories of homosexual England', *Historical Journal*, 52 (2009), 213–33, but nearly everything that follows is new. Whether the money expended on its research and writing could have been better spent on rolling stock or tracks for the Auckland–Wellington railway is up to the reader to decide.

Prologue

Suddenly Neal leaned to me earnestly and said 'Jack I have something to ask of you – very important to me – I wonder how you'll take it – we're buddies aren't we?' 'Sure are, Neal.' He almost blushed. Finally he came out with it: he wanted me to lay Louanne. I didn't ask him why because I knew. He wanted to test something in himself and he wanted to see what Louanne was like with another man. We were sitting in Ross Bar on Eighth Avenue when he proposed the idea; we'd spent an hour walking Times Square looking for Hunkey. Ross Bar is the hoodlum bar of Times Square; it changes names every year. You walk in there and you don't see a single girl, even in the booths, just a great mob of young men dressed in all varieties of hoodlum cloth – from red shirts to zoot suits: it is also the hustler's bar, the boys who make a living among the sad old homos of the Eighth Avenue night. Neal walked in there with his eyes slitted to see every single face. There were wild Negro queers, sullen guys with guns, shiv-packing seamen, thin non-committal junkies, and an occasional well-dressed middleaged detective posing as a bookie and hanging around half for interest and half for duty. It was the typical place for Neal to put down his request. All kinds of evil plans are hatched in Ross Bar – you can sense it in the air – and all kinds of mad sexual routines are initiated to go with it. The safecracker not only proposes a certain loft on Fourteenth Street to the hoodlum but that they sleep together. Kinsey spent a lot of time in Ross Bar interviewing some of the boys; I was there the night his assistant came, in 1945. Hunkey and Allen were interviewed. Neal and I drove back to York Avenue and found Louanne in bed. Hinkle was roaming his ghost around New York. Neal told her what we had decided. She said she was pleased. I wasn't so sure myself. I had to prove that I'd go through with it. The bed was the bed my father had died in – I had given it to Allen a week before . . .
(Jack Kerouac, 1951)[1]

This long extract from *On the Road*, Jack Kerouac's famous manifesto of the Beat generation, was written in 1951 but not published until 2007. The 1957 edition had changed names to protect the guilty: Neal

1. The Moss (Ross) Bar, 1949. From the Thomas Painter Collection. Reproduced by permission of The Kinsey Institute for Research in Sex, Gender, and Reproduction, Inc.

[Cassady] was Dean; Louanne or LuAnne Cassady was Marylou; the Ross Bar became Ritzy's; Herbert Huncke/Hunkey, a hustler, was called Hassel; Allen [Ginsberg], the poet, was Carlo; the bed was no longer Kerouac's father's but that of an anonymous big man. Kinsey's was the only unchanged identity – Alfred Kinsey, the well-known sex researcher.[2]

The Ross Bar was indeed a New York hustler haunt. We even have a picture (see Figure 1). The photographer, Thomas Painter, whom we will get to know intimately in the pages that follow, referred to it in 1952 as the 'the Ross-Moss-What-have-you Bar', noting that it had changed its name yet again.[3] And we have a photograph of one of the bar's inhabitants (see Figure 2). The man, a New Jersey packer, came to New York from time to time 'to make some spare change' as a hustler.[4] He is dressed in the photograph exactly as he was when picked up and photographed by Painter in 1952.

Prologue

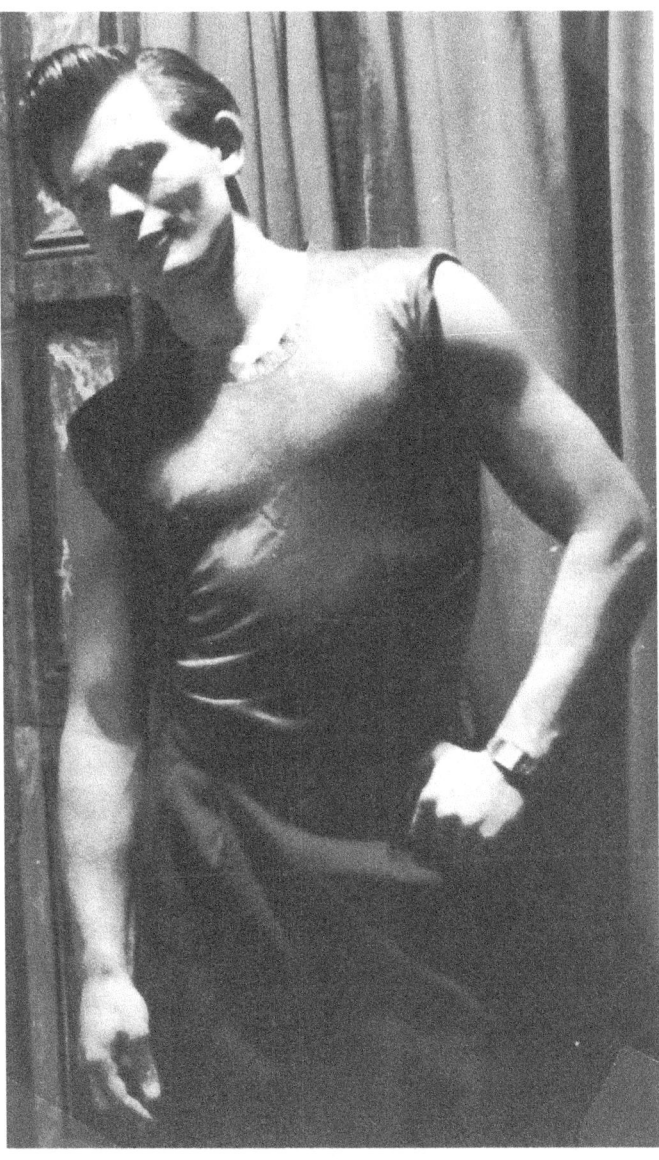

2. Moss (Ross) Bar hustler, 1952. From the Thomas Painter Collection. Reproduced by permission of The Kinsey Institute for Research in Sex, Gender, and Reproduction, Inc.

The original scroll of *On the Road*, breathless in its absence of paragraph and section, introduces characters and themes that may puzzle now but will become more and more explicable as the book in front of you progresses: the mad sexual routines, including the homoerotic possibilities of sex with a friend's wife while he watches; the lure of the hoodlum; the hustler bar and its 'boys'; the centrality of New York's Times Square; the shadowy presence of Huncke; Kinsey's visibility, even in the abridged edition; and, finally, the fact that this description exists in a Beat text. This is the lost world that we will be exploring.

Notes

1 J. Kerouac, *On the Road: The Original Scroll* (New York, 2007), pp. 231–2.
2 J. Kerouac, On the Road, 50th Anniversary Edition (New York, 2007), p. 131.
3 The Kinsey Institute for Research in Sex, Gender, and Reproduction, University of Indiana, Bloomington, The Thomas Painter Collection (hereafter, Painter), Box 1, Series 2, c. 1, Vol. 9: Painter Letters 1952: 8 November 1952.
4 Painter, Box 1, Series 2, c. 1, Vol. 9: 26 April 1952.

∽ 1
Introduction

> I know the scene: Chuck the masculine cowboy and Miss Destiny the femme queen: making it from day to park to bar to day like all the others in that ratty world of downtown L.A. which I will make my own: the world of queens and malehustlers and what they thrive on, the queens being technically men but no one thinks of them that way – always 'she' – their 'husbands' being the masculine vagrants – fleetingly and often out of convenience sharing the queens' pads – never considering theyre involved with another man (the queen), and as long as the hustler goes only with queens – and with other men only for scoring (which is making or taking sexmoney, getting a meal, making a pad) – he is himself not considered 'queer' – he remains, in the vocabulary of that world, 'trade'. (John Rechy, 1963)[1]

Though this opening quotation, by a hustler, is referring to Los Angeles and this book focuses on New York (see Figure 3), it captures the duality of male sex work that we will be dealing with. Effeminacy was part of this world but we will be concerned principally with the queens' counterparts, those commonly known as hustlers, the male prostitutes who paraded their masculinity and who were paid for sex with (nearly always) men. We will also deal with 'trade', ostensibly straight and similarly masculine men, often those in uniform, who would engage in same-sex sex. This world has not exactly been hidden from history. The psychiatrist George Henry's 1950s and 1960s guide to sex in US society picked male prostitution as 'one of the most serious' social problems of modern society: 'All large cities have areas and places where men congregate for the purpose of selling sexual favors.' New York, he claimed, was especially notorious.[2] In his 1965 study of victimless crimes, the sociologist Edwin M. Schur referred to the hustler as a 'well-institutionalized element in homosexual life'.[3] Nor was the hustler culturally invisible: critics have pointed to his role as 'sexual outlaw' in 1960s film and literary representations of perverse pleasures, more of which in a later chapter.[4]

New York hustlers

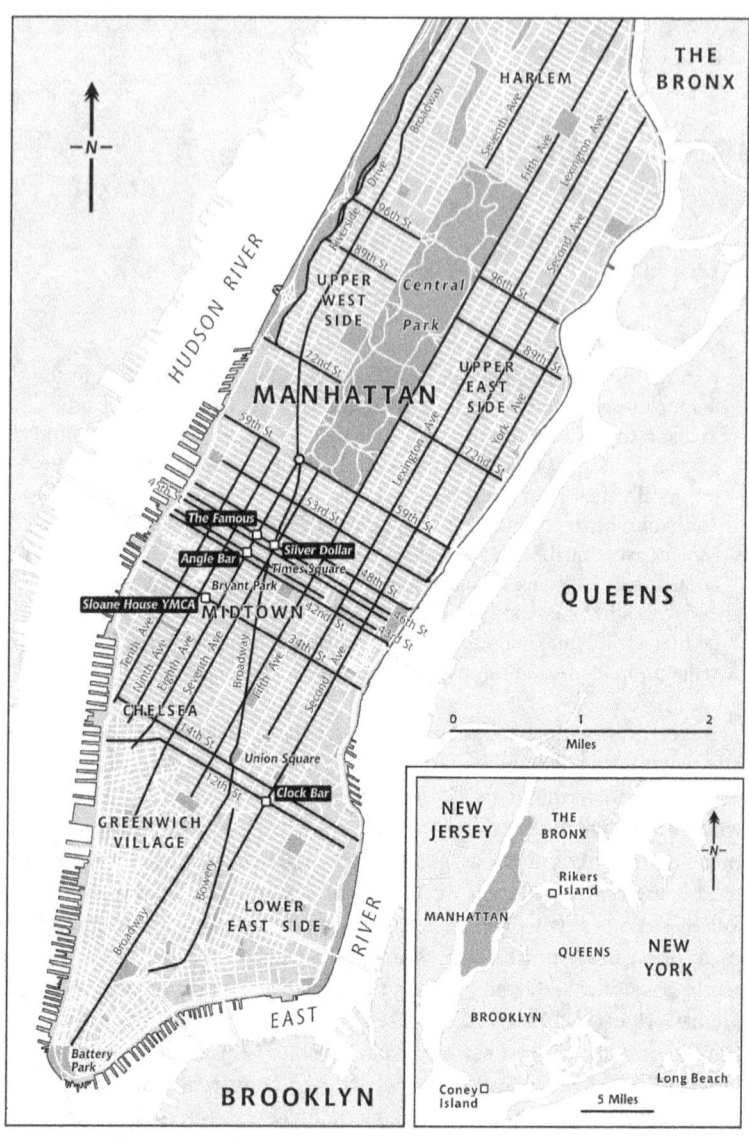

3. New York City, circa 1940–60. Map by Igor Drecki.

We meet hustlers and trade in memoirs and biographies. The New York writer, photographer, critic, and patron of the arts Carl Van Vechten was visited by an African-American male prostitute during 1929–30.[5] The Hollywood film director George Cukor is said to have 'preferred masculine heterosexual men'; from the 1930s onwards he had sex with sailors and trade, most of it paid.[6] The actor Tony Curtis recalled that 'George would throw a big, formal dinner party at his house. Then, after the party was over, George and his friends would go cruise Sunset Boulevard, looking for young men; they called them "after dinner mints".'[7] Though not actually named, the director appears in John Rechy's novel *City of Night* (1963) as a contemptuous user of hustlers.[8]

The hustler flits in and out of the science fiction writer Samuel Delany's account of life in the Lower East Side in the early 1960s and his recollections of 42nd Street cinema sex in the 1970s and 1980s, even though he claimed that 'Hustlers are just not my particular thing'.[9] Jim Carroll's *Basketball Diaries* described his teenage Times Square hustling in the early 1960s.[10] The artist and filmmaker Andy Warhol had fond memories of the San Remo bar in Greenwich Village in the early 1960s, 'all full of hustlers who usually sat on the railing of Washington Square Park who'd been taken to the San Remo for one-draft beer'.[11] Warhol associate, the transvestite Holly Woodlawn, fell in with the hustlers and queens of Bryant Park when he moved from Miami to New York in 1962 and lived for a time by (not very successful) hustling.[12] The writer John Cheever, his latest biographer tells us, was not above paid sex with young men.[13] The conservative lawyer Roy Cohn, famous for his public hostility to homosexuality and communism, used intermediaries to procure a string of hustlers and trade in the 1970s.[14]

The lure of trade recurs in homosexual chronicles and letters. The correspondence of the poet Hart Crane contains frequent references to his fondness for sailors in New York and elsewhere. 'If it weren't for the Fleet I should scarcely be able to endure it', he wrote during a visit to Hollywood in 1928.[15] When he lived in New York in the 1930s and 1940s, the aspiring early organizer of homosexuals Henry Gerber made full use of the Times Square hustlers (he refers in one letter to a string of prostitutes) and masturbated servicemen in picture theatres; these were his primary forms of sex.[16] Gore Vidal said of the 1940s 'that just about everyone, either actively or passively, was available under the right circumstances'.[17] Vidal, who had an appetite for trade, recalled the Astor Bar in New York's Times Square in the 1940s as 'the city's most exciting meeting place for soldiers, sailors, and marines on the prowl for one another'.[18] 'I did enjoy my daily meetings with strangers, usually encountered in the streets', he wrote of 1946.

> We would then go to one of the Dreiserian hotels around Times Square. Most were poor youths my own age, and often capable of an odd lovingness, odd considering the fact that I did so little to give any of them physical pleasure. But then, even at twenty, I often paid for sex on the ground that it was only fair. [19]

Tennessee Williams wrote in 1950 that, when Vidal stayed with him in Key West, Florida, he was dividing his time between the sailors and reviews of his latest book; 'I don't know which excites him the more but I suspect that the sailors taste better!'[20]

Hustlers and trade appear in a 1949 entry in the journals of the urbane Glenway Wescott:

> The rough trade and street boys of San Francisco have a peculiar habit or convention. There in Union Square they do not loll on the benches or stroll about – they stand separately, stock-still and upright, like sentries. Long after midnight, one here and one there, their expressions solemn, only their eyes lively – as though they had been mesmerized and the mesmerizer had gone off and forgotten them.[21]

The death of a hustler is recorded in the extensive New York diaries of the homosexual Donald Vining: 'FRIDAY, JULY 23, 1954 . . . the boy who fell (or was pushed) from an apartment window to his death was Douglas Locke. Seems he'd been sleeping around for a living and it may be that an attempted shakedown led to his death.' Vining's partner recorded a sardonic obituary: 'What a shame that such a good figure had to leave this world of so many ugly ones. At least you, and a few hundred others, had some pleasure from it while it was here.'[22] Vining's unpublished insider's novel about homosexual New York, 'The Unabashed', includes hustlers in its line-up of artists, copywriters, decorators, warehouse men, sailors, actors, rough trade, ex-marines, fairies, prisoners, and academics. 'Sailors have their points but they don't keep you in Bronzini ties', observes one of his (more refined) male prostitutes.[23]

Gay oral histories of the 1940s and 1950s invariably mention our subjects of interest. One was the 'handsomest young man I had ever seen: beautifully dressed, beautifully groomed . . . trade . . . picked up, polished up, dressed up. Straight.' Supported with his wife and child in New Jersey, he regularly came to New York to see his patron, a newspaper society columnist, who had bought the man his family house.[24] There are reminiscences of the Silver Dollar Bar with its 'wonderful selection' of hustlers, the more upmarket possibilities of the Astor Bar (hustlers with ties), and the young white and Puerto Rican men of 42nd Street available for $5 or $10. 'I couldn't believe that these beautiful, magnificent specimens of manly beauty would be so pliable and agreeable in bed.'[25] A man who claimed that he had sex with Montgomery Clift in the 1950s recalled the actor's interest in trade, 'an I-don't-give-a-fuck-who-you-are-do-you-want-to-suck-my-dick attitude'.[26] Samuel Steward was nostalgic about the hustlers he had known – 'a little Puerto Rican hustler in Chicago that I had a couple of hundred encounters with' – and claimed to have spent around $3,000 on one man over a five-year period.[27]

Male prostitutes, we will see, are centre stage in Steward's semi-fictional work.[28] And trade certainly features in his unpublished records of sexual interactions when he was a tattooist in Chicago in the 1950s. 'Norm . . . came over, wanting me to do the silhouettes of two dog heads for him, which I did, grumbling. But then he paid for it by letting me give him a blow job as usual. He continues to excite me – big and low-class as he is – and a punchpress operator at Bell and Howell.'[29] Steward kept a 'Stud File' of his sexual partners and contacts and the nature of their sexual interaction (he was an early exponent of S/M).[30] 'Trade' was a keyword in chronicles filled with references to truck drivers, taxi drivers, steel workers, construction workers, Marlon Brando look-alikes, and many sailors, 'a blur of sailors', like Kenneth Anger's film *Fireworks* (1947) (see Figure 26), and the incessant talk about blowjobs – one man told Steward that 'as many as 150 men had given him blowjobs'.[31]

Our subjects – and their European equivalents – are there in the diaries of the writer and poet Charles Henri Ford, who was still paying for sex in the 1960s.[32] 'With Fausto it was always a fee-for-a-lay – I wanted it that way, paid him after each love-bout. I wished to channel his eroticism to react to money.' 'No two boys react alike, whether their category is professional, semi-professional or amateur. Pick-ups are like restaurants – you go back to some.' Ford's long-term companion, the artist Pavel Tchelitchew, once told Charles Henri that he should be more concerned with 'making a name' than with 'making boys'.[33] But this did not prevent Tchelitchew from painting and drawing (and sharing) such young men.[34]

Tennessee Williams was another aficionado of trade: 'I went out cruising last night and brought home something with a marvelous body it was animated Greek marble and turned over even. It asked for money, and I said, Dear, would I be living in circumstances like this if I had any money?'[35] Gore Vidal recalled that he and Williams would 'pass boys back and forth'.[36] '[L]ine up some of that Forty-second Street trade for me when I get back', the playwright wrote to his friend Donald Windham in 1940.[37] Williams's *Memoirs* (1975) contains a 'free association' recollection of sex with a notable red-headed male prostitute, and his notebooks are peppered with entries concerning trade and hustlers – he even relates in-house gossip about the sexual proclivities of the long-dead writer Jack London 'that he was "trade" for "everybody"'.[38] 'Last night the apt. was filled with merchant marines – this a.m. F.'s electric razor was missing, which is *not* a *non sequiter* [sic].'[39] 'For sex', he wrote while living at the YMCA in Manhattan in 1942, 'a beautiful cold prostitute from Texas, and all that implies'.[40] 'Saturday Night I had the most beautiful (looking) lay of my entire experience', he wrote in 1943, 'Really flawless. Strange how little excitement I felt, however. Wanted money, paid $2. Then turned it over to Donnie [Windham] who was waiting his turn downstairs.'[41] The 'nightingale' was sometimes Williams's somewhat cryptic term for hired sex. 'The nightingales were on key' was an entry for 1953, 'though their tone has been sweeter on occasions. But those girls are costing me plenty: $40 for the past two concerts.' They were singing again in 1954: 'I got a little drunk and hired a nightingale to serenade me.'[42] After an awkward post-sex interaction with a prostitute in Rome in 1955, the playwright mused that despite the embarrassment and guilt involved in paid sex, 'I owe more pleasure to this circumstance in life than anything else, I guess'.[43] Dotson Rader, who got to know Williams in the 1960s, referred to the writer's fascination with male prostitutes and their 'life stories'. 'Tennessee . . . never did understand why bringing a hooker to a fancy dinner party wasn't good form.'[44]

Clearly, this milieu is central to the sexual histories of several generations of twentieth-century American homosexual men. The homoerotic scrapbooks of Van Vechten included sailor images, photographs, and drawings, sometimes in narrative form, 'unending stories of male types (such as sailors) having sex with each other and with other men'.[45] The Harlem Renaissance writers Richard Bruce Nugent and Wallace Thurman shared a 'taste for "rough trade"' in the 1920s and 1930s, and Nugent spoke later of his obsession with Italians, 'a "stable" of Latins who would come across the bridge from the Bronx into Harlem and yell up to my window "Bruce! Bruce!"'[46] Both men were paid for sex in their younger years.[47] Lincoln Kirstein, the arts critic and creator of the New York City Ballet and School of American Ballet, had, as his biographer puts it, a 'continuing penchant' for what Kirstein himself called 'low-life' sex with sailors, marines, and others.[48] He swapped stories about sailor tattoos: including one with a snake around the cock and another with an anchor chain around the waist with the anchor in the man's 'asshole'. A friend, presumably with oral sex in mind, suggested a tattoo of the 'Last Supper' on the belly.[49] Such contextual material complements some key art works of these early decades. Paul Cadmus's sailor trilogy, discussed in the following chapter, his *Y.M.C.A. Locker Room* (1933), Charles Demuth's watercolours *Dancing Sailors* (1917 and 1918), *Two Sailors Urinating* (1930), *Three Sailors Urinating* (1930), *Three Sailors on the Beach* (1930), and *On 'That' Street* (1932), the more sexually explicit intended only for private viewing, and Marsden Hartley's semi-naked, muscular, and sometimes hirsute prizefighter, lumberjack, and fishermen (circa 1938–41), including his *Christ Held by Half-naked Men* (1940–41), express the very desires that form the subject matter of this book.[50] Demuth's *Eight O'Clock (Morning #1)* (1917) very probably depicts a male prostitute asking for money.[51]

The American composers Virgil Thomson, Marc Blitzstein, David Diamond, and Ned Rorem all liked 'rough trade' in the 1940s.[52] Rorem's published New York diary refers to 1946 incidents of drunken, violent sex with strangers: 'beaten seven times this month, and room robbed twice . . . Picking my nose this morning was like applying a small sharp shovel to a shredded velvet carpet. The visitor didn't mind – even gave me a dollar, longshoreman from Jersey.'[53] The New York poet Frank O'Hara, according to his friend the artist Larry Rivers, liked 'guys who also like women'. A PhD student who rented his room in the 1950s remembered O'Hara bringing sailors back to the apartment.[54]

The influential magazine editor Leo Lerman recalled the birthday parties of the poet W. H. Auden in his apartment in the Village, attended by an incongruous mix of high-powered literary figures and 'street scum', boys whom Auden and his partner had picked up.[55] The early journals of another poet, Allen Ginsberg, record his amusement at Auden's partner Chester Kallman's story of picking up two sailors in 1947, the storyteller saying to himself 'Chester, No. Not two, Chester, No.'[56] The film critic Parker Tyler provided knowing comments about the dangers of sex with sailors ('Anyone who knows what cruising American sailors is . . .') and the ludicrousness of the dramatic premise of using a beautiful woman to lure trade for a homosexual man: 'all said visitor had to do is step outdoors alone to have boys drop from the sky and roll under his feet; they look up at one (I am told on reliable authority), flutter their lovely black eyelashes, and the deal is made'.[57]

The list could go on and on. The editor of a Swiss homosexual magazine lingered over the meat rack of Washington Square on his US trip in 1958, with the young hustlers all lined up: 'In close-fitting jeans with clear emphasis on certain body parts, in Levis, T-shirts, leather jackets (every taste is provided for), cigarette in the corner of the mouth and with the so often animal-like charming grace of the young American, to which nothing feminine is attached.'[58]

The historian Martin Duberman was engaging in sex with hustlers in the 1960s – '[T]he cash-and-carry ethic of a hustler bar had a persuasive appeal.'[59] Edmund White's *My Lives* (2005) begins in the 1950s with the young, T-shirted, Kentucky farmboys of Fountain Square, Cincinnati, sexually available for the right sum of money.

> [I]n Cincinnati there were *hired* men and the idea that twenty – or even ten – dollars could open their flies and make them lie back with a sneer and flex their muscles excited me. They were like dolls in a toy store that I could play with promiscuously but whose mechanisms would permit them to perform only one action – turn their head or open their arms – and that would exhaust their entire repertory.[60]

He later describes his period in New York in the 1970s, ghost writing college texts into the early hours (psychology and US history), then rewarding himself with a hustler at 4 am.[61] Structuring his past in terms of its influences – 'My shrinks', 'My mother' – White's autobiography significantly includes a chapter called 'My hustlers'. 'I have hired hustlers all my life', he wrote in 1980.[62]

The object of such attention was 'heterosexual'. The hustlers in the pages that follow were desired for their masculinity and their perceived sexual preference for women. *The Guild Dictionary of Homosexual Terms* defined both hustler and trade as understood in 1965. A hustler was 'A male prostitute to homosexuals, usually calling himself heterosexual'. Trade was 'Generic for the male of masculine type and body build, usually heterosexual, who takes the positive, leading, inserter role in sexual relations with the homosexual, and who does not make (or may pretend so) any identification with homosexuality'. To do for trade, the dictionary explained, was homosexual relations with 'any heterosexual male for the purposes of this male's sexual gratification only'.[63] George Henry was confident that the majority of hustlers 'are not homosexual by preference ... hustling appears to be an easy and exciting way of maintaining themselves'.[64]

The writer White is candid about the appeal of paying for sex with a straight male: 'We wanted a real man, a heterosexual man.'[65] A gay man, interviewed by the historian George Chauncey for his book *Gay New York* (1994), contrasted the world of the 1930s and 1940s with that of the 1960s and 1970s where the heterosexual–homosexual divide was far more pronounced: 'Most of my crowd [in the 1930s and 1940s] wanted to have sex with a straight man . . . And a lot of straight boys let us have sex with them. People don't believe it now. People say now that they must have been gay. But they weren't. They were straight.'[66]

A pioneering study of US male prostitution by Thomas Painter (more of whom later) estimated in 1941 that the nation's 'millions of homosexuals create and maintain a huge prostitution of boys and men; surely ten thousand *normal* boys are male prostitutes, a vicious, criminal, social life, while the number who casually prostitute themselves now and again to homosexuals must number several million'.[67] Hustlers, he explained in the opening pages of his survey, 'are – ninety per cent of them – sexual[ly] "normal" in the common use and understanding of the term. That is to say, they are heterosexual; they enjoy and prefer the sexual company of women rather than of men.'[68] His sexual matrix is of heterosexual hustlers catering for a homosexual market. Hence the only 'normal' patrons of a swinging 1930s Harlem homosexual/lesbian bar were the hustlers and female prostitutes! 'Not one of the men or women to be found there any evening is sexually normal, except those who come for the purposes of prostitution.'[69]

If the hustler and trade have a presence in the remembered sex lives of American homosexual men, they have had less effect on the writing of the history of sex. Mack Friedman's *Strapped for Cash* (2003) provides an overview of the history of American hustlers, but it is a popular rather than academic work, a history of hustling by a one-time hustler.[70] Hustlers turn up in the rather neglected but pioneering 1970s ethnography of a Seattle bar by Kenneth Read, an Australian anthropologist better known for his work on the New Guinea Highlands. One of them, 'Clint', even had a tattoo of a penis on his knee, revealed deliberately through a tear in his denims.[71] But Read never interviewed any of his hustlers: 'even in New Guinea I was often unnecessarily reticent about enquiring into sexual practices'.[72] Neither of these studies has had much impact on the actual historiography of sex.

Since the publication in English translation of Michel Foucault's *The History of Sexuality* (1978), it has been axiomatic in the history of sex to distinguish between sexual acts and sexual identities.[73] Modern sexuality moved from a situation where same-sex activity was merely excessive sex (sexual acts) to a regime where sexuality was linked to self (sexual identities). It was a shift that also saw the division into heterosexual and homosexual, a split that has been assumed in modern sexual paradigms, and an axiom reflected in the teleology of some influential gay histories. It explains the tendency of those who have commented on male prostitution to assign the male prostitute to their mutually exclusive categories of homosexual and heterosexual and/or to assume a rather uncomplicated twentieth-century making of these identities.[74] It accounts for the eagerness of gay historians to arrive at the making of a gay world: John D'Emilio's history of postwar America, for example, is a teleological account of the creation of a gay subculture that, even when it faced repression, moved neatly and inexorably towards the gay liberation of the late 1960s.[75]

But there has been a recent turn towards a rather more complex history of homosexuality, encompassing a variety of categories or sites for the location of same-sex desire. Eve Kosofsky Sedgwick wrote in 1990 of the limitations in thinking of a unitary homosexuality rather than 'overlapping, contradictory, and conflictual definitional forces' – though she gave little sense of what such histories might involve.[76] Diversity is certainly the theme of George Chauncey's *Gay New York* (1994), John Howard's *Men Like That: A Southern Queer History* (1999), and Matt Houlbrook's *Queer London* (2005), three historically grounded studies that have located divergent forms of queerness in twentieth-century rural and urban America and Britain.[77] Howard hypothesizes 'that throughout the twentieth century, queer sexuality continued to be understood as both acts *and* identities, behaviors *and* beings. It was variously comprehended – depending in part on place and race – along multiple axes and continuums as yet unexamined by historians.'[78] Both defenders of old paradigms and those celebrating new frameworks have highlighted this shift in historiography to the point where, as one recent commentator has put it, 'there is no such thing as a unitary history of homosexuality, sexuality, or of the self'.[79]

Taxonomy or classification has played an ambivalent role in this recent historiography. David Halperin has argued that, rather than assuming a single history of homosexuality, it is useful to consider a variety of categories of male same-sex desire in the period leading up to the nineteenth and twentieth centuries, when homosexuality was actually used as a word and became more closely related to what we mean by the term. The genealogy of male homosexuality consists of the five categories of effeminacy, sodomy, friendship, inversion, and homosexuality itself. Like Sedgwick, he gives little empirical sense of what this rethinking might entail, yet provides a significant theoretical reconceptualization of the history of homosexuality. Halperin allows for 'transhistorical continuities', writing of 'accumulation, accretion, and overlay', but these categories are historically situated and he maintains a conceptual distinction between modern homosexuality and what he terms pre-homosexual discourses.[80] Hence it could be argued that the structuring of his argument – with the focus on 'homosexuality before homosexuality'[81] – risks masking the multiplicity of homosexualities, the complexity and blurring of acts and identities contained in his important last category. This reading is not unassailable; H. G. Cocks has written approvingly of Halperin's 'flexible account of modern identity', where 'present homosexuality, with its variety of identities, ways of being, and sexual preferences, simply testifies to the traces of its past'.[82] The category of friendship, for example, is not incompatible with a complex discussion of layered, same-sex desire.[83] However, one recent critic has indeed charged that Halperin's taxonomies produce a somewhat 'totalizing impulse', with his final category 'homosexuality' precluding modern multiple forms of same-sex sexual expression.[84] Presumably, similar motivations lay behind Alan Sinfield's Freudian-inspired effort to widen the category 'homosexuality' to include androgyny, transgender categories, and the desires provoked by power differentials in class, race, and age.[85] Clearly there is further work to be done on unpicking that categorization 'homosexuality'.

As Laura Doan has observed, the focus on sexual identity had made it 'difficult to think more imaginatively about sexual subjects of the past who may have been less attuned to such modes of interiority'.[86] And Janet Halley has read Foucault's oft-quoted 'The sodomite had been a temporary aberration; the homosexual was now a species' as indicating not the replacement of one regime (acts) with another (identities) but rather as a displacement, with the two existing together. 'Thus sodomy – even sodomy between two people of the same sex or gender – is not necessarily the equivalent of acts or of identities; it is now unstably available for characterization as a species of act *and/or* as an indicator of sexual-orientation personality.'[87] Arguably, the most useful sexual histories are those that provide depth of context without either assuming sexual identity or anticipating its complete absence; and without forcing taxonomies. This book is an attempt to write such a history.

Trade is promising in this respect. Men so classified might have sex with women, fairies (effeminate men), or queers (homosexuals). Their public persona was that they assumed the male role and used the fairy or the queer much as they would a woman. As well as sailors, they were often soldiers, or the men who lived in the numerous lodging houses and the YMCAs.[88] 'Why, everyone knows that "Y's" are overrun with wolves out for chickens!' exclaims a character in a Tennessee Williams short story.[89] When John Rechy first headed to New York to begin his hustling career, he stayed at the Sloane House YMCA. 'They don't call this Y the French Embassy for nothing', he was told by a merchant marine.[90] Samuel Steward waxed eloquently on the attractions of the Embarcadero 'Y' in San Francisco, 'with its sailors, marines, dockhands, and truckdrivers running hot and cold down the corridors'.[91] It was, he wrote of a visit in 1953, 'A Christian brothel, a lupanar. Here, under the paternal and indulgent eye of the YMCA, more sins are committed per minute than were in the palmiest days of ancient Rome . . . Life here like a virus, a disease. When you get away from the place, you keep thinking: "Jesus, I ought to get back." Like life on the needle.'[92]

In London there were also men who had sex with other men (while continuing to have sex with women) and who did not consider themselves to be homosexual given their perceived dominance in such encounters. These usually working-class men, including sailors and the notorious guardsmen, might accept money or other forms of support, but their motivations were more involved than mere prostitution – Houlbrook writes convincingly of friendship, cross-class attraction, and the 'complexities' of desires. For some of these men, it was a phase that ceased once they married, but others continued with their same-sex liaisons.[93] 'The most remarkable thing about queer urban culture', he notes, 'is that it was, to a large extent, composed of and created by men who never thought themselves queer.'

> The boundaries between sexual difference and 'normality' were thus problematic, unstable, and contested, and discrete frameworks for interpreting male sexual practices and identities coexisted, intersected, and overlapped. Being queer was never simply the same as being 'homosexual', though it could be. Being 'normal' never simply denoted what would today be labeled 'heterosexuality', though in specific contexts and for certain men – particularly bourgeois men – it often did. Forms of understanding that we often assume to be timeless – the organization of male sexual practices and identities around the binary opposition between 'homo-' and 'heterosexual' – solidified only in the two decades after the Second World War. Remarkably, their origins lie within living memory.[94]

I will argue that the sexual culture of the New York hustlers and 'trade' mirrors the lack of binary division located in London during the same period – but that the American city demonstrates far more sexual fluidity than its English counterpart. The time span of my study is significant because it coincides with the solidifying of identities claimed even by those who argue for sexual diversity. Chauncey's *Gay New York* moves too quickly from the sexual practices of the early twentieth century to the gay culture and politics of the mid-century. Perhaps it is a structural consequence of the ordering of his material, but the varieties of same-sex interactions discussed for the opening decades of the twentieth century fade with his gay-world-making. My argument is that this making was rather more protracted and complex; that there are rich continuities of taxonomies missed by a tendency to categorize all same-sex sexual activity as 'gay' once the mid-century is approached.[95] The hustler – who was part of the sexual regime known as 'trade' – sexually traversed homosexuality and heterosexuality, continually negotiating the boundaries of pleasure and self through acts that refuse easy attributions of identity.[96] For I also hope to show that the history of the sexuality of the hustlers and their associates in twentieth-century New York challenges our notions of both heterosexuality and homosexuality.

I am helped in my task by a remarkable archive, that of a man called Thomas Painter (pictured in Figures 4 and 5). Painter's association with New York hustlers began in the 1930s when he started work on a never-published study of American homosexuality and his apartment was 'an open house' for 42nd Street hustlers: 'The place leaped with H's [homosexuals] and hustlers every moment of the day and night.'[97] He and several of his contacts featured as case studies in George Henry's pioneering *Sex Variants* (1941): 'Will G.' (Painter) said that he had 'had' about forty or fifty Times Square 'boys' in the less than two years since he had first discovered the male prostitution there.[98] But the documentation of Painter's association with the hustler world intensified after his contact with the soon-to-become-famous sex researcher Alfred Kinsey in the early 1940s. This valued Kinsey informant, friend, chronicler, and photographer of New York hustlers provided material to the Kinsey Institute until the early 1970s: letter-journals, home movies, about a thousand photographs, fiction, and drawings.[99] It is a unique archive of a particular type of male prostitution in the time before AIDS and crack cocaine.[100]

Throughout the postwar period, Painter regaled Kinsey with detailed

4. Thomas Painter and 'buddy' at Coney Island. From the Thomas Painter Collection. Reproduced by permission of The Kinsey Institute for Research in Sex, Gender, and Reproduction, Inc. Author's note: the photograph was taken in a booth and given to Painter (on the left) by his companion.

accounts of sex involving hustlers, servicemen, and various thugs and criminals.[101] These were, it seems, mostly handwritten letters that were later transcribed in typewritten form by Clara Kinsey, Kinsey's wife, for filing in the archive. One letter from 1950 contains instructions from Painter to 'Mrs Kinsey' not to capitalise words which are in capitals only to make their spellings clear. (She dutifully transcribed his instruction.)[102] One can only surmise what this most unlikely amanuensis must have thought of some of his material. She was surprised when she met one of the men described in Painter's correspondence; he was very different to the mental picture that she had formed, based on descriptions of his relationships with hustlers and penchant for trade.[103]

Painter was alert to the complexities of desire and individual identities, the little rules of engagement and denial that proclaimed varying blends of masculinity and sexuality. In the 1950s, he described a movie theatre in Spanish Harlem where fellators operated as a 'cooperative', some keeping watch on the stairs, the others observing the fellating. One was 'a horrid, campy, swishy, noisy old faggot' who irritated them all; another was 'a tough, rough, muscular, truck-driverish youth who

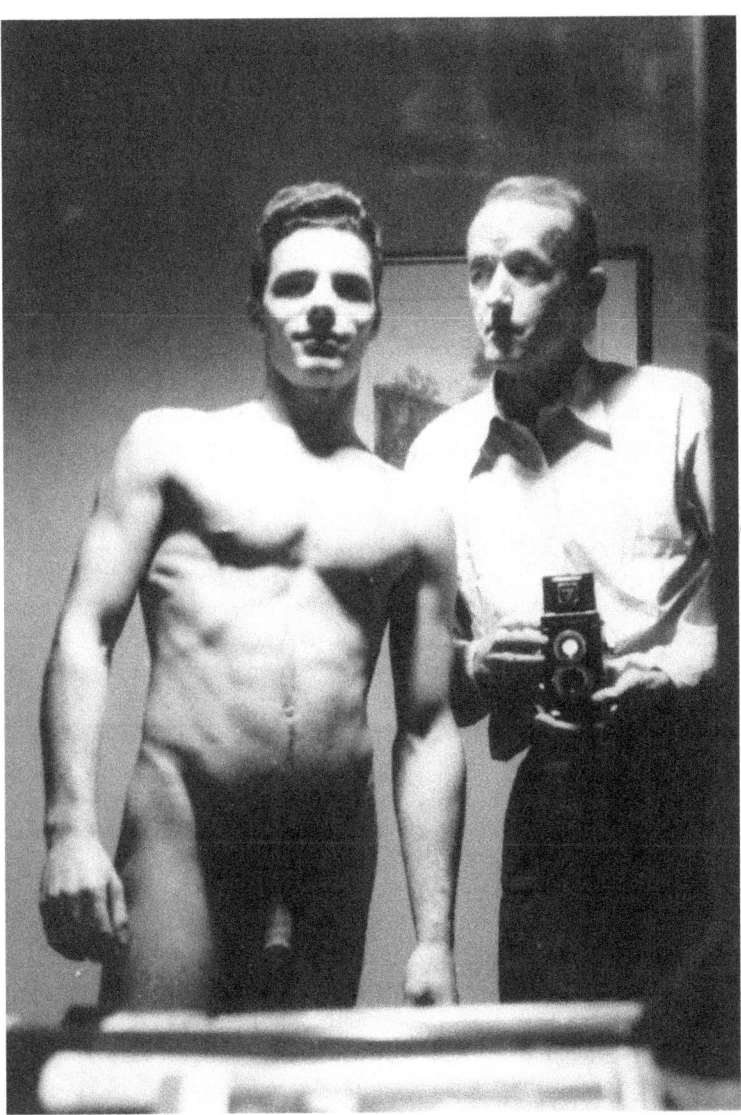

5. Thomas Painter and model, 1953. From the Thomas Painter Collection. Reproduced by permission of The Kinsey Institute for Research in Sex, Gender, and Reproduction, Inc. Author's note: the model (on the left), one of Painter's favourites, was a 'New York proletarian' who also worked as a hustler.

none-the less was also a fellator' and who said to the faggot, 'Thank God I'm just a cocksucker and not queer!' This, Painter wrote to Kinsey, 'I thought was one for your book in some chapter somewhere.'[104]

Kinsey's informant had an eye for the amusing anecdote. He wrote of the photographic subject who on browsing Kinsey's *Sexual Behavior in the Human Male* (1948) asked Painter what fellate meant – 'I told him it was what B... was going to do to him in a couple of hours'.[105] He told Kinsey (and Mrs Kinsey) about the hustler who was groped by a New York chaplain while hearing someone else's confession – 'holding Jimmy's cock in his hand while giving absolution'.[106] The correspondence even contains the earliest known twentieth-century description of fisting (1949), involving a close friend of Painter and a sailor. Historians of sex associate organized fist-fucking with the S/M scene of the 1960s, but Kinsey's informant implies that some sailors practised it earlier than this. Painter's friend mused 'that it had upset and disorientated him: he had been getting sadistic pleasure out of fucking people, just sticking his cock in them, but if you can potentially put your *arm* up, what's the fun in just a cock now?'[107]

Kinsey and his colleagues visited New York to meet Painter's contacts and to record their sexual histories. Kinsey knew a male brothel keeper prosecuted in 1948 for his involvement in male prostitution. When they raided the man's establishment, the police seized a copy of *Sexual Behavior in the Human Male*, and, amusingly, a clipping of a newspaper editorial about the dangers of Kinsey's book being in the wrong hands.[108] Painter also introduced Kinsey to the place that he shared with an artist friend, with 'its assorted denizens and visitants, pals and playmates. And they were as assorted a lot of toughs, criminals, thugs, pansies, literateurs, and plain cocksuckers as can well be imagined. And he [Kinsey] mesmerized them all.' Shortly before Kinsey's death, Painter took him to his fiftieth birthday party. He recalled that Kinsey was there with the tough Puerto Rican youths, and was driven back to his hotel by a drunken Irishman in what was probably a stolen car. Kinsey remained insouciant throughout the proceedings.[109]

Painter's archive is a reminder that Kinsey's sex research drew on more than quantification and the collection of life histories. It entailed the cultivation of key informants who provided a detailed sense of sexual interaction in process, and involved the researcher's own long-term personal relationships with these insiders and their contacts.

Painter felt able to comment on Kinsey's work. 'Your description of a woman's sex life sounds like a frightful bore, I must say', he wrote to the great man after the publication of *Sexual Behavior in the Human Female* (1953). 'It all seems just frightfully badly managed, somehow: I want men and can't get them, men want women and can't get them, while women just want to be left alone and are pestered all the time.' 'The silver lining... for us who happen to be homosexual, is that very peculiarity of women – which leaves the poor men frustrated, sex-starved and "willing to settle for anything" as that Marine so flatteringly informed me one night. Otherwise I'd have to "settle", myself, for "anything" – another homosexual probably, God forbid.'[110] Painter was amused by the contrast between his reaction above and the press response to Kinsey: 'They complain you say girls fuck too much. I remarked you pointed out they hardly fuck at all. I presume it all depends on one's frame of reference.'[111] Painter also provided Kinsey with gossipy information on individuals. 'X' says he is 'retired from that sort of thing, is devoting himself to study (drama, voice production, dancing, singing). Has found a patron who he insists is not queer, in the person of a French Count, who lives on Smith St here in Brooklyn and has a hobby of helping young men in the arts. Hm-m.'[112]

Painter was a key informant, a fact that was recognised both by Kinsey and by his main collaborators. When the sex researcher told Painter that he had helped 'materially' in the making of *Sexual Behavior in the Human Male*, he was doubtless referring to his brokering of subjects for interviewing.[113] But Kinsey also appreciated his ethnographic role. 'I feel an increasing indebtedness to you for continuing this record. It is a magnificent lot of material', Kinsey wrote in two separate letters in 1948, 'I have been seeing a good many diaries in the last few years', 'and there are only three or four which would be worth our keeping. Yours is one of the best two from any scientific standpoint.'[114] In 1950, he said of Painter's letters that they contained more insight 'than anything I have seen in the psychiatric literature'.[115] We have to allow for the flattery involved in maintaining a successful source; Kinsey was an expert in making contacts seem indispensible. However, his co-author Wardell Pomeroy later endorsed the importance of Painter to their project:

> Kinsey had a great many contacts among homosexuals and every other kind of group, not only in New York but virtually around the world, yet Will Finch [Painter's alias] was not like the others. A highly literate man with a truly extraordinary sexual history, of which he had kept a detailed record from the beginning, Will Finch was immensely valuable to the research. Not only did he produce a quantity of history givers, as the others did, but he supplied us with a constant flow of letters, diaries, journals and

statistical records of his own life, and some others as well, . . . His contributions . . . today are crammed into every corner of a large, locked steel filing cabinet at the Institute – probably the most complete record of human sexual life ever compiled, and much of it written with grace and style as well as factual accuracy.[116]

Pomeroy said that the correspondence between Kinsey and Painter read like 'one insider talking to another'.[117]

At times, it seemed that, given his other commitments, Kinsey was having trouble keeping up with the sheer volume of material that Painter sent. Moreover, he occasionally had to deal with the consequences of this close collaboration. One of Painter's hustler-criminals contacted the professor directly in 1951 from the Missouri State Penitentiary where he was serving time for armed robbery, requesting help to set up a leather-making business when he was released: 'if you want me to I'll write some case histories on some unatural [sic] sex acts which goes on in here that would make Times Square look like an old maids convention'.[118]

Painter sustained his unofficial research after Kinsey's death in 1956. He continued his gossipy interactions. On one occasion, referring to his dangerous exchanges with the New York Puerto Rican gang the Dragons, he wrote that one, Junior, had 'just gotten out of Riker's Island. Manuel is not only in Jersey but in jail in Jersey . . . Lobo is in the hospital with a gun wound. Philip . . . is in jail again, too. So here we all are.'[119] He retained his humour and self-reflective sense of irony, as in this 1961 comment on his sexual predicament: 'So if I reject girls and most other homosexuals, and most heterosexuals (not my sex objects) reject me because of my sexuality, and my sex objects ignore me unless I have money – well, you see where it lands me. With my hand. Talking to myself, or writing very long reports to you.'[120]

Painter went in the late 1940s to a Harlem bar where the occupants were black and male, 'homosexuals, mostly young and faggoty', and 'rough trade'. 'And I mean *rough*'; his companion joked that 'one might just as well go out and lie down in front of a truck – one gets less maimed with less trouble and expense'.[121] Painter's sexual reports were shaped by his personal preferences. He was not generally attracted to African-Americans, so such descriptions of Harlem bars are rare. Unmuscular hustlers did not affect him, even if their faces were appealing. Looking back from the early 1960s, Painter recognized the subjective nature of his earlier research, joking that it should have been called 'Professional

Heterosexual White Male prostitution of a Specific Age group in New York, with Notes on Allied Phenomena'. He ignored the prostitution of young boys, older males (that is, those in their mid-thirties), and what he called the 'prostitution of homosexuals to homosexuals'. His 1941 study did not focus much on casual prostitution, though his later correspondence more than compensated for this shortcoming.[122]

Painter's main silence related to 'prostitution of homosexuals to homosexuals', by which he meant sexual interactions involving effeminacy. He hated effeminacy, thus excluding a whole sexual category from his portfolio. His biases did not entirely prevent him from describing the patrons of the homosexual venues that he visited. He provided reports of the effeminate fairies precisely because he was so keen to distinguish himself from them – his masculinity was proclaimed constantly in this way – and because he had to compete with them for the kind of men that he desired. Nonetheless, homosexual effeminacy, a vital part of the sexual landscape of New York, has a somewhat shadowy existence in Painter's accounts.

It is important to be aware, however, that throughout the period covered in this study male prostitutes included the effeminate male (see Figure 6) as well as the more obviously masculine; the 1930s hustlers recalled in an oral history of a gay cabaret in Seattle, for instance, are effeminate: 'I'd have my hair curled and I'd look just like a girl.'[123] So too were the street fairies of the hustler bars, on the margins of Esther Newton's classic study of male transvestite performers in America in the 1960s.[124] The female impersonators of the stage liked to distinguish themselves from the street fairies who were, in a sense, always performing and were a constant reminder of what the former might become if their stage careers faltered: 'I asked . . . what drag queens do when they are out of work, he said, "They get their butts out on the street, my dear, and they sell their little twats for whatever they can get for them."'[125] Holly Woodlawn's memories of hustling in the early 1960s in and around Times Square were of 'girls', like him, effeminate boys, and the 'male' hustlers, 'usually of a rough breed'.[126] When the *New York Times* ran a feature article on homosexuality in New York in 1963, the hustlers that they identified were effeminate ones, 'the dregs of the invert world – the male prostitutes – the painted, grossly effeminate "queens"'.[127] The one-time hustler Herbert Huncke, another of Kinsey's New York contacts, a man we will encounter from time to time in this book, was quite clear about the different categories in his memories of this phase of Kinsey's sexual research.

New York hustlers

6. Transvestite prostitutes, 1960s. The Kinsey Institute for Research in Sex, Gender, and Reproduction, Inc. Author's note: these men were from Baltimore rather than New York but could be found there too.

Introduction

7. Times Square hustlers and johns (clients), 1966. Photography by I. C. Rapoport. Author's note: a rare photograph of both hustlers and clients.

I believe I was one of the first in New York to be interviewed by Kinsey, and certainly one of the first from Times Square. Kinsey had apparently seen me around the square and was fairly sure I'd have information to give, if he could get it from me. He had walked up and down Forty-second Street, and he realized there was action of some sort going on there. Of course, he didn't know too much about the underworld aspect of it, but it was still pretty obvious. One walked by doorways and saw young men in tight pants with their whole profile on display. And there were the many flagrant queens that used to fly up and down the street, not to mention the more sinister types that could be noticed if one paid attention, and they can still be seen to this day.[128]

I. C. Rapoport's brilliant photographs for *Life* magazine's exposé of criminal activity in Times Square in the mid-1960s capture this duality perfectly, including both a rare (previously unpublished) shot of masculine hustlers with their johns (clients) (see Figure 7) and the effeminate fairies or queens, the aspect of male prostitution relatively neglected by Painter (see Figure 8).[129] The effeminate working-class competition for rough trade so central to Hubert Selby's remarkable novel *Last Exit to Brooklyn* (1957) is peripheral to Painter though he must have encountered it on a daily basis.[130]

While effeminacy is discussed at length in the following chapters,

8. Times Square fairies/queens, 1966. Photography by I. C. Rapoport.

Painter's opacity on this subject was not unique. His self-critique for writing an account that 'dealt solely with prostitutes who were interesting to me' was no declaration of marginal taste.[131] His interests were those of large numbers of men attracted to paraded masculinity, and, as I hope to demonstrate, have significant implications for the way that we view the history of American sex. Kinsey observed in the early 1950s that he was puzzled by another expert's claim that male prostitution was comparatively rare when he (Kinsey) had friends who thought that the only way to have homosexual sex was by paying for it![132]

Notes

1. J. Rechy, *City of Night* (New York, 1984), p. 97. First published in 1963.
2. G. W. Henry, *Society and the Sex Variant* (New York, 1965), p. 149. A version of work first published in 1955.
3. E. M. Schur, *Crimes Without Victims: Deviant Behavior and Public Policy* (Englewood Cliffs, NJ, 1965), p. 91.
4. See M. Moon, 'Outlaw sex and the "search for America": representing male prostitution and perverse desire in sixties film (*My Hustler* and *Midnight Cowboy*)', *Quarterly Review of Film and Video*, 15 (1993), 27–40; reprinted

Introduction

  in M. Moon, *A Small Boy and Others: Imitation and Initiation in American Culture from Henry James to Andy Warhol* (Durham, NC, 1998), ch. 5.
5 C. Van Vechten, *The Splendid Drunken Twenties: Selections from the Daybooks, 1922–1930*, ed. B. Kellner (Urbana and Chicago, 2003), pp. 259, 276, 278, 301.
6 See the gossipy biography, P. McGilligan, *George Cukor: A Double Life* (New York, 1991), pp. 118–19, 120, 188–9, 206–7.
7 T. Curtis and P. Golenbock, *American Prince: A Memoir* (New York, 2008), p. 78.
8 C. Casillo, *Outlaw: The Lives and Careers of John Rechy* (Los Angeles, 2002), pp. 100–3.
9 S. R. Delany, *The Motion of Light in Water: Sex and Science Fiction Writing in the East Village* (Minneapolis, MN, 2004), pp. 217–18, 219, 232, 417, 434, 443, 452, 454; S. R. Delany, *Times Square Red, Times Square Blue* (New York, 2001), p. 46 (for quote).
10 For Carroll's hustling, see J. Carroll, *The Basketball Diaries* (New York, 1995), pp. 104–6, 114, 187–8. The book was first published in 1978, though parts had appeared in various magazines and anthologies throughout the 1960s and 1970s.
11 A. Warhol and P. Hackett, *POPism: The Warhol '60s* (New York, 1980), pp. 54–5.
12 H. Woodlawn and J. Copeland, *A Low Life in High Heels: The Holly Woodlawn Story* (New York, 1991), pp. 54–5.
13 B. Bailey, *Cheever: A Life* (New York, 2009), pp. 509, 540, 632.
14 N. Von Hoffman, *Citizen Cohn: The Life and Times of Roy Cohn* (New York, 1988), pp. 361–6.
15 H. Crane, *O My Land, My Friends: The Selected Letters of Hart Crane*, ed. L. Hammer and B. Weber (New York, 1997), p. 373. For other references, see pp. 274, 292, 301, 318, 335, 362, 363, 379, 382.
16 See J. Kepner and S. O. Murray, 'Henry Gerber (1895–1972): grandfather of the American gay movement', in V. Bullough (ed.), *Before Stonewall: Activists for Gay and Lesbian Rights in Historical Context* (New York, 2002), p. 31; J. T. Sears, *Behind the Mask of the Mattachine: The Hal Call Chronicles and the Early Movement for Homosexual Emancipation* (New York, 2006), p. 74.
17 G. Vidal, *Palimpsest: A Memoir* (London, 1996), p. 101.
18 Ibid.
19 Ibid., p. 115.
20 D. Windham (ed.), *Tennessee Williams' Letters to Donald Windham 1940–1965* (Athens, GA, 1996), p. 252.
21 G. Wescott, *Continual Lessons: The Journals of Glenway Wescott, 1937–1955*, ed. R. Phelps and J. Rosco (New York, 1990), p. 231.
22 D. Vining, *A Gay Diary 1954–1967* (New York, 1981), pp. 13–14.

23 New York Public Library Manuscripts and Archives Division, Donald Vining Papers, Box 2, Folder 6: 'The Unabashed', ch. 2, p. 4.
24 C. Kaiser, *The Gay Metropolis 1940–1996* (New York, 1997), p. 10.
25 Ibid., p. 83.
26 Ibid., p. 114.
27 T. Kissack (ed.), 'Alfred Kinsey and homosexuality in the '50s: the recollections of Samuel Morris Steward as told to Len Evans', *Journal of the History of Sexuality*, 9 (2000), 489–90. This interview was carried out in 1983.
28 S. M. Steward, *Chapters from an Autobiography* (San Francisco, 1981), ch. 8; S. Steward, *Understanding the Male Hustler* (Binghamton, NY, 1991); and S. M. Steward, *Bad Boys and Tough Tattoos* (New York, 1990).
29 The Kinsey Institute for Research in Sex, Gender, and Reproduction, University of Indiana, Bloomington (hereafter, KI), Samuel Steward Collection (hereafter, Steward Collection), Series 2, F: Diary 1955: 18 January. Steward's archive, including diaries kept for Alfred Kinsey in the 1950s, is in the Kinsey Institute but has limited access.
30 Steward Collection, Series 2, B: Diary 1924–52.
31 Steward Collection, Series 2, F: Diary 1955: 9 July, 10 July, and 21–4 August.
32 C. H. Ford, *Water from a Bucket: A Diary 1948–1957* (New York, 2001).
33 Harry Ransom Center, University of Texas, Austin (hereafter, HRC), Charles Henri Ford Papers (hereafter, Ford Papers), Box 21, Folder 2: 'Flesh and Marble: A Street Diary', 8a, 18 (diary of a trip to Greece in March 1962); Box 29, folder 2: 'Diary from Paris and New York 1962': November 1962, referring to a diary entry from December 1952.
34 See the drawings in D. Leddick, *The Homoerotic Art of Pavel Tchelitchev 1929–1939* (North Pomfret, VT, 1999).
35 A. J. Devlin and N. M. Tischler (eds), *The Selected Letters of Tennessee Williams: Volume 1: 1920–1945* (New York, 2000), p. 333. See also, Windham (ed.), *Tennessee Williams' Letters*, p. 17.
36 Vidal, *Palimpsest*, p. 177.
37 Windham (ed.), *Tennessee Williams' Letters*, p. 17.
38 T. Williams, *Memoirs* (New York, 1975), p. 154 (for the red-headed hustler); T. Williams, *Notebooks*, ed. M. B. Thornton (New Haven, 2006), p. 289 (for Jack London).
39 Williams, *Notebooks*, p. 285 (emphasis in original).
40 Ibid., p. 331. See also pp. 187, 255, 271, 333, 548, 551, 607.
41 Ibid., p. 341.
42 Ibid., pp. 607, 631.
43 Ibid., p. 677.
44 D. Rader, *Tennessee: Cry of the Heart* (New York, 1985), p. 18.
45 J. Smalls, *The Homoerotic Photography of Carl Van Vechten: Public Face, Private Thoughts* (Philadelphia, 2006), pp. 114–15.

46 R. B. Nugent, *Gay Rebel of the Harlem Renaissance: Selections from the Work of Richard Bruce Nugent*, ed. T. H. Wirth (Durham, NC, 2002), pp. 26, 270.
47 Ibid., pp. 26, 271.
48 M. Duberman, *The Worlds of Lincoln Kirstein* (New York, 2007), pp. 33, 93 (for quote), 138, 227, 567, 644, 688.
49 New York Library for the Performing Arts, Jerome Robbins Dance Division, Lincoln Kirstein Papers, Box 4, Folder 18: Diary 1932–3, p. 162.
50 See J. Weinburg, *Speaking for Vice: Homosexuality in the Art of Charles Demuth, Marsden Hartley, and the First American Avant-garde* (New Haven, 1993); J. Weinburg, 'The man in uniform', in his *Male Desire: The Homoerotic in American Art* (New York, 2004), ch. 2.
51 Weinburg, *Speaking for Vice*, p. 26.
52 N. Hubbs, *The Queer Composition of America's Sound: Gay Modernists, American Music, and National Identity* (Berkeley and Los Angeles, 2004), p. 69.
53 N. Rorem, *The New York Diary* (New York, 1967), p. 132.
54 B. Gooch, *City Poet: The Life and Times of Frank O'Hara* (New York, 1993), pp. 229, 276, 292.
55 L. Lerman, *The Grand Surprise: The Journals of Leo Lerman*, ed. S. Pascal (New York, 2007), p. 395.
56 A. Ginsberg, *The Book of Martyrdom and Artifice: First Journals and Poems, 1937–1952*, ed. J. Lieberman-Plimpton and B. Morgan (Cambridge, MA, 2006), pp. 187–8.
57 P. Tyler, *Screening the Sexes: Homosexuality in the Movies* (New York, 1993), pp. 253, 309. First published in 1972.
58 H. Kennedy, *The Ideal Gay Man: The Story of Der Kreis* (New York, 1999), p. 116.
59 M. Duberman, *Cures: A Gay Man's Odyssey* (New York, 1992), p. 84.
60 E. White, *My Lives* (London, 2005), pp. 114–15. Emphasis in original.
61 Ibid., p. 123.
62 E. White, *States of Desire: Travels in Gay America* (New York, 1980), p. 212.
63 *The Guild Dictionary of Homosexual Terms* (Washington, DC, 1965), pp. 23, 45.
64 Henry, *Society and the Sex Variant*, p. 150.
65 White, *My Lives*, p. 109.
66 G. Chauncey, *Gay New York: Gender, Urban Culture, and the Making of the Gay Male World, 1890–1940* (New York, 1994), pp. 21–2.
67 KI, Thomas Painter, 'Male Homosexuals and Their Prostitutes in Contemporary America' (New York, 1941), Vol. 1: 'American Homosexuals', p. 5. My emphasis.
68 KI, Thomas Painter, 'Male Homosexuals and Their Prostitutes in

Contemporary America' (New York, 1941), Vol. 2: 'The Prostitute', p. 8.
69 Ibid., p. 45.
70 M. Friedman, *Strapped for Cash: A History of American Hustler Culture* (Los Angeles, 2003).
71 K. E. Read, *Other Voices: The Style of a Male Homosexual Tavern* (Novato, CA, 1980), p. 47.
72 Ibid., p. 74.
73 M. Foucault, *The History of Sexuality, Volume 1, An Introduction*, trans. R. Hurley (New York, 1978). For a useful survey, see H. G. Cocks, 'Modernity and the self in the history of sexuality', *Historical Journal*, 49 (2006), 1211-27.
74 J. Scott, 'A prostitute's progress: male prostitution in scientific study', *Social Semiotics*, 13 (2003), 179-99; K. Kaye, 'Male prostitution in the twentieth century: pseudohomosexuals, hoodlum homosexuals, and exploited teens', *Journal of Homosexuality*, 46 (2003), 1-77. Kaye falls into the category of assuming an easy and early historical division into hetero and homo.
75 J. D'Emilio, *Sexual Politics, Sexual Communities: The Making of a Homosexual Minority in the United States, 1940-1970* (Chicago, 1998) (first published in 1983); J. D'Emilio and E. B. Freedman, *Intimate Matters: A History of Sexuality in America* (Chicago, 1998), pp. 288-95, 318-25 (first published in 1988).
76 E. K. Sedgwick, *Epistemology of the Closet* (Berkeley and Los Angeles, 1990), p. 45.
77 Chauncey, *Gay New York*; J. Howard, *Men Like That: A Southern Queer History* (Chicago, 1999); M. Houlbrook, *Queer London: Perils and Pleasures in the Sexual Metropolis, 1918-1957* (Chicago, 2005).
78 Howard, *Men Like That*, p. xviii.
79 For the former (a rather guarded defence), see J. Bristow, 'Remapping the sites of modern gay history: legal reform, medico-legal thought, homosexual scandal, erotic geography', *Journal of British Studies*, 46 (2007), 116-42. For the latter, see H. G. Cocks, 'Homosexuality between men in Britain since the eighteenth century', *History Compass*, 5 (2007), 865-89. The quote is from Cocks, 'Modernity and the self', 1222.
80 D. M. Halperin, *How to Do the History of Homosexuality* (Chicago, 2002), p. 106.
81 The term 'homosexuality before homosexuality' is not Halperin's. I am thinking here of the parallel concept of 'heterosexuality before heterosexuality': see J. A. Schultz, 'Bodies that don't matter: heterosexuality before heterosexuality in Gottfried's *Tristan*', in K. M. Phillips and B. Reay (eds.), *Sexualities in History: A Reader* (New York, 2002), ch. 3.
82 See Cocks, 'Modernity and the self', 1222.

83 B. Reay, 'Writing the modern histories of homosexual England', *Historical Journal*, 52 (2009), 213–33.
84 D. Seitler, 'Queer physiognomies; or, how many ways can we do the history of sexuality?', *Criticism*, 46 (2004), 82.
85 A. Sinfield, 'Lesbian and gay taxonomies', *Critical Inquiry*, 29 (2002), 120–38.
86 L. Doan, 'Topsy-turvydom: gender inversion, sapphism, and the Great War', *GLQ*, 12 (2006), 526, 537.
87 J. E. Halley, 'Reasoning about sodomy: act and identity in and after Bowers v. Hardwick', *Virginia Law Review*, 79 (1993), 1739–40.
88 Chauncey, *Gay New York*, ch. 3. For the YMCA, see J. D. Gustav-Wrathall, *Take the Young Stranger By the Hand: Same-Sex Relations and the YMCA* (Chicago, 1998), esp. ch. 7.
89 T. Williams, 'The killer chicken and the closet queen', in T. Williams, *Collected Stories* (New York, 1985), p. 555.
90 Rechy, *City of Night*, p. 22.
91 Steward Collection, Series 1, A: Samuel Steward's Letters 1950–55: 16 June 1953 (Letter to 'Mike').
92 Steward Collection, Series 2, D: Diary 1953–54: 'The Embarcardero Y'.
93 Houlbrook, *Queer London*, p. 171.
94 Ibid., p. 7.
95 I discuss this later. Perhaps Chauncey's forthcoming history of the period after the 1940s will address the problem.
96 For another recent exploration of twentieth-century heterosexual-homosexual divisions, dealing with an environment not unfamiliar to hustlers, see R. G. Kunzel, 'Situating sex: prison sexual culture in the mid-twentieth-century United States', *GLQ*, 8 (2002), 253–70; and R. Kunzel, *Criminal Intimacy: Prison and the Uneven History of Modern American Sexuality* (Chicago, 2008). See also C. Cagle, 'Rough trade: sexual taxonomy in postwar America', in D. E. Hall and M. Pramaggiore (eds), *RePresenting Bisexualities: Subjects and Cultures of Fluid Desire* (New York, 1996), ch. 10; and P. C. Rogríguez Rust, 'Heterosexual gays, heterosexual lesbians, and homosexual straights', in P. C. Rogríguez Rust (ed.), *Bisexuality in the United States: A Social Science Reader* (New York, 1999), ch. 17. All these works raise some of the issues dealt with in this book.
97 H. L. Minton, *Departing from Deviance: A History of Homosexual Rights and Emancipatory Science in America* (Chicago, 2002), pp. 128, 131. Minton provides the best scholarly account of Painter: ibid., chs 6–7.
98 G. W. Henry, *Sex Variants: A Study of Homosexual Patterns* (New York, 1941), Vol. 1, p. 378.
99 Minton, *Departing from Deviance*, pp. 178, 181, 185, 189. Minton has made fruitful use of the Painter archive, but is primarily interested in Painter's role (via Kinsey) in 'the promoting of homosexual rights through scientific

research' (p. 217), and in his life as a struggle against 'heterosexist domination' (p. 218). My focus is rather different.

100 For the hustler in the period after AIDS and crack, see R. P. McNamara, *The Times Square Hustler: Male Prostitution in New York City* (Westport, CT, 1994); Delany, *Times Square Red, Times Square Blue*, esp. pp. 10–13, 41, 48, 147, 158–9 (including photographs of hustlers on pp. 11, 13, and 147); and M. C. Clatts, 'Ethnographic observations of men who have sex with men', in W. L. Leap (ed.), *Public Sex / Gay Space* (New York, 1999), ch. 7. See also Bruce Benderson's novel *User* (New York, 1994).

101 For example, KI, The Thomas Painter Collection (hereafter, Painter), Box 1, Series 2, c. 1, Vol. 3: Painter Letters: 1 January and 7 November 1947.

102 Painter, Box 1, Series 2, c. 1, Vol. 7: 18 July 1950. See also, KI, Kinsey Correspondence Collection: Thomas Painter, 4 April 1949.

103 Painter, Box 1, Series 2, c. 1, Vol. 9: 4 February 1952.

104 Painter, Box 1, Series 2, c. 1, Vol. 10: 18 April 1953.

105 Painter, Box 1, Series 2, c. 1, Vol. 9: 28 January 1952.

106 Ibid., 17 November 1952.

107 Painter, Box 1, Series 2, c. 1, Vol. 6: 10 September 1949. It was called putting the arm up rather than fisting. The letter reads: 'Then (now hold your hat) the boy asked had Edward ever shoved his *arm* up anyone's asshole? No, Edward never had. But was always interested in obliging. (I measured Edward's hand at the thickest point and it, made narrow as he can, is 10 inches). So Edward puts in three fingers, four, the thumb, then over the thick part below the wrist at the thumb joint (where it is 10 inches) then on till the *whole hand* is in. Then there is a barrier. The boy makes a contortion, and the second, upper "sphincter" muscle opens and he progresses half way up his forearm, 11 inches. Upon request then he *clenches his fist* and *revolves* his hand and arm with a continuous motion, back and forth, while the boy jerks off, in extracy [sic].' For a recent discussion of the practice's genesis as a subculture: see Gayle Rubin's contribution to the History of Sexuality Discussion Network: Wed 11/7/2007 4:51 PM, H-HISTSEX@H-NET.MSU.EDU. John Loughery's rather good survey of US gay history dates the advent of fisting 'from 1969 to 1970': J. Loughery, *The Other Side of Silence: Men's Lives and Gay Identities: A Twentieth-century History* (New York, 1998), p. 364.

108 KI, Kinsey Correspondence Collection, Marty Deem to Alfred Kinsey, undated letter [1948].

109 Painter, Box 1, Series 2, c. 1, Vol. 18b: 28 September 1961.

110 Painter, Box 1, Series 2, c. 1, Vol. 10: 21 August 1953.

111 Ibid., 26 August 1953.

112 Ibid.

113 KI, Kinsey Correspondence Collection, Alfred Kinsey to Thomas Painter, 9 January 1948.

114 Ibid., 30 May 1948, 14 October 1948.
115 Ibid., 18 April 1950.
116 W. B. Pomeroy, *Dr. Kinsey and the Institute for Sex Research* (New York, 1972), p. 169.
117 Ibid.
118 KI, Kinsey Correspondence Collection, Jimmy Fox to Alfred Kinsey, 17 March 1951.
119 Painter, Box 1, Series 2, c. 1, Vol. 18b: 29 July 1961.
120 Ibid., 30 July 1961.
121 Painter, Box 1, Series 2, c. 1, Vol. 6: 19 November 1949.
122 A letter dated 2 September 1962, pasted into the front of the book: Painter, 'Male Homosexuals', Vol. 2: Minton discusses Painter's unpublished history in *Departing from Deviance*, ch. 6.
123 D. Paulson and R. Simpson, *An Evening at the Garden of Allah: A Gay Cabaret in Seattle* (New York, 1996), p. 125. See, especially, chs 1 and 7.
124 E. Newton, *Mother Camp: Female Impersonators in America* (Englewood Cliffs, NJ, 1972), ch. 1.
125 Ibid., p. 10.
126 Woodlawn and Copeland, *Low Life in High Heels*, p. 66.
127 R. C. Doty, 'Growth of overt homosexuality in city provokes wide concern', *New York Times*, 17 December 1963.
128 H. Huncke, *The Herbert Huncke Reader*, ed. B. G. Schafer (New York, 1997), p. 254.
129 J. Mills, 'The detective', *Life*, 3 December 1965. Figure 8 was used in the *Life* piece, but Figure 7 was not.
130 H. Selby, *Last Exit to Brooklyn* (New York, 1957). I discuss this book in the next chapter.
131 A letter dated 2 September 1962, pasted into the front of the book: Painter, 'Male Homosexuals', Vol. 2.
132 KI, Kinsey Correspondence Collection, Alfred Kinsey to Thomas Painter, 24 November 1951.

2

Contexts

> Mrs. Dodge with dark purple eyelids had joined the group, blinding everyone with the neck of her dress, a wide band of brilliants. She was laughing loud at Santiago who had just asked her if she had ever done anything with her breasts beside let them hang. He means have you ever had it between them Julian said. She liked Julian very much . . .
>
> Mrs. Dodge took off her clothes. She was short and fat and glowing. All three were nude. They got into bed, Julian between them.
>
> You're the only sissy I ever loved Santiago said to him. He's the only sissy I ever loved Santiago said to Mrs. Dodge. He put his arm around Julian who moved closer to Mrs. Dodge. Damn you he said and hit Julian, but not hard, on the top of the head.
>
> Be nice Mrs. Dodge said.
>
> Julian's eyes and lips were closed.
>
> Be nice now. (Charles Henri Ford and Parker Tyler, 1933)[1]

Kevin White has written perceptively of the working-class sexual cultures of America's largest cities in the first three decades of the twentieth century, where there were two noticeable types of men, the effeminate homosexual and the masculine 'straight':

> what is indeed most striking . . . is the extent of the overlap and interaction between the heterosocial and homoerotic worlds as well as the amount of homoerotic practice that resulted. It was in reality difficult to differentiate a heterosexual and a homosexual world. A kind of tolerance therefore developed among the working class. Not merely were the two worlds physically close to one another, but often both kinds of activities were pursued in the same bars.[2]

This book will be navigating such sexual cultures in New York with a focus on the period from the 1940s to the 1960s. It too will be concerned with a mingling of heterosexual and homosexual desire, a crossing of boundaries, indeed with boundaries that may not have existed. It has its male effeminates and masculine 'straights', though perhaps the term straight is hardly appropriate. The hustler will be our guide to this milieu. But before we can begin, we have to chart a longer sexual history. For our story begins in those first three decades of the twentieth century. And it starts in Rhode Island rather than New York.

> Mr. Secretary, did you know that in nine instances, between the 18th of March and the 14 April [1919] that certain naval operators had permitted sexual perverts in the naval service to suck their penis for the purpose of obtaining evidence to be used before the court of inquiry . . . which evidence resulted in a recommendation, by that court, to try by general court martial 19 enlisted men and to give two men undesirable discharges?[3]

That was the intriguing question posed to Franklin D. Roosevelt, the Assistant Secretary of the Navy and future US President. It was asked in a naval investigation in Washington in 1920. These enquiries into 'immoral practices and conditions' involving sexual activity and cocaine use in and around the naval bases at Newport (Rhode Island), and the subsequent trials, investigations, and generated outrage, provide an informative glimpse at sailor sex not far from New York in the immediate period at the end of the First World War. The affair, which involved young sailors acting as agents provocateurs for suspected 'perverts', is the subject of a path-breaking article by George Chauncey demonstrating the complexity of sexual categories at that time.[4] Those who engaged in what we would term homosexual acts in Newport (the immorality involved same-sex sex) were not necessarily homosexual.

> To classify their behavior and character using the simple polarities of 'homosexual' and 'heterosexual' would be to misunderstand the complexity of their social system. Indeed, the very terms 'homosexual behavior' and 'identity', because of their tendency to conflate other phenomena that other cultures may have regarded as quite distinct, appear to be insufficiently precise to denote the variety of social forms of sexuality we wish to analyze.[5]

It is worth pausing for a while to look more closely at these social forms, for they relate directly to the subject matter of this book. It is certain that the situation at this naval base was not unique. When a naval official first alerted his superiors, an admiral is reported to have exclaimed, 'My God! Now it's Newport!' He had received similar reports from other places in the USA.[6] As Margot Canaday has recently shown, 'perversion' in the military of this era was perceived to be a widespread problem.[7]

The sexual interactions involving the naval personnel and civilians in and around Newport were summarized in an examination at the very start of the inquiry when a witness listed off the names of naval men and their associates who were 'cocksuckers', 'pogues', and 'two-way artists'.[8] Cocksuckers, it was explained to the uninitiated, were those who 'took it in the mouth' ('French style') or who 'Frenched'. A pogue 'could be screwed in the rectum', that is 'browned'. And a 'two-way artist is a man that would receive the penis through the rectum or suck a man's prick'.[9] Inhabitants of this sexual world were quite specific about whether an individual was a cocksucker or a pogue, about who could or could not be 'browned'.[10] It was an important issue. 'And the other day they read off and said I was a two-way artist', an effeminate naval hospital apprentice complained in court, 'I want to say that I have never taken a penis into my mouth; only in the rectum, and I would not do that if I could help it.'[11]

Although Chauncey uses the word 'gay' in his analysis, it is never employed by any of those in the investigations.[12] 'Homosexual' is another word that almost never appears in this archive.[13] The word that does occur is 'queer', and those termed queer – both by queer and non-queer – were men who were effeminate in appearance and/or perceived sexual role.[14]

Q. What do you mean by 'queer'?
A. He is either a pogue or fairy. 'Queer' means either a pogue or a cocksucker.[15]

Effeminacy was the determining trope of their same-sex sexual activity. Described variously as pogues, cocksuckers, fairies, ladies, punks, fruiterers, faggots, and queens, they were perceived by those who had sex with them as 'giving pleasure the same as a girl'.[16] They were 'sissified', acting 'effeminate', or talking like 'a woman'.[17] They referred to one another as 'girls', 'us girls', 'she', and took on female names like Salome, Ruth, Blanche, Edith, Ethel, Rebecca, Theda Bara, Flora Finch, Mary Pickford, and Beckie.[18] They might use facial powder and lipstick, and pencil their eyebrows. Sometimes they went in drag.[19]

Clearly, these sailors and their civilian counterparts are part of the history of male prostitution. Money was a motive, although this is not to deny sexual desire on their part. 'All of us girls are out for the pennies', one fairy was reputed to have stated.[20] 'They published the fact that they were prostitutes and such stuff as that.'[21] And there are multiple references to payment in cash or kind – including drugs – for sexual services.[22] 'I suggested that to make me happy he would have to get some cocaine', an operative reported of a potential sting.[23] Another was told by a fairy that he followed the fleet because he could 'make lots of money on them'.[24] Sailors both paid for sex and were paid for it; a marine said that he was paid $5 by a fairy who wanted to 'suck his prick'.[25] A witness said that 'Ruth', one of the accused fairies, a seaman second class, had told him 'that he had a string of husbands and they were supporting him; that he made lots of money'. 'He told me that if I would go to New York with him, he would take me to a place near Times Square where the "queens" hung out and I could fuck him, if I so desired.'[26]

Cocksuckers were effeminate but it was not a consistent effeminacy, for there were troubling disruptions of gender. They were presented in rather aggressively masculine terms in one witness's account. 'Speedy' was a 'hard man' who, when he 'sucked a man off . . . would draw his brains down through the head of his penis'. Another 'had a nice chin to rest a pair of balls on and he was still a harder man'. These were people to be wary of; they were likely to roll their customers.[27] Nor was there a consistent homology of sexual roles. Cocksuckers could be sucked.[28] They might ask to penetrate rather than be penetrated.[29]

One fairy proclaimed that 'half the world is queer and the other half "trade"'.[30] This was an exaggeration. Not all non-effeminate men had sex with their effeminate counterparts, but those who did – providing the cocks for the cocksucking, so to speak – were not considered queer. Indeed the term 'straight' was employed in the enquiry.[31] These were 'men' not fairies, and, as long as they were the perceived penetrator in the relationship and presented a masculine demeanour, were not of the same genus as those they might have sex with. 'I am a man', stated an operative who was contrasting himself with his male sexual partner.[32] Witnesses testified that the cocksuckers gathered at the Army and Navy YMCA 'to solicit trade' and took them either to rooms in the building or to nearby lodging houses. 'Beckie', a ship's cook, was described as sitting in the lobby of the Y, tapping his fingers against the arms of his seat and calling out 'Trade, it's trade, trade is what I want'.[33] There are stories of fairies servicing multiple partners; parties where men had sex on the bed or in the bathroom.[34] 'There was a little cocksucking done there', a naval fireman recalled of one such gathering.[35] The masculine men – the 'husbands' to the 'girls' or 'ladies' – were known as 'trade'.[36] They might be paid for sex, or might pay for it, but their appeal for their partner was their masculinity. As Chauncey has explained, mere engagement in sexual activity with another male was not sufficient to categorize that man as 'homosexual'.[37] Fairies and trade and the court agreed on this serious matter, as emerges clearly in one interchange between a defendant and the judge advocate:

> Q. In your previous testimony you testified that a straight person was one who did not reciprocate in any way, did you not?
> A. Yes, I believe so.
> Q. Then during perverted sexual intercourse a straight man is one who doesn't reciprocate in any way?
> A. I believe so; yes.

The man questioned refused to classify himself as 'straight' because he admitted to having 'yanked someone off'. He considered the fact that he had 'reciprocated' in same-sex sex (by masturbating a sexual partner) meant that he could not be described as straight. He had, he said, 'a dash of lavender'.[38]

The whole basis to the proceedings at Newport hinged on this distinction between straight and queer homosexual activity, separating accused fairy seaman from straight, seaman witness. One operative agent provocateur outlined a rather unconvincing account of his brief:

> In investigating these conditions in and about Newport we were never to take the initiative in an immoral act . . . The method used was to allow yourself to be approached by one of these men, go along with him, follow his suggestions until I was certain in my own mind that the man was or was not a pervert. Of course, a great deal of that was involuntary inasmuch as a man placing his hand on my penis would cause an erection and subsequent emission. That was uncontrollable on my part.[39]

The same pharmacist's mate explained to the investigating court that he thought it necessary to engage in oral sex to the point of emission to make it entirely clear that the man providing the service was a pervert.[40] A parade of naval personnel, all enrolled to provide incriminating evidence against fairies, casually recounted receiving oral sex: 'I worked up a hard-on and he went to it. I gave him the load and he ate it.'[41] Less commonly the witnesses described sodomy. 'He took it in his mouth. Afterwards he wanted me to do it from behind, after some time which I did.'[42] The masculinity of these men – the fuckers and the sucked – was not compromised; nor were they charged with 'immoral practices'. While the spokesmen of the local churches were vocal in their condemnation of the irony of these proceedings, their opposition (and support of a minister accused of immorality) was based on the unreliability of the naval agents provocateurs rather than any suggestion of their homosexuality.[43]

Though on the eve of the period covered by this book, the Newport case anticipates many of its themes: the idea that the sexual expression of a man's masculinity or effeminacy might have economic value, that male prostitutes could be masculine or feminine in their demeanour, and the role of the sailor in this sexual traffic; that acts and identities that we might assume to be heterosexual or homosexual had very different sexual meanings, including the possibility that two men could engage in a sexual act with only one of them considered 'perverted'; that a world with seemingly clear-cut notions of active and passive in terms of its sexual interactions was in fact far more complex in terms of actual behaviour; and that what (again) we might term 'homosexuality' was so firmly fixed to ideas of effeminacy.

Steven Watson's introduction to a later edition of Charles Henri Ford and Parker Tyler's *The Young and Evil* (1933) notes that their New York of the 1930s was characterized by its polymorphous and labile sexuality. Their experimental novel, based on their own experiences in the city, did not 'present a strictly homosexual world'.[44] The young men and women in *The Young and Evil* have sex, including multiple-partnered sex, in varied combinations and present themselves in an array of masculinities and femininities – both male and female. 'The Lesbian said yes your face is so exquisite we thought you were a Lesbian in drag when we first saw you and for two long hours they insisted that he would do better for himself as a girl.'[45] Identities (though the word scarcely seems sufficient) shift. Homosexuality is a habit; 'my homosexuality is just a habit to which I am somehow bound . . . its not love or romance but a dim hard fetich [sic] I worship in my waking dreams'.[46] The sexual persona mutates: 'But Karel was thinking of Louis turning queer so beautifully gradually and beautifully like a chameleon like a chameleon beautifully and gradually turning.'[47] As Joseph Boone has observed, '*everything* is in transit: bodies, identities, desires'.[48] And the text's lack of punctuation heightens the 'polymorphous fluidity' of its described desires.[49] It is not surprising that recent critics have reclaimed Ford and Tyler as textual pioneers in the creation of a queer modernism.[50]

Though more experimental, *The Young and Evil* is not unlike Carl Van Vechten's elegant *Parties* (1930), an earlier work describing the, well, partying in New York during that era, its speakeasies, bootleggers, drugs and alcohol, and the wealthy who slummed it in Harlem. 'Just parties, that's all. The only happy people left in New York are the Lesbians and the pederasts, and they are so happy they are miserable.'[51] *Parties* has kept boys and gigolos ('He doesn't have affairs: he has transactions').[52]

It has easy sex of variant combinations. 'I never sleep twice with the same person any more and I have such a frightful memory, she went on.'[53] 'You're sure it isn't Noma or Rosalie . . . or Roy? she inquired, not without malice.'[54] Van Vechten's journals and day books show that *Parties* was no mere invention; 'they take off their clothes & give a remarkable performance', he wrote of a prominent American artist and his actress companion, 'Ralph goes down on Carlotta. She masturbates & expires in ecstasy. They do 69, etc. I leave about 12.30.'[55] Van Vechten and friends accompanied the British playwright and novelist Somerset Maugham and his longtime companion to a male brothel in Harlem – 'Why don't you boys do something together and amuse us?' was Maugham's reported request.[56] For years on end, Van Vechten's life as a man of letters was interspersed with early morning clubbing in Harlem and partying. 'Then to my house . . .where we have a very gay party & everybody takes off their clothes. In bed about 3' was an entry for 1927.[57] 'The Fitzgeralds [Francis Scott and Zelda] pass out. I go to bed about 4.'[58] The poet Langston Hughes thought that Van Vechten's own parties were far better than the ones in his book.[59] Men like Van Vechten, as Chad Heap has expressed it, 'led complicated sexual lives that defied simple categorization as either heterosexual or homosexual'.[60]

The inhabitants of Ford and Tyler's New York include masculine homosexuals, fairies – especially fairies – Tyler referred much later to it as his 'years among the fairies' – lesbians, cross-dressers, queens, prize-fighters and their girls, dancers, models, gangsters, sailors, trade, and, of course, writers and poets.[61] It also comprises the hustlers of Broadway and 72nd Street: 'And here *o murderpiss beautiful boys grow out of dung* . . . They push flesh into eternity and sidestep automobiles. I bemoan them most under sheets at night when their eyes rimmed with masculinity see nothing and their lymphlips are smothered by the irondomed sky. Poor things, their genitals only peaceful when without visiting cards.'[62]

We also catch glimpses of the sexual configurations of the 1930s in Kennilworth Bruce's novel *Goldie* (1933), about a fairy, the Goldie of the book's title, an effeminate male prostitute, inhabitant of 'Limbo, the land of twilight sex'.[63] '[H]omo-sexuals' and the 'homo-sexualist' are mentioned.[64] There is even reference to becoming '"queer" in the fullest meaning of the word', seemingly implying being attracted solely to the same sex.[65]

> Goldie came to know hundreds of people like himself. Men, and women, too, whom the world called queer. Goldie divided them into the two

accepted classes. There were those who affected a feminine exterior to the limit allowed by the law. Then there were those who remained essentially male in appearance but whose instincts were just as inverted as those who usurped the voice, occupations, and mannerisms of the female.[66]

(The female inhabitants of Limbo consisted of the 'decidedly masculine' 'Dike', in tailor-made suit, collar and tie, and cropped hair, and her 'delicately feminine', gown-clad 'Lesbian lover'.)[67]

Yet Goldie's world is not simply one of the homosexual versus the heterosexual. It is certainly a world of 'fairies' and 'wolves'.[68] That is, those that belong 'to Limbo' are the males (fairies like Goldie) who 'attempt at femininity', and the conventionally masculine (the wolves) with 'abnormal appetite[s]'.[69] The sexual tastes of the masculine are explained as sexual excess, acquired taste, ennui, 'vice', and 'degenerate passion' rather than any declaration of sexual identity.[70] When hustling in New York, Goldie's various contacts (or putative contacts) included a former Air Service captain whose resort to fairies was part of his 'unending search for thrills' (women and heroin were not enough), a young man who thought that he was not being unfaithful to his girl by getting 'French' from a fairy, a gangster who kept a 'moll' but who wanted a fairy as part of his range of available lovers ('I'm outside the law... So why give a damn if it's a skirt or a kid I sleep with?'), a middle-aged, married man who said that it was 'a fact that there were certain things a man couldn't do with his wife and certain things that a wife couldn't do at all'.[71] (There were women too who sought out female prostitutes for sexual service, 'women on the borderline, genteel some of them, others shop girls who wanted a different thrill and found it easier to ask members of their own sex to provide it'.)[72] For Goldie's world also contains those 'who lapsed occasionally into Limbo and its pleasures'.[73] One of these is a grocery clerk who worked as hustler to support a wife, his four younger sisters, and his mother.[74]

Though both Boone and Juan Suárez stress the elusive nature of the described sexual desires in *The Young and Evil*, Boone has a tendency to interpret in terms of a 'gay' taxonomy (writing of 'an unabashedly gay character', 'an almost entirely gay world', 'gay incognitos'), while Suárez reads through the lens of 'queer' (he refers to 'queer desires and subjectivities' and claims the work 'still has much to say to our queer life today').[75] Yet neither gay nor queer quite captures the text and its context. Chad Heap's impressive new history of sex and race in New York and Chicago during this very period likewise struggles to accommodate sexual diversity with his adherence to historiographical assumptions of an inevitable gay-world-making: thus one ('new sexual and racial identities') contributes to the other (the 'codification of a new twentieth-century hegemonic social order').[76] The person who comes closest to identifying the spirit of this period is Scott Herring in his deconstruction of works by Van Vechten and Richard Bruce Nugent – ironic given his declared antipathy to historical recuperation and advocacy of 'sexual unknowing' rather than knowing.[77] Herring refers to sexual admixtures rather than identities and emerging communities: 'entrenched boundaries between homosexuality and heterosexuality ... are purely imaginary'.[78] 'Scattering into oblivion – rather than congealing into community – is the key trope here', he notes of *Parties*.[79]

Contemporaries had trouble discussing 1930s sex too. Samuel Kahn, who had considerable experience as a psychiatrist in New York in the 1920s and 1930s, wrote: 'It is known for a fact that a number of normal individuals indulge sparingly in homosexual acts in the active capacity and, with less frequency, in the passive capacity.'[80] He used the terms homosexual and, elsewhere in the book, heterosexual; following Freud, he saw homosexuality as regression to an early stage of childhood development. But Kahn was also clear about the overlaps in desire and acts. His definition of homosexual included those whose sexual preference was for their own sex yet who 'may accept the opposite sex'.[81] Another New York psychiatrist, George Sprague, wrote in 1938 of 'persons whose sexuality varies, being at certain periods in their lives quite heterosexually adjusted, but in whom interludes of homosexual activity occur ... less frequently, we find persons who seem so ambivalent in their erotism [sic] that they desire and actually carry on homosexual and heterosexual relationships simultaneously and with satisfaction'.[82] Again, the languages of hetero–homo were employed while simultaneously demonstrating the complexity of such classifications.

The writer Glenway Wescott captured the era's sexuality well when, from the perspective of the end of the 1940s, he recalled that the homosexuality of the previous generation was more of a sin than a culture: 'I think there must not have been quite so unabashed and homogeneous and self-conscious a homosexual society as such. It was still rather a sin, with something of Byronic fatalism.'[83]

This not strictly homosexual world forms the context for my study. George Chauncey has described a sexual culture divided into 'fairies' and 'normal men', or 'queers' and 'men', rather than heterosexual and homosexual.[84] Leo, an eighteen-year-old, African-American, effeminate man in Chicago, thought in terms of fags, faggots, cats ('colored queers'), bells, and queer people (on the one hand) versus Jam people, straight people, squares, and those who were manly (on the other). He felt that he could be himself when 'among the faggots'. He became confused when men who appeared masculine – 'men' – tried to french him.[85] The terms that were used for men who had sex with other men, Chauncey explains, were fairy, queer, and trade. Some men were seen as woman-like and effeminate (the fairy), but those who sought them out for sex (trade) were not considered homosexual or unmanly. What was important in this culture was whether a person acted like a male or a female (that is, their gender performance) rather than their sexual orientation (whether they were homosexual or heterosexual). Chauncey has discussed the code of the men (trade) who had sex with homosexuals (fairies and queers) while maintaining that they were not homosexual themselves. The penetrator, because penetration was associated with dominance, did not compromise his masculinity. A fairy was a fairy not because she (he) engaged in what we would term homosexual activity but because she (he) was the passive partner or woman-like. Men went with fairies much as they went with female prostitutes; indeed might view sex with a fairy like sex with a woman. This was activity that we would doubtless call homosexual, but the attitudes, desires, and identities involved in this activity were not what most would now identify with homosexuality.[86]

The basic rules of sexual engagement in this regime are alluded to in accounts of 'normal men' who were paid for sex with other men. A conventionally masculine Chicago hustler outlined what he would and would not do for money and/or a 'good time' ('i.e., good shows, food, etc.'). Queens would french him and he would brown them.[87] In his unpublished history of male prostitution in the 1930s, Thomas Painter outlined what masculine-identified hustlers had to do and their attitudes to such acts. They were expected to get an erection, allow fellation, and be willing to pedicate (sodomize). The rest, as he put it, was optional but desirable. Being blown and actively sodomizing were perceived as 'normal and masculine'. Hustlers had to be 'men', 'accepted as "trade"' – what Painter called 'prostitute timber'.[88]

> A man can admit to having been fellated by a 'fairy' or having pedicated some 'faggot' or other, and he loses very little face, but it is a question which is considered more reprehensible: to be a 'punk' – to have submitted to pedication, that is – or to be a 'cock-sucker', which term is at present the most villainous epithet of which an American feels capable. To be forced

to kiss or lick another person's penis is considered the nadir of humiliation among ordinary normal men, and we might mention a rancorous passage-at-arms which we observed on the subway, at the conclusion of which one of the two men involved hissed to the other: 'If I had you alone, you'd *suck my cock!*'[89]

Eddie, an eighteen-year-old Chicago hustler who was also a prize-fighter, distinguished himself from the 'queers' that he had sex with, and stressed that he used the money gained to go out with women. 'I'd rather have a girl anytime', he said when interviewed in 1933. A fellow newspaper seller introduced him to prostitution when he was about sixteen; 'he told me that there were a lot of queer guys around, and if I let them suck me off I could make a buck or two each time'. He mentioned the sexual acts that he would engage in. It is a long list: mutual masturbation ('jerking'), kissing, fellation (both giver and receiver), penetrative anal sex ('browning'), and receptive intercrural sex ('I told him he could put it between my legs or nothing at all'). He told stories of multi-partnered sex, including that involving men and women. Receiving anal sex seemed to be the only act that he would not permit: 'He wanted to brown me, but I told him that I didn't go in for that.' Eddie still went to confession occasionally:

> I tell the priest about hustling, and he told me to stop it . . . But I told him, how can I? I got to have some money, to take my girl out on Sundays . . . And I haven't got a job . . . I told him I sucked guys off, and he told me to stop that and be like other boys. But I told him other boys had a home and went to school and had money. I didn't have nothing . . . he told me to say fifty rosaries, and gave me absolution. I said them.[90]

The way in which the young Chicago hustlers distinguished themselves from those with whom they had sex may seem strange to the post-Stonewall observer. An itinerant who had travelled the USA hustling in a variety of cities ('as queers seemed to be constantly present in every city') was unembarrassed about deriving pleasure from his same-sex contacts: 'I like to get on top and fuck them in the mouth.' He also referred to wearing a rubber while engaging in anal sex ('when you hose in the ass', is how he put it). However, he denied that he was 'queer' himself. 'No, I'm not queer. I don't do anything. I never fool with anyone else, but let them fool with me. I did jerk them off sometimes. No. I'm not queer myself; I'd tell you if I was.'[91] He told his questioner that he preferred girls. It is puzzling what he meant by 'fool with', given his somewhat unbounded repertoire. Perhaps he merely meant that he never made the first approach, did not seek other men out for sex. His sociologist interviewer commented that although his subject, Bill, obviously enjoyed sex with males he was not a 'true homosexual'. It is notable that Bill never used the term homosexual. He referred to 'fairies' and 'queer'.[92]

There is an argument to be made, then, for a very different sexual regime in America in the early decades of the twentieth century. As Chauncey has put it, it was 'a world divided into "fairies" and "men" on the basis of gender persona' that would later be replaced by 'one divided into "homosexuals" and "heterosexuals" on the basis of sexual object-choice'.[93] (See Figure 9.)

We will discuss the culture of male effeminacy later in the book, but it is worth stressing now its ubiquity. Both Chauncey and Heap have established what has been called a pansy craze in the nightlife of the 1920s and 1930s.[94] Heap, who also writes of a conterminous lesbian craze, has shown the geographical and historical shifts in a fascination with effeminate male entertainers and female impersonators (and their female counterparts), and with the fairies who attended the various venues of night-time leisure, the tearooms, speakeasies, cabarets, clubs, drag balls, and restaurants. When the craze faded in the Village it moved to Times Square and then to Harlem.[95]

That a man might seek sex from a fairy as much as from a woman was not considered especially significant. In 1917, a doctor published his notes on the Brooklyn fairy 'Loop-the-loop', a 'perfectly virile' young man who cross-dressed and had paid sex with numerous men as a 'passive pederast' (between the thighs and in the anus).[96] He mentioned satisfying 'as many as forty men in twenty-four hours' and a line-up of twenty-three men in a Brooklyn room; 'it was truly remarkable to hear this nervous, loquacious, foul-mouthed and foul-minded "fairy" of the most degraded slums of a multi-millioned city chatter about his experiences, just as though he were talking about the rearing of fancy pigeons, or anything of a similar nature'.[97] One of the man's 'husbands', a musician, who accompanied him to a session with the doctor, was unconcerned that the latter knew of their relationship.[98] It was Loop-the-loop's insouciance (and mental state) that surprised the medical expert rather than his congresses with men. There was never any suggestion that those who had had sex with him should undergo any sort of treatment – other than that for syphilis.

Most of the desire in Claude McKay's *Home to Harlem* (1928) is opposite-sex. Jake Brown, the book's main character, likes women.[99] But one of the more positively portrayed roles in the story is that of a wolf,

9. Two New York hustlers, 1930s/1940s. From the Thomas Painter Collection. Reproduced by permission of The Kinsey Institute for Research in Sex, Gender, and Reproduction, Inc. Author's note: the photograph, an undated movie still from the 1930s or 1940s, captures the hustling binary of masculinity and effeminacy. The man on the right in drag owned a male brothel patronized by New York celebrities and shared Thomas Painter's taste in men.

Billy Biasse, 'the happiest, well-feddest wolf in Harlem'.[100] Billy's preferences are commented on but never condemned. Nor are the pansies. They are part of the decor in the speakeasies and various clubs in the novel. 'The pansies stared and tightened their grip on their dandies. The dandies tightened their hold on themselves. They looked the favored Jake up and down . . . Dandies and pansies, chocolate, chestnut, coffee, ebony, cream, yellow, everybody was teased up to the high point of excitement.'[101] Even at the start of the novel, when the absent Jake yearns for the women of Harlem, their allure is framed in terms of the glamour of the fairy: 'Brown girls rouged and painted like dark pansies. Brown flesh draped in soft colorful clothes. Brown lips full and pouted for sweet kissing. Brown breasts throbbing with love.'[102] A. B. Christa Schwarz has commented on the 'inappropriateness of an unqualified transference of the concepts of hetero- and homosexuality into McKay's real and literary world'.[103] The lyrics to the African-American blues singer Ma Rainey's *Sissy Blues* (Thomas Dorsey, 1928) capture the situation perfectly:

> I dreamed last night I was far from harm
> Woke up and found my man in a sissy's arms . . .
>
> Some are young, some are old
> My man says sissies got good jelly roll . . .
>
> My man's got a sissy, his name is Miss Kate
> He shook that thing like jelly on a plate . . .
>
> Now all the people ask me why I'm all alone
> A sissy shook that thing and took my man from home . . .[104]

Her man had gone off with a fairy but it was no more remarkable than leaving her for another woman, the more common theme of such music. It was her man's infidelity that was the subject of comment, not his sexual identity or masculinity. Women had to worry about competition from fairies as well as other women. (See Figure 10.) When the white fairy Baby Face first met the masculine African-American Sammy in James T. Farrell's (Chicago-based) short story, 'Just boys' (1931–34), Sammy was on the hunt for 'girls' but was attracted by Baby Face's femininity: 'He was as pretty as a girl, with skin as tender.' And so he responded when the fairy said: 'You like boys . . . too?'[105]

The (effeminate) fairy and (masculine) trade, then, were key to this sexual world and featured also in commercial and casual sex. One of the subjects in George Henry's study of the 1930s told the psychiatrist

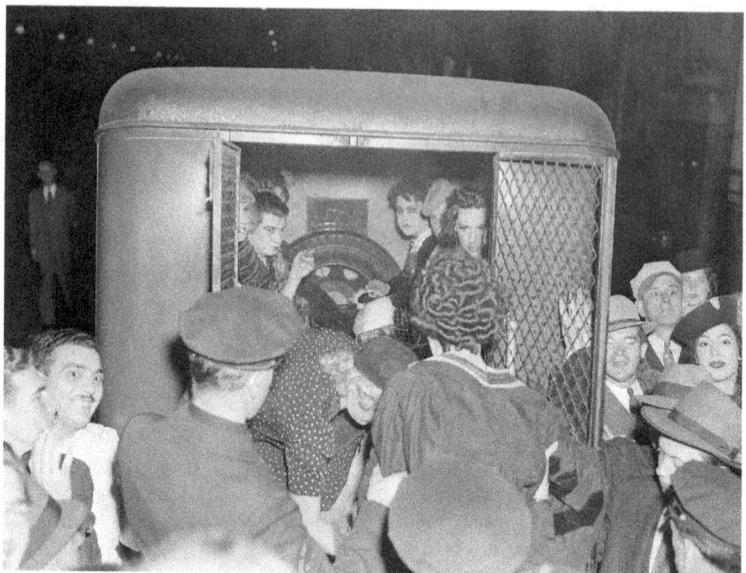

10. Groups of cross-dressed and effeminate men in police custody, New York, 1939. © Bettmann/CORBIS.

that 'There are two kinds of male prostitutes. One is heterosexual and prefers women but will sell his body to anyone for money. The other is the painted kind that has a feminine gait and hangs around Times Square.'[106]

Painter's account of male prostitution provided summaries of the lives of the first of Henry's types, more than twenty (heterosexual) hustlers. These young men do not speak to us direct but are heavily mediated through the longing of the cataloguer. Nevertheless, these brief life summaries tease out the ingredients of the hustler's appeal. One man had worked in hard manual jobs ('as a lumberjack, prize-fighter, truck-driver, barroom bouncer, seaman, etc'.), but hustled 'a year or more at a time – between jobs'.[107] Another was born in 'the meanest slum of New Jersey City, which is saying something'. He had been a hold-up man, bootlegger, pimp, hustler, and heroin addict.[108] Of another, Painter said that work never occurred to him as 'an alternative to homosexual prostitution, which was to him just another angle on robbery and chiselling, and which had little effect on his really vicious personality'.[109] Yet another, from Scranton, Pennsylvania, and of poor immigrant Polish background, drifted to Times Square in 1932. 'Young, well-built, sensuous looking, and quite lacking in moral scruples', he became a hustler. 'But after a few years at it, he consummated homosexual intercourse only as seldom as possible – being fervently heterosexual – and clipping, gambling, and mooching as much as possible.' 'Hustling and the homosexual world represent just another avenue of raising money by not working.'[110] Painter listed off cases of those who hustled through dissatisfaction with their low wages as dishwashers or busboys. One hustled occasionally to supplement his 'meagre income as a waiter'.[111]

Painter wrote of heterosexual/homosexual pleasure. One man claimed that he was a hustler because he liked the sex. He once took a girl to Coney Island and when he met a boy there could not decide whom he wanted to take to bed so had a 'threesome':

> He enjoyed active fellation [blowing] and passive pedication [being fucked], choosing large, muscular men . . . He also enjoyed normal coitus, cunnilinction, and being fellated by a girl; usually being attracted by the dark, petite, small-boned type of girl, but not really being very particular. He even enjoyed homosexual relations with homosexuals, again being very catholic in his taste. Sixty-nining – simultaneous mutual fellation-irrumation [fucking the mouth] – was his favorite diversion with these.[112]

Painter said that another had acquired a taste for sodomizing sixteen- and seventeen-year-old males, yet adjudged him to be 'primarily heterosexual' – 'Is now married and working as a stevedore, apparently settled down'.[113] We encounter a man described as 'strongly heterosexual' apart from a period as a 'wolf' (a sodomizer of youths). 'He is now happily married and has been working as a seaman for three years.'[114] One hustler was 'heterosexual, but didn't care much how he "got his nuts off"'.[115] Another, a Navaho, was 'strongly heterosexual, but admits to finding a dee[p] pleasure in active irrumation of a man (or woman); and with men this is what the act actually is'. He started life as a hustler in Times Square in the Depression in 1932 when he went with other transient boys to 'play the queers'.[116] Yet another was 'Generally quite heterosexual', but became 'exclusively a wolf for a period of two years, his sexual object being homosexual boys who submitted to pedication by him with pleasure'.[117] We encounter hustlers, on the one hand, who have sex with men though they are 'thoroughly heterosexual, and took no pleasure in homosexual intercourse', and others for whom 'homosexual intercourse is not unpleasant . . . he frequently enjoys it, but he is quite predominantly heterosexual, being very fond of girls'.[118]

George Henry and Alfred Gross conducted a study of 'homosexual delinquents' held in the Penitentiary of the City of New York, Riker's Island. One was 'Jimmy', a 'Drug-Addict Hoodlum Homosexual' and sometime hustler and seaman, who boasted that he had never fallen foul of the law for sexual offences: 'Mine have all been for junk, vagrancy, and disorderly conduct.' His persona was one of masculinity: 'Even in a homosexual group he strives to preserve the appearance of masculinity.' Henry was told by Jimmy's fellow inmates that he was a reluctant hustler but 'is said to make quite violent love to the effeminate boys who strike his fancy. There is no doubt that he spends much of his time reassuring himself of his masculinity.'[119] Henry observed of Jimmy (and his type), 'Like so many hoodlum homosexuals, Jimmy has convinced himself that he is not a homosexual because he enjoys the masculine rôle in homosexual intercourse. He finds it necessary to say to any one who will listen, "I'm no G[o]d da[m]n fag". Under protest he will accept identification of himself as a hustler.'[120] Henry and Gross also came across hustlers, what they termed the 'hoodlum homosexual', in another of their studies:

> The hoodlum homosexual waxes wrathy [sic] if he is regarded as a homosexual. He claims that he accepts the proposals of other homosexuals only as a source of revenue, and that he derives absolutely no pleasure from such relationships. The conduct of one or two of the toughest customers interviewed belied their protestations. These men make prostitution their profession, or at least a professional avocation. As time goes on, they derive not a little gratification from the satisfactory performance of their professional duties.
>
> So long as the hoodlum homosexual can exhibit to his public a rough, aggressive, 'hard-boiled' exterior, he is quite content. He preserves his *amour propre* among his kind by loudly protesting his masculinity, and perhaps by boasting a little of the 'fags' he has beaten and robbed. He seems to justify the fairies' description of him as 'rough trade'.[121]

'Just last night I went to a fag's house he wanted me to fuck him.' Such were the opening words of the sexual history of Walt Lewis, one of those collected by University of Chicago graduate student sociologists in the 1920s and 1930s, and used by White as an example of the movement between the worlds of homosexuality and heterosexuality.[122] We write of two worlds, but Lewis, an African-American, would have observed no such division. He nonchalantly (and without punctuation) referred to a 'fagish Bulldaggers fucking party a man frenching a woman a woman under him french him and a man frenching her'. He certainly never used the words homosexual or heterosexual. He talked of fags and 'bulldaggers' (or women-fuckers) rather than homosexuals and lesbians:

> Now the women fucker, she fucks women like men, if she fucks your wife, or girl, your girl will you cannot fuck good enough for her she will leave you are quit right away. The fags like to be fucked in the ass, just like when you fuck a woman some of them comes when you come, some of them jackoff when their are frenching you they like it that way they called that thrills, or seeking new thrills . . .[123]

Lewis was clear, and crude, about his enjoyment of sex with women – 'ways to fuck a girl' – and would pay for it. 'If I was rich I would never tire of fucking a nice good looking girl.' But he was also nonjudgemental and highly matter-of-fact about sex with men:

> he had me to lay between his legs and roll it to him like a man does to a woman when he jazz her. We laid there for about 2 hours and talked. We talked about was this He wanted me to fuck him, he said that he had an old man, and wanted me to he his old man, and said less get married I said when, he said right now,
> Some of them you cannot tell from a woman if they never have whiskers or mustash. They take in the ass, French you, like to be called girls names and if they like you will give you money, let you stay with them like a man and wife.[124]

Lewis had been paid for sex with men, sex with women, and sex with a woman while a man watched. As with all these men, however, there were things that he would not do. He would not provide oral sex, even to a woman.[125]

The cases collected by Painter, Henry and Gross, and the Chicago students testify to the mixture of heterosexual and homosexual desire associated with the hustler, their combination of what we (though not they) would call sex work with crime, violence, and other forms of getting by, their working-class background, and their other traded commodities – handsomeness, rugged masculinity, and muscularity. These verbal portraits are reinforced by Painter's photographic record, suffused with the same longing for masculinity. The unwary might think that these are simple images of gangsters and sailors, but they are of men who are also prostitutes. (See Figures 9, 11, 12, 13, 54, and 62.)

It was a complex sexual terrain. As we will see, women, fairies, homosexuals, trade (including seamen and those in the armed services), and hustlers attracted one another. Servicemen frequented New York's Central Park in search of women, and women went there to meet men. A serviceman might 'kid' with the women, some of them very young, but

New York hustlers

11. Irish-American hustler, 1937. From the Thomas Painter Collection. Reproduced by permission of The Kinsey Institute for Research in Sex, Gender, and Reproduction, Inc. Author's note: during the 1940s the man was in a ménage with his wife (and children) and a seaman.

12. A sailor/hustler, early 1940s. From the Thomas Painter Collection. Reproduced by permission of The Kinsey Institute for Research in Sex, Gender, and Reproduction, Inc. Author's note: the 'husband' of a man who ran male brothels in New York both before and after the war. The hustler later married (a woman) and moved to the mid-west.

New York hustlers

13. Bowery hustler, 1936–39. From the Thomas Painter Collection. Reproduced by permission of The Kinsey Institute for Research in Sex, Gender, and Reproduction, Inc. Author's note: the man was long-time 'husband' of a drag queen. They lived on the lower East Side.

end up having sex with the homosexuals who also frequented the park. The sexual activity there comprised group sex with individual girls – 'line-ups' – as well as homosexual encounters.[126] One restaurant at 48th Street 'was a very notorious rendezvous for "fairies" and their hangers-on until the police and management became bored and impatient with the noise and confusion and disorder and drunken fighting and screaming, and with the painted, mincing effeminates accompanied by soldiers, sailors and toughs'.[127] Riverside Drive was the haunt of Navy and Army men looking for female prostitutes and therefore attracting homosexuals and hustlers – a symbiosis of desire that, as we will see, was just as strong in the 1940s. 'Where homosexuals gather, hustlers will gather', and during the 1920s and early 1930s Riverside Drive at about 96th Street was 'a hive of homosexual activity every mild evening and even during the winter'.[128]

Painter recognised that this 'mixture' was captured in the paintings of Paul Cadmus and he thought that the hostility of naval officials to *The Fleet's In!* (1934) was motivated more by the recognition of its 'homosexual implication' than its portrayal of female prostitution.[129] Both *The Fleet's In!* and *Shore Leave* (1933) have Cadmus's trademark off-centre fairy propositioning a sailor. But the homoerotics of the picture are far more central than that, adhering to the bodies of the to-be-looked-at sailors.[130] Richard Meyer has noted the crotch-level positioning of the characters in *The Fleet's In!* and the cling of the women's dresses and the sailors' trousers in all three paintings.[131] Meyer writes perceptively of a 'complex knot of desire' in Cadmus's sailor trilogy: that of the women, the sailors, and the homosexuals.[132] Although neither the artist nor commentators have said so, two of the centrally positioned floosies in *Shore Leave* and *Sailors and Floosies* (1938) may have been male rather than female. (See Figures 14, 15 and 16.) If so, the knots of desire represented were even more complicated.

The effeminate had a presence both in the bars where homosexuals went to meet other homosexuals and in those more disparate ones where homosexuals – both masculine and effeminate – hoped to encounter servicemen and hustlers, and where the servicemen might end up with almost anyone of any sex, either paying or being paid! 'Soldiers and sailors were always ready prey', writes Kennilworth Bruce of the fairy Goldie's potential customers.[133] When young Eddie Owens Martin arrived in New York from Georgia in the 1920s, he quickly discovered that there was a living to be made from the Maltese on the Lower East Side. 'I learned to hustle them. You had to dye your hair blonde and use

14. Peg house owner in drag, 1930s/1940s. From the Thomas Painter Collection. Reproduced by permission of The Kinsey Institute for Research in Sex, Gender, and Reproduction, Inc. Author's note: the man's 'husbands' were hustlers.

that Peaches & Cream powder 'cause they wanted the more feminine type. And I'd live with one or another of these Maltese for two weeks three weeks, sometimes a month.'[134]

One popular bar on 42nd Street near Times Square was a 1930s 'rendezvous for homosexuals and for prostitutes to them, including the men of the nation's uniformed service'. The patrons of this bar included both boys in 'dungarees and polo shirts' and 'painted young effeminates'.[135] Another bar, in the Bowery, was described as loud and 'camp', its occupants 'always and forever noisily "camping" – doing *almost* anything and ostentatiously saying *absolutely* anything'. Painter identified a 'painted young homosexual male whore "swishing" and posing'. The described sexual possibilities were various but the clientele included effeminate hustlers.[136]

In the 1930s, 'painted faggots' were to be found on the blocks above and below 72nd Street between Central Park and Broadway – because the end of 72nd Street was where the sailors disembarked.[137] The future features editor of *Vogue*, seventeen-year-old Leo Lerman, knew the 'queer speakeasies' of West 72nd Street in the early 1930s and the young, effeminate, 'mincing' men who adopted the names of female stars (Mae

15. Paul Cadmus, *Shore Leave*, 1933. Oil on canvas, 33 × 36 in. Whitney Museum of American Art, New York. Gift of Malcolm S. Forbes. Photography by Geoffrey Clements. © The Paul Cadmus Estate.

West, Jean Harlow, Gloria Swanson), sometimes wore drag, and would have sex for money or for fun. Their beat included the west side of Fifth Avenue, starting at 42nd Street, the west side of Riverside Drive as far north as 89th Street.[138] Painter wrote in 1940 or 1941 that he thought that 'the personally homosexual hustler is disappearing, at any rate as a street phenomenon'. However, in the 1920s and 1930s 'the flaming homosexual was a common sight on the streets of mid-town New York':

> there were blatant, painted, 'flaming' young homosexuals (older ones seldom try to flame) with marcelled hair quite long and held in place with innumerable hair pins, with mascaraed [*sic*] eyelashes, powdered cheeks, lipsticked mouths, and riotously colored fingernails, their fingers vulgarly ornamented with large rings, their clothing femininely soft and loudly colored, their shoes suede, their whole appearance and manner calculated

16. Paul Cadmus, *Sailors and Floosies*, 1938. Oil and tempera on linen mounted to Masonite, 25 × 39½ in. Whitney Museum of American Art, New York. Gift of Malcolm S. Forbes. Photography by Geoffrey Clements. © The Paul Cadmus Estate.

to attract the attention of normal men. These were to be seen any night in Times Square.[139]

Henry and Gross included an effeminate male prostitute in their study of homosexual delinquents, referred to earlier. He was an eighteen-year-old, Puerto Rican 'male prostitute' called Santos, 'lisping' and 'excessively feminine in his movements', who had been a prostitute since the age of thirteen (and had rectal gonorrhoea).

> Santos measures his success by his earnings. He is sure that he has done as well, if not better, than most of the boys who loiter around Forty-second Street between Broadway and Eighth Avenue, a street known by homosexuals as the 'Meat Market'. Here hoodlum homosexuals meet prospective customers and arrange the details of payment, the form of sex play, and the place where it is to occur. Santos says that his usual fee is $1. On one evening he took in as much as $6 for three sexual experiences.
>
> A few flagrantly exhibitionistic fairies are able to make a living through the sexual gratification of men who are interested in their type of service. Ordinarily, however, the hustler is the one who is paid by the 'queen', 'bitch', 'fag', or 'fairy' – that is, by an effeminate exhibitionist who not only brazenly proclaims his homosexuality to the interested, but attempts to force it on the notice of others. Like the female prostitute, the effeminate male prostitute has a more masculine male prostitute somewhere in the

offing to whom he contributes and who serves as his protector. Sometimes these protectors are gangsters. Emotional attachments between fairies of Santos' type and their protectors are ephemeral affairs.[140]

Santos told Henry that his mother knew of his occupation and accepted money from him for the family coffer.[141]

Effeminacy and cross-dressing – the fairy and transvestite – are somewhat blurred in Painter's history of the 1930s. There are certainly references to male–'female' pairings: cross-dressing men with conventionally masculine hustler 'husbands'. Indeed there are photographs of both in Painter's collection (see Figures 9, 12, 13, and 14). Painter knew a hustler who lived with a heterosexual hustler (his 'husband'), and who dressed in drag and fellated 'her' customers or who engaged in anal intercourse, with the sexual partner under the misapprehension that they were 'copulating with a girl'.[142] He writes of a cross-dressing homosexual who tells a john that he is menstruating so can only have anal or (provide) oral sex, of the use of breast pads and a girdle to hold up tell-tale testicles and penis, of the strategy never to strip, and of the employment of a rubber vagina or the technique of slipping the penis into the anus instead of the (non-existent) vagina. 'This form of seduction – pretending to be a girl, wig, breast plumpers, false vagina, and all – is rather common, especially among male prostitutes who are themselves homosexual.'[143] Painter's early study of prewar hustling and homosexuality reflected his heavily gendered classifications of male prostitution: the masculine hustler was simply a 'hustler'; the effeminate hustler was a 'homosexual male whore'. In this worldview, *homosexual* male prostitutes were effeminate by definition – there are references to their womanish ways and need for a 'husband' – whereas *heterosexual* male prostitutes were represented as masculine, or hyper-masculine.[144]

That this somewhat simplistic division occluded the labile sexuality referred to earlier is clear even from Painter's own sources. A cross-dressed proprietor of a peg house (male brothel) was a 'pedicant – but extremely virile, both looking and acting. He is muscular and heavy set. Never camps or swishes, even in private.' His sexual tastes in men were 'almost identical' to Painter's.[145] Another owner of a male brothel, also with similar likes to Painter, had operated as 'Dolores', a hustler in drag, before he ran his own business. When he operated the peg house he reverted to a masculine name but still 'tried out all the trade that came to her place'.[146]

One of the best-known sources for the history of New York sex in the prewar period is George Henry's earlier-mentioned study of sex variants.

It has added significance for us in that Henry enlisted the assistance of the young Painter (in his pre-Kinsey years) to provide hustler contacts as well as his own sexual history. Henry's book, *Sex Variants* (1941), published under the aegis of the Committee for the Study of Sex Variants, consisted of a classification of sexual behaviour in terms of the extent to which the cases covered 'deviate from heterosexual adjustment'.[147] Henry was constructing heterosexuality at the same time he was charting deviance.[148] I will argue that his categories of 'bisexual', 'homosexual', and 'narcissistic' (a category that included hustlers and transvestites, by the way) not only fail to contain their case studies but also – through their very categorization – distort the sexual flexibility and multiplicity evident even within the confines of these limited sexual histories. In particular, one aspect of the Henry cases, the persistence of opposite-sex sexual interaction amidst the supposed same-sex deviancy, has direct bearing on what follows in this book. 'Heterosexuality' and 'homosexuality' continually interacted in all Henry's categories, the homosexual and the narcissistic no less than in the bisexual.

We might expect a labile sexuality from those described as bisexual. Donald H. described mutual masturbation and intercrural sex with sailors, and sex with a man and his wife (Donald H. sodomized the man while he had intercourse with his wife). He had sex with hitch-hikers, hoboes, and prizefighters, group sex with two young itinerants and three nurses (what he calls 'normal sexual relations'), and sex with a cross-dressed girl whom he had picked up thinking she was male. Though married, he took up with a 'very masculine looking' former gangster who alternated between fairies and women. The man, who had been married several times, and who still 'needed a girl' occasionally, let Donald H. bugger him.[149] Other bisexual cases included a man, Sydney H., who enjoyed being fellated by men, sodomy (of men), and sex with women: 'I like normal coitus and to use my mouth with women, the mouth first. I enjoy active sodomy but orgasm in the vagina is best. The sex act with men is not as interesting as with women who are really emancipated.' This man recounted how he had participated in a female friend's sexual marathon with two men hired expressly for their services. The men had sex with each other and with her; she enjoyed watching them have oral sex but they had to reserve their orgasms for her.[150]

We might also anticipate a more fluid sexuality in the cases classified as narcissistic (Henry's third category). Max N., who claimed that he had a 'new boy every night' some weeks, including the hustlers of Times Square and Central Park, was attracted both to virile men and to the 'obviously effeminate', but had also participated in 'mass sex relations', 'parties in which both men and women took part'. He claimed to appreciate beauty, whether it was male or female.[151]

The hustlers included in the narcissistic category also complicate Henry's categorizations. Victor R., the proprietor of a homosexual brothel, said that the masculine hustlers which he procured on Riverside Drive, 42nd Street, and various parks and cafés, rarely were homosexual; they just did it for the money. 'Some of these boys have mistresses and a few have wives and children whom they support with their earnings.'[152] Leonard R., a hoodlum hustler, was an experienced male prostitute, who plied his trade in the restaurants and bars between 43rd and 59th Streets. He claimed to charge from $20 to $150 for a night. 'All I do is to get in bed with them and perform active sodomy or let them go down on me.' 'During all this I was having relations with girls, mostly prostitutes. I just pick them up, have sex with them, and then turn them loose.' He had a long-term relationship with a young policeman's widow (who had paid sex with women to supplement her pension) and said that he got 'most pleasure' from sex with a woman, while acknowledging the 'excitement' of being picked up by a strange man.[153]

Clearly, these hustlers had sex with both males and females. Peter R., described by Henry as variously 'a delinquent, vagrant, hoodlum, prostitute, or criminal, depending upon the particular time in his career that he happened to be under observation', was working lucratively as a male model when interviewed for Henry's book. Although he claimed to have had sex with some prominent New York men, including actors and movie stars, his accounts of male–male sex were interspersed with stories of sex with women. 'For the past four years I've been having sex with both men and women.'[154]

This mix of the hetero and homo is unsurprising in such men. But sex involving women is by no means absent in Henry's *homosexual* cases. Michael D. recalled a woman that he knew who lived with a man but 'was attracted to homosexual men and to a few homosexual women'. She would arrange for men to have sex while she watched.[155] He referred to group sex, 'a daisy chain', in which women might well take part.[156] Another, Eric D., told his classifier that 'sodomy with a woman has opened up to him the possibility of sex with women'.[157] In fact these heterosexually involved homosexuals challenge their taxonomy, though Henry seemed oblivious to these inconsistencies. Eric D., who considered himself 'homosexual', who liked to perform pederasty and fellation at the same time, and who picked up sailors because they 'like pederasty', also knew people involved in mixed-sex 'orgies of pain', had 'quite a number of affairs with women', and considered heterosexual relations 'more thrilling'. He married a 'bisexual' woman shortly after he was interviewed for the survey.[158] Robert T., yet another classified as homosexual, said that he had had sex with many 'homosexual men, most of them pick-ups' but was also going out with women. 'In the past ten years it's been about the same. I have spasms now and then with men or women but mostly with men. This last week I slept with a different person every night. Some of them were women and none of them interested me.' He said that he had no 'special preference for either sex'.[159] Though popular with homosexuals, James D. had had some group sexual experiences with men and women; 'I enjoyed both the homosexual and heterosexual relations.'[160] Nonetheless, he, like several others, appears in Henry's homosexual cases.[161]

It is worth pausing for a moment and asking just what sorts of desires are being charted in Henry's catalogue of 1930s sex. When writing of Michael D., one of his homosexual cases, Henry noted his subject's ability to 'be aggressive or passive as he chooses'. His 'diverse desires and the ability to gratify them', Henry admitted, 'demonstrates the futility of rigid classification of sex variants'.[162] Yet the expert persevered with his categories, even though they were threatened with every detail of desire and act.

There are indications that the subjects themselves categorized their sexual acts. The word queer is used in the sense of homosexual.[163] But we also have same-sex sexual activity – from Henry's 'homosexual cases' moreover – where at least one of the participants was not 'conscious I was being homosexual', even though he had read about homosexuality.[164] There is the young man who had practised fellatio and had been fellated and had engaged in mutual masturbation before he ever knew the word 'homosexual'.[165] Eric D. 'knew what homosexuality was but I had no idea that it had any connection to me'. He said that he 'went around' with homosexuals for a year 'believing myself not to be one'.[166] Salvatore N. said

> I often ask myself whether I am really a homosexual or merely a person who performs homosexual acts through association. I never want to have an affair with another homosexual. Taking the penis in my mouth does not satisfy me. Homosexual practices disgust me. Men who speak with an effeminate voice, who refer to each other as 'she' or who make feminine gestures, are repugnant to me. My desire is for virile men who never think of such things and so I can see no hope of complete satisfaction.[167]

Painter, who appeared in Henry's book along with his hustler associates, later questioned the sexologist's categorizations. 'Dr. Henry obviously believes that participation in a homosexual act makes one a homosexual, and we do not believe any such thing.' He was especially critical of the doctor's characterization of the hustler Leonard R. as homosexual when he was not homosexual: 'most male prostitutes to homosexuals are themselves heterosexual'.[168]

It is tempting to read these cases as a direct entry to the sexual cultures of the 1930s and earlier. Henry Minton has interpreted the sex variant material as providing a 'window into the personal and cultural experiences of gay men and lesbians in the 1930s', referring both to the 'visible urban homosexual subcultures' of that period and to the narratives as 'personal and collective struggles for self-validation'.[169] Indeed he interprets the case histories as 'homosexual life stories', the title of a chapter in his book, *Departing from Deviance* (2002), and writes both of sexual identities and 'coming out'.[170] The episode, for him, is 'part of the history of gay and lesbian consciousness'.[171] The most blatant forcing of sexual identities on people who (on my reading of the material) did not clearly exhibit them in any recognizably modern sense of the word can be found in a co-authored earlier article by Minton that sees in these 'life stories' the construction of a 'queer' identity based on 'sexual object-choice', a prototype of the 'gay identity of the 1970s liberation movement'. Not only is the fairy replaced by 'queerness' in this teleology but also this visible identity work is effected against a 'newly established', fully-constituted (and assumed) *heterosexuality*.[172] My argument will be that male effeminacy continued as a powerful element in the same-sex sexual imaginary and that heterosexuality was as much in the process of construction as any of its supposed others.

Jennifer Terry recognizes that the accounts in the study are shaped by the psychiatric interviews and the doctor carrying out the interview, recording it, and writing it up as a 'connected history' (Henry's words), and is fully aware that understandings of homosexuality were being constructed in the text itself. Yet she also wants to use the cases ethnographically to read the accounts of the sex variants as guides to 'a shadowy subculture' and as 'an articulation of their variant subjectivity'.[173] Thus she sees the case studies as oppositional texts, capturing moments of interaction between resisting subject and scientific expert, and reads 'variant subjectivity' through the surviving reports of the interviews. However, it is debatable just how oppositional these texts really are. Notions of speaking back, confrontation, tensions between interviewee and psychiatrist, and dissonance must be tempered somewhat by the reader's realization that the only way that he/she knows about such 'resistance' is because the alleged discomforted medical expert recorded and published it in its complexity.[174] While the scientific expert's commentary, his authoritative gloss, attempted to impose parameters, Henry would hardly have recorded and relayed so much complexity had the impulse to control been uppermost in his thoughts.[175]

Yet Terry is certainly correct in observing that the case studies indicate sexual fluidity: 'the boundaries of sexual identity were not so clearly drawn along the lines of exclusive sexual orientation as we might presently conceptualize them in the light of the lesbian and gay liberation movements beginning in the 1960s'.[176] The complexity of these cases subverts the overall attempt to categorize.[177]

One of the principal shortcomings of the Henry material is that we do not have access to the direct statements and languages of those interviewed; we have only the printed summaries, or rather interviewers' interpretations of what their subjects said. Thus when those interviewed refer to being 'homosexual', to 'homosexual relations', 'homosexual desires', 'homosexual practices', and 'homosexual experiences', or to 'homosexual circles', and 'overt homosexuality', and reputedly talk of 'homosexuality', there is no way of knowing whether this is their language or their questioner imposing the term 'homosexual' on other ascriptions.[178]

The advantage of the earlier-cited Chicago study is that we do have entry not only to original statements and letters but to the sociologist's attribution of meaning to their findings. It provides an instructive comparison to Henry's New York data. In Chicago, as intimated earlier, the word 'homosexual' is rarely used – certainly not to the extent of the suspiciously edited Henry interviews. Even the jokes collected there in the 1930s invariably refer to queers, queens, and cocksuckers rather than homosexuals.

> A belle went to a priest to confess. She told him that she was a cocksucker and wanted penance. The father asked the other father, 'What shall I give her?' The other father answer[ed], 'Not more than $5.00.'
>
> A queer met another one on the boulevard and said, 'Oh Masie what a beautiful pearl you have on your tie.' The other queer answered saying, 'Why that isn't a pearl, that is just plain carelessness.'
>
> A queen was following a sailor all round the port. The sailor said, 'If you don't stop following me, I will stick my prick down your throat and choke

you to death. How loud can you holler help[?'] The queen in a meek voice said 'Help'.[179]

A glossary of homosexual terms drawn up by the Chicago researchers was heavily weighted towards effeminacy. 'Belle', 'Drag', 'Temperamental', 'Marjorie', 'Fish queen', 'Queen', 'Ella', 'Auntie', 'Lily', 'Bitch', 'Fairy-joint', 'Gay', 'Chorus moll', 'Girls', 'Fruiterer', 'Dearie', 'She', 'Swish', 'Camp', 'Fairy meat', 'Get her', 'Maude's back hair', 'Switch' all denoted feminine characteristics. Thus 'Swish' meant to 'walk and act with extreme effeminacy; shaking hips, rolling shoulders, walk mincingly'. 'Fairy meat' referred to a 'type of attractive youth . . . well built'.[180] The terms listed reflected the language of the streets. Letters collected by the interviewers and the life histories themselves all referred to a queer effeminacy rather than homosexuality per se: 'queer', 'Swishy bells', 'cock suckers', 'pansy', 'Nellie', 'Miss Millard', 'fellows that wore make up and had plucked eyebrows', '"Showy" people', 'Margie queen'.[181] But the actual glossary imparted academic meanings. Thus words that may have not actually have connoted the precise identity 'homosexual' became such in their gloss. A 'belle' was 'any homosexual person'. A 'Fairy-joint' was a 'place where homosexuals gather or can be found'. Most tellingly, 'Queer' became 'anything or anyone homosexual'. While the material they collected actually reflected a sexual world divided into the effeminate and the 'normal' man – there are also entries for 'Trade', 'Dirt', 'Wolf', 'Punk', and 'Jam' – the budding academics translated it as a world of homosexuals and 'normal' men.[182] They were only partially aware of this transmigration of meaning. One of the young researchers, Earle Bruce, observed in his dissertation that his sample favoured the 'more feminine, passive members of the homosexual group' but claimed that it reflected social reality.[183] He could not have anticipated contrary readings of his own collected interviews.

Bruce's collected life histories in fact convey a remarkably sexually fluid world, and one where few of the matrices of active/passive seem to have been observed in practice. One man had started experimenting with women's cosmetics as a teenager at a time he was having sex with an older girlfriend. He read *Twilight Men, Goldie, Strange Loves, Strange Brother* and other such literature, was attracted to the life described in this fiction, and sought out Chicago's fairies. He plucked his eyes to indicate his sexual availability and began to work as a hustler on the North Side. 'I did everything possible to imitate the effemininty [sic] of the queers that I had come into contact with. I began to wear flashy and obvious clothes, and use cosmetics to a greater extent.' His customers were 'all trade, masculine fellows'. He said that he preferred 'sissyfied' men but went with trade for money. He had worked the clubs as a female impersonator and recalled being called 'cocksucker, fruit, fairy', instead of being appreciated for his craft. This was a man who had been drawn into a lifestyle that seemed far more exciting than that of the 'jam'. Yet his effeminacy did not indicate a simple passivity translated into sexual practice. He did not like to be browned by his trade when he was an effeminate hustler so presumably provided manual or oral relief. His personal sexual preference was for effeminate men and he liked penetrative sex where he was the penetrator: 'I get the greatest kick out of browning someone.' He used the words 'queer' (which he associated with effeminacy) and 'sissies', and 'jam' and 'trade', but only once referred to 'homosexual'. When he used the word 'homosexual', it was to indicate an act – 'homosexual intercourse' – rather than a type of person.[184]

Another interview suggested a similar attraction to the excitement of queer life. The young man claimed that he had started off as 'very masculine' but had acquired the attributes of effeminacy: 'I have become bitchy.' He outlined the characteristics of being 'bitchy'. 'When a bitch is speaking to a bitch, they call one another by a bitchy name.' He discussed the use of feminine names (Maisie, Girl, Miss), the parading on the boulevard, constant gossip about lovers, the sexual banter – 'Oh go home, and clean your hole out Tessie' – and the oral sex and daisy chains (group sex). He worked as a hustler, 'frenching' his clients; he said that, unlike many of his effeminate friends, he did not enjoy providing oral sex but calculated having 'frenched about 100' in just two months. He, like so many we will encounter in this book, had boundaries that did not quite conform to the sexual rules that historians have come to expect. Here was an effeminate hustler who, along with fellow 'bitches' (they called themselves bitches rather than fairies or pansies), earned money fellating. His declared sexual preferences, however, were *being* fellated ('I have been frenched 10 times') and browning ('I have browned others at least 25 times'). He said that he liked 'men' rather than 'bitches' – 'if I can't have a man I just don't want them' – and would not let a 'flaming fag french me'. Even he was not always able to tell the sexuality of a man by his outward appearance, for he complained about clients who looked conventionally masculine 'and when I get them down to my room, I find they are a professional cocksucker'. His annoyance was from a professional point of view: it took more time and trouble to fuck them than to simply fellate them. This was a fairy who could tell trade, 'turn over and I will brown you like mad'![185]

While the 1930s have been characterized as a period of labile sexuality, we should not overdraw the contrast between it and the postwar period. Much the same could be said of the New York that greeted Painter when he returned from his military service in 1945: 'The succeeding four nights have proven that New York is still a Babylon and a Sodom – if not more so.'[186] After describing how he penetrated an infantry sergeant, Purple Heart, 'pleasantly muscular, quite masculine', Painter recounted an evening involving group sex, female-to-male, male-to-male, male-to-male-to-female, and golden showers (males-to-male): 'The next night at M's . . . was climactic, even for that dive.' Those participating included Painter, the infantryman, an attractive woman, an 'extremely homosexual Cuban' who dressed as a gypsy and had injected his pectoral muscles with paraffin to make them look like breasts, two 'Broadway sharpies talking jive talk', and M and G (G being M's 'husband'). At one point, G went down on the woman while 'Gypsy' sodomized him.[187]

We saw that Painter argued that the open fairydom of the 1920s and 1930s was a thing of the past, yet the effeminate presence was still visible around 72nd Street in the 1950s – indeed the street features in Hubert Selby's *Last Exit to Brooklyn* (1957).[188] Painter himself gave an account of the occupants of the Cork Bar on 72nd, 'the most pronounced faggots I have seen in years and years. Boys who, without noticeable make-up, are so like girls as to be sort of fascinating in a morbid sort of way. Until one decided to mince up, exactly like a female whore, and talk to me.'[189] The former gang member Claude Brown said that there were 'a whole lot of faggots' in Harlem in the 1950s. 'Nobody thought anything was wrong with faggots. Faggots were an accepted part of life.'[190]

The world evoked in the postwar novel *Last Exit to Brooklyn* would not be out of place in 1930s New York.[191] This hard-drinking, violent, criminal, blue-collar, woman-hating, bar-based environment was populated by workers, soldiers, sailors, and criminals, their women (girlfriends, wives), and fairies and female prostitutes. The worker was as liable to fuck a fairy as a wife or a female prostitute. He was most likely to receive oral sex from the fairy; that is, to 'be done' by a fairy. Indeed much of the sexual activity in the novel is between fairies and working-class toughs – referred to as 'rough trade' by the fairies. The fairies were paid but might also pay for sex: the young thug Vinnie and his friends expected recompense, if only in drugs, for their involvement with the fairy Georgette, but the brutal union official Harry soon found that his appeal with the effeminate Regina faded when his strike expense account finished. Homosexuality in *Last Exit* is expressed as effeminacy:

> Georgette was a hip queer. She (he) didnt try to disguise or conceal it with marriage and mans talk... leering sidely while seeking protection behind a carefully guided guise of virility... but, took a pride in being a homosexual by feeling intellectually and esthetically superior to those (especially women) who werent gay... and with the wearing of womens panties, lipstick, eye make-up (this including occasionally gold and silver-stardust-on the lids), long marcelled hair, manicured and polished fingernails, the wearing of womens clothes complete with padded bra, high heels and wig.[192]

Even when the masculine Harry becomes homosexual without becoming effeminate his same-sex desires are developed through his sexual interactions with fairies.

The attitudes expressed should already be familiar. Vinnie took pride in the fairy's public endorsement of his 'strength and virility', he felt good to be wanted, 'Even if it is a fag.'[193] If his friends thought that he was going to be paid to be done so much the better ('it takes loot tado me sweetchips').[194] Being done was to receive rather than to give oral sex; Harry suffered horrendous consequences when he became a cocksucker. Georgette, the fairy, was 'tolerated' rather than 'accepted' and there were limits to this tolerance: 'the code forbids drinking from the same glass as a fag'.[195]

It was the femininity of the fairy that was the lure for rough trade. 'Harrys eyes bugged when he saw Lee. She looked like one of the show girls you see in some of the magazines... a real doll.' Initially, Harry was confused by these men who looked and walked so much like women, better than any of the real women he knew. 'Vinnie was hip to Lee, but she still looked like a lovely doll and he thought of her as a dame.'[196] Fairies were fucked much as women were fucked: 'comon motherfucka. You wanna look like a broad ya gonna get fucked like one... Hey Vinnie, come-on. Lets throw a hump intaer.'[197] Of course, it was the masculinity of rough trade – the rough in rough trade – that held the appeal for fairies. 'Her eyes almost blurred with excitement. They had such hard looks. Why their eyes went right through you as if you were naked.' 'It is so refreshing to meet a man who will give you a good fucking.'[198] Yet there was the perpetual danger that, as one of Selby's fairies expressed it, 'the boys would simply become rough and not trade'.[199] A fairy and a female prostitute both suffer violent pack rapes in the novel.

I mention such continuities for both contextual and historiographical reasons. Chauncey is aware of the postwar material, and indeed uses it in his discussion of the prewar era. He also writes of 'traces of the prewar sexual regime' persisting into the postwar period.[200] But his division into prewar and postwar, with the book's endpoint in 1940, minimizes the possibilities for any consideration of such continuities, the subject of the book in front of you. Despite Chauncey's brilliance, the 'gay' in *Gay New York* elides the very distinctions that he has himself established.[201] It may seem a trivial point, but the word 'gay' operates like this in Part 2 of the book, 'The making of the gay male world'. Thus Chauncey describes Henry's *Sex Variants* as a study of 'forty gay men' when they were in fact 'sex variants' whose case studies – as we have seen – demonstrate a fluidity and indeterminacy masked by the designation 'gay'.[202] Marilee Lindemann has noted the 'slipperiness' of the meaning of 'queer' during the period to 1940, pointing out that it was less fixed than Chauncey has suggested, employed both by those keen to convey a homosexuality distinct from the effeminacy of the fairies *and* by those not so far from the fairies in terms of the slippage in their sexual desires and gender persona.[203] It is the untidiness of categories rather than gay-world-making that will form the focus of the following chapters.

Notes

1. C. H. Ford and P. Tyler, *The Young and Evil* (New York, 1996), pp. 104–6. First published in Paris in 1933.
2. K. White, *The First Sexual Revolution: The Emergence of Male Heterosexuality in Modern America* (New York, 1993), pp. 93–4.
3. National Archives and Records Administration, Washington, DC, RG 125, Courts of Inquiry (Kent, Samuel Neal), Boxes 254–8, Case 10821-1, File 26283/2591 (hereafter, USNARA Courts of Inquiry): 'Record of Proceedings of a Court of Inquiry . . . 22 January 1920', p. 2307.
4. G. Chauncey, 'Christian brotherhood or sexual perversion? Homosexual identities and the construction of sexual boundaries in the World War One era', *Journal of Social History*, 19 (1985–6), 189–211. Chauncey's article was reprinted in M. B. Duberman, M. Vicinus, and G. Chauncey (eds), *Hidden from History: Reclaiming the Gay Past* (London, 1991), pp. 294–317. I will refer to the original version of the article.
5. Ibid., 205.
6. USNARA Courts of Inquiry, 'Record of Proceedings of a Court of Inquiry . . . 22 January 1920', p. 1166.
7. M. Canaday, *The Straight State: Sexuality and Citizenship in Twentieth-century America* (Princeton, 2009), ch. 2.
8. USNARA Courts of Inquiry, 'Record of Proceedings of a Court of Inquiry . . . 18 March 1919', pp. 3–6.
9. Ibid., pp. 3, 4, 22, 24, 101, 119.
10. Ibid., pp. 57, 69.

11 Ibid., p. 68.
12 His use of the word 'gay' works against the very purpose of his analysis: see Chauncey, 'Christian brotherhood', 190. The same is true of a book-length account of the episode, in which it becomes (as in the book's title) a 'campaign against homosexuals', an 'anti-gay crusade', a 'homosexual scandal', a 'gay scandal', and the 'navy's systematic persecution of gays', with those accused characterized as 'gay' and 'homosexual'. The author is aware that the descriptions are freighted but employs them nonetheless: L. R. Murphy, *Perverts by Official Order: The Campaign Against Homosexuals in the United States Navy* (New York, 1988), esp. pp. 2–3, 16, 21, 45, 53, 67, 76, 97, 118, 153, 156, 168, 193, 209, 211, 226, 229, 249, 251, 253, 260, 283–99. Canaday does not make this mistake: Canaday, *Straight State*, ch. 2.
13 It was used by a lieutenant in the medical corps, the commander of the decoy section: USNARA Courts of Inquiry, 'Record of Proceedings of a Court of Inquiry . . . 22 January 1920', p. 1521.
14 USNARA Courts of Inquiry, 'Record of Proceedings of a Court of Inquiry . . . 18 March 1919', pp. 61, 63, 71, 76–7, 104, 120, 271–3, 298, 375.
15 Ibid., p. 63.
16 Ibid., p. 13. For some of these descriptions, see ibid., pp. 119–20, 359–60.
17 Ibid., pp. 73, 77, 153.
18 Ibid., pp. 20, 30, 33, 38, 253.
19 Ibid., pp. 29, 33.
20 Ibid., p. 7.
21 Ibid., p. 169.
22 Ibid., pp. 5, 27, 61, 187; USNARA Courts of Inquiry, 'Record of Proceedings of a Court of Inquiry . . . 22 January 1920', pp. 988, 1404; 'Exhibits . . . Court of Inquiry . . . 22 January 1920', pp. 152, 1361–2, 1365, 1371, 1380, 1401, 1447, 1448, 1458, 1510, 1514, 1525, 1562.
23 USNARA Courts of Inquiry, 'Exhibits . . . Court of Inquiry . . . 22 January 1920', p. 1557.
24 USNARA Courts of Inquiry, 'Record of Proceedings of a Court of Inquiry . . . 22 January 1920', p. 1895.
25 USNARA Courts of Inquiry, 'Exhibits . . . Court of Inquiry . . . 22 January 1920', p. 1381.
26 USNARA Courts of Inquiry, 'Record of Proceedings of a Court of Inquiry . . . 18 March 1919', p. 376.
27 Ibid., pp. 4, 5.
28 Ibid., p. 5.
29 Ibid., p. 22.
30 Ibid., p. 169.
31 Ibid., pp. 66, 269, 314.
32 USNARA Courts of Inquiry, 'Record of Proceedings of a Court of Inquiry . . . 22 January 1920', p. 1793.

33 USNARA Courts of Inquiry, 'Record of Proceedings of a Court of Inquiry . . . 18 March 1919', pp. 27, 28; 'Exhibits . . . Court of Inquiry . . . 22 January 1920', p. 1396.
34 USNARA Courts of Inquiry, 'Record of Proceedings of a Court of Inquiry . . . 18 March 1919', pp. 27, 33, 67–8, 183, 332, 375; 'Record of Proceedings of a Court of Inquiry . . . 22 January 1920', pp. 1404–5; 'Exhibits . . . Court of Inquiry . . . 22 January 1920', p. 1399.
35 USNARA Courts of Inquiry, 'Record of Proceedings of a Court of Inquiry . . . 18 March 1919', p. 185.
36 Ibid., p. 27.
37 Chauncey, 'Christian brotherhood', 190.
38 USNARA Courts of Inquiry, 'Record of Proceedings of a Court of Inquiry . . . 18 March 1919', pp. 314–15.
39 USNARA Courts of Inquiry, 'Record of Proceedings of a Court of Inquiry . . . 22 January 1920', p. 2113.
40 Ibid., p. 2115.
41 USNARA Courts of Inquiry, 'Record of Proceedings of a Court of Inquiry . . . 18 March 1919', p. 18. See also the operatives' reports in 'Record of Proceedings of a Court of Inquiry . . . 22 January 1920', pp. 1828–31, 1844, 1846–9, 1874–5, 1895, 1913, 1947–54, 1995–8, 2005–9; and 'Exhibits . . . Court of Inquiry . . . 22 January 1920', pp. 1360, 1461, 1464, 1470.
42 USNARA Courts of Inquiry, 'Record of Proceedings of a Court of Inquiry . . . 18 March 1919', p. 20. See also 'Exhibits . . . Court of Inquiry . . . 22 January 1920', pp. 1469, 1550.
43 USNARA Courts of Inquiry, 'Record of Proceedings of a Court of Inquiry . . . 22 January 1920', p. 391.
44 Ford and Tyler, *Young and Evil*, 'Introduction' by S. Watson, no pagination.
45 Ibid., p. 11.
46 Ibid., p. 170.
47 Ibid., p. 124.
48 J. A. Boone, *Libidinal Currents: Sexuality and the Shaping of Modernism* (Chicago, 1998), p. 258. His emphasis.
49 Ibid., p. 255.
50 Ibid., pp. 251–74; J. A. Suárez, *Pop Modernism: Noise and the Reinvention of the Everyday* (Urbana, IL, 2007), ch. 6.
51 C. Van Vechten, *Parties: Scenes from Contemporary New York Life* (Los Angeles, 1993), p. 70. First published in New York in 1930.
52 Ibid., p. 128.
53 Ibid., p. 71.
54 Ibid., p. 85.
55 C. Van Vechten, *The Splendid Drunken Twenties: Selections from the Daybooks, 1922–1930*, ed. B. Kellner (Urbana and Chicago, 2003), p. 97.

56 Ibid., p. 76.
57 Ibid., p. 165.
58 Ibid., p. 166.
59 L. Hughes, *The Big Sea* (New York, 1963), p. 253. First published in 1940.
60 C. Heap, *Slumming: Sexual and Racial Encounters in American Nightlife, 1885–1940* (Chicago, 2009), p. 162.
61 For the Tyler quote, see P. Tyler, *Screening the Sexes: Homosexuality in the Movies* (New York, 1993), p. 1. First published in 1972.
62 Ford and Tyler, *Young and Evil*, p. 74. Emphasis in original.
63 K. Bruce, *Goldie* (New York, 1933), p. 12.
64 Ibid., pp. 91, 108.
65 Ibid., p. 91.
66 Ibid., p. 169.
67 Ibid., pp. 181–2.
68 Ibid., p. 105.
69 Ibid., pp. 114–15.
70 Ibid., pp. 96, 115, 164, 174.
71 Ibid., pp. 164, 188–90, 193–6, 197.
72 Ibid., p. 173.
73 Ibid., p. 172.
74 Ibid.
75 Boone, *Libidinal Currents*, pp. 253, 261, 267; Suárez, *Pop Modernism*, pp. 187, 207.
76 Heap, *Slumming*, p. 3.
77 S. Herring, *Queering the Underworld: Slumming, Literature, and the Undoing of Lesbian and Gay History* (Chicago, 2007), pp. 3–4, 14, 20–1, 209–10.
78 Ibid., p. 145.
79 Ibid., p. 123.
80 S. Kahn, *Mentality and Homosexuality* (Boston, 1937), p. 135.
81 Ibid., pp. 15, 19.
82 G. S. Sprague, 'Varieties of homosexual manifestations', *American Journal of Psychiatry*, 92 (1938), 144.
83 G. Wescott, *Continual Lessons: The Journals of Glenway Wescott, 1937–1955*, ed. R. Phelps and J. Rosco (New York, 1990), pp. 248–9.
84 G. Chauncey, *Gay New York: Gender, Urban Culture, and the Making of the Gay Male World, 1890–1940* (New York, 1994), pp. 13, 20–2.
85 University of Chicago Library Special Collections Research Center, Ernest Watson Burgess Papers (hereafter, Burgess), Box 98, Folder 11: 'Homosexual Materials': 'Leo. Age 18. Colored'.
86 Chauncey, *Gay New York*, chs 2–4.
87 Burgess, Box 98, Folder 4: 'Homosexuality Interviews'.
88 The Kinsey Institute for Research in Sex, Gender, and Reproduction, University of Indiana, Bloomington (hereafter, KI), Thomas Painter, 'Male

Homosexuals and Their Prostitutes in Contemporary America' (New York, 1941), Vol. 2: 'The Prostitute', p. 75.
89 Ibid., p. 102. Emphasis in original.
90 Burgess, Box 145, Folder 8: 'Case Study of a Homosexual . . . 1933 . . . Boy Hustler'.
91 Burgess, Box 145, Folder 8: 'Case Study of a Homosexual . . . 1933 . . . Vagabond Boy'.
92 Ibid.
93 Chauncey, *Gay New York*, p. 358.
94 Chauncey, *Gay New York*, ch. 11; Heap, *Slumming*, ch. 6.
95 Heap, *Slumming*, pp. 83, 93, 175, 231, 241, 259, 260–3.
96 R. W. Shufeldt, 'Biography of a passive pederast', *The American Journal of Urology and Sexology*, 13 (1917), 451–60. In later times he might have been classified as transsexual, for he talked of having a 'vagina': ibid., 454.
97 Ibid., 457.
98 Ibid., 459.
99 C. McKay, *Home to Harlem* (Boston, 1987). First published in 1928.
100 Ibid., pp. 87–8, 92.
101 Ibid., p. 32.
102 Ibid., p. 8.
103 A. B. C. Schwarz, *Gay Voices of the Harlem Renaissance* (Bloomington and Indianapolis, 2003), p. 104.
104 A. Y. Davis, *Blues Legacies and Black Feminism: Gertrude 'Ma' Rainey, Bessie Smith, and Billie Holiday* (New York, 1999), pp. 242–3.
105 J. T. Farrell, 'Just boys', in *The Short Stories of James T. Farrell* (New York, 1945), pp. 50–1.
106 G. W. Henry, *Sex Variants: A Study of Homosexual Patterns* (New York, 1941), Vol. 1, p. 154.
107 Painter, 'Male Homosexuals', Vol. 2, p. 103.
108 Ibid., p. 104.
109 Ibid., p. 108.
110 Ibid., p. 116.
111 Ibid., p. 117.
112 Ibid., p. 109.
113 Ibid., p. 103.
114 Ibid., p. 104.
115 Ibid., p. 108.
116 Ibid., p. 109.
117 Ibid., p. 112.
118 Ibid., pp. 105, 106.
119 G. W. Henry and A. A. Gross, 'The homosexual delinquent', *Mental Hygiene*, 25 (1941), 431–2.
120 Ibid., 432.

121 G. W. Henry and A. A. Gross, 'Social factors in the case histories of one hundred underprivileged homosexuals', *Mental Hygiene*, 22 (1938), 606.
122 For historians who have made use of this archive, see White, *First Sexual Revolution*; K. J. Mumford, 'Homosex changes: race, cultural geography, and the emergence of the gay', *American Quarterly*, 48 (1996), 395–414; D. K. Johnson, 'The kids of fairytown: gay male culture on Chicago's near north side in the 1930s', in B. Beemyn (ed.), *Creating a Place for Ourselves: Lesbian, Gay, and Bisexual Histories* (New York, 1997), ch. 4; C. Heap, 'The city as a sexual laboratory: the queer heritage of the Chicago School', *Qualitative Sociology*, 26 (2003), 457–87.
123 Burgess, Box 98, Folder 11: 'Homosexual Materials': 'My Story of Fags, Freaks and Women Impersonators by Walt Lewis'.
124 Ibid.
125 Ibid.
126 Painter, 'Male Homosexuals', Vol. 2, p. 37.
127 Ibid., p. 21.
128 Ibid.
129 Ibid.
130 For Cadmus, see J. Weinberg, 'Cruising with Paul Cadmus', *Art in America*, 80, 11 (1992), 102–9; R. Meyer and A. D. Weinberg, *Paul Cadmus: The Sailor Trilogy* (New York, 1996) (an exhibition catalogue for the Whitney Museum of American Art); and R. Meyer, 'A different American scene: Paul Cadmus and the satire of sexuality', in his *Outlaw Representation: Censorship and Homosexuality in Twentieth-century American Art* (Boston, 2002), ch. 2.
131 Meyer, *Outlaw Representation*, p. 40.
132 Ibid., p. 42.
133 Bruce, *Goldie*, p. 174.
134 T. Patterson, *St. EOM in the Land of Pasquan* (East Haven, CT, 1987), p. 123.
135 Painter, 'Male Homosexuals', Vol. 2, pp. 40–1.
136 Ibid., pp. 42–3. Emphasis in original.
137 Ibid., p. 184.
138 L. Lerman, *The Grand Surprise: The Journals of Leo Lerman*, ed. S. Pascal (New York, 2007), pp. 309–12.
139 Painter, 'Male Homosexuals', Vol. 2, p. 183.
140 Henry and Gross, 'The homosexual delinquent', 433.
141 Ibid., 438.
142 Painter, 'Male Homosexuals', Vol. 2, p. 118.
143 Ibid., p. 90.
144 Ibid., p. 187.
145 KI, The Thomas Painter Collection (hereafter, Painter), Series 2, Vol. 4: Index of names O–Z.

146 Painter, Series 2, Vol. 2: Index of names A–F.
147 Henry, *Sex Variants*, Vol. 1, p. xii.
148 J. Terry, *An American Obsession: Science, Medicine, and Homosexuality in Modern Society* (Chicago, 1999), p. 214.
149 Henry, *Sex Variants*, Vol. 1, pp. 26–37.
150 Ibid., pp. 53–4.
151 Ibid., pp. 408–11.
152 Ibid., p. 445.
153 Ibid., pp. 457–60.
154 Ibid., pp. 471–7.
155 Ibid., p. 139.
156 Ibid., pp. 141–2.
157 Ibid., p. 147.
158 Ibid., pp. 147, 152–6.
159 Ibid., pp. 214–15.
160 Ibid., pp. 258, 263–5.
161 See also, ibid., pp. 298–9, 346.
162 Ibid., p. 146.
163 Ibid., pp. 30, 254, 286, 309, 398, 447, 474.
164 Ibid., p. 104.
165 Ibid., pp. 134–5.
166 Ibid., pp. 151, 152.
167 Ibid., p. 178.
168 Painter, 'Male Homosexuals', Vol. 2, pp. 216, 217.
169 H. L. Minton, *Departing from Deviance: A History of Homosexual Rights and Emancipatory Science in America* (Chicago, 2002), p. 57.
170 Ibid., pp. 58, 61. See also, his 'Community empowerment and the medicalization of homosexuality: constructing sexual identities in the 1930s', *Journal of the History of Sexuality*, 6 (1996), 435–58.
171 Ibid., 91, 93.
172 H. L. Minton and S. R. Mattson, 'Deconstructing heterosexuality: life stories from gay New York, 1931–1941', *Journal of Homosexuality*, 36 (1998), 52, 58.
173 Terry, *An American Obsession*, pp. 222–5.
174 Descriptions from ibid., pp. 224, 233, 237, 240, 242.
175 In an earlier analysis, Terry is more forceful in reading the opposition of subject to psychiatrist, referring to nodal points of resistance, 'resistant subjectivity', and 'sites of conflict, tension, and resistance between the doctors and subjects'. She even separates the commentary from the case descriptions in her quotations from Henry, using headings (DOCTOR: . . . FRIEDA: . . .) to imply that one (the former) is spoken by the psychiatrist and the other (the latter) by the subject when in fact both are the psychiatrist's summaries. See J. Terry, 'Theorizing deviant historiography', in

A.-L. Shapiro (ed.), *Feminists Revision History* (New Brunswick, NJ, 1994), pp. 290–2.
176 Terry, *An American Obsession*, p. 247.
177 Ibid., p. 263.
178 Henry, *Sex Variants*, Vol. 1, pp. 29, 56, 71, 99, 105, 298.
179 Burgess, Box 98, Folder 11: 'Homosexual Materials': 'Jokes'; 'Queer Jokes'.
180 Burgess, Box 145, Folder 8: 'Glossary of Homosexual Terms'.
181 For example, Burgess, Box 98, Folder 2: 'Homosexuality Interviews'; Box 98, Folder 11: 'Homosexual Materials'.
182 Burgess, Box 145, Folder 8: 'Glossary of Homosexual Terms'.
183 E. W. Bruce, 'Comparison of Traits of the Homosexual from Tests and from Life History Materials' (MA Thesis, University of Chicago, 1942), p. 12. He made very little use of his case studies in his dissertation.
184 Burgess, Box 128, Folder 7: 'Earl Bruce's Homosexuality Materials, Cases, Notes, etc.'
185 Burgess, Box 128, Folder 8: 'Earl Bruce's Homosexuality Materials, Cases, Notes, etc.'
186 Painter, Box 1, Series 2, c. 1, Vol. 2: Painter Letters: 4 October 1945.
187 Ibid.
188 H. Selby, *Last Exit to Brooklyn* (New York, 1988), p. 187. First published in 1957.
189 Painter, Box 1, Series 2, c. 1, Vol. 14: 9 February 1957.
190 C. Brown, *Manchild in the Promised Land* (London, 1966), p. 195.
191 I am here arguing the exact opposite of James Levin, who considers Selby's book a 'doubtful' reflection of sexual realities: J. Levin, *The Gay Novel* (New York, 1983), pp. 249–50.
192 Selby, *Last Exit to Brooklyn*, p. 23.
193 Ibid., p. 28.
194 Ibid., p. 74.
195 Ibid., pp. 25, 57.
196 Ibid., pp. 45, 47.
197 Ibid., p. 71.
198 Ibid., pp. 48, 59.
199 Ibid., p. 67.
200 See Chauncey, *Gay New York*, pp. 22–3.
201 Thus the ascription 'gay' sets up a quote in which the original source actually employs the term 'queer': ibid., p. 278. Compare with Henry, *Sex Variants*, Vol. 1, p. 398.
202 Chauncey, *Gay New York*, p. 360.
203 M. Lindemann, *Willa Cather: Queering America* (New York, 1999), pp. 2–3, 143–4.

3

Hustlers and trade

> My main desire to be supported lavishly – expensive clothes – an automobile – long and sleek – preferably a convertible – a Doberman pinscher sitting next to me – the top down – a beautiful woman – fashionably gowned – travel and debauchery on an international scale – my commodity in ex-change – my body. Unfortunately there were few buyers and those were far from able to supply any of the extremely choice luxuries I wanted. Also I soon learned I was unable to restrain myself sufficiently to give the impression that I was rare enough to merit high price – and could be had as easily for nothing – as long as the stimulants were many and in plenty and there was much laughter and I was free of even the slightest degree of responsibility . . . Soon I became a thief – no longer desirous of prostituting my body and discovering it was far simpler to sneak around here and there taking things I could convert into money – or money – and except for perhaps working with a partner, no need to deal in a so-called personal way with other people. (Herbert Huncke on hustling, 1961)[1]

This book deals with the history of straight men engaged in homosexual sex, and it is important to grasp this from the outset. It is true that during the prewar period some *women* paid male prostitutes for their sexual services. Some of the fairies at Newport in the 1910s were said to provide oral pleasure to women; one was called a 'cunt lapper'.[2] Those in the know referred to women hiring men for oral sex – fellatio as well as cunnilingus. Painter's history of male prostitution mentions female clients, society women and professionals, who either for contraceptive purposes or erotic choice preferred cunnilingus to sexual intercourse. There were said to be particular bars of assignation where women could meet these specialists. In the 1930s these men were called 'fish queens', 'the *oral male prostitute to women*', supposedly because some were homosexual men who, given their predilections, could only give oral satisfaction, or perhaps it was a statement about the status of those who placed

17. Jon Voight in *Midnight Cowboy*, 1969. © John Springer Collection/CORBIS.

themselves in an inferior sexual position to women (a version of the cocksucker).³ The providers of sexual services to female clients certainly included heterosexual hustlers: Painter mentioned a wealthy patroness of the arts who used the same trade as male homosexuals.⁴ The academic, tattooist, and pornographer Samuel Steward knew a truck driver in the 1950s, 'trade' that he met at his tattoo shop and later had sex with, who told him that he 'eats pussy all the time and is partly supported by the money the gals he eats give him'.⁵

However, as far as we know, this was a minority service. The bulk of male prostitution in the pages that follow is male–male sexual access. Readers should not make the same mistake as *Midnight Cowboy*'s Joe Buck in both the 1960s novel and film. With an irony not fully grasped by critics, Joe Buck is hoping to hustle women in a homosexual environment – dressed, moreover, in clothes calculated to appeal to a certain type of homosexual taste. (See Figure 17.) His friend Rizzo Ratso points out his miscalculation: 'he had not a hope in hell of making a living from women... The cowboy gambit wouldn't work on New York women. Not only was the costume an almost purely homosexual lure, it was severely specialized even within that group, attracting to it almost exclusively a very small masochistic element. ("Never mind *what* that is, you wouldn't believe it if I told you.")[6] The amusing thing about Buck is that, although he has been told to head for Times Square and 42nd Street when he reaches New York, his aim is to prostitute himself to women rather than men. He gets things wrong. He knows about New York homosexuality, but his logic is askew: 'The men . . . is just faggots mostly, and so the women got to buy what they want. They glad to pay for it 'cause it's just about the only way they can get it.'[7] However, it was the faggots, not the women, who were his potential clientele.

The character notes for Lanford Wilson's New York play *Balm in Gilead* (1965) introduce assorted fairies, heroin addicts, and hustlers, observing fluidity in definition: 'What they are now is not what they will be a month from now.' Hustlers, Wilson explains, would 'sell anything including themselves to any man or woman with the money, although they could not be described as homosexuals'.[8] As Wilson is intimating, the hustler is a shifting target, and we will be dealing with the world of the hustler rather than the hustler per se. Samuel Delany, drawing on decades of experience, was to write of the highly permeable line between commercial and non-commercial sex.[9] Strictly speaking, a hustler is a man who makes his body available in exchange for cash. But many men who traded on their looks or physical attributes did so for food, drink, or a room or bed for the night. One told Painter in 1949 that he was 'willing to live with a queer in exchange for the living accommodation and occasional entertainment ("going out" to bars, shows, etc.) and "help" on buying clothing'.[10]

The image of the hustler is a young man who either parades his body on the street or is available for private consultation in a male brothel or on call. A 1970s study of male prostitutes in Boston divided 'professionals' into street and bar hustlers and call-boys and kept men.[11] Yet the hustler had to contend constantly with seamen and sailors – and, especially in the 1940s, with military personnel – barely distinguishable from the semi-professionals in terms of their appeal. The 'angels' of John Rechy's fictional homosexual professor come in various forms, including the street angels (hustlers), truck drivers, marines, and the seafaring or sailor angels.[12] 'Sit down on your ass, or what's left of it after four years in the Navy', quips a William Burroughs character.[13] Allen Ginsberg's poem *Howl* (1956) referred to those

> Who blew and were blown by those human seraphim,
> the sailors, caresses of Atlantic and Caribbean
> love.[14]

Indeed a study of legal enforcement against homosexuality in Los Angeles County in the 1960s specified sailors, prompted by 'non-homosexually motivated reasons' including possible monetary gain, as especially susceptible to '"situational" violations'.[15]

Painter's 1941 account of male prostitution referred to the 'working boy or a boy temporarily or chronically unemployed', the casual 'resorting to it now and again as the necessity arises during period of unemployment or other financial ebb'.[16] Exactly thirty years later, the sociologist Laud Humphreys divided hustlers (the 'midnight cowboys') into the hustler proper, what he termed 'semiprofessionals', firmly part of a hustling 'subculture', and those described as pseudo-hustlers, who had sex for spare change or a packet of cigarettes and who seldom made 'a living from sexual activity'.[17] A 1971 study of prostitution in the USA, which touched briefly on its male forms, pointed out that if prostitution was considered as an occupation its numbers at any one time would be relatively small, but if 'defined as the exchange of sexual favours for cash, on an indiscriminate basis and with no emotional involvement, the number would be much higher'.[18] In fact nearly half the subjects of the Boston study referred to earlier were occasional sex workers.[19] Hence we cannot confine our account of hustling to the full-time prostitute; and it is therefore more useful to refer to hustlers and trade.

The dress of the hustlers reflected this blurring of identity. Photographs of hustlers show young men in casual garb, with shirts close fitting, transparent, or loosened to expose muscle and skin. We will discuss the hustler's self-presentation later, but one of its characteristics was that it mirrored the indeterminacy of male prostitution. Just as hustling merged imperceptibly with trade, the hustler's uniform was merely the work or leisure clothing of working-class youth. When the police rounded up 'undesirables' in Times Square in 1954 – 'organized bands of youthful hoodlums and perverts' – and the *New York Times* photographed them being charged at the 47th Street station house, it is impossible to tell youth from hoodlum from 'pervert' (see Figure 18).[20] The T-shirt and turned-up jeans are ubiquitous: what Rechy was to call the hustler 'uniform'.[21]

Those who did earn varied in their success. They were a commodity like any other, priced by their desirability and according to competition and demand. Painter's account of the 1930s referred to prices of $2 or $3 as a minimum and $5 (occasionally $10) as a good rate. (He thought that Los Angeles hustlers could be had for as little as $1.) In comparison, the price of New York female prostitutes was $2.[22] A hustler picked up

18. Times Square 'undesirables', 1954. AP Photo/Chris Daly.

by one of Painter's friends in 1953 was paid $10 for oral sex (plus a $1 cab fare), quite a good rate given that a week's rent plus utilities in a New York rooming house at that time was the same amount.[23] Painter himself usually paid $10 for 'both posing – and', in other words for photography and some form of sexual contact. But he would pay as little as $5 for touching.[24] These were the rates mentioned by Rechy in the early 1960s.[25] The successful earned more. An attractive young Italian body builder who became a movie actor was charging $25 'a throw' and was also being supported by a wealthy homosexual: 'went around with him in his Cadillac convertible to theatrical opening nights, the best night clubs, etc, sucked his cock and gave him a great deal of money and things'.[26] Another body builder was said to have earned up to $500 a week and put himself through college.[27] But they were middle-class Brooklyn boys rather than the typical working-class Times Square hustler. By the end of our period of interest, the amounts were higher; the hustler in the 1968 film *Flesh* referred to $20 to $30 as the rates for 'most jobs'.[28]

A few hustlers used their appeal, talent, and contacts to advance in various areas of endeavour. Marlon Brando and Cary Grant were said to have started their careers in such a milieu. One young Italian who traded on his body and looks in the 1950s changed his name and went to Hollywood.[29] Another film sex symbol began his working life as a New York artist's model and sexual partner.[30] Lesser mortals doubtless harboured similar – unfulfilled – ambitions, like the fellow hustler Herbert Huncke knew in the 1940s or 1950s:

> Johnie Pimples – a young cat – a typical Forty-second Street hustler – open for any suggestion where a dollar was involved but most of the time making it with fags for a place to sleep – a couple of bucks' eating and show money, occasionally scoring a ten spot or twenty – spending it on clothes – a chick – across the bar on his acquaintances – while he gave them a rundown on how smart he had been beating the queer – or how someday he was going to go to Los Angeles – maybe and try and get in the movies – if only he could get rid of all these goddamned pimples.[31]

Others moved from casual or professional prostitution to model work in the numerous physique magazines; it was not unusual for Painter to come across pictures of hustlers that he had seen in Times Square or sexually available young body builders that he had 'had'.[32] This symbiosis was not confined to New York. In Los Angeles, Bob Mizer mixed photography of body builders for *Physique Pictorial* with procurement for Hollywood clients; his subjects were classified by type and availability, with an inverted dollar as the code for hustler subjects.[33]

Donald Webster Cory and John P. LeRoy's brief consideration of hustlers in their influential account of homosexuality, *The Homosexual and His Society* (1963), referred to hustlers who moved from prostitution to the slightly more enduring status of 'kept boy'. 'Here a youth enters a permanent or semi-permanent quasi-marital union with another man for his money, his influence, or his prestige ... One-time street walkers and hustlers are transformed into well-dressed but ill-bred protégés.'[34]

Some 1930s and 1940s hustlers could be found in what were known as peg houses, the male equivalent of the female-staffed brothel. We have a photograph of one such group relaxing, rather incongruously, on the beach at Long Island (see Figure 19) and have seen other photographs of peg house owners (see Figures 9 and 14). Two such places gained some notoriety during the war, one, in Greenwich Village, as an FBI front for extracting information from foreign sailors; the other, near the

Hustlers and trade

19. Hustlers at the beach, 1930s/1940s. From the Thomas Painter Collection. Reproduced by permission of The Kinsey Institute for Research in Sex, Gender, and Reproduction, Inc. Author's note: a New York brothel owner and his hustlers at the beach at Long Island, circa 1937–47.

Brooklyn Navy Yard, as an alleged nest of German spies where the chairman of (appropriately) the Senate Naval Affairs Committee indulged his taste for sailors.[35] Painter's unpublished history described such houses as apartment-based male brothels, where the hustlers sat and played cards, listened to music, or read comics while waiting for clients. The 'boys' were usually in their late teens or their twenties. The New York peg houses employed Navy or Army hustlers, or as Painter expressed it, 'uniforms for trade'. One of the houses used the Navy and the other the Army. In the former, the sailors wore uniform but in the latter the soldiers were in civilian costume.[36]

The study estimated that there were fewer than a dozen such places in New York but that their proprietors supplied some well-known personalities. Hustlers' clients included American literary and artistic figures, a society photographer, actors, directors, producers, a celebrated songwriter, members of government, a Papal dignitary, foreign aristocrats, and businessmen of various kinds. There are stories of celebrity parties and orgies supplied with women, animals, soldiers, and assorted hustlers, including two of the original Dead End kids who swam at the end

20. 42nd Street hustler, 1940s/1950s. From the Thomas Painter Collection. Reproduced by permission of The Kinsey Institute for Research in Sex, Gender, and Reproduction, Inc. Author's note: photographed by Painter *in situ* on the corner of Seventh Avenue and 42nd Street.

at 53rd Street in the East River before the popular play, *Dead End*, was produced in the 1930s, but who later, as one succinctly put it in the late 1940s, 'suck and get sucked for a living'.[37]

However, most of the young men who form the subject of this book simply worked the bars and the streets. They stood on the kerb facing inwards on the sidewalk so that they could see those passing by and could be seen – like the man photographed by Painter in the 1940s or 1950s in place on the corner of Seventh Avenue and 42nd Street (see Figure 20). Or, like the hustlers photographed by I. C. Rapoport (Figure 7) and William Gedney (Figure 55) in the 1960s, referred to in other chapters, they stood on the opposite side of the sidewalk against the wall or a shop window, easily approached by potential johns who could always say that they were window shopping!

The sexual topography of the 'capital of the homosexual world' continually shifted but did so around recurring axes. In the 1920s, the centres had been Riverside Drive, Fifth Avenue, and Battery Park. In the early 1930s, the focus had moved to Bryant Park and Lexington Avenue. In 1940, it was Times Square and lower Central Park.[38] Times Square was described in 1941 as the busiest market, the 'grand-carnival', of homosexual prostitution, but its commentator noted that the uninitiated would hardly distinguish the hustler from the multitude of other loitering youths. The fairy was easily seen, but the hustler, apart from the fact that he usually stood at the kerb, was practically invisible.[39] Times Square, 'New York's service station of vice and crime', was the Mecca for hustlers and their clients. Its speakeasies of the 1930s, open after the legally operated bars had closed, and patronised by both male and female prostitutes, had been notorious for their unrestrained sex, with open groping in the bar and actual consummation in the toilets. Painter thought the post-1940s bars 'kindergartens' in comparison.[40] The concentrations of hustlers shifted within the broad parameters of the region of the Square, focused on 42nd Street but stretching up several blocks. The 'floating center' of hustlers moved from one street corner to another or from the north to the south side of the street, depending on the popularity of a given bar or the frequency of policing. Hustlers also cruised Fifth Avenue, en route to Central Park, another focus of homosexual activity.[41] There were topographical idiosyncrasies. In 1930, Fifth Avenue from 42nd Street to Central Park at 59th Street was 'popular homosexually, but only one side of the street – the west side'.[42]

The focus of male prostitution, then, was 42nd Street and Times Square (see Figure 21). Dotson Rader's compelling 1970s novel about hustling begins with its narrator gazing across the lawn of Bryant Park at the lights of 42nd Street while his score is 'down on me lapping up the groceries'.[43] 'From the thundering underground – the maze of the New York subways – the world pours into Times Square' wrote Rechy in the early 1960s,

> Like lost souls emerging from the purgatory of the trains (dark rattling tunnels, smelly pornographic toilets, newsstands futilely splashing the subterranean graydepths with unreal magazine colors), the newyork faces push into the air: spilling into 42nd Street and Broadway – a scattered defeated army. And the world of that street bursts like a rocket into a shattered phosphorescent world. Giant signs – Bigger! Than! Life! – blink off

21. Times Square, 1969. © Bettmann/CORBIS.

and on. And a great hungry sign groping luridly at the darkness screams: F*A*S*C*I*N*A*T*I*O*N.[44]

Rechy refers to the 'army of youngmen' outside the movie houses, along the streets, at the subway entrances, 'like photographs in a strange exhibition: slouched invitingly, or moving back and forth restlessly'.[45]

It is fitting that that temple of fantasy, the motion picture house, was so closely associated with hustler sex. Delany's nostalgic account of movie theatre sex in the days before Times Square's commercial transformation in the 1990s claimed the cinema, with its trade and hustlers, its commercial and non-commercial sex, as a primary site for homosexual contact.[46] The motion picture house of the 1930s and 1940s was said to be a 'popular resort' for homosexuals wishing to meet 'hustlers ... or transient boys'. It was a venue for the 'impecunious' to relax while waiting to be propositioned or taken to a hotel room; potential clients went there cognisant of this situation. Alternatively, a deal could be struck and the sex (usually oral sex or masturbation) would be carried out in the darkened seats or in the standing space found at the back of every theatre. Habitués claimed that groping was less conspicuous in a crowd.[47] Two of Tennessee Williams's short stories, 'The mysteries of the Joy Rio' and 'Hard candy', published in 1954 though written in the 1940s, feature such 'fleeting and furtive practices' in a movie theatre, with layers of meaning that draw on the knowingness of the reader.[48] Harry Benjamin and R. E. L. Masters's 1964 history of prostitution mentioned the all-night movie houses as 'favourite contact places for the younger hustlers', observing that they could be identified moving from seat to seat until a contact was made and a deal struck.[49] Rechy's hustler's very first customer meets him outside one such theatre in Times Square, and then later warns him against his new trade: 'Hell, youll become part of the 42nd Street army of punks – sleeping in movies, cant make it; everybody's had you.'[50] The hustler Joe Buck's first homosexual encounter in New York in the film version of *Midnight Cowboy* (1969) takes place in a picture theatre.[51]

Hustling, it has been intimated, merged with the wider sexual world of trade and involved the professional and casual. Any venue involving muscularity and bodily display attracted male admirers and the temptation of prostitution. Members of the swimming team at the pool of a large Manhattan hotel in the 1930s had been known to be casual prostitutes.[52] Painter and his friends had long maintained that boxers, secure in their physicality and virility, were the 'most relaxed queer-lovers' and that 'many boxers and wrestlers . . . do prostitute themselves to homosexuals'. 'Any boxing or wrestling match draws a large quota of homosexuals who come to see not the fighting so much as the fighters'.[53] Certainly boxers/hustlers/criminals appear with some regularity in the photographic portfolios of Painter and his artist friend Edward Melcarth. (See, for example, Figure 22.)

Then there were the young Brooklyn body builders. Their clients were mainly rich homosexuals, and a big name photographer in the physique and muscle-building scene brokered their availability. Though they were contemptuous of the common hustlers of Times Square, the muscle boys involved in selling sex were, in effect, semi-professional prostitutes. In 1950, Painter photographed a muscle man featured in some of the physique magazines but who also traded sex, and the man described a 'demi-monde of sex of all sorts and muscle-minded males, and females, and rich queers – a sordid world'.[54] Some years later, Painter went to the 'Mr. New York' show at the Brooklyn Central YMCA, and recognized five of the performers and several in the audience as former sexual contacts – including one that he had forgotten but when he had consulted his diaries discovered that he had 'had' him too.[55] 'It was the vogue at the time', Painter recalled in the 1960s, 'maybe it still is', that the muscle boys 'were all whores'.[56]

22. Italian-American boxer/hustler, 1954. From the Thomas Painter Collection. Reproduced by permission of The Kinsey Institute for Research in Sex, Gender, and Reproduction, Inc.

Coney Island has traditionally featured in histories of heterosexual leisure and courtship but it was also a centre for homosexual sex. It was not so much the professional (and nocturnal) hustler that frequented New York's resorts (though we do have a picture of some peg house boys on a Long Island beach) but rather the casual prostitute, the working-class boy out to supplement or earn an income, and the New York model and body-building set who were willing to have their photographs taken – and more – for the appropriate cash or support. Coney Island was listed as a site of homosexual promise in Painter's history of 1930s male prostitution – such boys 'if properly approached, may be won over to the homosexual's desires and financial proposition'.[57] Painter wrote of a bath house in 1930s Coney Island that backed on to the beach, with nude bathing on its roof – 'a hundred naked males practically all of them homosexuals, with a few hustlers and kept boys about, lying in the sun' – and open sex in its steam rooms.[58] Coney Island beach was a major cruising ground for Painter and his friends in the 1940s and 1950s, when they photographed and had sex with young men encountered on the beach, in bars, and at the baths.[59] At the very least, Coney Island provided an opportunity for looking, as Painter outlined to Kinsey, voyeur to voyeur, in 1949: 'my eyes are busy and appreciative'. 'Coney Island has been a Paradise for me that way – as it would be: my type goes there – the rough, tough proletarian; they dress for Coney Island in fetish clothing (to me), and they proceed to reduce that clothing to a fascinating minimum. And on the beach, ah the beach, with its beautiful Italians!'[60] (See Figure 23.)

A Puerto Rican gang member dictated his life story to Painter in 1957, a desperate catalogue of misfortune from his father's early death and the murder of his mother at the hands of a lover, through a young life of domestic violence, existence on the streets, passage through homes and orphanages, and eventual migration at the age of thirteen to live with a sister in New York. His life consisted of housebreaking, mugging, picking pockets, pimping his girlfriends, smoking 'pap' (marijuana), playing pool, gambling (with a loaded dice), drinking, sniffing and injecting heroin, drug dealing, and prison. Interaction with homosexuals had a vague presence in the narrative. A middle-aged homosexual photographer first gave him money for heroin and then supported him through what proved to be an inconsequential 'cold turkey'. And our very possession of his story is due to his relationship with another homosexual, Painter, who photographed him, had sex with him (or by means of him), took him away on holiday, and derived pleasure from his mere presence. Yet the truly interesting thing about this little story

23. Coney Island trade, 1950s. Collection of Richard Taddei, New York. Gifted to Edward Melcarth Collection, Archives of American Art, Smithsonian Institution, Washington, DC. Author's note: the photograph was taken by the artist Edward Melcarth. Painter and Melcarth knew the central subjects.

– as the ever-astute Painter noted – is its 'amazing lack of sexuality'. The twenty-one-year-old, who seemed already to have lived a whole life, had nothing to say either about his sexuality or that of his various partners. Associating with homosexuals was a means of getting by – like mugging, gambling, or housebreaking. Pleasure was expressed in terms of 'dressing well', drinking, dancing, playing pool, and taking drugs; sex was rarely mentioned.[61]

Some readers may be astonished that members of the Puerto Rican gangs were sexually available and that Painter had extended involvement with New York's notorious Dragons in the 1950s and early 1960s. But it is not really surprising. The social factors that drove impoverished, immigrant communities into gangs were the same that facilitated hustling.[62] (See Figure 24.) Tony Hernandez, one of the co-accused in the notorious Capeman murders in 1959, and member of the Vampires gang, was said to earn money as a hustler.[63] Salvador Agron, the so-called Capeman, later said that he had been living with older men in furnished rooms shortly before the killings; 'they paid for the room so that he would stay with them'. Agron and Hernandez and another

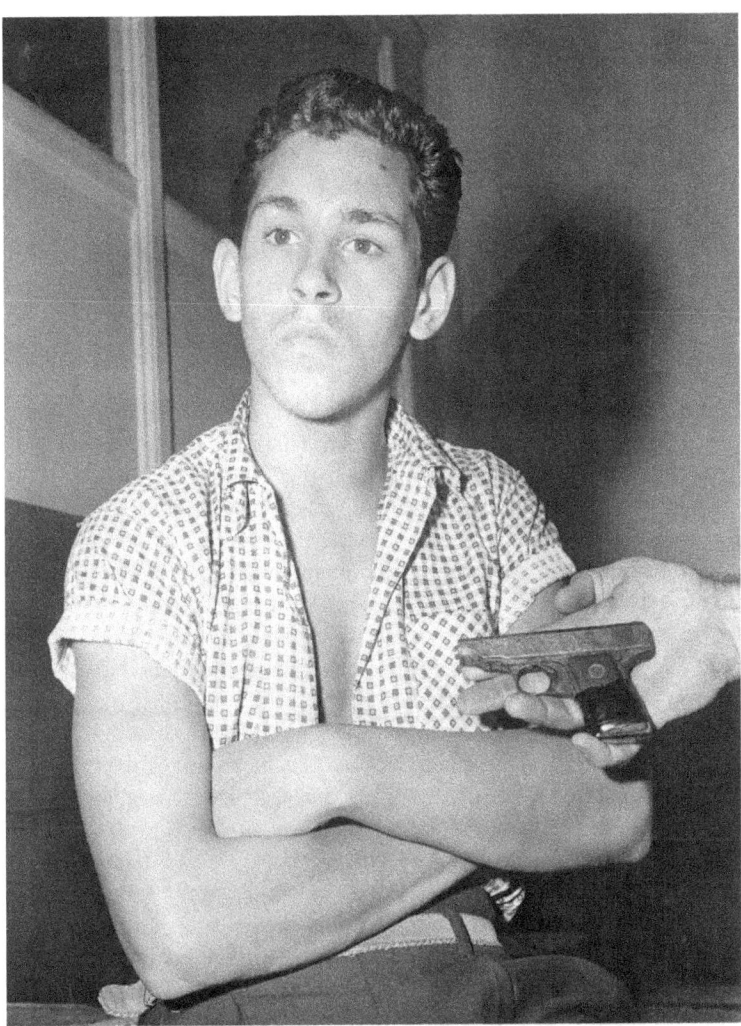

24. Bronx teenage gang member with gun at police station, 1954. © Bettmann/CORBIS. Author's note: his dress and pose is not unlike that of the Puerto Rican 'hustlers'.

youth called Ralphie were 'hustling on the streets'.⁶⁴ The playground in which the gang stabbed two boys to death was between 45th and 46th Streets at Ninth and Tenth Avenues in Hell's Kitchen and a reputed place where homosexuals from Times Square were lured and robbed.⁶⁵

Eric Schneider has outlined the gangs' engagement in same-sex encounters for money or drugs, being blown for cash, or simply picking up a queer and then beating and robbing him.[66] A man who worked closely with the gangs of the 1950s and early 1960s said that their main sexual outlets were gangbangs, sex with prostitute drug addicts, and 'perverts'.[67] While sex with a 'fag' might finish with theft and violence, that was not invariably the case. Sometimes it was for cash: 'I got my joint copped and five bucks. Is that bad?'[68] Or it could merely be quick sex. 'What the hell's so wrong about having a queer blow you? All the guys around here do it.'[69] The Boston study of 1970s hustling certainly included what it termed 'peer delinquents' among its part-time prostitutes, including members of a motorcycle gang. 'Although assault and theft of vulnerable homosexual men are the rationale for their prostitution, almost all of the peer-delinquents are willing recipients of fellatio (described by them as getting a "blow-job" or getting "blown").'[70]

Painter hesitated to call his gang contacts hustlers. Those who hung out at the Clock Bar on 12th Street in the early 1950s, Painter explained, were 'local, working, or temporarily unemployed youths, who go there because it amuses them, possibly also to get fellated, to get free drinks, as well as pleasure in the unusual atmosphere. If they happen to get paid too, so much the better.'[71] (The Clock Bar is mentioned in William Burroughs's *Interzone*, mostly written in the 1950s: 'Then one night I happened into a strange, equivocal place on Twelfth Street at Second Avenue. It was called the Clock Bar. The Clock had no regular crowd. It was not Bohemian or tough or Bowery. It was a place that anyone could happen in. The place was empty – except for you.')[72]

Puerto Rican youths replaced Americano trade in Glenn's Bar on 14th Street. 'Good looking boys, shirts wholly unbuttoned, cluster around middle aged Americans who buy them drinks and give them money for the juke box.'[73] (See Figure 25.) Painter classified the young Puerto Ricans as 'amateurs' in contrast to the Times Square hustler who was available to 'all comers'.[74] Ironically, when the sociologist Robert McNamara studied male prostitution in Times Square in the early 1990s, he found that the bulk of the hustlers were Puerto Rican.[75] We will return to the Puerto Ricans in the following chapter.

'Corner of 42nd Street and Broadway', Charles Henri Ford wrote in his diary in 1948, 'meatmarket in the rain: a seaman wearing tight light blue jeans and dark knitted cap. If I had gone up to him and said, "How much" and he'd have said, "For what?" and I'd have replied, "You know

Hustlers and trade

25. A Puerto Rican 'hustler', 1959. From the Thomas Painter Collection. Reproduced by permission of The Kinsey Institute for Research in Sex, Gender, and Reproduction, Inc.

for what", would he have told me?'[76] A character in one of Tennessee Williams's 1950s stories about a young man and a not-so-young woman with similar taste in males refers to the trade on the corner of 42nd Street and Broadway in Manhattan:

> Like everyone whose life is conditioned by luck, they had some brilliant streaks of it and some that were dismal. For instance, that first week they operated together in Manhattan. That was really a freak; you couldn't expect a thing like that to happen twice in a lifetime. The trade was running

as thick as spawning salmon up those narrow cataracts in the Rockies. Head to tail, tail to head, crowding, swarming together, seemingly driven along by some immoderate instinct. It was not a question of catching; it was simply a question of deciding which ones to keep and which ones to throw back in the stream, all glittering, all swift, all flowing one way which was toward you![77]

An article in the *American Journal of Psychiatry* in 1938 noted that 'Sailors and army men are known to indulge in homosexual activities when heterosexual opportunities are long absent, only to renounce homosexuality when normal conditions are restored'.[78] Some, of course, were slower in their renunciations. As already hinted, soldiers, seamen and sailors need to be included among the casual prostitutes. They were to be found wherever the homosexuals and hustlers congregated and vice versa. It was a sexual geography with a long twentieth-century history, captured, we have seen, in Painter's own account of the 1930s: the streets and bars of Times Square; Bryant Park (behind the New York Public Library); Central Park Mall and Columbus Circle, where the girls attracted the sailors and soldiers, who in turn drew the homosexuals and thus the hustlers; the waterfront bars on the Hudson and near the Battery, where the foreign seamen and stewards congregated, eager for American dollars; and the bars of Brooklyn near the US Navy Yard, where homosexuals went for 'sea food' (that is, sailors).[79] As Williams's couple knew, the servicemen were as likely to have sex with a man as a woman and thus competed for the hustlers' prey. It was something that Williams was familiar with from personal experience: 'Till 6 a.m. I tagged along with an attractive soldier but finally gave him up as he fell into the clutches of a female whore', he wrote in his notebook in 1941.[80] Other homosexual diaries refer to the availability of soldiers and sailors. One man told Donald Vining in 1942 that he had blown as many as three soldiers in a car, one by one, as the others looked on. 'Some of the fellows want money.'[81] Vining did not know the meaning of the word 'trade' until he went to New York to live, but before long he was picking up soldiers and sailors on a regular basis and both doing and being done by trade who often expected some form of payment, if only a bed for the night.[82] (See Figure 26.) Vining later wrote that he 'somewhat favored sailors over handsome men in other branches of the service'.[83]

Painter's history of the 1930s had referred to 'soldiers and sailors by the dozen' lining up 'before and across the street from the New York Times Building' and 'brazenly' offering themselves 'for prostitution to men'.[84] (See Figure 27.) He also recalled 'the men in the armed services

26. The erotic appeal and danger of sailor trade: Kenneth Anger's film *Fireworks* (1947).

27. Sailors in Times Square, 1950s. Collection of Richard Taddei, New York. Gifted to Edward Melcarth Collection, Archives of American Art, Smithsonian Institution, Washington, DC. Author's note: any of those in the picture (shoe-shine boy or sailors) may have been sexually available. The photograph was taken by Edward Melcarth.

28. Henry Faulkner and two sailors, 1950. From the Thomas Painter Collection. Reproduced by permission of The Kinsey Institute for Research in Sex, Gender, and Reproduction, Inc. Author's note: Faulkner gave Painter an extensive portfolio of photographs of sailors.

who sell themselves while on leave'. Camp Dix, near New York, was known by homosexuals as 'Camp Pricks'.[85] A study of sex offenders in military service in the 1940s identified a substantial group (just under a quarter of cases) that although not considered 'true homosexuals' were facing court martial for sodomy. The study also located what its author termed facultative homosexuals: those who 'function on either a heterosexual or homosexual level, depending on circumstances ... The orgasm however achieved, is the primary goal.' Such men 'frequently' declared histories of same-sex experiences in gyms, in baths, and in naval service. Presumably men like these were the hustlers' competitors.[86]

The artist Henry Faulkner ('a wild, blond, mincing faggot') had a voracious appetite for trade (see Figure 28). When he stayed with Painter and Melcarth, he amazed them with his success rate with seamen and sailors: 'And it takes a bit to astonish us.'[87] (Dotson Rader, who was in Key West, Florida, with Tennessee Williams and Faulkner in the 1970s, claimed that Faulkner would arrive every morning – like the milkman – with a jeep load of young men, usually sailors.)[88]

Painter opted for naval or military men when the hustlers were thin on the ground. In 1949 he described sex with a soldier picked up at the bar Diamond Jim's. The man was with a friend and Painter had to bargain for his services: '"Ten." "Five." "Ten." "Five." . . . (this is literal verbatim quotes). "Well, ten for the both of us . . ." "But I don't want him." He (the other one, the unattractive one) looks a little miffed . . . I ask him if he doesn't have types of girls. Yes. Well, I have my types too.'[89] The Silver Dollar Bar, at Broadway and 46th Street, was a sailor bar frequented by Melcarth and Painter in 1949 ('really an amazing place').[90] The Famous, on Eighth Avenue at 46th Street, started as a bar for sailors and their 'girls'. 'Then slowly the queers infiltrated. Then hustlers followed them . . . now the girls are swamped and crowded out by milling service men, queers and hustlers'.[91]

Hustlers and trade were also associated with violence. Tennessee Williams's letters recount such threatening situations as he moved throughout the country.[92] 'She picked up dirt and was so severely chastised that she was not recognisable', he wrote of a 'queen' beaten in Key West in 1952.[93] His notebooks recount an incident at the Hotel St George in Brooklyn in 1943 when a sailor beat him:

> My face is still swollen from [the] blow – the donor will remain in my memory always, and as a lover, not antagonist. There was something incredibly tender and sad in the experience. So much of life at its most haunting and inexpressible. Not that I like being struck, I hated it, but the keenness of the emotional situation, the material for art – these gave a tone of richness to it which makes the affair unforgettable among many that melt out of sight.[94]

After another episode in the same year – 'when my trade turned "dirt"' – Williams told himself that he would stay away from these situations: 'that is the end of my traffic with such characters'.[95]

Further afield, Truman Capote wrote amusing letters in 1949–50 about the robbing of American literary visitors by young men that they had picked up. Tennessee Williams's apartment had been stripped by 'some piece of Roman trade'.[96] Donald Windham had his money and clothing stolen in Taormina (Sicily): 'one of his many pickups broke into his room, and made a clean sweep. D. had to give the names of all the boys who came to his room to the police; my, it was a sordid list.' When Windham's long-time companion joined him there, he was greeted with visual reminders of 'D's infidelities'; 'How would you feel', Capote wrote mischievously, 'if every other boy you passed on the street was wearing a shirt or a tie that had once been presents from you to your lover?'[97] And, then, in Rome, Windham was robbed yet again by two young men whom he had met at the Coliseum and taken home with him: 'they told me they would show me the sights of Rome'. Capote joked that the Italian authorities might have to ask him to leave. 'After all, they can't throw every able-bodied male into prison.'[98]

Painter's letters likewise relate escapes from potentially dangerous situations (and some non-escapes), yet also make it clear that he was sexually attracted to such types and that the lurking danger was part of the appeal. '[H]e threatened me with a broken bottle...hung my cat...would appear nights...to tell me how he had burgled or, in one case, murdered someone', Painter recalled of a hustler, 'but the fascination was his outpourings – of his misery, of the horror of his life, his dreadful compulsions ...his confused sexuality.'[99] One of his 1950s hustlers had raped a woman, had robbed a bank, and was a wanted criminal: 'He was a nightmare of terror, horror and vice.'[100] Yet Painter returned again and again to such relationships, sometimes with the same person over a number of years. Photographs taken and collected by Painter and his friends record the iconography of sexual danger in the crudely tattooed bodies and sneering faces of their risky contacts (see Figures 29–31.) As he wrote rather ruefully, 'After all these years and all these psychopaths I still do get involved'. 'These boys are dangerous brutes and criminals, thieves and beaters-up by training. And we their natural prey. And I like danger.'[101]

'Rosario is the devil', Melcarth's young artist friend Richard Taddei wrote of his live-in hustler model, 'Maddeningly attractive ... strong, forceful, violent, potentially deadly, dangerous', 'a psychopath and the perfect model'.[102] Melcarth's fragmentary papers, housed in the Smithsonian's Archives of American Art, contain photographs of tough-looking young men, including one injecting heroin.[103] They also include letters from prison: 'Coming off the dirty streets of the West Side into an apartment filed with art was wonderful and I probably bothered you quite a bit', wrote one man from Virginia State Penitentiary in 1963. 'I will never sell Benzedrine again. I hope to be a useful citizen when I return to society.'[104] The artistic association with 'outlaw culture' was more than a figment of the cultural critics' imaginations. As another friend of Melcarth wrote, referring to a young tough that he was interested in but thought might have Mafia connections, 'so long as he presents more Ass than Assassin'.[105] In retrospect, Edmund White admitted that his sexual encounters with hustlers 'were as much an expression of fear as of desire'.[106]

Hustlers and trade

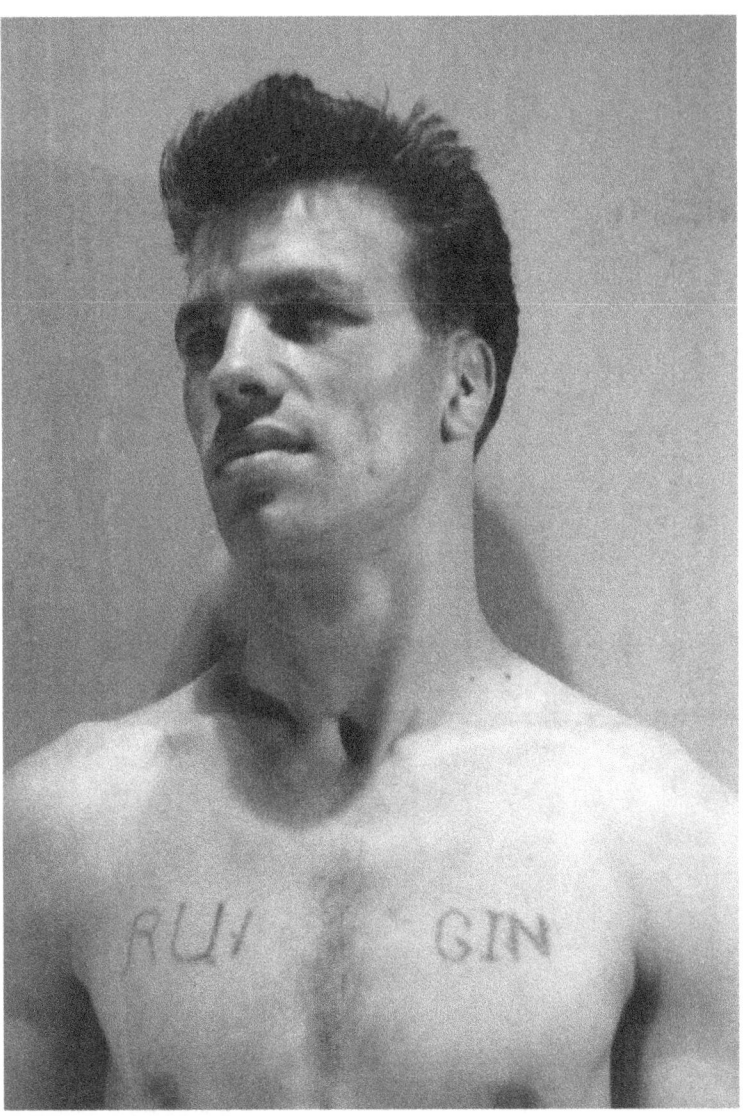

29. Times Square hustler and 'clip artist', 1950s. From the Thomas Painter Collection. Reproduced by permission of The Kinsey Institute for Research in Sex, Gender, and Reproduction, Inc. Author's note: Painter said that the man was arrested for robbery.

30. The hustler 'Biceps', 1948. From the Thomas Painter Collection. Reproduced by permission of The Kinsey Institute for Research in Sex, Gender, and Reproduction, Inc. Author's note: this photograph, taken in the home of a client, was given to Painter by the subject. Note the interesting juxtaposition between rough trade and classical homoeroticism. The image can also be read as a visual reminder of the potential dangers of engaging a hustler.

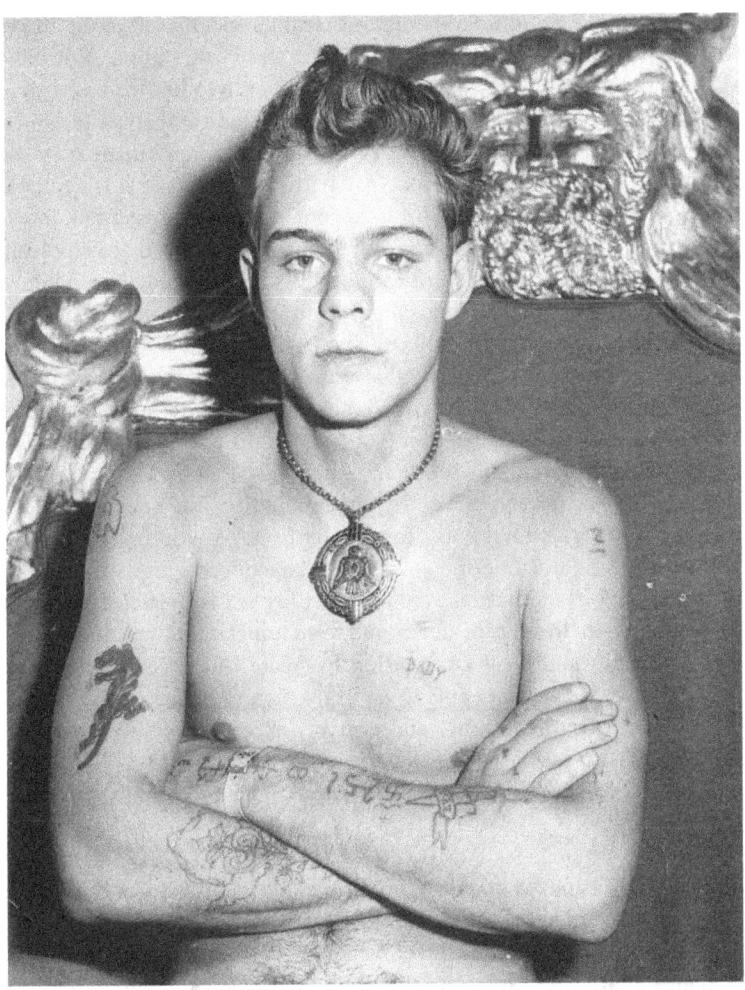

31. Hustler with jail tattoos, 1950s/1960s. Collection of Richard Taddei, New York. Author's note: the photograph was taken by Edward Melcarth. The chair, a Melcarth creation, was later housed in the famous New York 1970s gay bar The Anvil, on the corner of 14th Street and Eleventh Avenue.

Part of the appeal of the hustler, then, was his otherness, a class difference reinforced by his lack of education as well as his physicality. This was something that Rechy discovered early: 'And I learned too that to hustle the streets you had to play it almost-illiterate.'[107] Mart Crowley's play *Boys in the Band* (1968) contains a rather vicious riff along those lines. The hustler character Cowboy is beautiful but stupid; 'Not only can he not talk intelligently about art, he can't even follow from one sentence to the next.'[108] Likewise, Gus, the rough trade archetype in James Barr's novel *The Occasional Man* (1966) is 'appealingly inadequate in mind and emotions'; the uncle of Gus's patron complains to his nephew, 'Damn it, boy, can't you ever bring anyone up here who can talk intelligently?'[109] Painter said that one of his hustlers thought that Napoleon discovered America, had never heard of Julius Caesar, and did not know where Rome was. His mother taught him about Judgement Day, 'But fortunately she taught him nothing about sex.'[110] 'His attitude towards my sex play is, I feel, rather like that of the Russian peasant toward the noble's: incomprehensible, bizarre, but not for him to question any more than to understand, to cater to and allow tolerantly', he said of another. 'Being moronic and highly sexed add to his easy-going attitude. And he seems to have acquired none of the usual prejudices one finds, especially on what is queer and not queer for a queer to do. Anything I suggest he will try with the docility of a cow and no preconceptions as to what is proper or not.'[111] Painter referred to this either as his Galatea complex – a doomed desire to educate and mould from imperfect raw material – or, when he had money, his compulsion to create Cinderella stories: 'the use of money to "help" people or an expression of power or to impress people or to give them things and/or experiences they could never buy themselves – for the pleasure of their pleasure in it (I think)'.[112] Whatever the theory or the motivation, it is the distancing condescension of class that prevails.

The hustler was but an iconic figure in a much wider amorphous trade, although it is difficult to find a definitional term for the casual operatives. Times Square was packed with young men who traded their bodies occasionally or part time – some employed, some not. In 1951, Painter picked up a hustler who had quit boxing, was married, and was going to start work as a longshoreman: 'Meanwhile is . . . in need of money. Hence one hustles occasionally.'[113] In the following year, he encountered a packer from Union City in New Jersey who came to New York 'when the spirit moved to make some spare change or get fellated, or both'.[114] In 1961, he met an automobile mechanic, also from New Jersey, who visited New York about once a month when he needed to make extra cash.[115]

The hustler population changed over time: Painter thought that the Puerto Rican casual whoring of the 1950s was the sociological equivalent of the sexually available Italian working-class youth of earlier generations.[116] Painter compared the more respectable working-class hustler of the Depression years of the 1930s and immediate postwar with what he saw as the criminal, drug-dependent trade of the 1950s and 1960s.[117] His study of 1941 was confident that poverty was a 'great factor' in the making of the hustler of that earlier period. Most of these sexually available young men 'came from the most underprivileged class hailing from the depression-ridden industrial and mining areas of the East, especially Pennsylvania, from the "poor white" class of the South, or from the slums of Boston, New York or other great Eastern cities'. While some ended up in prison or dead, 'most finally become working-men and get married and raise families'. They are 'quite indistinguishable to the untrained eye from the ordinary run of American youth, a part of which, in fact, they are'.[118]

Painter's later file of sexual contacts, most of them hustlers, shows that a large number of them were either married or would marry later. Some put the hustling behind them and, as far as it is possible to know, enjoyed average working-class lives.[119] Gore Vidal said as much when bemoaning the decline in the quality of trade in an interview in the early 1970s: 'When I was young there was a floating population of hetero males who wanted money or kicks or what have you and would sell their ass for a period of their lives. Later they would marry and end up as construction workers or firemen or in the police department.'[120] Steven Maynard has argued that in Canada from the 1890s onwards there is evidence that working-class boys habitually traded sex for cash and access to the trappings of modernity.[121]

Young itinerants, tramps, were notoriously sexually available. The sexual regime of wolves and punks found in prison culture was also the pattern favoured by transients, so payment of cash or kind was but a logical extension of established practice.[122] The tramp and the boy were familiar figures. Nels Anderson, who knew the culture better than most, wrote in the 1920s of wolves and jockers, and punks, lambs, and fairies among the tramp population, the use of girls' names (Mabel, Dollie, Susan) to indicate sexual subordination, and descriptors such as 'my wife', 'my sweetie', or 'the old lady' to refer to male sexual partners.[123] The age profile of itinerants – Anderson estimated that 25 per cent of them were under twenty-one – and their practice of locating to the 'most undesirable' parts of the city was thought to increase their 'intimate contact with vice and immorality'.[124] Anderson claimed that 'Sex perversion is very prevalent among the tramp population', and one former tramp, who was working as a hustler when interviewed, said that 'I never saw a boy I couldn't get next to'.[125] Anderson's fieldwork identified many itinerants who moved into hustling.[126] Colin Johnson has recently re-examined the early twentieth-century environment of itinerant labour, hoboes, and tramps, a mobile homosocial world that linked city to city and town to country, where men had sex with each other and were also available for casual, same-sex prostitution.[127] And Margot Canaday has demonstrated what she calls the straight state's awareness of the problem in the Federal Transient Program and Civilian Conservation Corps men's welfare camps during the Depression.[128] John Worby's memoirs of itinerant life in the USA and England in the 1920s and 1930s includes sexual encounters with men who were better off than he was. Worby's description of an episode with an effeminate man is not without hints of reciprocation to his attentions, but Worby's essential manner was detached and his motive, in this and other encounters, was what gain could be gleaned from such men – theft was usually the outcome.[129]

The Chicago material discussed in the previous chapter contains details about young men who sold their bodies in the 1920s and 1930s as a means of getting by. 'I began to play the queers', a Chicago pugilist and stick-up man told an investigator, relating how he had travelled the country, providing sex for money to both men and women. At the time of the interview in 1933, he was back in Chicago, 'panhandling and playing queers to live'.[130] Others referred to 'playing queers' for money, sometimes to supplement their income.[131] One out-of-work man was 'frenched' by an older client in return for an expensive coat. 'I was down town looking for bitches in order to get some money.' 'I thought of the coat that he gave me [it cost $27.50] all for a piece of cock.' The man said that his dreams were about getting a job rather than sex: 'I dream that I am working at the Western Electric and of old times there... Most of my dreams are about working.'[132]

Bell hops and elevator boys were known to be available for paid sex.[133] Cab drivers sold more than their transport time; one aficionado of trade recounted his success – he would simply offer them $5 or $10.[134] Leo Adams, an executive for Fox Theatres in New York in the late 1920s, relayed the story of a 'notorious belle', known by all the 1930s Chicago cabbies for his willingness to purchase sex, who when he approached what he thought was a new driver was told 'Oh, I've been up your poop a couple of times!'[135] The Chicago investigators also came across references to hustling newspaper boys.[136] A woman who worked with those who appeared before the US juvenile courts noted the sexual accessibility of the boys who sold newspapers and confectionary on street corners. 'I confess', she wrote in 1949, 'that these lads taught me more about homosexual relations than I had ever wanted to learn.'[137] It is likely that the hustlers are part of a wider cultural history.

Hustling, then, was not some minority activity – it is important to be clear about this. Indeed it is interesting to compare male hustling with the charity girls of New York so skilfully illuminated by Elizabeth Clement, young working-class women who in the first half of the century might exchange sex for a night out or material gifts, in what was called 'treating'.[138] Although the female recipients of treating were keen to distinguish the practice from prostitution, and its male variant could hardly be termed a form of courtship, the money earned by males selling sex to other males might well be redeployed for that precise purpose: to pursue opposite sex interests, including dating. For several generations of American men, hustling was a way of making a living, though it is not an aspect of US working life that labour historians have been much interested in.

Notes

1. H. Huncke, *The Herbert Huncke Reader*, ed. B. G. Schafer (New York, 1997), pp. 24–5.
2. National Archives and Records Administration, Washington, DC, RG 125, Courts of Inquiry (Kent, Samuel Neal), Boxes 254–8, Case 10821-1, File 26283/2591, 'Exhibits . . . Court of Inquiry . . . 22 January 1920', pp. 1380, 1421.
3. The Kinsey Institute for Research in Sex, Gender, and Reproduction, University of Indiana, Bloomington (hereafter, KI), Thomas Painter, 'Male Homosexuals and Their Prostitutes in Contemporary America' (New York, 1941), Vol. 2: 'The Prostitute', pp. 3, 129.
4. KI, The Thomas Painter Collection (hereafter, Painter), Box 1, Series 2, c. 1, Vol. 6: Painter Letters: 16 February 1949; Vol. 18b: 29 July 1961.
5. KI, Samuel Steward Collection, Series 2, F: Diary 1955: 26 January.
6. J. L. Herlihy, *Midnight Cowboy* (New York, 1965), p. 170.
7. Ibid., p. 19.
8. L. Wilson, *Collected Plays 1965–1970* (Lyme, NH, 1996), pp. 5–7.
9. S. R. Delany, *Times Square Red, Times Square Blue* (New York, 2001), p. 148.
10. Painter, Box 1, Series 2, c. 1, Vol. 6: 2 March 1949.
11. D. M. Allen, 'Young male prostitutes: a psychosocial study', *Archives of Sexual Behavior*, 9 (1980), 404.
12. J. Rechy, *City of Night* (New York, 1984), pp. 63–4. First published in 1963.

13 W. S. Burroughs, *Queer* (New York, 1987), p. 21. *Queer* was written in the 1950s.
14 A. Ginsberg, *Howl and Other Poems* (San Francisco, 1959), p. 13. First published in 1956.
15 J. J. Gallo and others, 'The consenting adult homosexual and the law: an empirical study of enforcement and administration in Los Angeles County', *UCLA Law Review*, 13 (1965–6), 690.
16 Painter, 'Male Homosexuals', Vol. 2, p. 128.
17 L. Humphreys, 'New styles in homosexual manliness', in J. A. McCaffrey (ed.), *The Homosexual Dialectic* (Englewood Cliffs, NJ, 1972), p. 75. The essay was first published in 1971. He also drew attention to a newer category, the call-boys.
18 C. Winick and P. M. Kinsie, *The Lively Commerce: Prostitution in the United States* (Chicago, 1971), p. 89.
19 Allen, 'Young male prostitutes', p. 406.
20 *New York Times*, 1 August 1954, p. 1.
21 Interview with Rechy in 1973 in W. Leyland (ed.), *Gay Sunshine Interviews: Volume 1* (San Francisco, 1978), p. 260.
22 Painter, 'Male Homosexuals', Vol. 2, p. 100.
23 Painter, Box 1, Series 2, c. 1, Vol. 10: 2 May 1953.
24 Painter, Box 1, Series 2, c. 1, Vol. 13: 22 March 1956; Vol. 18a: 14 February 1961.
25 Rechy, *City of Night*, pp. 31, 33, 34, 38.
26 Painter, Box 1, Series 2, c. 1, Vol. 10: 7 December 1953.
27 Painter, Box 1, Series 2, c. 1, Vol. 13: 2 February 1956; Vol. 14: 10 March and 4 August 1957; Series 2, Vol. 4: Index of names O–Z.
28 *Flesh* (1968: Paul Morrissey).
29 Painter, Box 1, Series 2, c. 1, Vol. 9: 8 August, 28 September, 13 October, and 19 November 1952; Vol. 10: 18 April, 26 August, and 7 December 1953; Vol. 13: 31 December 1956.
30 Painter, Box 1, Series 2, c. 1, Vol. 14: 1 March 1957; Vol. 18b: 3 September 1961.
31 Huncke, *Herbert Huncke Reader*, p. 104.
32 Painter, Box 1, Series 2, c. 1, Vol. 10: 18 April 1953; Vol. 16: 17 September 1959; Vol. 18a: 2 January 1961.
33 See M. Friedman, *Strapped for Cash: A History of American Hustler Culture* (Los Angeles, 2003), pp. 154–69.
34 D. W. Cory and J. P. LeRoy, *The Homosexual and His Society: A View from Within* (New York, 1963), p. 13.
35 C. A. Tripp, *The Homosexual Matrix* (New York, 1986), pp. 204, 212–13; L. R. Murphy, 'The house on Pacific Street: homosexuality, intrigue, and politics during World War II', *Journal of Homosexuality*, 12 (1985), 27–49.
36 Painter, 'Male Homosexuals', Vol. 2, pp. 73–81.

37 Ibid. See also, Painter, Box 1, Series 2, c. 1, Vol. 6: 16 April, 5 November, and 13 November 1949.
38 Painter, 'Male Homosexuals', Vol. 2, pp. 20–1.
39 Ibid., pp. 29–31.
40 Ibid., pp. 27, 38, 47–8.
41 Ibid., pp. 22–4, 27, 29.
42 Ibid., pp. 20–1.
43 D. Rader, *Gov't Inspected Meat and Other Fun Summer Things* (New York, 1971), p. 3.
44 Rechy, *City of Night*, p. 30. For a history of Times Square during our period of interest, see W. R. Taylor (ed.), *Inventing Times Square* (Baltimore, 1996), esp. chapters by George Chauncey (ch. 15) and Laurence Senelick (ch. 16).
45 Rechy, *City of Night*, p. 29.
46 Delany, *Times Square Red, Times Square Blue*, pp. 83, 145–50, 175, 194.
47 Painter, 'Male Homosexuals', Vol. 2, pp. 63–5.
48 D. Savran, *Communists, Cowboys, and Queers: The Politics of Masculinity in the Work of Arthur Miller and Tennessee Williams* (Minneapolis, MN, 1992), pp. 111–14. For these deftly and humorously understated stories, see T. Williams, *Collected Stories* (New York, 1985), pp. 99–109, 335–46. The quote is from 'The mysteries of the Joy Rio', in Williams, *Collected Stories*, p. 102. Both these stories were first published in Williams's short story collection, *Hard Candy* (New York, 1954).
49 H. Benjamin and R. E. L. Masters, *Prostitution and Morality* (New York, 1964), p. 292.
50 Rechy, *City of Night*, pp. 26–7.
51 *Midnight Cowboy* (1969: John Schlesinger).
52 Painter, 'Male Homosexuals', Vol. 2, p. 67.
53 Ibid., p. 68; Painter, Box 1, Series 2, c. 1, Vol. 18b: 6 November 1961.
54 Painter, Box 1, Series 2, c. 1, Vol. 7: 5 December 1950. Steward knew of a similar gym-based scene in Chicago in the 1950s and 1960s: S. Steward, *Understanding the Male Hustler* (Binghamton, NY, 1991), pp. 26–7, 57–8.
55 Painter, Box 1, Series 2, c. 1, Vol. 10: 22 February 1953.
56 Painter, Series 2, Vol. 4: Index of names O–Z.
57 Painter, 'Male Homosexuals', Vol. 2, p. 66.
58 Ibid., p. 65.
59 Painter, Box 1, Series 2, c. 1, Vol. 7: 19 August 1950; Vol. 10: 5 July 1953.
60 Painter, Box 1, Series 2, c. 1, Vol. 6: 31 July 1949.
61 Painter, Box 1, Series 2, c. 1, Vol. 14: 29 March 1957.
62 For this context see E. C. Schneider, *Vampires, Dragons, and Egyptian Kings: Youth Gangs in Postwar New York* (Princeton, 1999), ch. 1.
63 Ibid., p. 15.

64 R. Jacoby, *Conversations with the Capeman: The Untold Story of Salvador Agron* (Madison, WI, 2004), pp. 110, 171.
65 Schneider, *Vampires, Dragons, and Egyptian Kings*, p. 3.
66 Ibid., pp. 134–5.
67 V. Riccio and B. Slocum, *All the Way Down: The Violent Underworld of Street Gangs* (New York, 1962), p. 90.
68 Ibid., p. 91.
69 Ibid., p. 92.
70 Allen, 'Young male prostitutes', 407.
71 Painter, Box 1, Series 2, c. 1, Vol. 10: 3 October 1953.
72 W. Burroughs, *Interzone* (New York, 1990), p. 122.
73 Painter, Box 1, Series 2, c. 1, Vol. 16: 9 October 1959.
74 Painter, Box 1, Series 2, c. 1, Vol. 14: 31 May 1957.
75 R. P. McNamara, *The Times Square Hustler: Male Prostitution in New York City* (Westport, CT, 1994), pp. 36–7.
76 C. H. Ford, *Water from a Bucket: A Diary 1948–1957* (New York, 2001), p. 19.
77 T. Williams, 'Two on a party', in Williams, *Collected Stories*, p. 287. It was written in 1951–52.
78 G. S. Sprague, 'Varieties of homosexual manifestations', *American Journal of Psychiatry*, 92 (1938), 144.
79 Painter, 'Male Homosexuals', Vol. 2, pp. 32–8, 46–7.
80 T. Williams, *Notebooks*, ed. M.B. Thornton (New Haven, 2006), p. 271.
81 D. Vining, *A Gay Diary 1933–1946* (New York, 1996), p. 274.
82 Ibid., pp. 286, 317, 322, 326, 401–2, 427–8; D. Vining, *A Gay Diary 1946–1954* (New York, 1980), pp. 318–19.
83 D. Vining, *How Can You Come Out If You've Never Been In?* (Trumansburg, NY, 1986), p. 4.
84 Painter, 'Male Homosexuals', Vol. 2, p. 198.
85 Ibid., p. 145.
86 L. H. Loeser, 'The sexual psychopath in the military service', *American Journal of Psychiatry*, 102 (1945), 93, 98.
87 Painter, Box 16, Series 4 A. 1. b., box 1: Photographs from the collection of Henry Faulkner (c. 1940s); Painter, Box 1, Series 2, c. 1, Vol. 6: 13 November 1949; Vol. 7: 26 March, 8 April, and 20 April 1950.
88 D. Rader, *Tennessee: Cry of the Heart* (New York, 1985), pp. 235–6.
89 Painter, Box 1, Series 2, c. 1, Vol. 6: 19 February 1949.
90 Ibid., 5 March 1949.
91 Ibid., 13 November 1949.
92 D. Windham (ed.), *Tennessee Williams' Letters to Donald Windham 1940–1965* (Athens, GA, 1996), pp. 45, 132.
93 A. J. Devlin and N. M. Tischler (eds), *The Selected Letters of Tennessee Williams: Volume 2: 1945–1957* (New York, 2004), pp. 420–1.

94 Williams, *Notebooks*, p. 339.
95 Ibid., p. 343.
96 G. Clarke (ed.), *Too Brief a Treat: The Letters of Truman Capote* (New York, 2004), p. 67.
97 Ibid., pp. 114, 116–17.
98 Ibid., p. 145.
99 Painter, Box 3, Series 2, d. 2, Folder 1: Autobiographical sections: # viii Biography.
100 Painter, Series 2, c. 1, Vol. 10: 14 September 1953.
101 Painter, Box 1, Series 2, c. 1, Vol. 14: 4 September 1957; Box 1, Series 2, c. 1, Vol. 18b: 29 July 1961.
102 Archives of American Art, Smithsonian Institution, Washington, DC, Edward Melcarth Papers (hereafter, Melcarth Papers), Box 2 of 2: Riccardo [Richard] Taddei to Edward Melcarth: 20 January and 12 March 1972.
103 See Melcarth Papers, Box 1 of 2: Folder – 1970s; Box 1 of 4: Folder – Contact Sheets.
104 Melcarth Papers, Box 3 of 4: Joseph Newlin to Edward Melcarth: 20 June 1963; see also Box 2 of 2: Edward Tortora to Edward Melcarth: 7 September 1973.
105 Melcarth Papers, Box 2 of 2: Gary Spokes to Edward Melcarth: 13 October 1971.
106 E. White, *My Lives* (London, 2005), p. 14.
107 Rechy, *City of Night*, p. 32.
108 M. Crowley, *The Boys in the Band* (Harmondsworth, 1970), p. 52. First published in New York in 1968.
109 J. Barr, *The Occasional Man* (New York, 1966), pp. 79, 211.
110 Painter, Box 1, Series 2, c. 1, Vol. 6: 17 January 1949.
111 Painter, Box 1, Series 2, c. 1, Vol. 6: 21 June 1949.
112 Painter, Box 1, Series 2, c. 1, Vol. 8: 17 September 1951; Box 1, Series 2, c. 1, Vol. 18a: 27 May 1961.
113 Painter, Box 1, Series 2, c. 1, Vol. 8: 9 June 1951.
114 Painter, Box 1, Series 2, c. 1, Vol. 9: 26 April 1952.
115 Painter, Box 1, Series 2, c. 1, Vol. 18b: 17 August 1961.
116 Painter, Box 1, Series 2, c. 1, Vol. 14: 31 May 1957. Chauncey discusses the Italians: G. Chauncey, *Gay New York: Gender, Urban Culture, and the Making of the Gay Male World, 1890–1940* (New York, 1994), ch. 3.
117 Painter, Box 1, Series 2, c. 1, Vol. 18a: 26 June 1961.
118 Painter, 'Male Homosexuals', Vol. 2, pp. 4, 9, 125–7.
119 For their later histories, see, for example, Painter, Series 2, Vol. 2: Index of names A–F.
120 Interview with Vidal in 1974, in Leyland (ed.), *Gay Sunshine Interviews*, p. 291.

121 S. Maynard, '"Horrible temptations": Sex, men, and working-class male youth in urban Ontario, 1890–1935', *Canadian Historical Review*, 78 (1997), 191–232.
122 University of Chicago Library Special Collections Research Center, Ernest Watson Burgess Papers (hereafter, Burgess), Box 127, Folder 1: Document 30; Folder 2: Document 82; Folder 3: Document 110; Folder 4: Documents 120, 122, 124, 125, 127.
123 N. Anderson, 'The juvenile and the tramp', *Journal of the American Institute of Criminal Law and Criminology*, 14 (1923–24), 305, 306.
124 Ibid., 292, 293.
125 Ibid., 301, 302.
126 Ibid., 302–8.
127 C. R. Johnson, 'Casual sex: towards a "prehistory" of gay life in bohemian America', *Interventions*, 10 (2008), 303–20. See also his 'Columbia's Orient: Gender, Geography, and the Invention of Sexuality in Rural America' (PhD Thesis, University of Michigan, 2003), ch. 3.
128 M. Canaday, *The Straight State: Sexuality and Citizenship in Twentieth-century America* (Princeton, 2009), ch. 3.
129 J. Worby, *The Other Half: The Autobiography of a Tramp* (New York, 1937), pp. 32, 38, 185–6.
130 Burgess, Box 98, Folder 5: 'Homosexuality Interviews'.
131 Burgess, Box 98, Folder 11: 'Homosexual Materials': 'Supplement to Jack's History'.
132 Burgess, Box 98, Folder 11: 'Homosexual Materials': 'As told to me by Sidney'.
133 New York Public Library Manuscripts and Archives Division (hereafter, NYPL), Donald Vining Papers, Box 2, Folder 6: 'The Unabashed', ch. 3, p. 7.
134 Burgess, Box 128, Folder 9: 'Earl Bruce's Homosexuality Materials, Cases, Notes, etc.': 'Robert – Age 33 Years'.
135 NYPL, Leo Adams Papers, Box 1, Folder 1: Correspondence with Merle Macbain, 19 April 1937.
136 Burgess, Box 130, Folder 5: 'Paul Cressey's Report on Summer Work with the Juvenile Protective Association of Chicago, 1925', pp. 37–8; Box 145, Folder 8: 'Case Study of a Homosexual . . . 1933 . . . Boy Hustler'.
137 H. K. Branson, '"Street trades" and their sex knowledge', *Sexology*, April 1949.
138 E. A. Clement, *Love for Sale: Courting, Treating, and Prostitution in New York City, 1900–1945* (Chapel Hill, NC, 2006).

4

Sexualities

> I met him [Alfred Kinsey] on 42nd Street. I was living off the largesse of the public... I was a hustler. He asked me... if I had ever had sex with another member of my own sex, you know, and I said, oh, definitely. And, did you like it? Yes, I liked it. Do you think you're homosexual? I said not really. He was kind of taken aback by that. He said well how could you have a homosexual relationship without not thinking you're homosexual? I said, well, I think sex is sex. (Interview with Herbert Huncke, referring to the 1940s.)[1]

> Dear Doctor,
> Sex... is peculiar, odd, unpredictable, or, as my mother used the word, queer. This week I have cornered two of such examples: I have had sexual relations with two 'normal' young men, one of whom dislikes being fellated [blown] (but allows it for money) but liked being pedicated [fucked]; the other won't be pedicated, but voluntarily fellates, without being asked. Both were in the Marine Corps, in action on islands in the Pacific. Both are tough, muscular, virile youths. (Thomas Painter to Alfred Kinsey, 1947)[2]

One of the most notable aspects of Alfred Kinsey's research was his recognition of the variability of human sexuality in his seven-point continuum of sexual activity, ranging from heterosexuality (0) at one end to homosexuality (6) at the other.[3] Kinsey's collaborator Wardell Pomeroy later claimed it as one of their major contributions, 'of prime value in breaking away from the confines of classifying homosexual and heterosexual behavior as two separate, compartmentalized types'.[4] Kinsey wrote to one of his informants that he thought that it was societal pressure that forced people into rigid categories, and that he considered that 'most people would carry on both homosexual and heterosexual activities coincidentally'.[5] *Sexual Behavior in the Human Male* (1948) argued that about half the population had sexual experiences exclusively heterosexual and a few per cent were exclusively homosexual; therefore, as he put it, 'one must learn to recognize every combination of heterosexuality and homosexuality in the histories of various individuals'.[6]

Where might the hustler and the inhabitants of the wider world of trade fit on Kinsey's scale? What can we say about the sexualities of hustlers? Looking for hustlers in the Kinsey data is like searching for the proverbial needle in a haystack. *Sexual Behavior in the Human Male* refers to 'several hundred' male prostitutes having given their histories; Kinsey mentioned this when discussing the ability of such men to achieve ejaculation five or six times a day over many years.[7] We know from other sources that hustlers were among those interviewed by Kinsey and his team for their work on male sexual behaviour (before and after 1948): the Herbert Huncke of this chapter's opening quote and Puerto Rican gang members (we will see shortly) were among them. Unfortunately, it is not possible to isolate such men in the Kinsey data because individual identities in the sexual histories remain confidential. However, we know that they fall within the 'Underworld' classification, those 'Deriving a significant portion of their income from illicit activities ... bootleggers, con men, dope peddlers, gamblers, hold-up men, pimps, *prostitutes*, etc'.[8] So we can employ this category as a rough proxy for our subject, given also that many hustlers had experienced prison or were involved in criminal or semi-criminal activities.[9]

Using this proxy to rework the Kinsey data, it is possible to calculate the extent of this group's homosexual experience, plotted against a control, white non-college-educated (that is, working-class) males. See Table 1.[10] It is important to note that this measurement makes no claims for homosexual identification but merely charts homosexual experience. Whereas 60 per cent of the comparative group claimed no homosexual experience, only 14 per cent of criminal males made the same claim. Well over half (57 per cent) of the criminal proxy group had had what was described as 'extensive' homosexual contact involving a total of 21 or more males and/or 51-plus incidents. Just over 70 per cent had had sex with a total number of five or more males or had been involved in more than twenty sexual contacts. The figure for the control is 17 per cent.

The other calculation that we can make is of hustler/trade rankings on the Kinsey 'Heterosexual–homosexual' scale. See Table 2.[11] We do not need to use any proxy here, for the Kinsey team asked Painter to classify his hustlers and other male contacts retrospectively (131 in all) according to the seven-point grid, and we have the results. If we compare them with Kinsey's figures for the general male population aged 16–25 years, we see that the hustlers group (as one would expect) has a much lower

Table 1: Extent of homosexual experience

Extent	Criminal males (Kinsey data): percentages	Kinsey data tabulations: Table 379: White non-College educated males
Never	13.8	60.2
Rare (1 male and/or 1–5 times)	6.0	10.9
Incidental (2–4 males and/or 6–20 times)	8.5	10.3
More than incidental (5–20 males and/or 21–50 times)	13.5	4.6
Extensive (21+ males and/or 51+ times)	57.2	12.7
Occurred, unknown amount	0.9	1.1
Total number	318	764

Table 2: Heterosexual–homosexual rating

Rating on Kinsey Scale	Painter's files: percentages	Kinsey book: Table 149: Population aged 16–25: percentages
0 no same-sex contact/response	8.4	69.0
1 incidental same-sex contact/response	43.5	4.2
2 response to homo but hetero stronger	26.7	7.1
3 midway on homo/hetero scale	16.0	4.7
4 more overt homo than hetero	4.6	3.5
5 almost entirely homo	0.0	3.0
6 exclusively homo	0.8	6.5
Total number	131	2539

weighting in the purely heterosexual rating of zero, indicating no same-sex contact. Most, some 70 per cent, fall into the 1–2 rating, signifying both same-sex and opposite-sex sexual response but that their heterosexual experience outweighs homosexual contact. (The corresponding figure for the general male population is only 11 per cent.) Few, only 5 per cent, were rated 4–6 (the homosexual range). And some 16 per cent were in the midpoint at 3.

What this rather minimal quantitative data indicates is the existence of a group rated as predominantly 'heterosexual' that was also involved in 'extensive' homosexual sex. The nearly 60 per cent of the proxy group with wide same-sex experience would have had even more comprehensive heterosexual sexual histories and would have been likely to have been ranked at 1–2 on the Kinsey scale. As we have seen, most of Painter's paid sexual contacts were rated as such. Without labouring the point, these statistics agree with Pomeroy's observation to a fellow researcher that most hustlers were rateable at a 2 on the Kinsey scale and with an early 1970s study of forty-one Los Angeles hustlers that classified 72 per cent as 'basically heterosexual'.[12]

But these bare statistics give us little sense of the nature of that activity. One of the Los Angeles hustlers, a former marine, had had five heterosexual experiences compared to two hundred homosexual contacts yet insisted that he was 'heterosexual'.[13] To gain a deeper understanding we need to turn to qualitative evidence. It is here that Kinsey's informant Painter came into his own.

Painter's experience with the young Puerto Ricans confirmed his (and Kinsey's) belief in natural omnisexuality – 'polysexual, pansexual', he was grasping for the best description. 'Strict heterosexuality is as abnormal as strict homosexuality.'[14] Painter explained the Puerto Ricans' availability as cultural: females were supposed to be virgins before marriage so young men had to have sex either with a man or with a female prostitute. 'So they fuck one another.'[15] Penetration of males was accepted and 'habitually practiced' by Puerto Rican males and just as acceptable as heterosexual coitus; 'it is very important to note this "homosexual" trait in this extremely heterosexual people'.[16] Pedication was of no consequence provided that the man was the pedicator and not the pedicant; hence the popularity – as sexual objects – of effeminate Puerto Ricans and passive Americano homosexuals. One of Painter's long-term Puerto Rican associates took him to a Puerto Rican party where the queers were dancing with 'macho' gang members.[17] Even homosexual men who were not actual pedicants were assumed to be so by a young man's friends; as Henry Minton has noted, Painter was continually negotiating himself out of being fucked by his Puerto Rican gang friends.[18] One of the Dragons said that he loved faggots, meaning, Painter glossed, that he loved to pedicate them.[19] Another boasted that Painter was 'his queer' and paid for all the girls he wanted, even though the two men had never actually had sex.[20] At the party it had been taken for granted that Painter was the gang member's queer. Although Painter was puzzled by the way in which a young Puerto Rican took him home to meet his parents after they had spent the day together and had sex, he was doubtless assumed either to be an innocent friend or a passive partner.[21] It was the public face that was all-important. There are indications that Painter was incorporated into community mores. When he and a gang member shared accommodation on 20th Street West, his companion 'proceeded to interpret [this] as a marital act, and he became, thereby, my *marido* [husband]'. Painter later asked for a 'divorce', which he granted but 'continued for a very long time to contend we were still "married"'.[22]

The arrangements that the gang members entered into with homosexual Americanos varied around a common axis: sex and money. Some were merely paid to be fellated – as Painter expressed it somewhat indelicately of his friend's relationship with two Puerto Ricans, they came around to get their cocks sucked and were paid for it.[23] One hustler, photographed by Painter, had worked shining shoes but then discovered that he could earn a better living 'letting queers suck his cock'.[24] Or there might be longer-term scenarios. Painter was persuaded to rent rooms, accommodate gang members, take them on holidays to Puerto Rico and on road trips in the USA (he even took a party to Indiana so that Kinsey could take their sexual histories).[25] In return, Painter expected photographic access and occasional sex of varied forms (though often merely bodily contact or companionship). Painter was aware of the sensibilities of his partners, modifying his sexual practices to meet their mores. He preferred frictation (rubbing against the body) but often masturbated when he thought that they would be uncomfortable with the acts that he desired.[26] He had several relationships with Puerto Ricans that did not involve any overt contact whatsoever, though Painter still saw their interactions as sexual.[27] Companionship was important for him and, he was convinced, his tough friends: 'these "brutes and thugs and hoodlums" bare to me, as to no one, . . . the terrors and agonies and fears that swirl and snarl within them, behind their masks of toughness and brutality and criminality'.[28] (See Figures 32 and 33.)

None of these relationships was exclusively homosexual as far as Painter's Puerto Rican contacts were concerned. One man stated some ground rules: 'The sex part is all right with him: I would have no other boys – and he would keep his girls away from me.'[29] Another gang member suggested that Painter live with one of his associates while the man's wife was away, paying the rent, presumably in return for sexual favours.[30] Hector, described by Painter as his 'lover, chauffeur and procurer', had both a wife and mistress and was constantly in trouble for 'fucking other men's wives'.

32. Puerto Rican gang members, 1956. From the Thomas Painter Collection. Reproduced by permission of The Kinsey Institute for Research in Sex, Gender, and Reproduction, Inc.

Hector's personal life was confused. He was married and had two legitimate children, but constantly preferred living with other men's wives. This kept him in hot water, both with the wife . . . and with the husbands who now and then pursued him with knives. He also had an Italian girl in Astoria by whom he had a son, and she was jealous. He was a conscienceless seducer, doing it for the pleasure of it – and perhaps for the danger. One time he told me of was when he was living with this woman who had a daughter living with her. He seduced the daughter, too, unknown to the woman, and kept them both serviced for a while; like walking on explosive eggs.[31]

Dionysio had five sons by two women (including two called Danny!); 'he never lived with me – any more than with one woman'.[32] Johnny, who drove Painter around in the 1950s in return for sex and a down payment on the car, 'came out heterosexually' and married a girl who owned a beauty shop.[33]

The Puerto Ricans appear to have conformed to the sexual regime outlined by experts on Latino cultures, sexuality based on penetrative masculinity: the masculine penetrator versus the effeminate penetrated.[34] Don

33. Puerto Rican 'hustler', 1950s. From the Thomas Painter Collection. Reproduced by permission of The Kinsey Institute for Research in Sex, Gender, and Reproduction, Inc. Author's note: Painter wrote on the back of the photograph, which he took, 'dressed just as he was when I picked him up on 14th St. The primary reason is visible, just as it was as he walked about the Clock Bar'.

Kulick has observed of Brazilian male sexual culture (in its most exaggerated form) that the elemental distinction was between those who penetrate and those who are penetrated rather than between male and female. The sex of the penetrated was not of great concern to those effecting the penetration. Men who enjoyed being penetrated, on the other hand, 'belong to the same classificatory category' as women.[35] That Painter's Puerto Rican gang associates had sex with both men and women did not mean that they were bisexual; as commentators on Costa Rican mores have put it, 'sex with men is not important enough to affect their identity'. In short, 'practice is more important than the object of sexual desire'.[36] (In Costa Rican prison culture the nearest to bisexual would have been a man who was both active and passive with other males.)[37] Painter's New York Puerto Ricans are not unlike the Costa Rican male prostitutes in a 1990s study. They paraded their attraction to women, were paid for active sex with men, saw this means of economic survival as a temporary situation, and preferred older clients (*pagadores* [payers] or sugar daddies) because they were generous and because it would be obvious to any observer that the relationship was based on material gain rather than mutual attraction – a key perhaps to Painter's successes with the Puerto Ricans.[38]

Many of the other inhabitants of the Americano hustler's world shared similar sexual codes. A twenty-three-year-old sailor from Iowa expressed what were common guidelines. He would penetrate but would not be penetrated. 'He is not passionate, or cooperative even, but has no objection to any amount of pawing . . . "I don't care what you do so long as you don't try to stick it . . . in anywhere".'[39] One of Painter's favourites, an illiterate young tough, was willing to live with him for companionship and limited sexual contact, but was far less willing to enter into a similar set-up with Edward Melcarth because he kept trying to 'fuck him and he positively will not be fucked'.[40] Another, a truck driver and former prizefighter, a divorced Irishman who was violent and abusive towards women, enjoyed a 'heterosexual life' that was 'extensive, rough and primitive, promiscuous and obscene – and wholly contemptuous of all women'. He bragged of drinking and fucking to 5 am and continually talked about 'fucking women'. While his code of male–male interaction had included being fellated when he was in the Navy, there were clear boundaries: 'Jimmy says he does *not* want to be fucked.'[41] The ex-hustler John Rechy claimed an even more limited repertoire in keeping with his defined masculinity as trade. He would not kiss, blow, or even fuck. '*So the only thing you did was get a blow job*? That's all.'[42] Although he revelled in being provided with homosexual oral sex, the principal rough trade character in James Barr's novel *The Occasional Man* (1966), repeatedly proclaimed 'I never went down on a guy in my life.'[43]

Painter provided a long account of the morality of one of the men that he picked up in Diamond Jim's, a favourite haunt. The twenty-one-year-old had come to New York from Detroit to join the merchant marines and had gone to the bar because he was broke and needed to make some money. Painter offered him $5 to go home with him and he did. Over the following weeks, he lived with Painter, worked for Melcarth, and posed naked for a photographer friend. Another of Painter's associates fellated the man for $50 a week 'plus entertainment'. The former seaman enjoyed being fellated, although he thought it 'dirty', and preferred frictation because it was less 'queer'. 'Sees nothing at all wrong, shameful or deplorable about the homosexual. Just less fun, that's all.' He was married but separated, talked incessantly about women, and went out 'cunt hunting' with a friend. Painter informed Kinsey that the man insisted that he was heterosexual but thought that the Professor would have classified him as a 1–2 on his scale.[44] (See Figures 34 and 35.)

34. Hustler, circa 1940. From the Thomas Painter Collection. Reproduced by permission of The Kinsey Institute for Research in Sex, Gender, and Reproduction, Inc. Author's note: one of Painter's heterosexual/homosexual hustlers, the man worked as a chauffeur when not hustling and was married and had a child. He was posing as a merchant seaman for the photograph but normally wore a suit.

35. Hustler, circa 1950. From the Thomas Painter Collection. Reproduced by permission of The Kinsey Institute for Research in Sex, Gender, and Reproduction, Inc. Author's note: another of Painter's heterosexual/homosexual hustlers.

On the face of it, then, there were simple rules. We have discussed the focus on active/passive in Chapter 2 but it is worth pointing out that it was something that Kinsey was aware of when he wrote his section on 'Homosexual Outlet' in his survey of male sexual behaviour. 'There are persons who insist that the active male in an anal relation is essentially heterosexual in his behavior, and that the passive male in the same relation is the only one who is homosexual.' He continues in his characteristically clinical style: 'Some males who are being regularly fellated by other males, without, however, ever performing fellation themselves, may insist that they are exclusively heterosexual and that they have never been involved in a truly homosexual relation.'[45]

Although personally critical of the view, authors of a classic account of 1960s homosexuality were aware of its influence:

> there is no denying that our society views the role of insertion as bound up with the traditional concept of masculinity; so much so that many people who have performed sexual acts with partners of the same sex and who have confined themselves to insertor performances do not conceive of their

experiences as being homosexual *for them*, but only for their partner! In this country, such men are often referred to in gay slang as 'trade'.[46]

The Kinsey Institute's own study of American sex offenders in the 1940s and 1950s outlined a sexual philosophy shared by psychologist, psychiatrist, law enforcer, and sexually active males alike. The Institute's researchers pondered the illogicality of a policing that resulted in the man who fellated, or masturbated, or provided anal sex being considered homosexual, whereas the man being brought to orgasm by these means was neither homosexual or culpable. 'The attitude is widespread. We have interviewed many men who disapproved of homosexuality and hotly denied homosexual activity, but freely admitted that they had been brought to orgasm by other males. Such men felt that since they made no attempt to bring the other man to orgasm they could not be said to have displayed any homosexual behavior.'[47]

The sociologist Albert Reiss was similarly clear about the sexual code of young delinquents in Nashville in the 1950s, and, he thought, in large and small cities throughout the USA. Getting 'blown' by queers for money was taken for granted in this milieu. Provided there was payment in cash or alcohol, and the only contact was oral (with the youth as the fellated), there was no stigma. 'Adolescent boys in delinquent gangs quite commonly seek out older males –"queers" – to perform mouth-genital fellatio in exchange for money. These boys, however, have no conception of themselves as homosexual, although they view the fellator as a "gay" or "queer boy".'[48] Such attitudes, Reiss argued, were in keeping with wider American sexual mores:

> An extremely important element determining public reaction to acts of sexual deviation is the *degree to which the status and role of the participants in the sexual act depart from the status and role expectations for these persons apart from the sexual act itself.* In American culture, the male is expected to assume active roles and the female passive roles. The degree to which the male departs from the masculine, active sex role or the female departs from the feminine, passive sex role, therefore, is a factor in public reactions to the deviating sexual act. The 'pansy' and the 'castrating female' both seem more likely to be sanctioned for homosexual deviation than are the participants who fulfill [sic] conventional active-passive sex-role expectations.[49]

Pederasty ('corn holing') and frictation ('slick-legging') were accepted in an incarcerated environment (the Training School for Boys) but never with one of the gang and only in an active role. 'Boys who accept the female role in sexual transactions occupy the lowest status position among delinquents. They are "punks".'[50] Reiss's delinquents would grow up to either a life of crime or a 'conventional' working-class existence; 'A small proportion of them undertake hustling careers, but most assume the typical lower-status adult male role of husband and father.' 'They become neither hustlers nor queers.'[51]

George Henry and Alfred Gross's study of men held at the Penitentiary of the City of New York had noted a gap between public persona and private sexual practice. 'Many men who are known as "wolves" themselves submit to a feminine rôle in sex play. This, however, they will do most guardedly and never among their intimates, before whom they must preserve the appearance of masculinity.'[52] Appearances, a man's sexual demeanour, could be misleading, even to the experienced. The poet W. H. Auden's long-term partner Chester Kallman complained in 1941 that he had picked up a merchant sailor from Brooklyn: 'Wildly attractive, young, strong, perfectly built and large. I was all prepared for an absolutely relentless fucking, – but – as it turned out in the end, that is what I had to provide him with.'[53]

The New York homosexual diarist Donald Vining likewise recorded breaches in anticipated sexual rules. In 1948 he encountered a man in Central Park whom he was certain was trade and would therefore engage sexually in the role required. But the man, dressed in dungarees, 'gave me such a blow job as had me gripping the trees'. 'The most expert eye can be fooled.'[54] This vignette shows both the acceptance of certain rules of sexual engagement based on concepts of paraded masculinity *and* the breaching of such rules. Vining himself oscillated between 'playing trade', that is being approached by others, and being 'aggressive' in his pursuits as in the recorded contact in 1950 that occasioned such reflection: 'a fellow who looked as if he might be rough trade'.[55] He also referred to what he called the 'absurd talk about active and passive, male-role and female-role homosexuals', countering that 'one may be both in the same act of intercourse, or vary from person to person or from time to time'.[56] He elaborated in far more detail years later in 1969, when emphasizing 'how much more homosexuality can be than any theory':

> I, for instance, like to suck AND fuck, but do not care much for being fucked and am so indifferent to being sucked that I frequently cannot reach orgasm that way. Now one of the things I like involves having a penis in me and one involves inserting my penis in someone else, and the things I don't like are equally mixed. Furthermore, I know many people who have these mixed tastes. My sexual preferences are both aggressive acts and the

passive acts don't interest me much, tho on occasion they can if performed by masters. We're a varied lot and I've seen few theories that fit many of the people I know.[57]

It is interesting that he saw sucking as aggressive rather than passive.

The best-selling expert on homosexuality, Donald Webster Cory, co-author of an insider's guide, was similarly dismissive of the 'confusing and absurd concepts of "active" and "passive" homosexuals' and 'using masculine-feminine concepts' to understand sexual relations.[58] He favoured the more neutral terminology of inserter and receptor when discussing oral and anal sex, and pointed out that actual sexual practice made a mockery of such simple divisions. Effeminate men could insist on insertive sex. Fellatio – with its 'diversity of meanings' – could be both or either active or passive. Pederasty was open to role reversal and sexual flexibility, 'with no significant correlation between the degree of manliness in the individual's non-sexual personality and the sexual activity he prefers'. In group sex, by no means an unusual practice, 'it is possible for a man to be receptor and insertor at the same time . . . Any attempt to make active-passive distinctions under such circumstances is doomed to absurdity.'[59]

The composer Ned Rorem also mused on the indeterminacy of active and passive, provoked, strangely enough, by a panel discussion in 1971 on woman as a sex object:

> To homosexuals rough-trade is an object though his role is hardly passive: he does the work, ramming the twitching lips, and is paid off without a word (what could he possibly *say?* Verbal intercourse personalizes). But who's to prove he's a 'thing' without knowing what goes on behind the scenes of all concerned?
>
> That 'passive' homosexual deals the cards, purchases the merchandise (I command you to dominate me!), writes the sonnet, ends up literarily if not literally on top. Yet the trade, when he murders his client, does so for having been sucked off or sucked into, verbs indicating passivity.[60]

And indeed many of the postwar hustlers and trade that Painter encountered exhibited sexual taxonomies somewhat more complex than we might expect from Reiss's sociology. The men adjudged 'heterosexual' varied in what they would permit. One 'New York proletarian' was 'totally amoral' and longed to be fellated. Another of his favourite partners and models, also heterosexual, refused to be fellated because he was afraid that he would like it.[61] Not all observed the non-penetration rule. When Painter was in the Army in Dayton, Ohio, he ran into an old New York hustler contact who had since joined the Army and been fighting overseas: 'We discussed the old times, and I, apologizing and explaining a psycho-sociological interest, asked him if he in those days allowed himself to be pedicated. He said yes, he did – because then his gypsum was not used up, and with the money he could then go and get a girl and have his own fun . . . He liked being fellated, but . . . not so much as normal coitus.'[62] Another, Howie, who looked like a prizefighter, muscular and tattooed, enjoyed passive penetration as well as frequent heterosexual sex. 'Told me he came five times the other night with the woman he is living with' was the caption for one of his homoerotic photographs.[63] But even these heterosexual, homosexual pedicants had some limitations. Fear of effeminacy was the great constant – I was about to say inhibitor but inhibition is scarcely the right word. Those who had to be reassured were persuaded that they were not 'queer': that is, effeminate. Eddie, who was being pedicated by both Painter and Melcarth and had begun to worry about enjoying it – 'Eddie . . . fucks girls avidly' – was easily convinced that it merely enlarged his sphere of enjoyment and did not make him 'queer'.[64] (Eddie, whom Painter dubbed the 'voice of the urban proletariat', said that he was more at ease socially with males; 'But girls are lots of fun to fuck'.)[65] This slippage in the penetrator/penetratee rule, the gap between public presentation and private practice (recall earlier comments about the sexual accessibility of boxers) is something that observers of Latin American sex have also noted.[66] Arnaldo Cruz-Malavé has written that 'dominant/passive, macho/*pato* (*maricón*) [duck or faggot], hustler/*pargo* [fish or dupe], top/bottom are not fixed, stable, or equivalent binary pairs that designate equally fixed, stable, or analogous sexual identities and practice' but rather 'sexual scripts' subject to constant negotiation and dependent on 'specific social contexts'.[67]

One young man managed to combine homosexuality and heterosexuality without any need to declare his sexual identity. He lived with his widowed mother but had 'gone steady' with queers for nearly three years, one at a time rather than hustling indiscriminately. 'Has a girl who is a "nice girl", whom he doesn't fuck. Fucks other girls – has for years – but has never been to bed with one. Would like to. But since they are all local girls where is there to go? And they must be home to mother early. All very frustrating, it seems. Which is one reason he goes with queers – to round out his sadly circumscribed sex life.'[68] A hustler in Times Square said that he did not mind a blowjob from a queer when he felt like it. He had a 'steady girl, whom he does not fuck'. Painter tried to make sense of the 'mores' which permitted this man to have sex with other 'babes' provided they were not seen together socially, and to gang-rape. The youth's 'buddies' would join him in a 'gang-fuck' but disapproved when he took another girl to a picnic. 'Hustling queers also is all right, not unfaithful or improper (says his girl knows he does it) (and his buddies know: in fact he offered me his buddies).'[69] (See Figures 36 and 37.)

After a graphic description of fellation, irrumation (fucking the mouth), and masturbation, Painter wrote of a soldier he picked up in 1949: 'he dresses, is paid, and leaves. He is getting his discharge in a couple of weeks, going back to Newcastle, Pa., to marry his girl who is a virgin, he says. He is being faithful to her. An Italian name I don't quite remember.'[70] That engaging in homosexual sex indicated heterosexual fidelity is a curious twist of logic, but the soldier was obviously not alone in believing it.

The sexual practices and codes of the hustler's world trouble tidy sexual taxonomies. Gershon Legman's 1941 glossary of the languages of homosexuality continually interposed descriptions of heterosexual acts and identities in its explanations of homosexual culture, especially in relation to male prostitution. 'Hustler', 'it', 'jam', 'man', 'one-way man', 'rough trade', 'straight', 'trade', 'two-way man', 'uniform' all referred to male heterosexual sexual partners of homosexuals. The entry for 'cruise' contained numerous examples of this slippage with its references to heterosexual pedicators and heterosexual-to-heterosexual homosexual sex!

> To avoid confusion it should be remembered that the homosexual prostitute may be heterosexual (in which case his prostitution usually consists of allowing homosexuals to fellate him, or allowing pedicators – who may be heterosexual – to pedicate him) or homosexual (in which case his prostitution usually consists of submitting to passive pedication by possibly heterosexual pedicators, or performing fellation upon entirely heterosexual persons). Furthermore, the client may be a homosexual, or a complete heterosexual (who may wish to be fellated because of a superstitious belief that he may be cured of acne in that way, or because women are not available or too costly). This is quite complex...[71]

The Guild Dictionary of Homosexual Terms (1965) confirmed such overlaps but added further examples of its own. 'Bronco', 'bugle boy', 'floater', 'fruit picker', 'goofer', and 'scalp hunter' referred to sex between heterosexuals and homosexuals.[72] A fruit picker, for example, was a term 'used to describe men who both think of themselves as "straight" and who are so considered by those who know them, but who seek out homosexuals for sexual gratification at the moment'.[73]

'P', selected as a representative hustler in H. Benjamin and R. E. L.

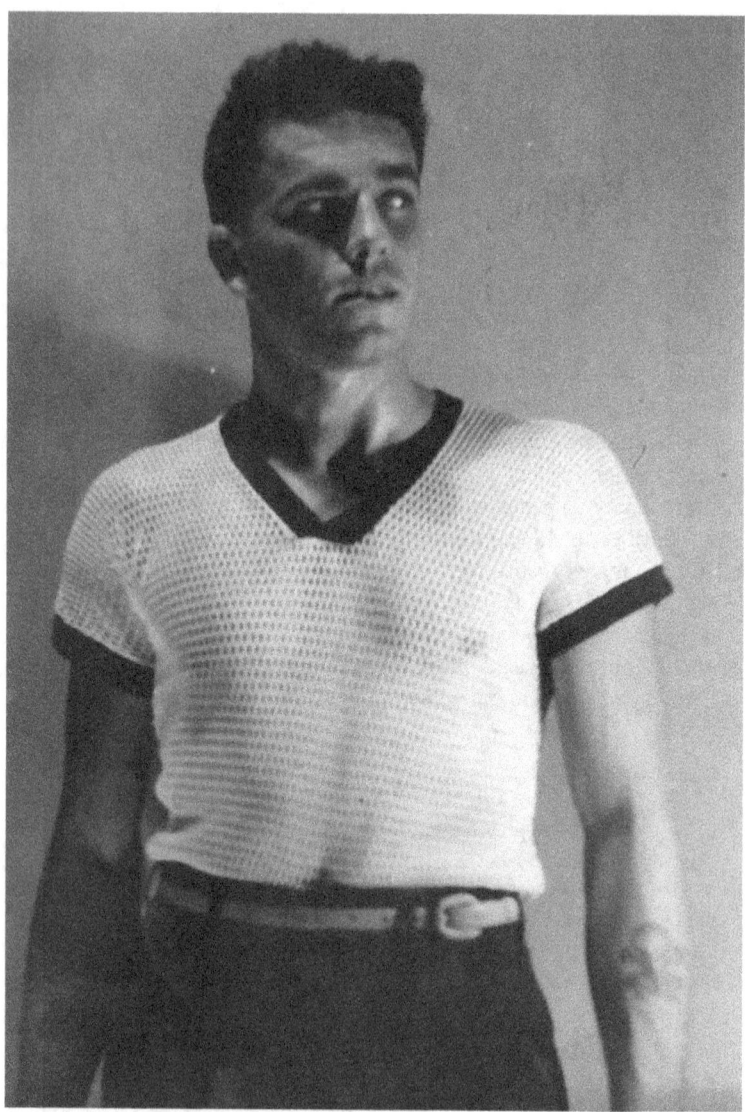

36. Times Square hustler, 1951. From the Thomas Painter Collection. Reproduced by permission of The Kinsey Institute for Research in Sex, Gender, and Reproduction, Inc. Author's note: the man, described by Painter as a 'typical rough trade Times Square hustler', is wearing the shirt he wore to attract johns (clients).

37. Italian-American hustler, circa 1951. From the Thomas Painter Collection. Reproduced by permission of The Kinsey Institute for Research in Sex, Gender, and Reproduction, Inc. Author's note: 'rough trade' who hustled Times Square.

Masters's 1960s study of male prostitution, described himself as 'mainly heterosexual' and bragged of his successes with women, but had actually had more homosexual experience ('active or passive') and had derived 'considerable pleasure' from such contact. He constructed his own boundaries: he would perform fellatio but would not swallow: 'That is really queer, you know.' 'Q', another of their case studies, had had 'too many girls to remember' and was 'no lousy queer', but would 'slip it to a cocksucker if the price is right'. He too had his limits: 'The thought of kissing another male is more abhorrent to him than is the idea of committing fellatio.'[74] Benjamin and Masters attempted to move beyond their subjects' protestations of their heterosexuality, reasoning that their ability to function sexually with men demonstrated 'at least a minimal amount of homosexual interest'. Their hustlers were divided into those who became 'primarily homosexual' and those who married and 'are able to function in an apparently normal, heterosexual fashion'. They floated uneasily between heterosexual and homosexual, the very categories to which they did not seem to conform.[75]

Painter's history, on the other hand, admitted the difficulty in determining 'just who is homosexual'. How did one classify a hustler who in his private life 'alternated in choice between delicate, small-boned girls, and big tough truck drivers'? Others enjoyed the sexual company of women but also got pleasure from fellating or active homosexual pedication and irrumation. 'Confusingly, we have encountered heterosexuals who intensely enjoyed active fellation or others who much enjoyed being pedicated.' 'We can hardly term as normally heterosexual any male who actually enjoys fellating other males. Still we do not class these individuals as homosexual.'[76] Painter knew many men of ambivalent sexuality. One announced that he was heterosexual and in love with a woman in Wisconsin, yet still cruised Times Square. 'And he wound up the night in bed with a male person (of dubious virility, but male). So his heterosexuality is open to question. He may have meant that, as he remarked, he was not *falling in love* with males anymore, just fuck 'em and leave 'em.' Several years later, the same man was indeed married and invited a previous sexual contact ('trade') home to dinner, probably with impure motivations. But the outcome was that his wife got involved with the guest and left her husband for him. Moreover, the guest was none other than the earlier-mentioned Howie, the 'very active' heterosexual who enjoyed passive pedication – and one of Painter's sexual partners![77] As the anthropologist Roger Lancaster once expressed it, sexual practice is 'more complex than the enactment of a norm, the realization of a code, or the performance of a script'.[78]

Laud Humphreys's study of anonymous sex in US public restrooms in the 1960s has relevance to this sexual uncertainty. This archetypal, non-verbal, impersonal sex ('you can always find someone to suck your cock') involved homosexual acts by men, a majority of whom had 'no homosexual self-identity'.[79] Humphreys found a flexibility of roles that took him by surprise with their refusal to fit his preconceived gendered assumptions of active and passive. Instead, he found that it was impossible to predict sexual act from personal appearance: 'The players (insertor and insertee) are identifiable only in the sex act.' Nor did the categories correspond to active/passive in any predictable way. The insertee was as likely to be the 'aggressor' as was the inserter. Participants would change roles, whatever their preferences and intentions; no given scenario of encounter was certain. He noted cases where an insertee was later an inserter. Although Humphreys refers to 'mutually understood identities', he was in fact dealing with sexual acts cut adrift from identity. 'The point is that insertee and insertor are not sex roles as such, but parts into which actors step as they approach the payoff of a sexual encounter.'[80] And just over half of his subjects (traced by nefarious means that we will not go into here) were married and living with their wives; 'Many suburban housewives may think their husbands delayed by the traffic when, in reality, the spouses have paused for a tearoom encounter.'[81] The sociologist's classifications by 'Type' are rather confused but indicate that over 60 per cent of these men engaging in homosexual sex were still living with or having sex with women.[82] Such men were able to justify a recognizable separation of sexual acts in a way that did not threaten either their identity ('I'm not some sort of sick queer') or their masculinity ('normally masculine in appearance, he has never been publicly labeled as a deviant'). Even their perceived fidelity was intact: 'That's not really sex. Sex is something I have with my wife in bed. It's not as if I were committing adultery by getting my rocks off – or going down on some guy – in a tearoom.'[83]

So we are dealing with a sexual fluidity wider than Painter's hustler culture. Indeterminacies abound too in the recorded sexual contacts of the writer and poet Charles Henri Ford, spanning our very period of interest. Although he claimed in 1963 to be unashamed in his homosexuality, and his sexual preferences were clearly same-sex, Ford had earlier extolled the pleasures of the 'polymorphous-erotic' and had participated in group sex with both women and men.[84] A 'cunt feels better [to the cock], from a purely local physical point of view', he wrote in 1948,

> it's the best thing yet I've found [to stick my prick in] – a mouth is not as pleasurable – except from the mental-image point of view ... I think after all the most important part of sexual feeling is the actual feeling you get out of it, rather than whether the object acted upon is male or female. I can conceive of lovemaking together with a boy and girl – threesome combinations – being more exciting than alone with either – the erotic images are multiplied![85]

The males he was involved with certainly proclaimed their desire for women. Bert, a former sailor whom he shared with the artist Pavel Tchelitchew, enjoyed receiving oral sex from men, would masturbate Ford and permitted intercrural and anal sex. Yet he also bragged of his female conquests and talked of his continual need for heterosexual sex. Interestingly, this experienced recipient of male oral gratification had not been fellated by a woman (or tried cunnilingus) until he had sex with Ford and a woman they picked up at a party. Bert had a girlfriend during the time of his relationship with Ford but was not having intercourse with her.[86] From the 1940s to the 1960s, Ford was involved with men who also had sexual relationships with women. Al, described by Ford as 'rough trade', a 'rare beauty' (Ford recommended him to George Platt Lynes and Carl Van Vechten as a photographic model in 1949), would talk about girls to arouse himself before he and Ford had sex. Al and Ford also participated in a 'fucking party' with six men and women.[87] Renzo, an Italian lover who joined Ford in New York in the 1960s (nicknamed 'Beauty' by Andy Warhol), reduced his benefactor to obsessive jealousy because of his continuing relations with women.[88]

Samuel Steward's Chicago archive, likewise, contains traces of sex that was not confined either to same- or opposite-sex encounters. It was that of his various contacts rather than his, for although he 'had a woman who I screwed two hundred and eleven times', Steward's preferences were clearly male.[89] His diaries for the 1950s refer to a sailor he was tattooing who said he was going to 'jack off, then go down the street and let a homo give him a blow job, and then he'd be properly heated up to screw a woman'.[90] Steward noted the overheard conversations of teenagers: 'Cheez, if you wanna pick up a queer, go to Mark's restaurant. Up there they give you ten bucks if you let 'em give you a blow job, or twenny if you fuck 'em in the ass.'[91]

The Prologue to this book began with an epigraph hinting at the polysexual possibilities of the Beat culture of the 1940s and 1950s. Herbert Huncke, the Beats' Beat, the man interviewed by Kinsey in the anecdote quoted at the start of this chapter, left a statement to this effect in his unpublished papers:

> Even though my first experiences at a heterosexual level were great my homosexual desires had been effectively aroused and I was unable to continue a consistently heterosexual sex life finally giving it up entirely for a period of several years. I did this several times and it wasn't until I reached my late thirties I succeeded in combining the two in a manner of being heterosexual today and homosexual the next – allowing neither to influence me more than the other.[92]

'Here in the city your lovers are all women but your friends are all fairies', the Beat writer Irving Rosenthal wrote of a New York acquaintance. 'How you thrived in prison. You want to give up your marriage scene out here in the city and go back to your jailboy . . . dig "boy-flesh is girl-flesh".'[93] Rosenthal refers to fucking a man who 'last week' had been 'putting down queers', and to his friend Riggsy who has sex with men but refuses to acknowledge it – 'He asks if he can stay overnight ("Me and the old lady are having a hassle"). In bed if I move just barely to touch him, he will whisper "Go down on me man, please? Aw come on!"' Riggsy never mentions these episodes the following morning.[94]

Neal Cassady, reputedly a one-time hustler, was best known for his sexual exploits with women, but he was sexually involved with the homosexual poet Allen Ginsberg. Ginsberg's love poem, describing sex with the former hustler, invokes Cassady's heterosexuality at the moment he is engaging in homosexual sex. His experience with the opposite sex is written on his body – 'his belly a thousand girls kissed in Colorado'. Cassady's sexual history is summoned in a manner that indicates its centrality to his appeal for Ginsberg:

> I first touched the smooth mount of his rock buttocks, silken in
> power, rounded in animal fucking and bodily nights over
> nurses and schoolgirls . . .

The poem even contains a moment of negotiation, a pause, when the rules of dominance and submission are simultaneously declared and negated:

> –And confessed, years later, he thinking I was not a queer at first to
> please me & serve me, to blow me and make me come,
> maybe or if I were queer, that's what I'd likely want of a
> dumb bastard like him.[95]

Ginsberg had sex with Jack Kerouac as well as Cassady. And the Beats Ginsberg and William Burroughs (primarily homosexual in their tastes) and Jack Kerouac (primarily heterosexual) enjoyed sex with both men and women.[96]

Cassady also engaged in group sex. A letter to Jack Kerouac in 1949 provides a graphic description of one encounter with a woman he met and an African-American couple, '4 way orgy – goes on for hours'.[97] He wrote to his friend again in 1950, 'get a cunt & your cunt & us'll have a *real* orgy unless you want to go "lonely fucker"'.[98] 'I love skinny women & strong chinned (queer's ideal) men', he wrote to Ginsberg in 1948, 'I love all – sex – yes all; all, sex, anyway I can get it.'[99] Cassady was unusual in his promiscuity but was not untypical in his polymorphous perversity. Ned Polsky, who interviewed over three hundred Greenwich Village Beats for a study in 1960, observed their encouragement of 'socially disapproved forms of sexual behavior', claiming that an 'extraordinary number of male beats . . . are fully bisexual or in some cases polymorphous perverse'. He elaborated:

> They accept homosexual experiences almost as casually as heterosexual ones. Even beats with numerous and continuing post-adolescent homosexual experiences typically do not feel the need to define themselves as homosexuals and create some sort of beat wing of the homosexual world. Nor do they give up heterosexual involvements. Beats not only tolerate deviant sex roles but, to a much greater extent than previous bohemians, display a very high tolerance of sex-role ambiguity.[100]

Polsky estimated that most would fall at a 2, 3, or 4 on Kinsey's heterosexual–homosexual scale.[101] Significantly, a few Beat men were part-time hustlers in uptown Manhattan, 'making enough money to stay straight in the Village the rest of the week'.[102]

The artist Larry Rivers, who played in a 1940s jazz band in New York before he took up painting, said later that he was 'so convinced of being heterosexual I could be homosexual'. Thus this 'heterosexual' had sex with men, including the poet Frank O'Hara in the 1950s.[103] 'Sex with men wasn't exactly my bag, but if they got my cock hard they could have it.'[104] Rivers wrote a song called 'Headhunters', which the 'hip' knew referred to blowjobs; as 'the initiated of the jazz world knew', headhunters were 'hip guys constantly seeking to receive or administer blow jobs'.[105]

Although a little outside our period, the sexual contacts that occurred in Samuel Delany's darkened Times Square cinemas in the 1970s, where homosexual men watched hour upon hour of heterosexual and lesbian sex, also trouble the hetero–homo divide. The visual absence of homosexuality on the screen was more than compensated for by its presence in the audience. The films showed porn aimed at a heterosexual audience but the sexual activity in the theatre was less sharply defined. Men masturbated to the moving images of women while other men masturbated to the sight of their pleasure. Those who were 'getting off on the straight screen action' were fellated by those 'who enjoyed sucking cock'. Money might or might not change hands.[106]

Finally there is prison culture. Richard Jacoby, who befriended Salvador Agron, the celebrated Capeman, the young Puerto Rican gangster imprisoned in 1959 for murder, observed that it did not take him (Jacoby) very long to 'figure out that male to male sexuality in prison had little to do with whether a particular convict was "heterosexual" or "homosexual". Instead, and with rare exceptions, active sexuality was always a matter of power and control.'[107] Agron already knew this from a young lifetime acquaintance with remand centres and gang life; *'already scheming how to fuck him without him fucking me'*.[108] Agron was unembarrassed about his same-sex relationships in prison in the 1960s and 1970s. Shortly after he was sentenced, a death-row prisoner gave him a blowjob through the bars and behind a book entitled *American History*. Agron thanked him for the lesson and the man replied, 'That's what American history is all about.'[109]

A legal expert who carried out an investigation into systematic rape in the Philadelphia prison system in the 1960s reported that 'the typical sexual aggressor does not consider himself to be a homosexual, or even to have engaged in homosexual acts. This seems to be based upon his startlingly primitive view of sexual relationships, one that defines as male whichever partner is aggressive and as homosexual whichever partner is passive.'[110] A teacher in the Tennessee Department of Correction, who studied prison language in the 1980s, observed that while 'homosexuality is widespread in the prisons, those men who take the male role do not consider themselves to be gay: "I'm a man – I don't catch; I just pitch", such a person says.' In such prison talk, the vocabulary for the dominator was limited: taken for granted, he was a man or 'daddy'. However, the dominated was more extensively connoted as 'boy', 'chicken', 'gal-boy', 'little girl', 'punk', and 'sissy'.[111]

As Regina Kunzel has recently demonstrated, the prison, with its situational same-sex activity involving men (and women) who would not usually be classified as homosexual, demonstrates the existence of 'an unexpectedly plural, varied, and contradictory sexual world' with implications for the way in which we view both heterosexuality and homosexuality and demonstrating the instability of these categories.[112] This environment has particular relevance for my study, given that, as we have seen, the hustler was no stranger to prison. They were intersecting milieus: attitudes in incarceration reflected wider working-class sexual mores, and desires and practices from the forcing ground of prison returned to the local community with the released prisoner.[113]

Here it was certainly possible for men to engage in sex with their own sex without thinking themselves homosexual. George L. Kirkham, who studied inmates at California's Soledad prison for a study published in 1971, referred to prisoners exempting many of those who 'indulge in homosexuality... from the odious ascription of a "homosexual" status'.[114] As Jack Abbott informed *The New York Review of Books* in 1981:

> It really was years, many years, before I began to actually realize that the women in my life – the prostitutes as well as the soft, pretty girls who giggled and teased me so much, my several wives and those of my friends – it was years before I realized that they were not women, but men; years before I assimilated the notion that this was unnatural . . . It was difficult for me to grasp the definition of the clinical term 'homosexual' – and when I finally did it devastated me.[115]

For Abbott, who was in prison from the early 1960s, sex was linked to power and dominance. He observed that during prison riots guards were sodomized as an act of contempt: 'The normal attitude among men in society is that it is a great shame and dishonor to have experienced what it feels like to be a woman.' Abbott thought that by sentencing him to time in the main penitentiary both judges and police anticipated that he would be raped and thereby 'shorn of my manhood', reduced to a 'punk', and turned into a 'cocksucker'.[116] Dominance was everything. 'In prison, if I take a punk, *she is mine*.' He insisted that he was never a 'punk'. Naked violence meant that he was the dominator rather than the dominated; one of his first acts was to force a would-be fucker to fellate him.[117] In this logic – which Abbott insisted was merely a more blatant expression of wider attitudes – it was only the penetrated who was homosexual. The penetrator was merely inscribing his masculinity. 'The majority of prisoners I have known – something like ninety per cent – express sexual interest in their own sex. I hesitate to call this "homosexual" because American society recognizes *only* the passive homosexual – the one who plays the female role – as being a "homosexual". So it is really the same outside as in prison, but open in prison.'[118] Abbott thought that much of the violence in prison sex was fuelled by these distorted meanings, the mismatch between men's own same-sex desires and their hostility to homosexuality.

Edwin Johnson, who had spent three years in San Quentin in the 1960s, was quite clear about the gendered homosexuality of the prison. Those considered homosexual were referred to as bitches, broads, whores, girls, punks, 'the old lady', and (less commonly) fags. Johnson's analysis was functionalist. He saw prison life, prison homosexuality, as replicating heterosexual life on the outside, with stable (and unstable) marriages, dysfunctional rapes, and prostitution and pimps. (He even argued that this sexual system contributed to prison stability.) The difference was that it was a world of men where some men – those deemed homosexual by the very nature of their subservient role – were functional females, what he termed 'a class of substitute women'. He describes it as actual life rather than theatre: 'So well has the inmate culture created the concept of [the] "broad" that it is accepted as if it were real (in the sense that women are there).' (Recall Abbott's comments about prison 'women'.) The 'submissives' or homosexuals were social women; they kept house, provided receptive sexual services, and might adopt a feminine 'style'. On the other hand, what he persists in calling the 'male partner' (the article sometimes reads as though it is about chromosomal males and females) was not considered homosexual: 'As the designation of a homosexual was feminine, the male aggressive was never self-defined or societally defined as homosexual.' In fact both his masculinity and his status were enhanced by the extent to which he was 'in demand by homosexual "women"'.[119]

A generation earlier, Haywood Patterson, an African-American imprisoned for alleged rape in the notorious Scottsboro case, said that, when he was first propositioned in prison, he claimed to have told the wolf 'If any of that stuff goes on with me in on it I'll do all the fukking [*sic*] myself. I been a man all my life.' Patterson, who prided himself as a 'man who wanted women' and totally uninterested in same-sex activity, was nevertheless 'drawn more into this life'. 'It went against all my nature. But it set me as a man amongst the prisoners, not a gal-boy.' He had his own gal-boy, even though he was only young himself. He described this milieu of hybrid sex: 'There were men who came into prison leaving wives and families on the outside, and they became gal-boys. I saw men learn to love boys harder than they could any woman. I saw beatings and jealousy and killings over it.'[120]

One of the most articulate cartographers of prison sex – from the punk perspective – was the one-time nightclub pianist, drug-addict, male nurse, and long-time prison inmate James Blake. Blake's letters to the American writer Nelson Algren and others in the 1950s and 1960s contain graphic descriptions of what he called 'days of heart-tearing labor and nights of dreary bestiality', and 'aberrant sex run wild'.[121] References to reading Gide, Bowles, and Colette and writing for *The Paris Review* are interspersed with allusions to forced sex in the showers ('he detained me in the shower room for the old and sickeningly familiar reason and I was numb with helpless rage for the rest of the day') and stories about the gang rape of new inmates ('sounds accompanying this noble group therapy were something to saw the nerves in half') and the man who quoted scripture and threatened perdition to his young cellmate during the day and sodomized him at night.[122] Blake had a series of protectors in prison, whether by coercion or choice, and, although he considered himself mentally superior to them, he was physically dominated and brutalized. 'You ask who the Muskie is. I thought I made that clear. He is simply the brass-brained, muscle-bound Golden Boy who appointed himself my jailhouse Daddy-o. Between beatings and brainings he implores me not to take off.'[123] 'That's how it goes', Blake was told by one of his protectors, 'Either you're my old lady or you're a whore. If you're a whore, they'll grind you up.'[124] Indeed Blake was informed that he was known as 'The Whore' by the assistant warden at one prison, but he saw himself as vastly different to the effeminate 'pussyboys, galboys, fuckboys' with their earrings and painted faces and girls' names, housed separately from the other prisoners yet available for sex. When asked by the admissions officer if he was homosexual, Blake always said no.[125]

If Blake was forced into a kind of enraged passivity, he distanced himself from effeminacy (hence the homosexual denial). Yet he was homosexual in his desires. As he said of one of his sexual partners in 1956, 'What I feel is beyond shame or guilt, or even embarrassment: I know that his homosexuality is like my own, in that it is a matter of attraction between two masculine minds, and not a tinsel thing in which one of them must pretend to be a woman.'[126] He wrote a harrowing letter about a lifer called George who had shot an FBI man in a Manhattan hotel and, on a separate occasion, a prison warden: 'The Warden's last words: "Jesus, Mary and Joseph, Shitfire I'm dying."' George asked Blake to spend the night with him for Benzedrine-fuelled sex:

> Lust, pity, fright, love, bewilderment. We talked for a good part of the night. That is, George talked. What was it like, what it meant, I have to walk up and down when I think about it. Can a pigeon say what a raven is . . . What was he like, Montgomery Cliftish on the outside, inside unbearably taut, aluminium and Vesuvius. He was a destroyer, a malign force. And yet

in fellatio my tears fell into his groin hair. What was I crying about? Myself? Him? Everybody?[127]

However, the men that Blake was sexually and emotionally involved with in prison were not so channelled in their sexual preferences. One of his favourites, a heroin-addicted trumpet player, was 'as howling a hetero as they get' and was living with a woman when he was paroled. Blake refused to move in with them, though 'sex with him was pure sorcery as always'.[128] Another, Blake mused, just needed love; 'that it was homosexual love was, in my opinion, of no importance'.[129]

'The application of middle-class concepts of homosexuality to prisoners produces much absurdity and little understanding', an ex-prisoner (and former punk) warned a lecture group at Columbia University in the early 1990s. Self-identified homosexuals are a minority, an effeminate minority, highly sought after as women. The 'Men' or jockers are heterosexual, as are the coerced punks. 'For the majority of prisoners, penetrative sex with a punk or a queen remains a psychologically heterosexual and, in the circumstances of confinement, normal act; the relationships involved are also psychologically heterosexual to them (as well as to most of their partners, willing or not).'[130] Hence the man repeatedly raped by other men in prison, who formed same-sex sexual alliances for protection from indiscriminate predation, and who classed himself as 'heterosexual'.[131] Hence the 'heterosexual' jocker who, in the words of his interviewer, had been 'orally copulated' 150 times, performed anal intercourse 200 times, and had had sex with men outside prison: 'Ed considers himself to be heterosexual.'[132]

> Q: Do you think that you'll get down with homosexuals on the street?
> A: Do you mean fuck punks? Sure, that's some of the best pussy there is.[133]

Like hustler sex, prison sex challenged the taxonomies both of heterosexuality and of homosexuality. 'Revealing the border between homosexuality and heterosexuality to be blurred and permeable', concludes Kunzel, 'sex in prison suggested that desire and even sexual subject positions were unfixed and unstable, produced at certain moments and in certain circumstances, rather than inhering in the psyche or body.'[134]

We started this chapter with Alfred Kinsey's measurement of the variability of sexuality in his seven-point 'Heterosexual-homosexual rating' from exclusive sexual contact or response with the opposite sex (0) to exclusive homosexuality (6). The ratings in-between indicated degrees of same-sex or opposite-sex sexual activities or reactions.[135] Kinsey observed of the categories heterosexuality and homosexuality:

> It would encourage clearer thinking on these matters if persons were not characterized as heterosexual or homosexual, but as individuals who have had certain amounts of heterosexual experience and certain amounts of homosexual experience. Instead of using these terms as substantives which stand for persons, or even as adjectives to describe persons, they may better be used to describe the nature of the overt sexual relations, or of the stimuli to which an individual erotically responds.[136]

Although Kinsey and his co-researchers did not precisely use the terms 'act' and 'identity', heterosexuality and homosexuality were best envisaged as acts ('to describe the nature of the overt sexual relations') rather than identities ('substantives which stand for persons').

Painter did not provide the statistical support that gave Kinsey's sexual grid its intellectual validity, but *conceptually* he anticipated Kinsey's influential scale by several years. As early as 1941, he was discussing the complexity of definitions and demonstrating sexual multiplicity. Painter's proposed 'workable terminology' – true homosexual, homosexual (predominantly), homosexual bisexual, true bisexual, heterosexual bisexual, heterosexual (predominantly), and true heterosexual – was very similar to what would become Kinsey's. 'Almost any gradation or complex of characteristics can be covered by one or another of these categories, it being born in mind that homosexual and heterosexual are rather elastic terms that can and do include many degrees of preference and many types of behavior.'[137]

Even attempts to recognise the importance of sexual acts by categorizing them are destabilized by the performances enacted on a daily basis in the hotel rooms, parks, toilets, apartments, rooming houses, streets, bars, and clubs of New York. Painter's material on homosexual acts implies not only that acts can be more important than identities but also that their sheer range challenges simple sexual classifications. Of course acts were central to Kinsey's measurement of sexual activity in *Sexual Behavior in the Human Male*. Counting the number of orgasms attained from predetermined means of sexual release – masturbation, nocturnal emission, heterosexual petting, heterosexual intercourse, homosexual relations, and intercourse with animals – gave his basic unit of measurement, an individual's *total sexual outlet*. Kinsey's classification took masturbation seriously, used the words homosexual and heterosexual to describe acts (same sex or opposite sex) rather than declarations of self, and drew attention to heterosexual activity other than straight intercourse (so to speak). But it was an idiosyncratic taxonomy that nonetheless inscribed the heterosexual/homosexual division that he had treated with more subtlety elsewhere and which ignored a huge range of sexual acts. It is a great irony that Kinsey's best-selling work did so much to cement 'heterosexual' and 'homosexual' as words and categories in public discourse.[138] Kinsey's legacy was the basic categories rather than their complexities.

Prompted by Kinsey's findings on heterosexual petting, Chapter 16 in *Sexual Behavior in the Human Male*, Painter set out a series of definitional conundrums, testing the sexual expert's categories:

> [H]aven't I ever had sexual intercourse (except for the times I have pedicated and fellated)? Yet, if the partner in frictation 'comes' too (as has happened), and both are naked in bed, both sexually satisfied – it certainly seems as if it should be dignified (if that is the term) as full sexual intercourse . . .
> Have you got definitions ready yet for these things?
> Or for these: if I jerk off a boy [he used the term for men in their twenties], or he jerks himself off as part of my arousal of him by my sexual act, and does so in bed with me, with my help, is it masturbation or sexual intercourse? If I masturbate us both off at once, both penises in my one hand, naked in bed with various erotic foreplay, is it intercourse or masturbation and which for whom? If I come in midair (as I have done) while naked in bed with a boy as a result of some very erotic nuance of activity, is that intercourse, or petting to climax or what? If intercourse, then what was it when I 'came' just watching that boy undress to pose for me . . . I touched him, saw him, was aroused, came. But he didn't even know it. Or the men who masturbate . . . watching a boy strip before them? Or who 'come' being beaten, or cursed, or urinated on. Are those intercourse? If pedication is intercourse, what about 'leggins'?[139]

Warming to the complexity of his subject, Kinsey's correspondent continues:

> Yet some homosexuals (I assume) do 'pet to climax' in the true sense of the word. Two fellators 'come' as a result of just loving up, kissing and groping, in a theatre or park bench, say. But for a frictator this would be termed justly 'intercourse', I should think. Is it this: for those who 'come' by other means, habitually, to 'come' by frictational means is 'petting to climax' – be the parties clothed or nude, in or out of bed. For the frictator petting to climax is sexual intercourse. Does the other party have to be conscious of it to have it intercourse? Consider my model who did not know I came, or even that I was homosexual . . .

Or don't homosexuals *ever* have intercourse (except with a woman). They fellate, pedicate, frictate, actively and passively, masturbate and mutually masturbate – and sometimes make combinations of these acts. They pet to climax if they 'come' short of their habitual mode of sexual climax. It is masturbation if their usual climax is not masturbation, whether with another's penis 'coming' simultaneously in their hand with their own or whether their object is absent. But one can have several 'usual' modes, though usually one is preferred . . . I have come being fellated, fellating, pedicating, frictating, mutually masturbating, in mid-air at some obscene or erotic phase in the fore-play, or watching a handsome boy strip, or masturbating, clothed and partially clothed and nude. But frictation is my forte, my preference, my habitual mode.[140]

Painter's long description of homosexual sex makes nonsense of Kinsey's act of containment. It is indeed confusing: groping is foreplay for the fellator, but for the frictator it is the principal goal (his 'sexual intercourse', as Painter puts it). Moreover, much of this activity was carried out with individuals who were 'heterosexual'; 'my model . . . did not know I came, or even that I was homosexual'. 'Perhaps it's the theologian in me that delights in minutiae of definition', he continued, 'and maybe the above is all irrelevant to you, but I think it's interesting. At least it proves what does not need to be further proven, that sex is complex.'[141] Sex, to use that word of Painter's mother, was indeed queer.

Notes

1 *Reputations: Alfred Kinsey*, produced and directed by Clare Beaven, BBC, London, 1996. Huncke was referring to a meeting in the early 1940s.
2 The Kinsey Institute for Research in Sex, Gender, and Reproduction, University of Indiana, Bloomington (hereafter, KI), The Thomas Painter Collection (hereafter, Painter), Box 1, Series 2, c. 1, Vol. 3: Painter Letters: 7 November 1947.
3 A. C. Kinsey, W. B. Pomeroy, and C. E. Martin, *Sexual Behavior in the Human Male* (Philadelphia, 1948), pp. 636–66.
4 W. B. Pomeroy, *Dr. Kinsey and the Institute for Sex Research* (New York, 1972), p. 467.
5 J. Gathorne-Hardy, *Sex the Measure of All Things: A Life of Alfred C. Kinsey* (Bloomington and Indianapolis, 1998), p. 138.
6 Kinsey, Pomeroy, and Martin, *Sexual Behavior in the Human Male*, pp. 616–17.
7 Ibid., pp. 216–17.
8 Ibid., p. 78.

9 This is Code 10 in the Kinsey demographic data, those whose 'primary occupational rating' was 'Criminal'. See T. A. Albright (ed.), *The Kinsey Interview Kit Code Book* (Kinsey Institute for Research in Sex, Gender, and Reproduction, 2nd Edition, 2006), p. 3. The material in the pages above and below also will, hope, persuade the reader that this is not a fanciful connection.
10 The original Kinsey data have been coded and – with the Institute's permission – are available for specified analysis: see Albright (ed.), *Kinsey Interview Kit Code Book*, p. i. I am most grateful to the Director for giving permission and to Thomas Albright for carrying out the custom analysis that forms the 'Criminal Males' data in Table 1. The data on white non-college-educated males come from P. H. Gebhard and A. B. Johnson (eds), *The Kinsey Data: Marginal Tabulations of the 1938–1963 Interviews Conducted by the Institute for Sex Research* (Bloomington and Indianapolis, 1979), p. 428.
11 The figures for Painter's ratings come from Painter, Box 1, Series 2, c. 1, Vol. 13: 22 January 1956. The comparative figures for the male population aged 16–25 are from Kinsey, Pomeroy, and Martin, *Sexual Behavior in the Human Male*, p. 653.
12 N. R. Coombs, 'Male prostitution: a psychosocial view of behavior', *American Journal of Orthopsychiatry*, 44 (1974), 787.
13 Ibid.
14 Painter, Box 1, Series 2, c. 1, Vol. 14: 23 July 1957.
15 Painter, Box 3, Series 2, d. 2, Folder 1: Autobiographical sections: # viii Biography.
16 Painter, Box 1, Series 2, c. 1, Vol. 14: 23 July 1957.
17 Painter, Box 1, Series 2, c. 1, Vol. 18a: 21 March 1961.
18 H. L. Minton, *Departing from Deviance: A History of Homosexual Rights and Emancipatory Science in America* (Chicago, 2002), pp. 197, 198, 200.
19 Painter, Box 1, Series 2, c. 1, Vol. 18b: 29 July 1961.
20 Painter, Series 2, Vol. 2: Index of names A–F.
21 Painter, Box 1, Series 2, c. 1, Vol. 14: 17 June 1957.
22 Painter, Series 2, Vol. 2: Index of names A–F.
23 Painter, Box 1, Series 2, c. 1, Vol. 14: 9 February 1957.
24 Painter, Box 1, Series 2, c. 1, Vol. 16: 17 September 1959.
25 For example, Painter, Box 3, Series 2, d. 2, Folder 1: Autobiographical sections: # viii Biography; Box 1, Series 2, c. 1, Vol. 18a: 6 March, 28 March, and 30 March 1961.
26 Painter, Box 1, Series 2, c. 1, Vol. 18b: 22 August 1961.
27 For example, Painter, Box 1, Series 2, c. 1, Vol. 18a: 30 March and 19 April 1961.
28 Painter, Box 1, Series 2, c. 1, Vol. 18b: 19 November 1961.
29 Painter, Box 1, Series 2, c. 1, Vol. 18a: 19 June 1961.
30 Ibid., 3 June 1961.

31 Painter, Box 3, Series 2, d. 2, Folder 1: Autobiographical sections: # viii Biography; Series 2, Vol. 2: Index of names A–F.
32 Painter, Box 3, Series 2, d. 2, Folder 1: Autobiographical sections: # viii Biography; Box 1, Series 2, c. 1, Vol. 18b: 26 August 1961.
33 Painter, Series 2, Vol. 3: Index of names G–N.
34 See, for example, T. Almaguer, 'Chicano men: a cartography of homosexual identity and behavior', *Differences*, 3: 2 (1991), 75–100; F. L. Cardoso, '"Fishermen": masculinity and sexuality in a Brazilian fishing community', *Sexuality & Culture*, 6: 4 (2002), 45–72; H. Carrillo, *The Night Is Young: Sexuality in Mexico in the Time of AIDS* (Chicago, 2002), ch. 2; A. Rubenstein, 'Locating male sexualities in Latin American history: two anthropological models', *History Compass*, 1 (November 2003), 1–8.
35 D. Kulick, *Travesti: Sex, Gender and Culture Among Brazilian Transgendered Prostitutes* (Chicago, 1998), p. 229.
36 P. Kutsche, 'Two truths about Costa Rica', in S. O. Murray (ed.), *Latin American Homosexualities* (Albuquerque, 1995), p. 120; J. Schifter, *Macho Love: Sex Behind Bars in Central America* (Binghamton, NY, 1999), p. 61.
37 Schifter, *Macho Love*, p. 61.
38 J. Schifter, *Lila's House: Male Prostitution in Latin America* (Binghamton, NY, 1998), chs 2–3.
39 Painter, Box 1, Series 2, c. 1, Vol. 10: 26 January 1953.
40 Painter, Box 1, Series 2, c. 1, Vol. 3: 30 July 1946.
41 Painter, Series 2, Vol. 2: Index of names A–F; Box 1, Series 2, c. 1, Vol. 7: 2 May, 18 July, 22 July, 7 August, and 10 August 1950.
42 C. Casillo, *Outlaw: The Lives and Careers of John Rechy* (Los Angeles, 2002), p. 84.
43 J. Barr, *The Occasional Man* (New York, 1966), p. 97 and elsewhere.
44 Painter, Box 1, Series 2, c. 1, Vol. 6: 14 January, 17 January, 29 January, and 21 June 1949.
45 Kinsey, Pomeroy, and Martin, *Sexual Behavior in the Human Male*, p. 616.
46 D. W. Cory and J. P. LeRoy, *The Homosexual and His Society: A View from Within* (New York, 1963), p. 44. Emphasis in original.
47 P. H. Gebhard, J. H. Gagnon, W. P. Pomeroy, and C. V. Christenson, *Sex Offenders* (New York, 1965), pp. 324–5.
48 A. J. Reiss, 'The social integration of queers and peers', *Social Problems*, 9 (1961), 102–20; A. J. Reiss, 'Sex offenses: the marginal status of the adolescent', *Law and Contemporary Problems*, 25 (1960), 323.
49 Reiss, 'Sex offenses', 319. Emphasis in original.
50 Reiss, 'Social integration of queers and peers', 115.
51 Reiss, 'Sex offenses', 324; Reiss, 'Social integration of queers and peers', 120.
52 G. W. Henry and A. A. Gross, 'The homosexual delinquent', *Mental Hygiene*, 25 (1941), 422.

53 Quoted in R. Davenport-Hines, *Auden* (London, 1995), p. 212.
54 D. Vining, *A Gay Diary 1946–1954* (New York, 1980), p. 107.
55 Ibid., p. 278.
56 Ibid., p. 352.
57 D. Vining, *A Gay Diary 1967–1975* (New York, 1983), p. 111.
58 Cory and LeRoy, *The Homosexual and His Society*, p. 43.
59 Ibid., pp. 38–40, 43.
60 N. Rorem, *The Later Diaries 1961–1972* (New York, 2000), pp. 360–1.
61 Painter, Box 1, Series 2, c. 1, Vol. 10: 3 October 1953.
62 Painter, Box 1, Series 2, c. 1, Vol. 2: 9 August 1945.
63 Painter, Box 10, Series 4, A. 1. a: Photographs: 135–8.
64 Painter, Box 1, Series 2, c. 1, Vol. 6: 7 July 1949.
65 Ibid., 8 August 1949.
66 See Schifter, *Macho Love*, pp. 29–33; Schifter, *Lila's House*, pp. 83–9; and also C. Girman, *Much Macho: Seduction, Desire, and the Homoerotic Lives of Latin Men* (Binghamton, NY, 2004), ch. 1. For boxers, see Chapter 3 above.
67 A. Cruz-Malavé, *Queer Latino Testimonio, Keith Haring, and Juanito Xtravaganza: Hard Tails* (New York, 2007), p. 167. For explanation of the Spanish terms, see ibid., pp. 185–6, 189, 191.
68 Painter, Box 1, Series 2, c. 1, Vol. 7: 5 October 1950.
69 Painter, Box 1, Series 2, c. 1, Vol. 8: 23 June 1951.
70 Painter, Box 1, Series 2, c. 1, Vol. 6: 19 February 1949.
71 G. Legman, 'The language of homosexuality: an American glossary', in G. W. Henry, *Sex Variants: A Study of Homosexual Patterns* (New York, 1941), Vol. 2, pp. pp. 1161–2.
72 *The Guild Dictionary of Homosexual Terms* (Washington, DC, 1965), pp. 5, 6, 16, 17, 19, 40.
73 Ibid., p. 17.
74 H. Benjamin and R. E. L. Masters, *Prostitution and Morality* (New York, 1964), pp. 326–32.
75 Ibid., pp. 294–5.
76 KI, Thomas Painter, 'Male Homosexuals and Their Prostitutes in Contemporary America' (New York, 1941), Vol. 2: 'The Prostitute', pp. 187–8.
77 Painter, Box 1, Series 2, c. 1, Vol. 6: 15 May 1949; Vol. 9: 2 April 1952. Emphasis in original.
78 R. W. Lancaster, 'Sexual positions: caveats and second thoughts on "categories"', *The Americas*, 54 (1997), 14.
79 L. Humphreys, *Tearoom Trade: Interpersonal Sex in Public Places* (New York, 1975), pp. 10, 11.
80 Ibid., pp. 50, 52, 58.
81 Ibid., pp. 78, 105.

82 Ibid., pp. 112–13. Of the 50 subjects, 12 (24%) were bisexual ('Ambisexual'), and the rest were divided equally between 19 (38%) heterosexual ('Trade'/straight) and 19 (38%) homosexual ('Gay' or 'Closet Queens').
83 Ibid., pp. 119, 121, 122. For a fascinating follow-up of Humphreys's work, based on police surveillance and prosecutions in 1980s Canada, see F. J. Desroches, 'Tearoom trade: a research update', *Qualitative Sociology*, 13 (1990), 39–61. The majority of those arrested for committing indecent acts in (mainly) shopping mall washrooms were married (58%) and most said that they were heterosexual. 'No I'm not gay! I never gave blow jobs': ibid., 57.
84 Harry Ransom Center, University of Texas, Austin (hereafter, HRC), Charles Henri Ford Papers (hereafter, Ford Papers), Box 29, folder 3: 'New York Diary 1963': 10 February 1963; Box 22, folder 4: 'Diary 1948–9', p. 154 (some diary entries are paginated and others are just dated). For an example of group sex, see C. H. Ford, *Water from a Bucket: A Diary 1948-1957* (New York, 2001), pp. 30–1.
85 Ford Papers, Box 20, folder 3: 'Record of Myself', pp. 153–4 (typescript of a memoir, 1948). The words in square brackets were later crossed out by him.
86 Ford, *Water from a Bucket*, Index: 'Bert'.
87 Ford Papers, Box 22, folder 4: 'Diary 1948–9', pp. 131, 136, 191, 262–3.
88 Ford Papers, Box 29, folder 2: 'Diary from Paris and New York 1962', passim; Box 29, folder 3: 'New York Diary 1963', passim (for Warhol, see 12 February 1963).
89 T. Kissack (ed.), 'Alfred Kinsey and homosexuality in the '50s: the recollections of Samuel Morris Steward as told to Len Evans', *Journal of the History of Sexuality*, 9 (2000), 490.
90 KI, Samuel Steward Collection, Series 2, F: Diary 1955: 1 May.
91 Ibid., 22 July.
92 Department of Special Collections, Stanford University Libraries, Stanford, California, Irving Rosenthal Papers, Box 16, Folder 1: Typescript of 'Huncke's Ching or Book of Changes', p. 19.
93 I. Rosenthal, *Sheeper* (New York, 1968), p. 15. First published in 1967, but drawing on earlier experiences.
94 Ibid., pp. 45, 81–2.
95 See Ginsberg's poem about sex with Cassady, 'Many Loves' (1956): in B. Miles (ed.), *The Beat Collection* (London, 2005), pp. 103–6.
96 This is summarized, amidst more than a touch of gossip, in E. Amburn, *Subterranean Kerouac: The Hidden Life of Jack Kerouac* (New York, 1998), pp. 44, 50, 74, 93, 95, 97, 140, 257, 261, 338. See too, Index: Kerouac, Jean Louis 'Jack': 'heterosexuality of'; and 'homosexuality of'.
97 N. Cassady, *Neal Cassady: Collected Letters, 1944–1967*, ed. D. Moore (New York, 2004), pp. 77–8.

98 Ibid., p. 187. Emphasis in original.
99 Ibid., p. 104.
100 N. Polsky, 'The Village Beat scene: summer 1960', *Dissent*, 8 (1961), 347, 348.
101 Ibid., 348.
102 Ibid., 342.
103 L. Rivers, *What Did I Do? The Authorized Autobiography* (New York, 1992), p. 233.
104 Ibid., p. 110.
105 Ibid., p. 57.
106 S. R. Delany, *Times Square Red, Times Square Blue* (New York, 2001), p. 79.
107 R. Jacoby, *Conversations with the Capeman: The Untold Story of Salvador Agron* (Madison, WI, 2004), p. 266.
108 Ibid., p. 269.
109 Ibid., p. 116.
110 A. J. Davis, 'Sexual assaults in the Philadelphia prison system and sheriff's vans', *Trans-action*, 6 (1968), 15.
111 C. G. Karhu, 'Tennessee prison talk', *American Speech*, 63 (1988), 127.
112 R. Kunzel, *Criminal Intimacy: Prison and the Uneven History of Modern American Sexuality* (Chicago, 2008), pp. 6–7, 109, 237.
113 Ibid., p. 63.
114 G. L. Kirkham, 'Homosexuality in prison', in P. C. Rogríguez Rust (ed.), *Bisexuality in the United States: A Social Science Reader* (New York, 1999), p. 253.
115 J. H. Abbott, 'Two notes by Jack H. Abbott', *The New York Review of Books*, 11 June 1981.
116 J. H. Abbott, *In the Belly of the Beast* (London, 1982), pp. 78–9.
117 Ibid., pp. 79–80. Emphasis in original.
118 Ibid., p. 80. Emphasis in original.
119 E. Johnson, 'The homosexual in prison', *Social Theory and Practice*, 1: 4 (1971), 85, 87, 90, 91.
120 H. Patterson and E. Conrad, *Scottsboro Boy* (New York, 1950), pp. 79, 80, 83.
121 J. Blake, *The Joint* (New York, 1971), p. 16.
122 Ibid., pp. 44, 45, 46, 66, 120.
123 Ibid., p. 24.
124 Ibid., p. 81.
125 Ibid., pp. 37, 67, 68,
126 Ibid., p. 139.
127 Ibid., pp. 328–9.
128 Ibid., pp. 315, 355.
129 Ibid., p. 120.

130 S. D. Donaldson, 'A million jockers, punks, and queens', in D. Sabo, T. A. Kupers, and W. London (eds), *Prison Masculinities* (Philadelphia, 2001), pp. 124, 125.
131 Anonymous, 'The story of a black punk', in Sabo, Kupers, and London (eds), *Prison Masculinities*, pp. 127–32.
132 W. S. Wooden and J. Parker, *Men Behind Bars: Sexual Exploitation in Prison* (New York, 1982), p. 84.
133 Ibid., p. 86.
134 Kunzel, *Criminal Intimacy*, p. 109.
135 Kinsey, Pomeroy, and Martin, *Sexual Behavior in the Human Male*, pp. 636–66.
136 Ibid., p. 617.
137 KI, Thomas Painter, 'Male Homosexuals and Their Prostitutes in Contemporary America' (New York, 1941), Vol. 1: 'American Homosexuals', pp. 127–8, 131. Minton has already noted this anticipation of Kinsey: Minton, *Departing from Deviance*, pp. 139–40. In an interesting recent article, Chris Brickell has argued that Kinsey's flexibility built on a classificatory fluidity inherent in the sexology of the late nineteenth and early twentieth centuries (Casper, Krafft-Ebing, Moll, Ellis, and Freud): C. Brickell, 'Sexology, the homo/hetero binary, and the complexities of male sexual history', *Sexualities*, 9 (2006), 437.
138 For two useful recent accounts of Kinsey and his impact, see J. Gilbert, *Men in the Middle: Searching for Masculinity in the 1950s* (Chicago, 2005), ch. 5; and M. G. Reumann, *American Sexual Character: Sex, Gender, and National Identity in the Kinsey Reports* (Berkeley and Los Angeles, 2005).
139 Painter, Box 1, Series 2, c. 1, Vol. 6: 21 May 1949.
140 Ibid.
141 Ibid.

5
Effeminacy

After a wasted night in Sacramento the fag slyly bought a room in a hotel and invited Neal and I to come up for a drink, while the couple went to sleep at relatives, and in the hotel room Neal tried everything in the books to get money from the fag, submitting finally to his advances while I hid in the bathroom and listened. It was insane. The fag began by saying he was very glad we had come along because he liked young men like us, and would we believe it but he really didn't like girls and had recently concluded an affair with a man in Frisco in which he had taken the male role and the man the female role. Neal plied him with businesslike questions and nodded eagerly. The fag said he would like nothing better but to know what Neal thought about all this. Warning him first that he had once been a hustler in his youth, Neal proceeded to handle the fag like a woman, tipping him over legs in the air and all and gave him a monstrous huge banging. I was so non-plussed all I could do was sit and stare from my corner. And after all that trouble the fag turned over no money to us, tho he made vague promises for Denver, and on top of that he became extremely sullen and I think suspicious of Neal's final motives. He kept counting his money and checking on his wallet. Neal threw up his hands and gave up. 'You see man, it's better not to bother. Give them what they secretly want and they of course immediately become panic-stricken.' (Jack Kerouac, 1951)[1]

There is a strong argument that homosexuality was conceived in terms of effeminacy in the sexual culture of interwar America. The young government employee Jeb Alexander certainly returned to it in his diary attempts to chart his sexual desires in the 1920s in Washington, DC. Variously, he noted the tendency of others to label ('*There goes a fairy*', '*a damn fairy*', '*does* he have sissified ways?'), his own adherence to such classifying ('I became friendly with a bare-headed boyish fellow of the athletic normal type, with no suggestion in manner or looks of the homosexual'), dislike of such types ('effeminacy repels me'), yet the fact that he was sometimes seen as such himself ('*That's* a fairy').[2] Though somewhat inconsistent in their overall message, the point about these recorded comments and reactions, both in their affirmation and denial, is the focus on the fairy.

The fairy also dominates the homosexuality portrayed in Mae West's controversial plays of the 1920s, *The Drag: A Homosexual Comedy in Three Acts* (1927) and *The Pleasure Man* (1928). The effeminate (often cross-dressing) male, and his object of desire – 'rough trade', the 'normal man', the seemingly straight taxi-driver, and the policeman – were the recurring subject of light relief.[3] 'So that's how I met the taxi-driver and he's been riding me ever since.' 'I can at least go through the navy yard without having the flags drop to half mast.' 'Oh, I get down on my knees – and sing a couple of Mammy songs . . . you see I'm a character imperson-eater.' 'PEACHES: Paradise, did you ever have a platonic love affair? PARADISE . . . Oh yes, but his wife found it out.'[4] A New York district attorney's memorandum observed that the men in *Pleasure Man* 'were not mere female impersonators, but degenerates, who, even off-stage, when not performing, adopted the mannerisms of women'.[5]

Those 'who plucked their eyebrows, blondtinted their hair, or rouged their faces' appeared in novels from the 1930s.[6] And these were books, David Johnson has pointed out, that enjoyed considerable success, in terms of both the tens of thousands of copies sold and the even greater numbers borrowed from the commercial lending libraries.[7] Surviving records relating to the rental stores and libraries in Chicago, for example, indicate that multiple copies were rented scores of times each. In one store, six copies of Blair Niles's *Strange Brother* (1931) were borrowed about a hundred times each: 'They were read so much they were worn out.' The manager of a large supplier of books to several thousand drug stores explained that people tended to rent rather than buy such literature because they did not want to keep these books permanently at home. Circulation was impressive. He purchased from 300 to 350 copies of Andre Tellier's *Twilight Men* (1931) and 200 copies of *Strange Brother*, estimating rental rates of from 15 to 25 times per copy. The spokesperson of a smaller rental library indicated readers' disappointment with Robert Scully's *Scarlet Pansy* (1933): 'They expected to see the person in the book suck a penis. The name is what put the book over.'[8] As Johnson and George Chauncey have claimed of Chicago and New York respectively, the sexual culture of male effeminacy was remarkably open.[9] Medical experts and showgirls alike proclaimed the ubiquity of the 1930s fairy. 'Today there is scarcely a school boy who doesn't know what a "pansy" is. On every vaudeville stage and in every sophisticated review we hear broad references to "fairies". Many realistic novels are written around the activities of homosexual characters.' 'Twenty years ago "queers" were a rarity – today they are quite the fashion. They are undoubtedly the heaviest drawing cards in the night clubs of today.'[10]

The main protagonist in *Goldie* (1933) is a golden-haired, fairy prostitute, operating in Times Square, his 'hunting grounds': 'There's the actors and musicians when the shows break; there's the gamblers and guys with small-time rackets; and there's the highbrow sots when they leave the speakeasies in the wee hours. Fairies work up a regular trade.'[11] Karel (Parker Tyler) in *The Young and Evil* (1933) is a fairy with long black hair, plucked eyebrows, and makeup – used 'achingly but unobtrusively'. 'His eyebrows . . . might cause an Italian laborer to turn completely around.' His eyelashes were 'long enough now to catch in the boughs (should he go for a walk in Washington Square)'.[12] ('My dear . . . You wouldn't believe the amount of time I spent on my hair', Tyler later told his partner Charles Boultenhouse.)[13] Sailors on Riverside Drive sexually assault Karel and another fairy: 'thissailorsaidhefuckedhiminthemouth'.[14]

Fay Etrange, the fairy protagonist of *Scarlet Pansy*, is referred to as 'she' and 'her' from the opening lines of the book.[15] (The unwary reader could be forgiven for thinking that it is the story of a woman; indeed we know that some Chicago readers were unable to fix on the sex of the main character.)[16] Fay found that 'the more virile the man, the more readily he succumbed to her open advances'.[17] She went to a Greenwich Village restaurant, where the 'aunties' went with their good looking clerks and the fairies sat with 'their sailors or marines or rough trade' and exchanged crude banter: 'Sailor boy, if you don't take back those indecent words, I'll bring my longshoreman over here and he'll almost choke you to death. He's big enough. He's done it to me several times. At first I thought I'd never get over it.'[18]

> After a lull, with time between for drinks, a fat boy with a high-pitched voice delivered a patter song, with exaggerated rolling of eyes, shimmying movements of shoulders, swaying of hips, wriggling, and overdone femininity. 'I cannot make my eyes behave, nor my lips either', he sang.
>
> Here one heard fruit, banana, meat, fish, tomato, cream, dozens of everyday words, used with double meaning. With their voices pitched high and in imitation of the effusive type of woman, the guests declaimed with the utmost exaggeration possible, each and all trying at the same time to be the centre of interest. Without meaning to, they burlesqued all life.[19]

Other acknowledged classics of homosexual literature likewise portrayed the homosexual as effeminate. Armand Bironge, the French protagonist of *Twilight Men* – half the book is set in New York – is introduced as a beautiful man with tapered fingers, golden eyes, and long blond hair. He is fragile, dainty, 'dangerously near the feminine'. Armand's appalled father 'observed the almost effeminate gesture with which the boy smoothed back his curls, and the coquettish manner he had of narrowing his eyes as he talked'.[20] His demeanour, which features in the first section of the novel, is intended as a clue to his sexual temperament. While the truth of his nature is clear to all those around him – 'You're one of those creatures who prefer your own sex' – Armand's innocence survives until he reaches New York.[21] Only then is he able to declare, 'I'm what the world considers queer.'[22]

The fairy is central to *Strange Brother*, though in a different way. Fairies appear early in the novel in a club in Harlem: 'June gave a little gasp, for the five young men had carefully marcelled hair, all had their eyebrows plucked to a finely penciled line, all had carmined lips, all were powdered and rouged, all had meticulously manicured nails, stained dark red, all had high voices and little trilling laughs, and all expressed themselves in feminine affectations and gestures.'[23] They provide the foil for the main protagonist's less visible (though no less doomed) homosexuality. While Mark Thornton is masculine in his persona, his very masculinity is framed in contrast to the exaggerated effeminacy of the pansy, Nelly. Through his conversations with the sympathetic female character, June Westbrook, we encounter another type of homosexuality:

> Then there was the gallery of a well-known Broadway moving picture house, where you saw only men, never any women, though the men up there were seldom the flossy wench sort like Nelly, but an altogether different kind, men who were outwardly completely masculine, simple rough fellows with no understanding of themselves. In the summer time, Mark said, you would see them sitting in the gallery in their shirt sleeves. When they looked at you, you saw that they had the eyes of hungry animals. They had a driven look that Mark could never forget. They stirred him to a profound pity.[24]

The fairy and his 'tribe' revolt Mark. 'The Nelly type disgusts me. They make me feel uncomfortable. They seem to caricature what I am.'[25] The sting is in that word 'caricature': the fairy is merely an exaggerated parading of Thornton's essential womanliness. Just as the masculinity of the hungry-eyed men in the movie house balcony was *outward*, he sees himself as incompletely male, a 'half man'. 'It's as though I had the body of a man and the psychology of a woman! I'm what you might call a half-man.'[26] *Strange Brother* attempts to blur the inexorable pairing of homosexuality and male femininity yet actually reinscribes the link. Thornton is an archetypal sad young man, and, of course, has to die.

The focus on male effeminacy is remarkably widespread. The 1930s magazines *Brevities* and *Broadway Tattler* contained a strange visual and textual mix of representations of assertive female sex and male effeminacy. The oral sex more than hinted at in its cartoons and stories was as likely to be cunnilingual as fellatory, with the provider of the latter as liable to be male as female. The two stock figures of their caricatures were the busty blond and the fairy. Much of the knowing banter featured the pansy. The effeminate (though not cross-dressed) man – identified by his unconventional clothing, pose, cosmetics, and coiffure – appeared regularly in cartoons that played on the pansy's gender ambiguity and desire for 'real' men.[27] (See Figures 38 and 39.)

The implied woman-like nature of men with homosexual desires surfaces repeatedly on the American stage in productions – and in reviews of those plays – from the 1920s to the 1950s: from Eugene O'Neill's rather strange *Strange Interlude* (1928) to Robert Anderson's *Tea and Sympathy* (1953).[28] Unsurprisingly, it was there in film too, in what Thomas Doherty has aptly termed 'Queer Flashes'.[29] *Variety* wrote in 1933 that 'producers are going heavy on the pans stuff in current pics, despite the watchful eye of the Hays office, which is trying to keep the dual-sex boys and lesbos out of films'.[30] What the magazine called 'pans stuff' was evident both in the uncertain masculinity of late 1920s and 1930s actors such as William Haines (see Figure 40), Edward Everett Horton, and Franklin Pangborn and in the succession of effeminate males providing comic vignettes in a surprising number of movies – David Lugowski and Richard Barrios have established the ubiquity of such representation.[31] Barrios writes of scores of such films.[32] *Palmy Days* (1931), for example, begins with an obvious fairy ordering a chocolate birthday cake ('I *love* chocolate') and asking for it to be decorated with 'a pansy' rather than a rose.[33] *Our Betters* (1933) finishes with the 'mincing' Ernest (Tyrell Davis), described by Barrios as 'the nightmare that haunts those threatened by effeminacy' and by *Variety*'s reviewer as 'the most broadly painted character of the kind yet attempted on the screen'.[34] The homosexual–pansy link is evident in the complaints of studio executives: 'I think the quicker we get away from degenerates and fairies in our stories, the better off we are going to be.'[35] From 1934, it features in Production Code censorship correspondence; Lugowski quotes a letter regarding a Fred Astaire sailor dance routine in *Follow the Fleet* (1936), requesting that there be 'no attempt to inject any "pansy" humor into the scene'.[36]

38. Fairies and sailors, 1932–33. The Kinsey Institute for Research in Sex, Gender, and Reproduction, Inc. Author's note: cartoons from *Brevities*, 7 March 1932 and 19 October 1933 dealing with the sexual interactions of fairies and sailors. The upper caption reads: 'Oh, shucks! There goes my hankie again.' The lower one, headed 'Pickled corned beef', has the caption: 'Rivalry!'

Effeminacy

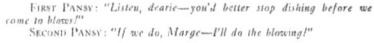

39. Fairies and pansies, 1932–33. The Kinsey Institute for Research in Sex, Gender, and Reproduction, Inc. Author's note: cartoons from *Brevities*, 28 November 1932 and *Broadway Tattler*, August 1933, featuring fairies or pansies, and assuming some knowledge of sexual terms, including oral sex. The upper caption reads: 'First pansy: "Listen, dearie – you'd better stop dishing before we come to blows!" Second pansy: "If we do, Marge – I'll do the blowing!"' In the lower caption, the woman asks the fairy, 'Just had a trip round th' world?' He replies in the affirmative. She asks, 'Been to Lapland?' He replies, 'Hell *No*!'

40. William Haines, 1920s. Photofest.

Though strongest in film in the early 1930s, male homosexual effeminacy was a theme of the 1940s too. Steven Cohan has discussed the influence of the 1930s 'sissy' on the Bob Hope and Bing Crosby buddy movies of the 1940s and Gene Kelly's sailor musicals.[37] Ambivalent masculinity – 'What do you think I am with this carnation, a float in the rose show?' – was also a comic motif in the work of Jack Benny and his collaborators, first on radio and then on television, continuing the sissy theme through the 1940s and 1950s in these highly popular shows.[38]

The same identification of homosexuality with effeminacy occurs in other discourse. John Worby's *The Other Half* (1937), the memoirs of a hobo in the USA and England in the 1920s and 1930s, includes an encounter with a young man from Buffalo who picked up the itinerant and took him home. The man is described in terms of his effeminacy. 'I was beginning to marvel at the queer way in which this young man spoke. His strain of speech was getting more and more affectionate, in fact so much so that I was beginning to compare him with a lady I had known where I last stayed.' 'He was painted up, too, with eyebrow pencil, rouge, lipstick and powder and just saturated in scent.'[39] This chapter is called 'A queer evening' in the English edition of the book; and in the US version it is 'A curious friend'.

La Forrest Potter's *Strange Loves* (1933) was unambiguous in its linkages. 'Queers', 'queerness', 'inversion', 'homosexuality in males' – all these terms were used – equalled the fairy, pansy, sissy.[40] Potter was aware that the European sexologists recognized the 'virile homosexual', but quickly moved on to the 'female man' and 'why the invert swings his hips': 'My personal experience, and I believe this conclusion is general among American physicians, is that there is a decided preponderance of the *feminine* type of invert in this country.'[41] In case readers did not grasp that the fairy represented male homosexuality, a glossary reiterated the core message. '"Fairy" – Male homosexual.' '"Pansy" – A male homosexual.'[42] When the artist Thomas Hart Benton penned his farewell to New York in 1937, criticizing an art scene dominated by 'precious fairies', he too was clear about homosexuality's 'feminine characteristics': 'Our New York aberrants are, for the most part, of the gentle feminine type with predilections for the curving wrist and outthrust hip.'[43]

The former Inspector of Federal Prisons, Joseph F. Fishman, repeatedly slipped between homosexuality and effeminacy in his book-length account of sex in the US prison system: 'there is a greater percentage of homosexuals within the prison than on the outside. The actual presence of so many "fairies" with their feminine carriage, gestures and mannerisms, in itself tends to keep aglow the fire of sex in even the most heterosexual of the prisoners.'[44] The prison sexual environment, like the streets of New York, was divided into the 'passive', those known as 'fags', 'fairies', 'girls', 'pansies', 'punks', and the 'active', the 'wolves' or 'top men'. 'Invariably, the "passive" homosexuals are attired in women's clothes when arrested. The inexperienced person finds it difficult to distinguish them as males. They rouge their faces and lips, walk with mincing steps, usually have high pitched voices, and wear feminine ornaments such as earrings, bracelets, and other trinkets which we are in the habit of associating with women.' In prison, Fishman explains, they have to improvise with their make up and adornment. They are segregated to prevent temptation for the other inmates.[45] The hustlers in Fishman's account are all fairies, selling their sexual services in the guise of women. He relates the case of one: 'When dressed in women's clothes it was impossible to admit that he was not a woman. He had brown hair that he had bleached with peroxide to make it blonde. His hair was long and thick at the back, like a woman's hair, bobbed. His skin was fair and smooth, while his eyes were unusually large and soft looking. He had the homosexual characteristics of the narrow waist and the wide hips.' He lived with a succession of men as their 'wife' and when not supported in this manner, or when he required money, would 'solicit men on the street'.[46] Another had been working the streets for ten years (since the age of fourteen); 'I don't know how many men I have let use me ... I guess it would add up to a couple of hundred.'[47] In the big penitentiaries at that time these openly effeminate homosexuals were segregated from the other prisoners, but were importuned and secretly courted by the other inmates in the same manner they would the inhabitants of a women's wing in a prison.[48] The New York prison doctor Louis Berg was especially disparaging of the fairies whom he encountered in the Welfare Island penitentiary in the 1920s and early 1930s, what he called 'men like women'. Indeed he considered them a corrupting presence in the prison population. 'At first glance they appear like women with their long hair and painted cheeks and mincing gait. But as soon as they come quite close, you recoil; this can't be true! It is. These are men like women, the "fags" returning from the laundry ... We stand for a moment and watch them in a kind of horrified fascination.'[49]

However, even the misnamed 'secret' homosexuality of the prison – what sexologists called situational homosexuality – was conceived of in terms of the masculine normal and the homosexual effeminate. As Haywood Patterson said of his experience in prisons in the South in the period 1937–43, inmates had to choose between being 'a man or a gal-boy'; 'You had to prove you were a man or become a woman.'[50] The dominant pattern of prison sexuality was of the wolf (or 'jocker' or 'daddy') and his 'girl', 'punk', 'lady', 'fag', or 'gonsil'.[51] The prisoner Victor Nelson further divided them in 1933 into the 'oral copulators' – 'muzzlers', 'fairies', 'fags', 'pansies' – and the 'passive partners in sodomy' – 'punks', 'gonsils', 'mustard pots'. The 'active participants' were the 'wolves', 'jockers', and 'daddies'.[52] But the logic was the same. The 'top men' sought out younger inmates for sexual gratification, offering protection in return. Though no doubt the erotics of interaction were complex – we know as much from at least one prisoner's letters – the logic of both penologist and inmate dictated that the inevitable result was the perversion and effeminacy of the dominated partner. The 'girl' became a woman with a woman's desire for men.[53] The African-American prisoner Patterson wrote of 'a young woman being born' every time a wolf selected his punk and he believed that the gal-boys of the Northern cities were a product of the prisons of the South – 'The Southern prisons breed them.'[54] However, the wolf remained a man for all concerned. As Fishman reported, 'The active participant in homosexuality, that is the "wolf" is accepted with tolerance by the officers, while the prisoners do not consider him abnormal at all.'[55] Nelson, who had served considerable time in prison and knew from experience, wrote that wolves were treated with 'comparative respect': 'the "wolf" (active sodomist) . . . is not considered by the average inmate to be "queer" in the sense that the oral copulist, male or female, is so considered'.[56] What he called 'active homosexuality', he explained in his prison memoir, 'is the form of sexual abnormality which meets with the least disapproval'. It was approval, even respect, based on recognition of the wolf's masculinity, his toughness.[57] When he pursued the object of his desire, courting them 'exactly as a normal man "courts" a woman' – Nelson recalled one wolf who acted like 'a Wall Street broker with a Broadway chorus-girl mistress' – it merely reinforced his gendered role at the same time it confirmed his prey's femininity.[58]

Fishman allowed for degrees of 'abnormal behavior'. He advised wardens to distinguish between the corrupting influences of the 'chronic' wolf and those merely practicing homosexuality in the absence of women and warned against branding the latter as 'queer'. Similarly, passive participants should be divided into the 'congenital homosexual', who should be separated from other prisoners, and those who (again) were situationally placed and should not be branded 'as a "fairy"'.[59] Berg likewise separated the punks from the truly effeminate, what he termed the 'constitutional homosexual' or 'constitutional pervert': 'the one the man in the street recognizes under the optimistic title of "fairy"'.[60] Samuel Kahn, psychiatrist to the Department of Correction for New York City, who, in the 1920s, studied prisoners on Blackwell's Island, the clearing house for all prisoners and repository for all those classified as homosexual, wrote that there were three types of male homosexual: the effeminate; those without 'female traits'; and the homosexual with both masculine and feminine characteristics. He pronounced the last the most common but nevertheless discussed this type's stereotyped effeminacy. 'He appears and acts effeminately.'[61] Even the more nuanced positions essentialized homosexuality as effeminacy.

We could return also to the research sponsored by the Committee for the Study of Sex Variants (dealt with in Chapter 2). As Jennifer Terry has discussed, the assumption of the Committee and those involved with its work, including George Henry, was that homosexuality was marked by gender inversion: male homosexuals were effeminate in both the physical and the psychological sense, and female homosexuals exhibited masculine characteristics. And these researchers had trouble accommodating homosexuals who did not fall into their perceived pattern.[62] Furthermore, this inversion was inscribed on the body. Terry refers to the study's obsession with bodies – measured and photographed – as 'a kind of scientific scopophilia'.[63]

Henry's *Sex Variants* (1941) classified according to gender – male versus female – even in the face of evidential logic. In the case of males (we can leave women aside for the moment, though the reasoning is the same) homosexuality becomes merely a matter of effeminacy. This is what, in an earlier article, Henry termed 'constitutional factors' in homosexuality. Thus

> The homosexual male is characterized by a feminine carrying angle of the arm, long legs, narrow hips, large muscles, deficient hair on the face, chest and back, feminine distribution of pubic hair, a high-pitched voice, small penis and testicles and the presence of the scrotal fold. Not uncommonly there is an excess of fat on the shoulders, buttocks and abdomen. Occasionally the penis is very large and the hips are unusually wide. [64]

Men's (or women's) deviancy was also determined by their scores on the heavily gender-determined M–F scale. Lewis Terman, the originator of the Masculinity–Femininity Test, was insistent that his measurements were not a diagnosis for homosexuality and that 'perfectly normal heterosexual' males might rate low on the masculinity scores. But the rationale of the test, that 'male homosexuals of the passive type as a rule earn markedly feminine scores', must have tempted clinicians to prognosis.[65] Nearly all of the 'homosexuals' tested in *Sex Variants* ranked low in the masculinity test and most are described as 'Passive, effeminate, homosexual'.⁶⁶ The will to classify as masculine or effeminate is so insistent that, even if a subject's demeanour does not conform to the usual stereotype, some hidden propensity will betray him – a 'sensual mouth', a 'feminine' interest in personal appearance – and his homosexuality will be classified as 'an expression of innate effeminacy'.⁶⁷ Hence the violent, hoodlum hustler, Leonard R., with his extensive sexual relations with women, was supposedly betrayed by his 'sensual mouth' and the 'suggestion of the feminine in the uncertainty of his gait'.⁶⁸ It is interesting that penis size is not axiomatic in these notions of masculinity and femininity. In Henry's 1934 article quoted above, the homosexual penis is both large and small, and in the sex variant cases it is not unusual for a subject to have a large phallus yet still be classified as effeminate.⁶⁹

The effeminacy of those in Henry's homosexual category is clear from the initial cases. It is a powerful trope: 'On closer inspection, he is a tall, gentle young man with a pretty unlined face, a sensual mouth, slender, delicate hands and well-kept fingers. The hair over his forehead constantly falls in his eyes and is flung back with a girlish gesture. His voice is high pitched and his gait is a little mincing . . . an air of effeminacy pervades all his actions and gestures.' The giveaway phrase, 'on closer inspection', demonstrates that the observers knew exactly what they were looking for. The verdict was that this man's homosexuality was 'a manifestation of innate lack of virility'.⁷⁰ The terms used to describe this homosexuality were consistent in their association with effeminacy. Voices are 'soft', 'gentle', 'high-pitched', and 'feminine' in modulation or tone. Steps are 'mincing'. Hand and wrist movements are delicate, and hands are small and fingers long and/or tapered. Hair is fine or 'scanty'; eye lashes are long. Such men are characterized by sensitivity, delicateness, and 'soft manners'.⁷¹ They are 'sissies', 'pansies', 'girlish', 'feminine', 'swish', with 'marked effeminacy', and 'girlishness'.⁷² That homosexuality is proclaimed by effeminacy is a stereotype promulgated by several of the subjects themselves. Paul A. claimed that he could tell a homosexual by his exaggerated speech and intonation or 'high-pitched voice'. 'Sometimes I tell by the walk, its effeminate prissiness or swagger.'⁷³ Gene S., himself described as girlish and feminine by Henry, thought that paraded effeminacy gave homosexuality a bad name. He made it clear that he did not like 'pansies'; 'I detest the obvious, blatant, made-up boys whose public appearance and behavior provoke onerous criticism.'⁷⁴

Several articles in the *American Journal of Psychiatry* in the 1940s reflect the thinking of that period. Two officers in the United States

Naval Reserve claimed rather unambiguously that there was a 'predominance of female characteristics' in male homosexuals: 'it has been our experience that the majority of inverts display evidences of physical as well as psychic traits of effeminacy'. The logic of the study was self-selective. Non-effeminate men who engaged in homosexual acts – even when they claimed homosexuality – were seen as engaging in 'acts of perversity rather than true homosexuality'. But the link between homosexuality and effeminacy is clear. 'Emotionally, the invert is very similar to the average woman.'[75]

Another study, dealing with military sex offenders, was aware that homosexuality was more complex than division into active and passive and masculine and feminine (the author was critical of some of the terminology employed in discussing sexual roles), but nevertheless betrayed the influences of such a classificatory mindset. Those men defined as 'true' homosexuals were fairly evenly divided between those deemed masculine and those termed feminine in their 'make up and temperament and mannerisms'; but almost none of those not considered homosexual – although facing court martial for sodomy – was considered 'feminine in personality traits'. While effeminacy was not sufficient to define homosexuality, it was clearly necessary.[76]

A similar necessity surfaces in a highly successful, New York-set, novel of the period, Charles Jackson's *The Lost Weekend* (1944). Although it is billed as 'Five shocking days in the life of an alcoholic' in the 1948 Signet paperback edition of the novel, Don Birnam, the drunk at the centre of the story, is also a tortured homosexual. There is no suggestion that Birnam is effeminate; he is a regular guy, conventionally masculine ('Anyone ever tell you that you look like Ronald Colman?').[77] But his essence is unmanly, personified in the effeminate figure of the alcoholic ward male nurse Bim who calls Don 'baby' and offers to visit him at home with an illicit supply of drugs: '"Listen, baby." The voice was so low and soft he could scarcely hear it. "I know you."'[78] Bim, the man with the body of a truck-driver yet the voice of Marlene Dietrich, and who walks 'softly, insolently, like a dancer', represents the truth of Don's being: 'The flower of the ingrown seed he had in him was here shown in unhealthy bloom, *ad terrorem* and *ad nauseam*. It was aspiration in its raw and naked state, aspiration unenobled, a lapse of nature as bizarre and undeniable as the figures of his imagined life were deniable, bizarre, beyond reach.'[79]

We could probably take Donald Webster Cory's influential study, *The Homosexual in America* (1951), as a statement of received wisdom at the end of the 1940s, for it was aimed at the psychiatric community and law enforcers as well as the educated public and homosexuals themselves. Effeminacy, he wrote, was axiomatic in psychiatric and sociological theories of homosexuality, and indeed in the attitudes of many homosexuals themselves.[80] He was alert to the languages used to describe homosexuality, counting references to the homosexual in dictionaries of slang and criminal jargon and its recurrent association with the effeminate and passive.[81] He was critical of such stereotypes; indeed favoured the word 'gay' as a term used by homosexuals themselves with 'no odium of the effeminate stereotype'.[82] He argued that the 'extremely effeminate homosexual is a rarity even in gay circles'. Nevertheless, he could not quite relinquish the correlation between homosexuality and effeminacy. 'In my opinion, based upon close observation, the majority of homosexuals have some slight characteristic that will betray their inclinations to an astute and experienced observer: an unusual inflection of the voice, a movement of the hands or shoulders, a characteristic walk.'[83] Indeed another study, publicized in less nuanced terms in the popular magazine *Sexology* in 1949, linked homosexuality with identifiable feminine characteristics in a man's drawing and used The Goodenough Drawing-a-man Test to plot roles in homosexual activity against the clinicians' perceived indicators of masculinity and effeminacy. The *Sexology* article merely made more prominent the original premise of the more scholarly piece: a man's homosexuality was revealed in the effeminacy of his drawing.[84] (See Figure 41.)

The psychoanalyst Robert Lindner was at pains to separate what he termed the 'true homosexual' from the 'queens and weight-hefting homoerotics', yet recognized the popular power of stereotyping in the early 1950s. 'According to this definition, a homosexual is a person who demonstrates publicly and, it is assumed, privately, the behavioral characteristics of the opposite sex. Thus the invert is a *pansy, nance, sissy* or *fairy*.'[85]

'What is your name, Miss?' says Groucho Marx to a sissified Benny in the quiz sketch in a Jack Benny programme in 1953.[86] Clearly this oversimplified conception of homosexuality persisted into the 1950s and early 1960s. As Kaier Curtin has put it, the successful *Season in the Sun* (1950) provided Broadway with a stereotypical view of homosexuality in the form of 'two, silly effeminate males'. The fairies, obvious figures of derision ('I take the window screens off so's they can *fly* in and out'), literally had brief walk-on, walk-off roles, but were invariably mentioned

New York hustlers

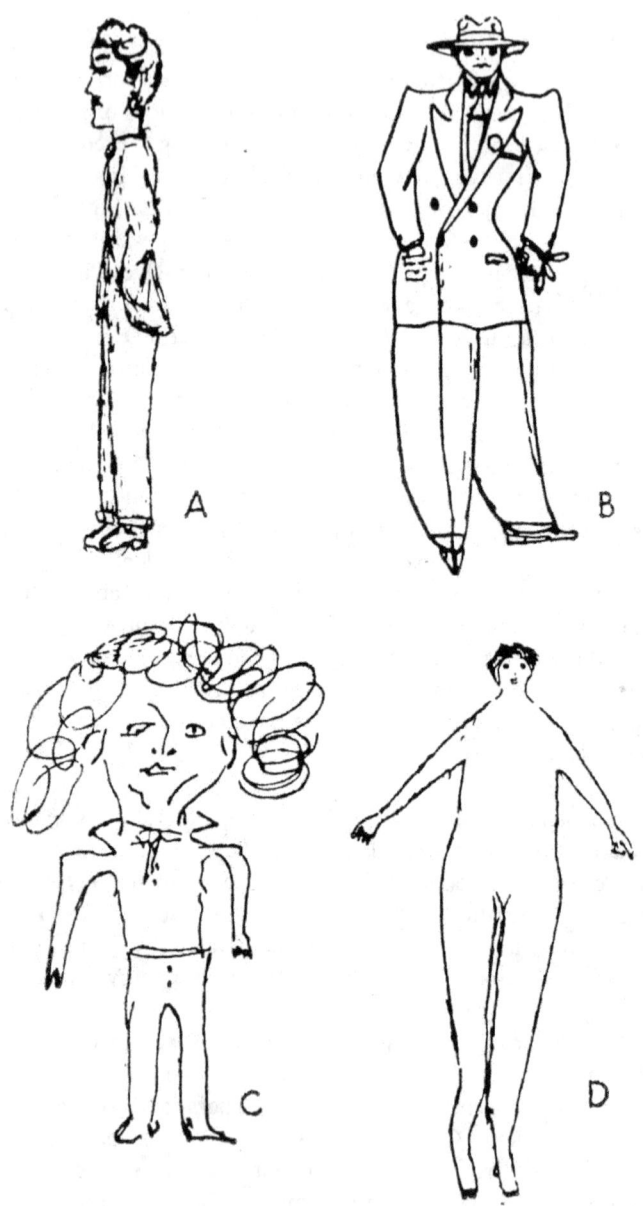

41. Supposed femininity disclosed in homosexual drawings of men. *Sexology*, 1949.

in reviews of the hit.[87] More seriously, Arthur Miller's *A View from the Bridge* (1955), set in a community of longshoremen in Red Hook, pits conventional masculinity against perceived homosexual effeminacy. Eddie Carbone, the stereotypical longshoreman, cannot make sense of his adopted niece's immigrant Italian boyfriend, Rodolpho, with his blond hair (Eddie thinks that it is dyed), singing (tenor), piano-playing, cooking, dress making skills, and love of clothes. For Eddie, all the markers are awry. He is not 'a man' like his brother; 'Then why don't his brother sing? Marco goes around like a man; nobody kids Marco.' 'And with that wacky hair; he's like a chorus girl or sump'm.' 'Is that a workin' man?' 'I mean he ain't right . . . He's a blond guy. Like – platinum. You know what I mean?' 'I mean he looked so sweet there, like an angel – you could kiss him he was so sweet.'[88] And that is exactly what Eddie does in a moment of jealous rage, derision, and assertion of his masculinity – reminiscent of the conflicted masculinity in another work of literature from the 1950s, *Last Exit to Brooklyn*, discussed in Chapter 2.

The whole purpose of the highly successful play *Tea and Sympathy* (1953) had been to counter assumptions about the association between homosexuality and effeminacy and manliness and normality. The most homosexual figure in the play is the swaggering, persecuting schoolmaster Bill, not the supposed effeminate queer, the 'fairy' Tom, who has a very heterosexual affection for Bill's wife, Laura. But the stereotype has to exist in order to be countered: 'He's a fairy. A homosexual.' 'Look at the way he walks, the way he sometimes stands . . . a man knows a queer when he sees one.'[89] At much the same time, the adaptors of André Gide's *The Immoralist* (1954) were concerned that the director of their dramatic version of the novel, with its homosexual character, was going to have one scene played 'swishy or with limp wrists'.[90]

What has been termed the 'Lavender Scare' of America's Cold War, where thousands of federal employees lost their positions for their alleged homosexuality, inextricably associated with communism in the minds of their harriers, reflected (as the term lavender suggests) an association between same-sex activity and gender inversion still rampant in the 1950s.[91] The men dismissed, or suspected, though logically indistinguishable from the general male population, were invariably represented as pansies (or 'pink pansies'), fairies, fruits, and fags.[92] The State Department's *Investigative Manual* advised interviewers of prospective employees to look out for 'any unusual traits of speech, appearance and mannerisms'.[93] The best selling *U.S.A. Confidential* (1952), which fanned such fears, wrote of many men who 'aren't men', and of 'the feminization of men'. 'The fairy situation is a pronounced problem', they reported of New York, 'in addition to our own, we get the pick of the nation's pansy crop'.[94] So homosexuality's association with effeminacy remained strong, even in the face of counter argument; *U.S.A. Confidential* was able to write of the 'unsophisticates who think of queers as prancing nances with rouged lips and bleached hair' on one page while confirming its own unsophistication on practically every other one![95]

We can see this quite clearly too as we enter the 1960s with Jess Stearn's *The Sixth Man* (1961). This book, which enjoyed months on the *New York Times* best-seller list, proclaimed the ubiquity and normality of homosexuality on its cover illustration and banner caption. The undetectability of the homosexual was conveyed in the pictures of six suited men (the same man) on the front and back covers. His prevalence was stressed in capitals: 'ONE OUT OF EVERY SIX MEN IN AMERICA IS A HOMOSEXUAL.' Ostensibly, this was a popular account countering popular stereotypes, 'the homosexual as an effeminate individual whose every gesture and mannerism clamors for attention . . . the effusive, preening, smirking exhibitionist – that the man in the street mistakenly judges all homosexuals'.[96] Yet the man in the street was unlikely to find his prejudice confronted in Stearn's book. *The Sixth Man* is steeped in the very stereotypes that it professes to counter. Its author achieves this with a rather crude two-handed representation, continually finding individuals who do not conform to the effeminate stereotype ('George looked like anything but the popular conception of a homosexual') but whose repeated exception reinforces the very attitude it is supposed to challenge, and by a rather sickening barrage of anecdote and commentary that merely perpetuates the old associations: 'Once as I watched a luncheon companion become an effeminate caricature of himself, he apologized. "It is hard to always remember that one is a man."'[97]

Martin Meeker sees *Life* magazine's 1964 'Homosexuality in America' article as pivotal in the media's 'discovery' of homosexuality in its different forms, including its masculine-presented, leather-garbed representatives.[98] It begins with a huge, double-page photograph of men in San Francisco's Tool Box bar. They are wearing caps, leather jackets and tight jeans, and stand in front of a bar mural of similarly masculine men, some of whom have conventional haircuts and are dressed in suits and ties. 'A San Francisco bar run for and by homosexuals', its caption explains, 'is crowded with patrons who wear leather jackets, make a show of masculinity and scorn effeminate members of their world.' The co-owner of the bar was quoted as saying, 'This is the antifeminine side of homosexuality

... We throw out anyone who is too swishy. If one is going to be homosexual, why have anything to do with women of either sex? We don't go for the giddy kids ... This is a place for men, a place without all those screaming faggots, fuzzy sweaters and sneakers.'[99] With its circulation of some 7.3 million copies in the USA, *Life* certainly publicized homosexuality, and Meeker has discovered fascinating evidence that it helped many young homosexuals make sense of – give a name to – the desires that they were experiencing. It became part of the same-sex communications network that Meeker has charted so successfully.[100] Yet, as already hinted, the fairy is by no means absent. There is also a full-page image of two effeminate men, the subject of the disapproving stares of a passing middle-aged man and woman, and, presumably, many *Life* readers. The caption is: 'Two fluffy-sweatered young men stroll in New York City, ignoring the stares of a "straight" couple. Flagrant homosexuals are unabashed by reactions of shock, perplexity, disgust.'[101] This influential piece also presented homosexuality as effeminacy, to quote Meeker, the 'image ... that most heterosexuals were familiar and comfortable with in 1964'.[102]

Meeker's thesis is that the 'new image of the masculine male homosexual ... became dominant by the end of the decade', evident in similarly high-profile articles in *Esquire* and *Time* magazines in 1969.[103] The theme of Tom Burke's 'The New Homosexuality', the piece in *Esquire*, was that the popular view of (male) homosexuality, reflected in the spectacular success of Mart Crowley's play *The Boys in the Band* (1968), was hopelessly dated. The new homosexual, he argued, was indistinguishable from the heterosexual hippie.[104] However, the *Time* article, 'The Homosexual: Newly Visible, Newly Understood', was rather more equivocal. True, it engaged with the multiplicity of same-sex sexual interactions and provided case studies to support that claim. It stated that 'stereotype "queers" were a distinct minority', quoting Paul Gebhard, Director of the Kinsey Institute, to that effect. But the article still referred more generically to 'swirling belles', homosexual 'self-indulgence', superficiality and shallowness, camp, and 'sissyhood', maintaining that 'authorities agree' that homosexuality was 'somewhat more common among so-called "pretty boys"', and finished with a discussion 'Are Homosexuals Sick?' in which the psychoanalyst Charles Socarides portrayed homosexuality as a failure to function according to the 'appropriate gender identity'.[105]

Commentary on *Boys in the Band* certainly fastened on the stereotyped homosexual effeminacy of the mincing character Emory, 'the show's only swishy, 42nd Street stereotype fag – the pathetic kind

42. Cliff Gorman in Times Square in the film *Boys in the Band* (William Friedkin: 1970). National General Pictures/Photofest.

that most people associate with homosexuality'. 'Flitting and floating and fluttering, he reminds you of a butterfly in heat. The Definitive Screaming Queen.'[106] Cliff Gorman, who played the role in both stage and film versions of *Boys in the Band*, did little to undermine such thinking, playing along with a profile that stressed his real-life heterosexuality, 'his incredibly beautiful wife', and 'his very butch, real-life voice'. 'There's no question in my mind of my gender' was his off-the-cuff endorsement of the logic that saw homosexuality as inversion.[107] Doubtless the film critic of the *New York Times* was right when he criticized the 1970 film version of *Boys in the Band* for perpetuating the same stereotypes as its stage version, namely 'the mannerisms of a certain kind of fake-elegant, American homosexual . . . patterned after fashions set 30 or 40 years ago on the Broadway stage'.[108] But the point was that those stereotypes were there in William Friedkin's movie. (See Figure 42.) Sissyhood was far from dead.

When the Beat anthologist and journalist Seymour Krim set out a pro and con piece on homosexuality, 'The Revolt of Homosexuality', an invented dialogue between a 'homosexual' and a 'straight guy', the main marker of late 1950s to early 1960s homosexuality was an imputed effeminacy. That was the message – despite the denials of the homosexual guy. 'Why have so many fairies come out in the open recently? Wherever I go I run into them – the Village, East Side, Harlem, even the Bronx. The whole thing seems to have exploded like a queer Mount Vesuvius.' 'Let me be blunt. Do you think it does your cause any good to see platinum-haired freaks swishing along 8th Street screaming at the top of their voices?'[109]

This was also the impression conveyed by the *Dictionary of American Slang*, a guide to the language of 'a rather large portion of the American public' in 1960.[110] Fag, fairy, fruit, Mary, nance, Nancy, pansy, queen, queer, and swish were all defined in terms of male homosexuality and feminine traits.[111] *The Guild Dictionary of Homosexual Terms* (1965), while pointing out that words such as pansy and fairy were rarely used any more (especially by homosexuals themselves) nevertheless provided a breathless list of synonyms for the term homosexual, including a great many denoting perceived degrees of effeminacy: amy-john, androgyne, angel, auntie, belle, bessie, birdie, bitch, blueberry pie, buttercup, camp bitch, capon, catamite, chicken, closet queen, cockeater, cocksucker, crushed fruit, daffodil, daisy, dicky licker, doll, drag queen, dreamboat, elegant, fag, faggot, fairy, fairy lady, fanny bellhop, faunet, fish queen, flaming bitch, flaming queen, flit, flossy, fluff, fluter, flutterer, fruit, fruitcake, funnyacting, gazooney, girl, gonsil, grandma, gunsil, hair fairy, jam fag, jeanie boy, la, lamb, lavender, lavender boy, lily, lily white, limp wrist, lizzie, ma, maricon, mary, milksop, mintie, miss, moll, molly, mother, mother superior, muffin, nance, nancy, nelly, nola, pansy, passion fruit, peepee lover, petal, pinky, pixie, pogue, poof, powder puff, pretty boy, princess, prissy, punk, quail, queen, queen bee, queer, quince, screaming bitch, sea pussy, she, sis, sissy, sister, swish, temperamental, tip, wife, yoo-hoo boy, and zanie.[112]

The lexical link was unambiguous. A recent study of the repertoire of jokes collected and used by Whitey Roberts, a popular American comedian and entertainer in the 1950s and 1960s, found that most of those dealing with male homosexuality favoured the imagery of passivity and femininity. A 'Faggot who went into a florist's . . . said "Do you send flowers?" The clerk said "Yes". He said, "Well, will you please send me to California . . . I'm a pansy."' One of the binders in Roberts's collection was labelled 'Nance', and the terms used – nance, swish, sissy, pansy, faggot, fruit, fairy – and the focus on providing oral sex – 'Queer bank robber who was so absent-minded that he tied up the safe and blew the teller' – would not have been out of place in the 1920s and 1930s.[113] The much-prosecuted 1960s comic Lenny Bruce likewise referred to fags, fruits, faggots (a favourite word of his), and screaming queens. His routine included a joke about an effeminate truck driver ('he's wearing an Anna Mae Wong dress') whose Jewish mother did not understand why he was taking so long to find a nice girl to marry, given his good nature: 'A night don't go past he don't bring some poor serviceman home'. Though Bruce challenged the men in his audience to deny that they had had at least one homosexual experience, his faggot riffs were in terms of lost masculinity. 'Somehow queens have always, like, swung'. 'I challenge your manhood ... That's the worst thing you can call us, right? Goddamn, man. It really bugs guys to call them faggot.'[114]

A New Yorker who had served in the Office of Naval Intelligence in the mid-1960s, responsible for detecting homosexuals as a potential security risk, explained the logic behind such investigations. Apart from the evidence of an actual homosexual act, 'they'd note it if a guy seemed effeminate to them, if he had no beard and didn't shave, if he minced or in any other way seemed not masculine to them. I can't tell you what they thought, really, because I considered the whole damn thing so absurd.'[115]

If the massive-selling – and crazed – *Everything You Always Wanted to Know About Sex – But Were Afraid to Ask* (1969) is any sort of guide to popular thinking, homosexual men were 'part-time women'. While its author, Dr David Reuben, admitted that not all homosexuals dressed and acted like women – 'There is a wide range of variation in homosexual behavior' – he was rather less varied in his associations: 'most homosexuals at one time or another in their lives act out some aspect of the female role'.[116] The recurring pattern when male effeminacy was discussed was a denial of stereotypes (as myth or popular superstition) accompanied by the very inscription of those caricatures. 'No picture of the "gay" life would be complete without some mention of the "fairy" or "faggot", or "queen"', was how one study broached the subject in 1967. 'It is these individuals who have come to personify the "real homosexual" to the masses, and the masses tend to think that "real homosexuals" are fairies.'[117] When the Kinsey associate C. A. Tripp wrote his classic study of homosexuality in 1975, he claimed that in learned circles the association between homosexuality and gender inversion was an outmoded concept. 'For several decades biologists and experimental psychologists have recognized that these are distinctly different phenomenon, though they may or may not occur together.'[118] Yet he was aware that inversion and homosexuality were still synonymous in 'popular thinking'. 'In both heterosexual and homosexual relations', he wrote, 'many men feel their manliness would be jeopardized (in their own eyes and in the eyes of others) if they inverted their dominant role, even for a moment.'[119] He even reluctantly provided a chapter on the psychology of effeminacy – explaining the finer points of 'Swish', 'Nelly', and 'Camp' – necessary, he argued, because so many people associated male homosexuality with effeminacy and vice versa.[120]

Midge Decter's piece in *Commentary* in 1980, wickedly demolished by Gore Vidal in *The Nation*, wrote sardonically of the impact of 'Gay Lib' on the culture of the early 1960s: 'Homosexuals were no longer to be called "fags", "queers", "pansies", or (how archaic the word seemed even then) "fairies".' Yet she proceeded to ignore her own edict, lingering on the 'smooth feminine skin', woman-like obsession with consumerism, pretty-girl-like narcissism, mincing, and general feminine artifice of homosexual men of Fire Island Pines and the 'swishing pansies' of Cherry Grove.[121]

We have to acknowledge the advent of what became known as 'gay macho', the 'gay clone', the hyper-masculine homosexuality of the 1970s and 1980s with its stylized masculinity – military, uniformed, blue-collar, leather, denim, cowboy – prefigured in that *Life* magazine exposé and modelled on the earlier look of trade (discussed elsewhere in this book), when many homosexuals became what they had formerly desired.[122] (Vidal wrote that Decter's portrayal of 'fags' as 'imitation women' ignored the 'present generation' who looked more like 'off-duty policemen or construction workers'.)[123] As John Loughery has observed of this period of US gay history, 'All around, gay men looked like the embodiment of fantasies that in adolescence had been associated exclusively with heterosexuals'.[124] As early as 1965, the pioneering sex researcher Evelyn Hooker was talking of a fight against the 'stereotype of the effeminate' in the homosexual world: 'In some, the result is a caricature of masculinity.'[125] Laud Humphreys in 1971 noted the 'virilization' of the gay scene, though what he had in mind was its merger with the masculinity of the hippies.[126] 'Where have All the Sissies Gone?' was a chapter in Seymour Kleinberg's personal account of gay life in the 1970s. He wrote of the new masculinity, the abjuration of effeminacy. 'The universal stance is a studied masculinity. There are no limp wrists, no giggles, no indiscreet hips swiveling.'[127] Edmund White's report card on gay America in the same decade included the New Yorkers in 'jeans, cowboy shirts, and workboots', with all the appearance of a new 'class of gay indigents'.[128] He recorded the antipathy of some homosexuals to drag queens ('they have become the outcasts of gay life'), warning that such hostility represented a failure of self-acceptance.[129] In John Rechy's *Rushes* (1977) about a tough, macho homosexual bar in the meatpacking district, a doorman 'nightly discards the "sissies" and other undesirables'; even hustlers do not measure up to the new standards of masculinity.[130]

Yet White also thought that Americans outside New York and the larger cities thought of homosexuality as comprised of 'pissy queens and fun-loving fags'.[131] It was, despite the clones, a persistent association. The existence of late 1970s books referring both to the new machismo and to their rejection of the stereotype of the 'nelly queen' demonstrates the latter's durability.[132] The academic studies of the 1960s and 1970s emphasizing the multiplicity of *homosexualities* and the inapplicability of masculine/feminine sex roles in such relationships were likewise reacting to oversimplified conceptions.[133] The well-known sociologist of masculinity R. W. Connell was still able to write of the 1980s that 'To many people, homosexuality is a *negation* of masculinity, and homosexual men must be effeminate'.[134] Similarly, a meticulously documented article in the *California Law Review* in 1995 charted the pervasive conflation of sex, gender, and sexual orientation – lesbians perceived as masculine and gay males as feminine – 'encoded in the heritage and life of the United States' and exerting 'a divisive force on society and a destabilizing influence in law'.[135] The gay theorist Alan Sinfield concluded in a book published in 1998 both that it was 'doubtful whether, without a huge change in hetero-normative patterns, the system could afford to concede masculinity to gays' and that 'effeminacy remains crucial in our subculture'.[136]

While these examples of the adherence of effeminacy to homosexual image and identity may seem repetitious, they reflect a historical persistence still insufficiently grasped by most historians. The history of effeminacy is yet to be written. Margot Canaday's important new book on the role of the state's immigration, military, and welfare agencies in the forging of US homosexuality and heterosexuality has many references to the effeminate strands in the making of the homosexuality that she assumes is made by the mid-twentieth century – 'War . . . is not a powder puff affair' was the quoted response of a congressman when the anti-homosexual implications of the 1944 GI Bill were discussed.[137] But effeminacy is never the focus of her interrogations and she does not sufficiently explore whether the homosexuality that includes the masculine homosexual as part of the hetero-homo binary by the 1950s was, for many, even in the 1950s, still homosexuality as effeminacy.[138]

Richard Dyer once observed that the hustler novels of the 1960s were obsessed with manliness and its performance, and we can certainly be confident that masculinity was central to this culture.[139] Dotson Rader wrote perceptively of 'the need for triumph and command and the strange ways in which young men have been twisted, made to turn away from themselves. Manhood. The need to affirm it and possess it and abuse it and transcend it. Manhood burlesqued and sought after and elevated like the Host.'[140] Rader's hustler narrator derided faggots, fags, and queers, writing of 'the browning queens ... fluttering out like deadly veiled widow-birds, winged-faggot carrion peering for meat'. He made it clear that he was no 'FAGGOT', 'no miss mary pansy'. 'HUSTLERS ARE NOT QUEER.'[141]

Hostility to homosexual effeminacy crossed the gay/straight divide. It was a feature of the otherwise avant-garde literature of the 1950s. As Catherine Stimpson has noted, the Beats 'often feminized invective to scorn the fag'. Their attitude to effeminate men reflected a far from radical attitude to women and, indeed, their conservative adherence to the division of the cosmos into active masculine and passive feminine.[142] John Clellon Holmes's Beat *roman à clef*, *Go* (1952), is dismissive of the 'affected gibberish of a dwarfish fairy' and 'mincing' homosexuals, who seem to have no real role in this celebration of life lived on the edge.[143] It is important, then, not to confuse antagonism to effeminacy with antipathy towards homosexuality, a mistake that some modern critics make.[144]

William Burroughs, a homosexual, was notoriously dismissive of pansies, fags, and swish: 'Burroughs may be gay, but he's a man', was Norman Mailer's endorsement.[145] 'I don't mind being called queer', Burroughs wrote to Allen Ginsberg in 1952, 'But I'll see him [his publisher] castrated before I'll be called a Fag ... That's just what I been trying to put down uh I mean *over*, is the distinction between us strong, manly, noble types and the leaping, jumping, window dressing cocksucker.'[146] 'All complete swish fairies should be killed', he told Ginsberg and Jack Kerouac in 1955, 'not as traitors to the cause of queerness, but for selling out the human race to the forces of negation and death.'[147] *Interzone*, written though not published in the 1950s, refers to 'a queen-repellent smelling of decayed queen flesh'.[148] 'A room full of fags gives me the horrors', writes the narrator (Burroughs) in *Junky*, first published in 1953.

> They jerk around like puppets on invisible strings, galvanized into hideous activity that is the negation of everything living and spontaneous. The live human being has moved out of these bodies long ago. But something moved in when the original tenant moved out. Fags are ventriloquists' dummies who have moved in and taken over the ventriloquist. The dummy sits in a queer bar nursing his beer, and uncontrollably yapping out of a rigid doll face.[149]

Effeminate homosexuality makes an occasional entry in *Naked Lunch* (1959) too. 'Cut that swish fart off the air and give him his purple slip.' 'So this piss elegant fag comes to New York from Cunt Lick, Texas, and he is the most piss elegant fag of them all.'[150] In *Queer*, written in the 1950s, though published much later, there is a firm distinction between the masculine queer and the effeminate fag. 'I shall never forget the unspeakable horror that froze the lymph in my glands – the lymph glands that is, of course – when the baneful word seared my reeling brain: *I was homosexual*. I thought of the painted, simpering female impersonators I had seen in a Baltimore night club. Could it be possible that I was one of those subhuman things?'[151] *Queer* rehearses stereotypes of homosexuality – 'It did not occur to him that Lee was queer, as he associated queerness with at least some degree of overt effeminacy' – while simultaneously challenging them.[152] Indeed the relationship between the novel's Lee (Burroughs) and Allerton (A. L. Marker) is remarkably similar to that of Painter and his masculine-presented hustlers. Lee pays Allerton and allows him to have sex with women.[153]

Craig Loftin has demonstrated the antipathy of organized homosexuality – ONE, Inc. and the Mattachine Society – towards its effeminate elements during the 1950s and 1960s.[154] The future secretary of ONE, Inc. once said that he never had 'anything to do with a man whose actions and appearance give people reason to believe that he's "abnormal"'.[155] 'In America', explained a *ONE* magazine editorialist, 'the "man in the street" instantly classifies all homosexuals as "swishes" with long fingernails, painted eyebrows, and exaggerated clothing, . . . to correct this impression locally it is almost requisite that we eliminate [magazine] references to such individuals'. *ONE* readers indicated their disapproval of effeminacy: 'It is irritating to see a nelly faggot and it is death to be seen WITH one.'[156] The aim of the Mattachine Society, Meeker has argued, was not just to make homosexuality more visible but also to provide it with a strategic public face of respectability.[157] The message that their spokesperson conveyed to the more mainstream readership of Stearn's *Sixth Man* was Mattachine's opposition to 'the stereotyped faggot who brought the third sex contempt and derision' (these words were Stearn's rather than those of the Society). Accordingly, they wanted homosexuals (in their own words) 'to adopt a behavior code which would be beyond criticism'.[158] The targets of this quest for normality included exaggerated forms of male effeminacy.

Crowley's play *The Boys in the Band* (1968) can also be read as an extended dialogue between manliness and its negation, whether in the homosexual, jocular, insider use of the feminine for the masculine ('she', 'Anything for a sis, Mary') or the invective of threatened heterosexuality: 'Faggot, fairy, pansy... queer, cocksucker! I'll kill you, you godamn little mincing swish!'[159] The merchant marine in the early pages of the hustler John Rechy's *City of Night* (1963) states his preferences: 'I dont like em queer: If I did, Id go with a woman – why fuck around with substitutes?'[160] The patrons of a gay bar in postwar Baton Rouge in the Southern pulp writer Carl Corley's semi-autobiography, *A Chosen World* (1966), are divided firmly into the admired, hustler-like, 'hard, healthy, utterly masculine' 'rough looking boys', and the ridiculed 'Friuts [sic] – Fairies', 'little faggots', 'silly faggots', 'screaming faggots', 'feminine queers', more like women than men, 'the gays, the faggots, the gueens [sic], the nellies', 'girlish creatures who fluttered about the juke-box, giggling, flinging their muscle-less arms'.[161] Corley's protagonist thought the word 'Gay' too feminine – 'utterly too feminine to fit properly the masculine homosexual which dominated, and made up my private world'.[162]

Our informant Thomas Painter was similarly hostile towards overt signs of effeminacy. When he worked undercover for the military in Dayton, identifying homosexuals for cashiering by 'posing' as one himself in a risky double sexual game, he justified it to Alfred Kinsey (and himself) in terms of his victims' overt campiness: 'public conduct unbecoming a soldier – such as screaming, camping and flirting with men at a public bar'. Effeminate, unrestrained fairies were his targets, not controlled, masculine homosexuals like himself.[163] Painter was disparaging about effeminate homosexuality, candid in his disgust at 'the painted, mincing, swishing faggots' of 42nd Street. 'I found them revolting, in fact literally nauseating – and why not, I who adored machismo, extreme virility.'[164] In 1961, he wrote of a 'queer' Union Square hustler, acting out 'all the horrid little gestures and pseudo-feminine mannerisms of the extreme faggot – with, what made it so gruesome, the almost solemnity of a priest at Mass'.[165] Painter deplored 'camping', the word 'gay', and 'traits which proclaim one's homosexuality': 'I am a very queer sort of queer.'[166]

Gore Vidal's notorious antipathy towards his literary rival Truman Capote proclaimed a similar (homosexual) masculine distancing from the recognized popular stereotype of the effeminate queer: 'he thinks he's a very rich Society lady'. 'The only thing that they [the reviewers] respect ... is a freak like Capote, who has the mind of a Kansas housewife, likes gossip, and gets all shuddery when she thinks about boys murdering people.' The 'fag' Capote was the stereotypical homosexual as far as national prejudices went; if he did not exist, he would have had to be invented.[167]

Vidal's prejudices were clear in his own literary creations. The masculine Jim Willard continually pits his same-sex desires against those of the effeminate fairies in the first edition of Vidal's *The City and the Pillar* (1948). The 'severe and masculine' Jim is not at all like the 'mincing', 'feminine', 'abnormal', 'effeminate' others.[168] 'He did not like men who acted like women', he elaborated in a passage excised in the reworked edition of 1965. 'He was repelled by the queens and the willowy long-haired young men with sensitive girlish faces ... Everyone deliberately tried to destroy the last vestiges of the masculine within himself, and this Jim found to be the worst perversion of all, the only perversion.' Accordingly, he sought sexual comfort with 'natural' young men like himself rather than the 'overly corrupted' ones.[169] Masculinity needed less distinguishing in the new world of respectable gayness. The fairies have either mysteriously vanished in the 1960s version of Vidal's youthful novel or have been transformed into the more restrained queen.[170] The fairy bar where Jim takes Bob in 1948 is merely a bar where 'men hunted men' in 1965.[171] Robert J. Corber's analysis of Vidal's novel seems unaware of the sexual context of the work. He treats it as 'utopian' when in fact Vidal was describing the experiences of himself and many others.[172]

Ricardo Brown's retrospective look at 'gay life' in St Paul, Minnesota, in the 1940s established a hierarchy of homosexuality. At the bottom were the tired old sissies, the aunties. Slightly above them were the younger sissies and the 'elegant bitches'. At the top were those whose masculinity rendered them unremarkable: 'the Regular Guys' like the author. When, young, naive, and full of hope, Brown had visited New York, he had been shocked by men 'who made a mockery of everything I'd been told was masculine'.[173] Donald Vining was yet another masculine homosexual who was disparaging about obvious effeminacy. When he went to Long Beach, New York, in 1947, initially he was disgusted by the 'flagrant and unashamed' 'screaming belles' but adjusted quickly and became amused at their banter. Nonetheless, his praise was reserved for the body builders and the companion of a friend whom 'You'd never suspect . . . was gay'.[174] The obviousness of effeminate queerness was repeatedly contrasted with a privileged masculine homosexuality: 'The boy is not the bitchy type and I can say of him what he said of me', Vining confided to his diary, 'I wouldn't have to be the least embarrassed to introduce you to my parents or to any friend I've ever known. You don't look gay, you don't sound gay or act gay.' The young man did not mix with 'the obvious types'.[175] In 1949 Vining was arrested while engaged in anonymous sex in Central Park and processed at Riker's Island. Again his diary records bemused horror at the encountered effeminacy of the fairy hustlers detained for stealing from their customers. 'Bleached hair, wildly arranged hair, and screaming voices made it seem like a scene from THE SNAKE PIT.' The homosexual block, which he was consigned to, was divided into the 'girls', fairies, 'whores', on the one hand, and, on the other, the 'men', among whom the diarist included himself.[176] His attitude was reflected in his unpublished novel about homosexual life, written in the late 1940s, with characters such as Brud Emerson, full of 'masculine charm' – 'There are too damned many bitches at this party . . . Let's get out of here before we're suffocated with cologne' – and the ex-marine Bob Tattersall who avoided 'soft people' because he 'wanted everyone to know he was "jam", completely masculine and normal'.[177]

The cultural impresario Lincoln Kirstein, encountered earlier for his taste in trade, disliked effeminacy. His biographer Martin Duberman notes that Kirstein's diary 'periodically disparaged "effeminate" men'. This co-founder of the New York City Ballet and the School of American Ballet disliked fairies.[178] Despite the linguistic camp of his correspondence, Tennessee Williams was unattracted by the 'swish and camp' of the 'very obvious types', homosexuality that was 'a travesty of the other sex'.[179] Similar sentiments lay behind Robert Rauschenberg and Jasper Johns's alleged distance towards their fellow homosexual artist Andy Warhol: 'You're too swish, and that upsets them . . . the *major painters* try to look straight; you play up the swish.'[180] Cory had been aware of these kinds of internal tensions when he published his insider survey of American homosexuality in 1951, writing that the effeminate was but a subgroup of male homosexuals, *'persona non grata* among the more virile'.[181] While Gavin Butt interprets Johns and Rauschenberg's caution as evidence of their closeted homosexuality, it may merely have indicated a simple dislike of swish.[182]

Although he certainly uses the contrast of effeminacy to highlight his own, carefully crafted, masculinity, and could be disparaging of queens 'prematurely sentenced to a purgatory of half-male, half-female', Rechy's powerful account of 1950s hustling is less hostile.[183] His 'femmequeens' are noisily defiant in their effeminacy.[184] 'IN THE BEGINNING GOD CREATED FAIRIES & THEY MADE MEN': this graffito on a Los Angeles toilet wall captures Rechy's celebration of the sexual dialectic of hustler/trade masculinity and fairy effeminacy.[185] His hustling world is one of 'painted sallow-faced youngmen, artificial manikin faces like masks' and 'tough-looking masculine hustlers, young fugitives from everywhere and everything'; 'the handsome masculine ones desired alike by men and women; the gushing swishes, hands aflutter like wings'.[186] The queens have names like Miss Destiny, Darling Dolly, Lola, and Trudi: the hustlers are called Tiger, Skipper, Buddy, Chuck, Duke, Lance: 'names, you will notice, as obviously emphatically masculine as the queens' are emphatically obviously feminine and for the same reason: to emphasize the roles they will play'.[187]

Recent commentators have discussed homosexual male distancing from effeminacy but have not fully captured the historical context and depth of this same-sex division. Jamie Russell's discussion of William Burroughs's championing of homosexual masculinity both exaggerates his subject's role in this fashioning and underestimates its longer history.[188] Craig Loftin's analysis of the hostility of the homophile organization ONE, Inc. towards effeminate homosexuality, 'swishes and swishiness', seems unaware that it had much wider cultural origins than a claimed 1950s pressure 'to pass as heterosexual'.[189]

The obsession with masculinity and femininity was such that the basic distinction in the world that we have been exploring was between an assumed masculinity and the 'queer' or 'gay' other. The sex researchers used the terms homosexual and heterosexual to classify or complicate the behavior that they were observing, but this was not the language of the streets. Painter found it worth recording when a young man used the word 'homosexual' to him in 1945 that 'that word is getting around'.[190] Corley's pulp character, although experiencing considerable male–male sex (he was raped repeatedly when in the marines), claimed never to have heard the term 'masculine homosexual' until it was mentioned in that Louisiana bar; he was certainly familiar with the term fairy.[191] Albert Reiss's delinquents talked repeatedly of fags, queers, and gays.[192]

A fictional young New York Puerto Rican hustler in the 1980s novel

Saul's Book said 'it don't mean that you're a faggot just because you let a faggot give you a blow job once in a while. I know a lot of big guys that go with faggots too. Plenty of them.' Although he knew from experience that there were exceptions to the stereotype, 'faggots' were usually 'swishy'.[193] It was a world of fine distinctions. Fellating and being pedicated were treated differently. Though 'cock sucker' was certainly a term of abuse in American slang, and fellating 'in bad repute among normal men', the fellator's status seems to have been more ambiguous than that of the pedicated. The former was more acceptable than the latter because it was perceived as less passive and feminine as being penetrated (though the passivity of the penetratee is questionable). Gershon Legman's glossary explained as early as 1941 that 'cock-sucker' had lost 'much of its sting'.[194] A fellator could be active.[195] Hence, perhaps, the earlier-quoted 'Thank God I'm just a cocksucker and not queer!'[196] This ambiguity may explain what might otherwise appear inexplicable, the writer Jack Kerouac's alleged boasting about having 'blown' Gore Vidal at the Chelsea Hotel. And would account for Vidal's later settling of scores: Kerouac's fellating was 'a pro forma affair', which Vidal put 'a quick stop to' before restoring his palimpsested dominant masculinity – 'classic trade meets classic trade' – by flipping Kerouac on to his stomach.[197]

The epigraph of this chapter, from Jack Kerouac's manifesto of the Beat generation, *On the Road*, was written in 1951 but not published until 2007. Its significance for us is its place in the cultures of masculinity and effeminacy that we have been discussing, with the added bonus of the ex-hustler, the womanizing Neal Cassady, who also engaged in homosexual sex. More flipping occurs in the extracted passage as the feminized 'fag', despite his protestations of male role capability, is treated 'like a woman' and given a 'monstrous huge banging'. The version of *On the Road* published in 1957 excised this sexually explicit section at the same time it introduced chapters, sections, and paragraphs. The fag remains a fag but is not given that monstrous, huge banging. Cassady (now Dean) remains a former hustler but merely demonstrates it through a quest for money rather than engaging in homosexual sex – even active homosexual sex.[198]

The ubiquitous association of homosexuality with effeminacy meant that activities that we might assume to be homosexual by definition were not seen as such by some participants – or rather were not necessarily seen as being queer. Perhaps this is what David the Korean War veteran meant in the film *Flesh* (1968) when he assured the hustler Joe Dallesandro, 'We're not queers', as he rubbed his leg and promised to blow him!¹⁹⁹ It is almost certainly the logic behind the denials of the conservative lawyer, Roy Cohn, Joseph McCarthy's chief counsel in the anti-communist and anti-homosexual 1950s. He could not be homosexual, he argued, 'my, ah, aggressiveness, . . . toughness, of everything along those lines is just totally . . . incompatible with anything like that'.²⁰⁰

Such denials provide a vital key to understanding a lost sexual domain. What seemed to perplex the son of the well-known American writer John Cheever about his father's sexuality – was he bisexual or homosexual? – makes perfect logical sense. How did a son respond to his dying father's admission: 'I wanted to tell you . . . your father has had his cock sucked by quite a few disreputable characters'?²⁰¹ Benjamin could not reconcile Cheever senior's declared hostility to 'homosexuals' and his adulterous relationships (with women) with his admissions of sex with (or rather, over) the equally well-known photographer Walker Evans and his claim that the composer Ned Rorem 'sucked my cock three times a day for three days'.²⁰² Cheever's letters include one to a young man in the 1970s where he declares his love and writes that he wants his cock while simultaneously declaiming, 'Neither of us is homosexual'.²⁰³ He could do this because, in the world in which he had operated during the 1950s and 1960s (the 1970s is rather late for this rationale), a homosexual was woman-like.²⁰⁴ This much is clear in another letter where Cheever parodies 'homosexuality' represented by an 'old fairy' and his youthful companion: 'The old one was very skinny with a few strands of hair, dyed a marvelous yellow. The youth had all this hair and everything else, I guess, and he might have seemed quite beautiful if he didn't have a mouth like an asshole. The old one would be seen to walk as if his asshole were a mouth.'²⁰⁵ Earlier, in a journal for 1966, Cheever mused about his sexual instincts and early upbringing, about a father's 'fear of having sired a fruit' and a son's determination to prove his masculinity through sexual contact with women. 'In order to prove my maleness, I resorted to such absurd strategies as not letting my eye rest on the woman's page in the morning *Times*.'²⁰⁶ By these criteria, where homosexuality was marked by effeminacy, by a failure of manliness, men like Cheever, whatever their same-sex cravings, were not homosexual.

Notes

1 J. Kerouac, *On the Road: The Original Scroll* (New York, 2007), p. 307.
2 I. Russell (ed.), *Jeb and Dash: A Diary of Gay Life, 1918–1945* (Boston, 1993), pp. 63, 73, 74, 82, 91, 142.

3 L. Schlissel (ed.), *Three Plays by Mae West: Sex, The Drag, The Pleasure Man* (New York, 1977), pp. 101, 103, 131, 132, 171, 194.
4 Ibid., pp. 121, 132, 152, 162.
5 Quoted by M. Hamilton, *'When I'm Bad, I'm Better': Mae West, Sex, and American Entertainment* (Berkeley and Los Angeles, 1997), p. 141.
6 The quote comes from K. Bruce, *Goldie* (New York, 1933), p. 121.
7 D. K. Johnson, 'The kids of fairytown: gay male culture on Chicago's Near North Side in the 1930s', in B. Beemyn (ed.), *Creating a Place for Ourselves: Lesbian, Gay, and Bisexual Histories* (New York, 1997), p. 100.
8 University of Chicago Library Special Collections Research Center (hereafter, UCL), Ernest Watson Burgess Papers (hereafter, Burgess), Box 98, Folder 11: 'Homosexual Materials': 'Rental Library'.
9 Johnson, 'The kids of fairytown' p. 101.
10 L. F. Potter, *Strange Loves: A Study in Sexual Abnormalities* (New York, 1934), pp. 4-6. The second quote is Forrest quoting the showgirl Evelyn Nesbit.
11 Bruce, *Goldie*, pp. 105, 111.
12 C. H. Ford and P. Tyler, *The Young and Evil* (New York, 1996), pp. 16, 56. First published in Paris, 1933.
13 New York Public Library Manuscripts and Archives Division, Charles Boultenhouse and Parker Tyler Papers, Box 12, Folder 13: C. Boultenhouse, 'Parker Tyler's Own Scandal', p. 13.
14 Ford and Tyler, *Young and Evil*, pp. 182-4.
15 R. Scully, *Scarlet Pansy* (New York, 1952), p. 5. First published in 1933.
16 Burgess, Box 98, Folder 11: 'Homosexual Materials': 'Rental Library'.
17 Scully, *Scarlet Pansy*, p. 95.
18 Ibid., pp. 97-8.
19 Ibid., p. 100.
20 A. Tellier, *Twilight Men* (New York, 1931), pp. 7-8, 11.
21 Ibid., p. 105.
22 Ibid., p. 163.
23 B. Niles, *Strange Brother* (New York, 1949), p. 49. This is a reprint of the 1931 edition.
24 Ibid., p. 196.
25 Ibid., pp. 50, 154.
26 Ibid., p. 153.
27 See the file on *Broadway Tattler* and *Broadway Brevities* (1930s) held in The Kinsey Institute for Research in Sex, Gender, and Reproduction, University of Indiana, Bloomington (hereafter, KI).
28 K. Curtin, *We Can Always Call Them Bulgarians: The Emergence of Lesbians and Gay Men on the American Stage* (Boston, 1987), pp. 117, 184, 186, 215, 228, 293-4, 297.

29 T. Doherty, *Pre-Code Hollywood: Sex, Immorality, and Insurrection in American Cinema 1930–1934* (New York, 1999), p. 120.
30 *Variety*, 28 February 1933.
31 D. M. Lugowski, 'Queering the (New) Deal: lesbian and gay representation and the Depression-era cultural politics of Hollywood's Production Code', *Cinema Journal*, 38: 2 (1999), 3–35; R. Barrios, *Screening Out: Playing Gay in Hollywood from Edison to Stonewall* (New York, 2003). See also Vito Russo's pioneering *The Celluloid Closet* (New York, 1995), pp. 3–59 (originally published in 1981); and W. J. Mann, *Behind the Screen: How Gays and Lesbians Shaped Hollywood 1910–1969* (New York, 2001), pp. 121–35.
32 Barrios, *Screening Out*, pp. 5, 71–4.
33 Lugowski, 'Queering the (New) Deal', 16; *Palmy Days* (1931: Edward Sutherland). The movie opening is on YouTube: www.youtube.com/watch?v=ci271zFXrmw.
34 Barrios, *Screening Out*, pp. 99–101; *Variety*, 28 February 1933.
35 Mann, *Behind the Screen*, p. 127.
36 Lugowski, 'Queering the (New) Deal', 10.
37 S. Cohan, 'Queering the Deal: on the road with Hope and Crosby', in E. Hanson (ed.), *Out Takes: Essays on Queer Theory and Film* (Durham, NC, 1999), pp. 23–45; S. Cohan, *Incongruous Entertainment: Camp, Cultural Value, and the MGM Musical* (Durham, NC, 2005), ch. 3.
38 A. Doty, 'The gay straight man: Jack Benny and *The Jack Benny Program*', in his *Making Things Perfectly Queer: Interpreting Mass Culture* (Minneapolis, MN, 1993), ch. 4. The quote comes from the *Jack Benny Christmas Show*, 1960. The quoted lines are from Frank Nelson's pansy-like department store floorwalker; see YouTube: www.youtube.com/watch?v=JA_r1Ynl4Ls.
39 J. Worby, *The Other Half: The Autobiography of a Tramp* (New York, 1937), pp. 28, 33.
40 Potter, *Strange Loves*, pp. 49, 79, 93.
41 Ibid., pp. 99–100.
42 Ibid., pp. 241, 242.
43 T. H. Benton, *An Artist in America* (New York, 1951), p. 265. First published in 1937.
44 J. F. Fishman, *Sex in Prison: Revealing Sex Conditions in American Prisons* (Washington, DC, 1934), p. 22.
45 Ibid., pp. 59–60.
46 Ibid., pp. 61–3.
47 Ibid., p. 64.
48 Ibid., pp. 69–70.
49 L. Berg, *Revelations of a Prison Doctor* (New York, 1934), pp. 137, 141.
50 H. Patterson and E. Conrad, *Scottsboro Boy* (New York, 1950), p. 80.
51 Berg, *Revelations of a Prison Doctor*, p. 59; Fishman, *Sex in Prison*, p. 142.

52 V. F. Nelson, *Prison Days and Nights* (Boston, 1933), pp. 149–50.
53 For an informative prisoner's account, see James Blake, *The Joint* (New York, 1971), based on prison letters from the 1950s and 1960s. For the penologist's logic, see Fishman, *Sex in Prison*, chs. 4–5; and Berg, *Revelations of a Prison Doctor*, ch. 10.
54 Patterson and Conrad, *Scottsboro Boy*, pp. 82–3.
55 Fishman, *Sex in Prison*, p. 143.
56 Nelson, *Prison Days and Nights*, pp. 150, 157.
57 Ibid., p. 158.
58 Ibid., pp. 158–9.
59 Fishman, *Sex in Prison*, pp. 151–2.
60 Berg, *Revelations of a Prison Doctor*, pp. 153, 163.
61 S. Kahn, *Mentality and Homosexuality* (Boston, 1937), pp. 70–2.
62 J. Terry, *An American Obsession: Science, Medicine, and Homosexuality in Modern Society* (Chicago, 1999), pp. 181–2.
63 Ibid., p. 196.
64 G. W. Henry and H. M. Galbraith, 'Constitutional factors in homosexuality', *American Journal of Psychiatry*, 90 (1934), 1265.
65 L. M. Terman, *Sex and Personality: Studies in Masculinity and Femininity* (New York, 1936), p. 9. For the gendered nature of the types of questions asked, see ibid., pp. 269–71: 'Inverts probably have more interest in flowers.' 'Lack of interest by inverts in things mechanical.' 'Inverts are notoriously little interested in games and sports.' 'Inverts are more given to the use of cosmetics.'
66 G. W. Henry, *Sex Variants: A Study of Homosexual Patterns* (New York, 1941), Vol. 1, pp. 5–10, 145, 168, 182, 217, 229, 240, 256, 301, 312, 340.
67 Ibid., pp. 229–30.
68 Ibid., p. 451.
69 Ibid., p. 435.
70 Ibid., pp. 117, 119, 127.
71 Ibid., pp. 127, 142, 184, 208, 219, 231, 242, 255–6, 283, 291, 303, 330, 342, 350, 477.
72 Ibid., pp. 132, 143, 192, 211, 221, 242, 254–5, 268, 296, 345, 477.
73 Ibid., p. 226.
74 Ibid., pp. 254–6.
75 H. Greenspan and J. D. Campbell, 'The homosexual as a personality type', *American Journal of Psychiatry*, 101 (1945), 682–9.
76 L. H. Loeser, 'The sexual psychopath in the military service', *American Journal of Psychiatry*, 102 (1945), 92–101.
77 C. Jackson, *The Lost Weekend* (New York, 1944). I am quoting from the London edition of 1945: Jackson, *Lost Weekend*, p. 135.
78 Ibid., p. 146.
79 Ibid., p. 140.

80 D. W. Cory, *The Homosexual in America: A Subjective Approach* (New York, 1951), pp. 60-4.
81 Ibid., pp. 111-12.
82 Ibid., p. 107.
83 Ibid., p. 63.
84 R. A. Darke and G. E. Geil, 'Homosexual activity: relation of degree and role to the Goodenough Test and to the Cornell Selectee Index', *Journal of Nervous and Mental Disease*, 108: 3 (1949), 217-40; H. W. Secor, 'Homosexuals known by their drawings', *Sexology*, July 1949.
85 R. Lindner, *Must You Conform?* (New York, 1960), pp. 34, 50. First published in 1955.
86 *Jack Benny Program*, 3 April 1955, available on YouTube: www.youtube.com/watch?v=3wNK1Jt4JLg.
87 Curtin, *We Can Always Call Them Bulgarians*, pp. 293-4. The quote is from W. Gibbs, *Season in the Sun* (New York, 1951), p. 27.
88 A. Miller, *Collected Plays 1944-1961* (New York, 2006), pp. 526, 527, 533, 534.
89 R. Anderson, *Tea and Sympathy* (New York, 1953), pp. 48, 70, 172.
90 See Curtin, *We Can Always Call Them Bulgarians*, p. 312.
91 See D. K. Johnson, *The Lavender Scare: The Cold War Persecution of Gays and Lesbians in the Federal Government* (Chicago, 2004).
92 Ibid., pp. 37, 47, 68, 69, 70, 89, 90, 121.
93 Ibid., p. 128.
94 J. Lait and L. Mortimer, *U.S.A. Confidential* (New York, 1952), pp. 44, 313.
95 Ibid., pp. 44-5.
96 J. Stearn, *The Sixth Man* (New York, 1963), p. vii. The book was first published in 1961.
97 Ibid., pp. 29, 123. However, examples can be found on many other pages: ibid., pp. 31, 33, 51, 52, 55, 75, 82, 84, 88, 91, 104, 114, 116-17, 121, 125, 147, 149, 157, 176, 180.
98 M. Meeker, *Contacts Desired: Gay and Lesbian Communications and Community, 1940s-1970s* (Chicago, 2006), ch. 4.
99 P. Welch and E. Havemann, 'Homosexuality in America', *Life*, 26 June 1964. The photographer was Bill Eppridge.
100 Meeker, *Contacts Desired*, pp. 152, 178-84.
101 *Life*, 26 June 1964.
102 Meeker, *Contacts Desired*, p. 165.
103 Ibid., p. 190.
104 T. Burke, 'The new homosexuality', *Esquire*, December 1969.
105 'The homosexual: newly visible, newly understood', *Time*, 31 October 1969.
106 J. Klemesrud, 'You don't have to be one to play one', *New York Times*, 29 September 1968.

107 Ibid.
108 V. Canby, 'Screen: "Boys in the Band"', *New York Times*, 18 March 1970.
109 S. Krim, *Views of a Nearsighted Cannoneer* (New York, 1961), p. 76.
110 S. B. Flexner, 'Preface', in H. Wentworth and S. B. Flexner (eds), *Dictionary of American Slang* (New York, 1960), p. vi.
111 Ibid., pp. 176, 203, 334, 351, 374, 415, 533.
112 *The Guild Dictionary of Homosexual Terms* (Washington, DC, 1965), p. 22.
113 P. M. Nardi and N. E. Stoller, '"Fruits", "fags", and "dykes": the portrayal of gay/lesbian identity in "nance" jokes of the '50s and '60s', *Journal of Homosexuality*, 55 (2008), 396, 397.
114 L. Bruce, *The Essential Lenny Bruce*, ed. J. Cohen (London, 1975), pp. 178, 180, 181.
115 A. Karlen, *Sexuality and Homosexuality: A New View* (New York, 1971), p. 101.
116 D. Reuben, *Everything You Always Wanted to Know About Sex – But Were Afraid to Ask* (New York, 1969), p. 129. David Allyn refers to it as 'one of the most inaccurate and misleading "sex education" books of all time': D. Allyn, *Make Love, Not War: The Sexual Revolution: An Unfettered History* (New York, 2001), p. 175. It was on the best-seller list for eighteen weeks.
117 W. Churchill, *Homosexual Behavior Among Males: A Cross-Cultural and Cross-Species Investigation* (Englewood Cliffs, NJ, 1971), p. 185. First published in 1967.
118 C. A. Tripp, *The Homosexual Matrix* (New York, 1987), p. 20. First published in 1975.
119 Ibid., pp. 20, 21.
120 Ibid., ch. 9.
121 M. Decter, 'The boys on the beach', *Commentary*, 70: 3 (1980), 35, 38–9. For Vidal, see G. Vidal, 'Some Jews and the gays', *The Nation*, 14 November 1981, pp. 508–17.
122 See D. Harris, 'A psychohistory of the homosexual body', in his *The Rise and Fall of Gay Culture* (New York, 1997), pp. 86–110; M. P. Levine, *Gay Macho: The Life and Death of the Homosexual Clone*, ed. M. S. Kimmel (New York, 1998), esp. chs 1–5. See also P. M. Nardi, '"Anything for a sis, Mary": an introduction to *Gay Masculinities*', in P. Nardi (ed.), *Gay Masculinities* (Thousand Oaks, CA., 2000), ch. 1; I. Tattelman, 'Staging sex and masculinity at the Mineshaft', *Men and Masculinities*, 7 (2005), 300–9.
123 Vidal, 'Some Jews and the gays', p. 514.
124 J. Loughery, *The Other Side of Silence: Men's Lives and Gay Identities: A Twentieth-century History* (New York, 1998), p. 393.
125 E. Hooker, 'Male homosexuals and their "worlds"', in J. Marmor (ed.), *Sexual Inversion: The Multiple Roots of Homosexuality* (New York, 1965), p. 102.

126 L. Humphreys, 'New styles in homosexual manliness', in J. A. McCaffrey (ed.), *The Homosexual Dialectic* (Englewood Cliffs, NJ, 1972), pp. 70-1. The piece first appeared in 1971.
127 S. Kleinberg, *Alienated Affections: Being Gay in America* (New York, 1980), pp. 145-6.
128 E. White, *States of Desire: Travels in Gay America* (New York, 1980), p. 268.
129 Ibid., p. 51.
130 J. Rechy, *Rushes* (New York, 1977), pp. 14, 26.
131 White, *States of Desire*, p. 253.
132 For example, M. P. Levine (ed.), *Gay Men: The Sociology of Male Homosexuality* (New York, 1979), pp. 1-2, 156-7, 193, 329-30.
133 See Marmor (ed.), *Sexual Inversion*; A. P. Bell and M. S. Weinberg, *Homosexualities: A Study of Diversity Among Men and Women* (New York, 1978).
134 R. W. Connell, 'A very straight gay: masculinity, homosexual experience, and the dynamics of gender', *American Sociological Review*, 57: 6 (1992), 736. Emphasis in original.
135 F. Valdes, 'Queers, sissies, dykes, and tomboys: deconstructing the conflation of "sex", "gender", and "sexual orientation" in Euro-American law and society', *California Law Review*, 83: 1 (1995), 7, 8.
136 A. Sinfield, *Gay and After* (London, 1998), pp. 57-8.
137 M. Canaday, *The Straight State: Sexuality and Citizenship in Twentieth-century America* (Princeton, 2009), pp. 12, 34-5, 37, 42, 62, 79, 82-3, 88, 100, 115, 147, 170 (for quote), 219, 239.
138 While Canaday recognizes that homosexuality at mid-century contained both the 'gender invert' and the 'normal' masculine man who had sex with men, by the end of the book these complexities have gone and homosexual sex indicates homosexual identity: 'one was either heterosexual or one was homosexual': ibid, pp. 12, 216. The two are not the same.
139 R. Dyer, *Now You See It: Studies on Lesbian and Gay Film* (London, 1990), pp. 140-1.
140 D. Rader, *Gov't Inspected Meat and Other Fun Summer Things* (New York, 1971), p. 197.
141 Ibid., pp. 3, 43, 44, 62-3, 74, 174, 196.
142 C. R. Stimpson, 'The Beat generation and the trials of homosexual liberation', *Salmagundi*, 58-9 (1982-1983), 378. For two recent accounts of the Beats that discuss their sexual attitudes, see R. Kozlovsky, 'Beat spaces', in B. Colomina, A. Brennan, and J. Kim (eds), *Cold War Hothouses: Inventing Postwar Culture, from Cockpit to Playboy* (New York, 2004), pp. 191-215; M. P. Carden, '"Adventures in auto-eroticism": economies of travelling masculinity in autobiographical texts by Jack Kerouac and Neal Cassady', *Journeys*, 7 (2006), 1-25.

143 J. C. Holmes, *Go* (New York, 1997), pp. 95, 119.
144 For example, M. Davidson, *Guys Like Us: Citing Masculinity in Cold War Poetics* (Chicago, 2004), pp. 46–8.
145 Quoted in J. Russell, *Queer Burroughs* (New York, 2001), p. 2. This book is the best account of Burroughs's antipathy to effeminacy: see especially, Introduction and ch. 1.
146 W. S. Burroughs, *The Letters of William S. Burroughs 1945–1959*, ed. O. Harris (New York, 1993), pp. 119–20.
147 Ibid., p. 298. See also p. 235 for further negative comment about a fairy: 'Beneath this camp, I can feel incredible evil.'
148 W. Burroughs, *Interzone* (New York, 1990), p. 93.
149 W. S. Burroughs, *Junky: The Definitive Text of 'Junk'*, ed. O. Harris (New York, 2003), p. 60.
150 W. S. Burroughs, *Naked Lunch: The Restored Text*, ed. J. Grauerholz and B. Miles (New York, 2001), pp. 53, 107. *Naked Lunch* was first published in Paris in 1959 and in New York 1962.
151 W. S. Burroughs, *Queer* (New York, 1987), p. 39. Emphasis in original.
152 Ibid., p. 27.
153 Russell, *Queer Burroughs*, pp. 20–1; Burroughs, *Queer*, p. 80.
154 C. M. Loftin, 'Unacceptable mannerisms: gender anxieties, homosexual activism, and swish in the United States, 1945–1965', *Journal of Social History*, 40 (2007), 577–96. See also J. T. Sears, *Behind the Mask of the Mattachine: The Hal Call Chronicles and the Early Movement for Homosexual Emancipation* (New York, 2006), pp. 404–5
155 Sears, *Behind the Mask of the Mattachine*, p. 448.
156 Quoted in Loftin, 'Unacceptable mannerisms', 581, 582. See also R. Streitmatter, *Unspeakable: The Rise of the Gay and Lesbian Press in America* (Boston, 1995), pp. 37, 38
157 Meeker, *Contacts Desired*, p. 35. See also his 'Behind the mask of respectability: reconsidering the Mattachine Society and male homophile practice, 1950s and 1960s', *Journal of the History of Sexuality*, 10: 1 (2001), 78–116.
158 Stearn, *Sixth Man*, p. 157.
159 M. Crowley, *The Boys in the Band* (Harmondsworth, 1970), pp. 27, 44. First published in New York in 1968.
160 J. Rechy, *City of Night* (New York, 1984), p. 22. First published in 1963.
161 C. Corley, *A Chosen World* (Agoura, CA, 1966), pp. 158–67. For further discussion of Corley, see J. Howard, *Men Like That: A Southern Queer History* (Chicago, 1999), pp. 192–220.
162 Corley, *A Chosen World*, p. 167.
163 See KI, The Thomas Painter Collection (hereafter, Painter), Box 1, Series 2, c. 1, Vol. 2: Painter Letters: 17 June, 24 June, 25 June, 13 July, and 17 July 1945. This is an episode in Painter's life glossed over in H. L. Minton's

    Departing from Deviance: A History of Homosexual Rights and Emancipatory Science in America (Chicago, 2002), pp. 133, 178.
164 Painter, Box 1, Series 2, c. 1, Vol. 18a: 28 May 1961.
165 Painter, Box 1, Series 2, c. 1, Vol. 18b: 28 July 1961.
166 Ibid., 22 August 1961.
167 G. Vidal, *Sexually Speaking: Collected Sex Writings* (San Francisco, 1999), pp. 131–2, 209, 215.
168 G. Vidal, *The City and the Pillar* (New York, 1948), pp. 90–1, 95–6, 100, 106, 138, 236, 242, 247, 268, 277, 287.
169 Ibid., p. 247. Compare G. Vidal, *The City and the Pillar* (New York, 1965), p. 179.
170 Compare Vidal, *The City and the Pillar* (1948), pp. 90–1, 95–6, 100, 106, 138, 236, 242, 247, 268, 277, 287, with Vidal, *The City and the Pillar* (1965), pp. 72, 75–6, 79, 83, 106, 174, 175, 179, 191, 197, 204.
171 Vidal, *The City and the Pillar* (1948), p. 302: Vidal, *The City and the Pillar* (1965), p. 214.
172 See R. J. Corber, *Homosexuality in Cold War America* (Durham, NC, 1997), p. 157. Corber's constant use of the word 'gay' when discussing this postwar culture clouds rather than sharpens his conceptual vision: see ibid., ch. 5.
173 R. J. Brown, *The Evening Crowd at Kirmser's: A Gay Life in the 1940s* (Minneapolis, MN, 2001), pp. 20, 23–4.
174 D. Vining, *A Gay Diary 1946–1954* (New York, 1980), p. 44.
175 Ibid., p. 111.
176 Ibid., p. 238.
177 New York Public Library Manuscripts and Archives Division, Donald Vining Papers, Box 2, Folder 6: 'The Unabashed', ch. 2, p. 17; ch. 3, p. 5.
178 M. Duberman, *The Worlds of Lincoln Kirstein* (New York, 2007), p. 33.
179 T. Williams, *Memoirs* (New York, 1975), p. 50.
180 Quoted in K. E. Silver. 'Modes of disclosure: the construction of gay identity and the rise of Pop Art', in R. Ferguson (ed.), *Hand-painted POP: American Art in Transition 1955–62* (Los Angeles, 1992), p. 193.
181 Cory, *The Homosexual in America*, p. 92.
182 G. Butt, *Between You and Me: Queer Disclosures in the New York Art World, 1948–1963* (Durham, NC, 2005), p. 113.
183 Rechy, *City of Night*, p. 284.
184 Ibid., p. 151.
185 Ibid., p. 89.
186 Ibid., pp. 101, 207.
187 Ibid., p. 102.
188 Russell, *Queer Burroughs*, pp. 86–7.
189 See Loftin, 'Unacceptable mannerisms', 577.
190 Painter, Box 1, Series 2, c. 1, Vol. 2: 19 August 1945.
191 Corley, *A Chosen World*, pp. 160–1.

192 A. J. Reiss, 'The social integration of queers and peers', *Social Problems*, 9 (1961), 102–20.
193 P. Rogers, *Saul's Book* (New York, 1983), pp. 27, 51.
194 G. Legman, 'The language of homosexuality: an American glossary', in G. W. Henry, *Sex Variants: A Study of Homosexual Patterns* (New York, 1941), Vol. 2, p. 1161.
195 KI, Thomas Painter, 'Male Homosexuals and Their Prostitutes in Contemporary America' (New York, 1941), Vol. 2: 'The Prostitute', pp. 101–2.
196 Painter, Box 1, Series 2, c. 1, Vol. 10: 18 April 1953.
197 G. Vidal, *Palimpsest: A Memoir* (London, 1996), pp. 231–3.
198 J. Kerouac, *On the Road*, 50th Anniversary Edition (New York, 2007), p. 210.
199 *Flesh* (1968: Paul Morrissey).
200 C. Kaiser, *The Gay Metropolis 1940–1996* (New York, 1997), p. 76.
201 J. Cheever, *The Letters of John Cheever*, ed. B. Cheever (New York, 1988), p. 359.
202 Ibid., pp. 300, 304, 338.
203 Ibid., p. 341. There is a comparable scene in his prison novel, *Falconer* (1975), when two prisoners become lovers: '"I'm so glad you ain't homosexual", Jody kept saying when he caressed Farragut's hair.' See J. Cheever, *Falconer* (London, 1977), p. 91.
204 For some examples of Cheever's hatred of effeminacy, which he saw as the essence of homosexuality, see B. Bailey, *Cheever: A Life* (New York, 2009), pp. 207, 480, 481, 543, 574, 594.
205 Cheever, *Letters*, p. 335.
206 J. Cheever, *The Journals of John Cheever*, ed. R. Gottlieb (New York, 2008), p. 219.

6

Hustler hustled

I went out at around six-thirty, for no good reason; in the Rue de Rennes noticed a new hustler, hair in his eyes, a tiny earring; since the Rue Bernard-Palissy was completely deserted, we discussed terms; his name was François; but the hotel was full; I gave him some money, he promised to be at the rendezvous an hour later, and of course never showed. I asked myself if I was really so mistaken (the received wisdom about giving money to a hustler *in advance!),* and concluded that since I really didn't want him all that much (nor even to make love), the result was the same: sex or no sex, at eight o'clock I would find myself back at the same point in my life; and since mere eye contact and an exchange of words eroticizes me, it was that pleasure I paid for. Later in the evening, at the Flore, not far from our table, another hustler, angelic with his long hair falling on either side of a part down the middle of his head; now and again he glances at me; I am attracted by the way his white shirt opens down his chest; he is reading *Le Monde* and drinking a Ricard, I think; he doesn't leave, finally smiles at me; he has coarse hands, which belie the sweetness and delicacy of the rest; it is from his hands that I deduce his hustlerdom (he ends up by leaving before we do; I stop him, because he smiles, and make a vague rendezvous). (Roland Barthes, 1979)[1]

Hustlers are for watching. In the epigraph above, Roland Barthes attested to the pleasure of eye contact and exchange of words with a hustler outweighing the joys of any actual physical connection. (Note also that the hint of 'rough' in this class-inflected trade lies in the hustler's hands.) Although the encounter occurred in Paris, and involves a French hustler, it captures the fantasy surrounding this figure. The actual sex becomes almost incidental. As the cruiser or the cruised, the hustler is the figure of desire in the highly charged yet not necessarily realized encounter.[2] It is an encounter that may take place in the street, but also on screen, stage, the written page, the photographic print, and in painting and sculpture.

Thomas Waugh has described the role of trade in the 'gay-male imaginary' of the 1960s, especially in the films of Andy Warhol, where, in the dualism of the effeminate queen versus the masculine hustler, trade is the object of desire (for both queens and women): the to-be-looked-at. 'The queen looks, the trade is looked at.'[3] This visual consuming of the ostensibly heterosexual male star by both the viewer outside the film and the actors in the film, that is, on and off screen, is a feature of Warhol-influenced films, as we will see. In *Bike Boy* (1967–68), Joe Spencer, as Jennifer Doyle puts it, 'is explicitly offered up as a spectacle for our enjoyment'.[4]

For the hustler and trade are surprisingly ubiquitous in the literary and visual arts of postwar America.[5] As we have seen, the hustler stars in several iconic movies from the 1960s and early 1970s: the real hustlers Paul America in Andy Warhol's *My Hustler* (1965) and Joe Dallesandro in Paul Morrissey's *Flesh* (1968), the acting hustlers Jon Voight in John Schlesinger's *Midnight Cowboy* (1969), and Robert La Tourneaux, in William Friedkin's *The Boys in the Band* (1970), who later reputedly really had to hustle in order to survive.[6]

There were literary explorations too: *Midnight Cowboy* was based on James Leo Herlihy's 1965 novel of the same name, far more bitingly evocative than its film adaptation.[7] But Herlihy's hustler novel was not the first in the genre. Charles Wright's *The Messenger* (1963), a powerful first-person narrative of an African-American from Missouri trying to survive in New York, is also about a hustler.[8] So too is K. B. Raul's lesser work *Naked to the Night* (1964), though his protagonist has to die as warning to heterosexual youth.[9] Duke Custis, the teenage African-American gang leader in Warren Miller's *The Cool World* (1957), hustles in Central Park in an effort to get the cash to buy a gun; he has a childhood friend who is a 'kept boy' in a big building in the 70s on the East Side ('Did I tell you Duke I got 2 suits an 2 sport jackets with side vents?').[10] Times Square hustlers, in the form of Puerto Rican gang members no less, make a fleeting appearance in Paul Goodman's *Making Do* (1963), a novel about early 1960s academics and anarchists who slip easily between homosexual and heterosexual sex. The story's Harold is a Thomas Painter-like character who befriends the hustlers (car thieves and burglars) who end up robbing him.[11]

One of the principal narrative strands of *The Occasional Man* (1966), a novel by James Barr, involves a prolonged exploration of the attraction and repulsion of rough trade, men who alternate between homosexual oral sex and heterosexual sex with minors, appreciate the homosexual's lingual technique – 'you're better than a woman' – and ability to provide money and sustenance, and think nothing of such encounters – '"You ever let a queer go down on you, Gus?" "Sure, who ain't?"'[12] Hustlers also get an occasional mention in the Beat writer and literary editor Irving Rosenthal's *Sheeper* (1967): 'he scoreth with hustlers one time apiece only, visions of love and skin, sweet confidence'.[13]

And, as we are aware, a male prostitute speaks directly in the 1960s and 1970s literary interventions of John Rechy, whose hustling becomes a form of sexual revolution: 'He prepares his body for the hunt. A dancer at the bar. A boxer in the ring. Prepares ritualistically for the next three days of outlaw sex. The arena will be streets, parks, alleys, tunnels, garages, movie arcades, bathhouses, beaches, movie backrows, tree-sheltered avenues, late-night orgy rooms, dark yards.'[14]

The New York hustler is there on stage too in Lanford Wilson's *Balm in Gilead* (1965), set in New York's Needle Park and first performed at the Café La Mama Experimental Theatre Club, an Off-Off-Broadway venue.[15] As Cowboy, 'a midnight cowboy' hired as a birthday present and subjected to ongoing jokes about his brainlessness and beauty, the male prostitute has a minor (inter textual) part in Mart Crowley's *The Boys in the Band* (1968).[16] He has roles in long-forgotten productions – for example, Chuck, the 'midnight cowboy' (the phrase was infectious) in Ted Harris's *Silhouettes* (1969), who spends the entire play in bed, the object of affection for both a middle-aged woman and a homosexual man, and Erich, the male prostitute in Dennis Turner's *The Rapists* (1972), played by the already typecast Robert La Tourneaux.[17]

The hustler even appears in popular music in Lou Reed's reference to Joe Dallesandro:

> Little Joe never once gave it away
> Everybody had to pay and pay
> A hustle here and a hustle there
> New York City is the place where they said
> Hey babe, take a walk on the wild side
> I said hey Joe, take a walk on the wild side . . .[18]

The hustler provoked both horror and fascination in the pulp exposés of the 1960s, and there is almost little point in reading further than the covers. 'No details of this sordid vice are spared' was the promise of Johnny Shearer's *The Male Hustler* (1966), a not untypical example of the genre, 'Stud: The sex-hardened kid who has seen a million perverted images in a thousand bedrooms and felt the hot mouths of 10,000 lustful queers nibbling at his body.'[19] 'He was young, tough and beautiful . . . a prize stud in the shadowy underworld of strange sex and macabre pleasures' was the pitch for potential readers of *McCaffery* (1970), a rather dire reissued 1960s pulp about a New York male prostitute.[20] 'On Sunset Strip, Kenny was known as a wild piece of "rough trade". Five bucks and a shower, no need to scrub your own back': purchasers would have been disappointed given the lure of the cover, for the delightfully named Kenny Strange in *Queer Hustler* (1965) actually had little to do with male-to-male sex.[21] The hustler was an object of fantasy in gay adult fiction like *$tud* (1969), *My Brother, the Hustler* (1971), *San Francisco Hustler* (1971), and *Renegade Hustler* (1972). Samuel Steward listed nearly eighty such works, including his own, published during the period 1965–85.[22]

'I should like to start some sort of school for young men, a school where I would teach them how to make the most of certain situations which otherwise, due to inexperience and vanity, they badly mismanage. They are usually too truculent, too unbending.' Thus mused Michael, a fictional young man on the make in Key West. The best tactic when with a quarry was 'not to talk at all, to remain silent and smiling, enigmatic, waiting for the moment to assume the character of the other's dream'.[23] Gore Vidal's finely crafted short stories of masculine homosexuality have their hustlers, the 'cold and defiant angels', 'treacherous angels', liable to 'fall from beloved angel to treacherous monster'.[24] Mostly they are middle and up-market types, like the aforementioned Michael, posing as a former Princeton footballer, and the opiate-raddled Texan male prostitute, Elliott Magren, the consort of European aristocrats.[25] Rough trade is a backdrop (beautiful but dangerous sailors) rather than a focus of his fiction.[26] (Thomas Painter's hustlers knew all about other people's dreams, though they were unlikely to remain enigmatic in their understanding!)

Tennessee Williams's novella *The Roman Spring of Mrs. Stone* (1950) begins and ends with a hustler or gigolo (it is set in Rome), poor but beautiful, standing like a statue waiting for an offer. And the tale itself is about a wealthy American, Mrs Stone, and another young man, Paolo, who lives far more prosperously off both men and women, 'a boy who has no work and no money but lives very well without them'.[27] (Warren Beatty played Paolo in the 1961 film by José Quintero.)

Unsurprisingly, young men who sell their bodies have roles in other

Williams short stories and plays: the indistinguishable trade in 'Two on a party' (1954), about Cora and Billy and the various sailors that they share; the unnamed, beautiful youth in 'Hard candy' (1954); Christopher Flanders in *The Milk Train Doesn't Stop Here Anymore* (1964), played by Tab Hunter in the New York production; the two leather-jacketed hustlers in *Now and at the Hour of Our Death* (1970), one of Williams's lesser-known dramas; Bill McCorkle, the heterosexual hustler in the play *Small Craft Warnings* (1972) ('He has a name for his thing. He calls it Junior. He says he takes care of Junior and Junior takes care of him . . . Thinks the sun rises and sets between his legs'); Jack Jones, the 'extraordinarily well paid' bellhop in 'Miss Coynte of Greene' (1973); Clove, the hilarious, though scary, 'killer chicken' in 'The killer chicken and the closet queen' (1978); Tye – 'No goddam faggot messes with me, never! For less'n a hundred dollars!' – in the play *Vieux Carré* (1977); and Karl, the hustling merchant seaman in Williams's posthumous *And Tell Sad Stories of the Deaths of Queens . . .* (2005), who uses the money he gets from queens ('You can have what you want, now, for ten dollars') to purchase women and drink.[28] A hustler-priest, blond, tight-jeaned, and threatening to expose himself, is the main character in the playwright's fragmented *Kirche, Kutchen und Kinder (an outrage for the stage)*, performed (as a work in progress) in New York in 1979. 'His costume is the kind commonly worn by young male hustlers' was Williams's scene description.[29]

The best-known of these literary hustlers, however, is Oliver Winemiller in 'One arm', the story of a former sailor and boxer who took up male prostitution after he lost his arm in an accident, condemned to electrocution for killing and robbing a client. The young man, who had once relied on his physical strength and skill with his fists, was reduced to trading on his remaining bodily attributes. 'Now he looked like a broken statue of Apollo, and he had also the coolness and impassivity of a stone figure.' Like some real-life hustlers (and indeed the two protagonists in *Midnight Cowboy*), Williams's character lived in New York in the summer, moving south to Miami when the cold set in. It was said that he was based on a hustler the author had encountered in New Orleans's Canal Street in the late 1930s.[30]

Then there is Williams's literary rough trade. In one of his later plays, *Kingdom of Earth* (1968), the crude masculinity of Chicken, with his large hands and bulging crotch, is posited against the effeminacy of his frail, bleached-blond, half-brother Lot, who, on his own admission, looks like a 'fairy'.[31] Though the dramatic interactions of Chicken and his like are principally with women, their raw masculinity and sexuality is of the kind associated with trade. Williams's notes for Stanley Kowalski in *A Streetcar Named Desire* (1947) state that 'Animal joy in his being is implicit in all his attitudes and movements' and that his easy sexuality determined all his interactions, or, as his creator wrote, 'all the auxiliary channels of his life'.[32] (See Figure 43.) It is puzzling why

43. Marlon Brando as Stanley Kowalski in Elia Kazan's 1952 film version of Tennessee Williams's *A Streetcar Named Desire*. © Bettmann/CORBIS.

critics who discuss this playwright's homosexuality focus on his fictional women rather than their men.[33] The desires being conveyed were more straightforward than mere ventriloquism. A string of male leads in the stage and film versions of Williams's plays and short fiction – a veritable roll-call of heterosexual idols – conveyed precisely the homoeroticism associated with trade that blended same- and opposite-sex sexualities: Marlon Brando and Ralph Meeker as Stanley Kowalski in *A Streetcar Named Desire* (1947 and 1951); Ben Gazzara and then Paul Newman as Brick Pollitt in *Cat on a Hot Tin Roof* (1955 and 1958); Burt Lancaster as Alvaro Mangiacavallo in *The Rose Tattoo* (1955); Cliff Robertson and Marlon Brando as Val Xavier in *Orpheus Descending* (1957) – 'I learned that I had something to sell besides snakeskins' – and its film version *The Fugitive Kind* (1959); and Paul Newman as Chance Wayne in *Sweet Bird of Youth* (1959), the young man in white silk pyjamas, with 'the kind of body that white silk pajamas are, or ought to be, made for', who made a living by his love-making, 'I gave people more than I took'.[34] When trade literally consumes Sebastian Venable in *Suddenly Last Summer* (1958 and 1959), conceivably it is an exaggerated metaphor of the dangers of such sexual interaction rather than the open homosexual self-loathing that some critics take it as.[35] Dismissing Williams's drama as closeted is to miss the historical sexual context entirely.[36] Searching for an 'unequivocally homosexual character', likewise, is a futile search.[37] The critic who came closest to understanding the playwright's perspective was one who was writing contemporaneously. 'The play', he observed of *Cat on a Hot Tin Roof*, 'is really about that shadowy no-man's-land between hetero- and homosexuality.'[38]

There is also a study to be written on the role of the hustler and trade in modern American art.[39] Edward Melcarth does not appear in the published memoirs of either Tennessee Williams or Gore Vidal, but both were acquainted with the artist and his close friend, Thomas Painter, who had the same fondness for hustlers and trade and swapped photographs and contacts in the 1940s and 1950s.[40] The artist once said that he needed daily sex for his creativity, cruising every night 'like a mad thing', sometimes all night, leaving little time for actual work![41] Melcarth's art is saturated with hustler imagery. He used hustlers and trade as models, helpers, and sexual partners (he did not distinguish between the roles). Ironically, Melcarth is best known for designing and manufacturing the Peggy Guggenheim surrealist sunglasses, the labour for which was provided by these very helpers.[42] One of Melcarth's planned works of a union picket portrayed as the fallen Christ was modelled on a sailor that he had picked up. Trade as Jesus Christ is an interesting juxtaposition that provides an added dimension to American socialist art (Melcarth was a communist).[43] It was a theme continued in *Last Supper* (1962), his most intriguing work, with trade as Christ and the Apostles. If the iconography of gay visual culture can be divided into the classical and that of 'the rougher physical types', then Melcarth combined categories.[44] (See Figures 44–47.)

Melcarth is not an especially well-known artist – and his sculpture and photography are arguably superior to his painting – but his art sets the scenes both in a 1972 article on the Chelsea Hotel rooms of the composer Virgil Thomson (Thomson owned a sculptured head of a hustler) and in one of the very first celebrity 'outings', that of the billionaire Malcolm Forbes in 1990.[45] Forbes, the owner of *Forbes* magazine, purchased several of Melcarth's 1960s paintings of working-class

44. Edward Melcarth, sculpture of heroic (hustler) head, 1968. Author's collection.

45. An Italian-American hustler, 1950. From the Thomas Painter Collection. Reproduced by permission of The Kinsey Institute for Research in Sex, Gender, and Reproduction, Inc. Author's note: the man is standing in front of a painting by Edward Melcarth and one of Melcarth's sculptured, heroic hustler heads (like the one in Figure 44).

masculinity, including *Manhole* (men at the entrance to a manhole), *Trouble* (youth at Coney Island), *Movers* (men carrying a heavy box), and *Last Supper*.[46] (He also owned Paul Cadmus's *Shore Leave* (1933) and *Sailors and Floosies* (1938) – described earlier (see Figures 15 and 16) – before gifting them to the Whitney Museum of American Art.) A 1967 Melcarth mural, worked on by the artist and his assistants, still forms the back-drop in the rotunda of New York's Hotel Pierre.[47]

This aesthetic was not limited to the artistic fringe. Trade flits in and out of the famous artist and filmmaker Andy Warhol's 1960s *Screen Tests*.[48] We can see it in the never-named, leather-jacketed young man

46. Hustler, 1950s. Collection of Richard Taddei, New York. Author's note: the man has been photographed (hustler-like) in front of a mirror. The light, in the shape of a torch-bearing arm with flexed biceps, another example of trade imagery, was one of Edward Melcarth's creations. The photograph was taken by Melcarth.

in *Blow Job* (1964) whose face is shown for a full forty-one minutes at silent speed as he is fellated by those of unknown number or gender.[49] (See Figure 48.) Douglas Crimp has observed that the true withholding in the film is not the fact we never see the oral sex but the fact that

47. Edward Melcarth, *Last Supper*, 1962. Oil on canvas, 40 × 44 in. Private Collection, New York. Photography by Camerarts, Ali Elai.

the viewer cannot visually connect with the man: 'We cannot make eye contact. We cannot look into this man's eyes ... We cannot take sexual possession of him.'[50] Crimp cleverly contrasts the trade in Warhol's *Blow Job* with the seductive performance of the transvestite Mario Montez in Warhol's *Mario Banana* (1964), the blowjob that we *do* see (of a banana) and where eye contact is definitely made.[51] The former is detached, performed upon, and oblivious to emotional connection: the latter seduces and beckons. The trade in *Blow Job*, regardless of whether the man was a 'real' hustler, resides in his actions and demeanour as well as with his haircut and the collar of his leather jacket.

Trade also appears in person or similitude in the form of Warhol's numerous 'boys'. Wayne Koestenbaum has noted the visual appearances of some of Warhol's assistants: the gangster's son Victor Giallo, who looked 'like friendly "rough trade"'; and the poet Gerard Malanga, with the face of 'a seraphic piece of trade – a slim, versifying Brando', the heterosexual who has homosexual sex in *Couch* (1964), another Warhol film.[52] Philip Fagan, a short-term Warhol boyfriend, was a tattooed ex-marine.[53]

Warhol's censored mural *Thirteen Most Wanted Men* (1964), with its images of gangster masculinity, and his linked film *Thirteen Most Beautiful Boys* proclaimed desires that should now have significance for the readers of this book. While Richard Meyer has eloquently located the same-sex desire that informs these examples of Warhol's visual art, he has not quite captured the importance of its trade aesthetic. *Thirteen Most Wanted Men* was explicit rather than connotative in its message: hence, one assumes, the censoring. Whereas Meyer has referred to the suppression of the visibility of homosexuality, I am suggesting that – for the knowing – it was precisely the opposite.[54] (See Figure 49.)

48. The unknown star of *Blow Job* (1964).

A case could be argued that what I have termed the trade aesthetic exerted an influence wider than Warhol's boys and Tennessee Williams's rough heterosexuals. Van Hefflin and then Robert Duvall as Eddie Carbone in Arthur Miller's *A View from the Bridge* (1955 and 1965) and Ralph Meeker and William Holden, respectively, as Hal Carter in the stage and film versions of William Inge's *Picnic* (1953 and 1955) exhibit the same type of masculinity.⁵⁵ In his scene instructions Inge originally envisaged Carter as younger than the more-than-thirty-year-olds who played him: 'an exceedingly handsome, husky youth dressed in T-Shirt, dungarees and cowboy boots. In a past era he would have been called a vagabond, but Hal today is usually referred to as a bum.'⁵⁶ It is a familiar profile. In the play, Carter claims that when he was picked up by two women in a convertible while hitch-hiking ('Get in, stud!') he paid them for the ride with sex – 'this is the easiest way I know'.⁵⁷ Such archetypes of masculinity, engaged in heterosexual interactions, recur in Inge's early 1950s plays: the rugged, leather-jacketed cowboy Bo in *People in the Wind*; the young coast guard of 'almost god-like handsomeness' in *Memory of Summer*; the sailor Bus Riley in *Bus Riley's Back in Town* ('I'm in this business now strictly for kicks, Doll'); another sailor in *The Mall*; and the taxicab driver in *An Incident at the Standish Arms*, a 'big dark

49. *Thirteen Most Wanted Men No. 11 John Joseph H.* (1964) © Andy Warhol.

man of rough good looks' who is not adverse to taking his fares in kind: 'Look, baby, this happens to me a lot.'[58]

The attraction of youthful trade is obviously a factor in the appeal of the star James Dean. Michael De Angelis has analysed Dean's allure as a gay fantasy figure but surely it was more direct than the kind of displaced desire for identification with rebellion that he argues for.[59] The

50. James Dean and Frank Mazzola in *Rebel Without a Cause* (1955). © Bettmann/CORBIS.

lure, quite simply, was Dean as trade. The young gang members in *Rebel Without a Cause* (1955) were admired less as proxy homosexual rebels than as leather-jacketed heterosexuals, even allowing for the meaningful glances and homosexual subtexts. One of the cast, Frank Mazzola, was a member of a real gang.[60] (See Figure 50.) The same could be argued for the appeal of Tony Curtis and Mickey Knox in the earlier gang film, *City Across the River* (1949). Frances Negrón-Muntaner has written of the homoerotics of the gang musical, the Hollywood classic *West Side Story* (1961), with its Puerto Rican gang subject matter and the potential for 'gay spectators' to be able to 'enjoy the surfaces of rough trade without any of the risks'.[61] The roughness of the trade is further smoothed by what Negrón-Muntaner terms 'a musical feast of gay style'.[62] They are, after all, dancing Jets and Sharks.

Juan A. Suárez's identification of the biker and sailor in the underground cinema of Kenneth Anger, and the role of such figures in what he terms 'the iconography of homosexual desire', locates these icons – and understands the significance of the combined violence and eroticism

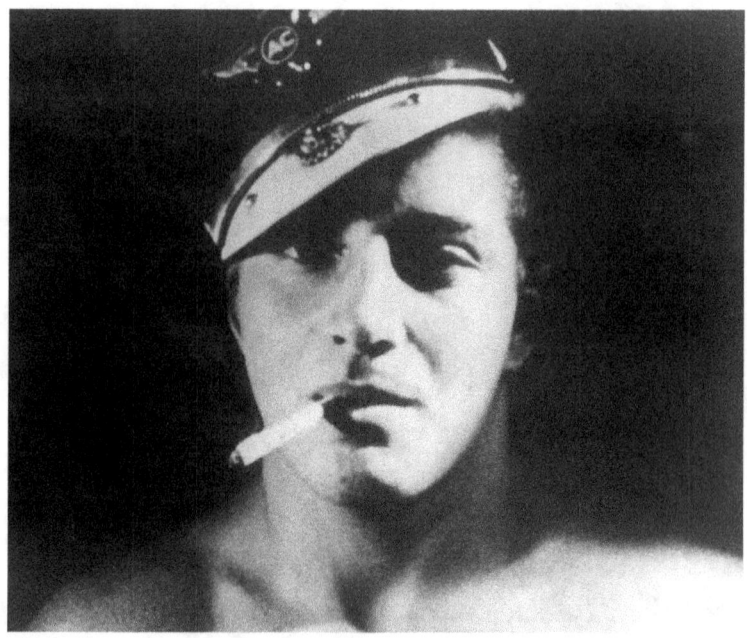

51. Victor Childe in Kenneth Anger's *Scorpio Rising* (1964). Photofest. Author's note: the word written on the cigarette is 'youth'.

– without fully explaining (or even naming) their role as *trade* in this sexual economy.[63] Suarez's discussion of cultural contestation, gay affirmation, the role of camp, and even Nazi influences treats this imagery as a novel construction, fashioned out of the elements of popular culture rather than the reflection of sexual practices and desires that I am stressing.[64] The lure of trade explains most of this imagery. Brando and Dean, as we have seen, already represented more than 'youth rebellion'.[65] Anger's avant-gardism is not really so avant-garde. (See Figure 51.)

Richard Hickock and Perry Smith, the murderers immortalized by Truman Capote in his book *In Cold Blood* (1966), were not hustlers as far as we know, though their time in prison and general delinquency corresponded to a familiar profile, and their appearance, captured in *Life* magazine in 1966 in photographs by Richard Avedon, conformed to the hustler aesthetic. Avedon's lens, with his trademark white backdrop and expert lighting, captures the men's tattoos, presenting bodies more akin to the homoerotic photography of Melcarth and Painter than any police mug shot.[66] Hickock reportedly said to the photographer, who was lingering over his tattoos, 'be patient. Maybe they'll send you my skin . . . later.'[67] The research notes for Capote's masterpiece, compiled by both Harper Lee and Capote, linger, like Avedon's camera, on the murderers' bodies: Hickock's dot tattoo under his right eye, the Lansing prison 'fraternity pin', identifiable by members of the club; and their other tattoos, some self-made, others carefully wrought – crosses, tigers, a dagger, a dagger with serpent, the words PEACE, MOTHER, DAD, and COOKIE ('a girl I once knew').[68] While not always flattering to their subjects, the researchers sexualize them. Death and sex intertwine like the serpent and the dagger on Perry Smith's arm. The killers reputedly said that preparation for the murders was 'like a long fuck'.[69] Smith was 'attracted' to Hickock in prison because he and his friends were 'all the more masculine type'.[70] Smith, an ex-marine, told Capote that he had been pursued by queers all his life.[71] The writer noted that he was 'one of those types (au M. Brando) who "sees" homosexuals everywhere, and is convinced that he is ever the object of their desire', whether in the merchant marine or in prison.[72] Smith had spent a winter in a hotel off 42nd Street in 1955, hiding out from the FBI, so was probably familiar with the hustling world.[73] And the attraction of trade may explain Capote's fascination with the murderers. Ned Rorem thought that Capote was in love with Perry Smith.[74]

We can even argue for trade's role in the student protest of the late 1960s and early 1970s – at least as relayed by a participant, the writer and former student radical Dotson Rader. Rader, also a self-claimed former hustler and friend of Tennessee Williams, was not above a little literary hustling so it is never clear how much of his work is pure fabrication. In one anecdote, the radical Abbie Hoffman talks politics with Tennessee Williams, while a hustler-pusher, Rader's friend, fondled his own nipples. 'Abbie and Tennessee talked of revolution . . . while a hustler sat stoned on the floor playing with himself.'[75] Rader's collection of essays, *Blood Dues* (1973), is steeped in a kind of posturing masculinity ('I was a joy-boy and violence was the john').[76] Fancifully, he compared hustling to radical street violence: 'to fuck another man was to gamble with your manhood as surely as you wagered it in political confrontation. That too was a kind of lovemaking between men.'[77] And we may be sceptical of his claim that he was drawn into activism by the plight of the hustler and his like, 'all the youths who have no place in postindustrial America', those with no place in society, 'America done over and lost'.[78] However, Rader writes interestingly of the 'rough-trade tough guy number' of the American male radicals and their appeal to rich left-liberals:

there was a strong sexual element at work. Radicals like myself, through media-created environments, were given a violent image. And since in America violence was so often associated with courage (it was in my mind) and therefore with manhood, there was a definite aura of slumming sexuality around radical males. That should not have been surprising, since the tradition of sexually slumming beneath and outside your class was strong among the leisure classes in the West, most clearly to be seen in the piss-elegant homosexual's taste for rough trade.[79]

The reputed lure of trade was surprisingly pervasive.

'You're a man, friend, a workin' man. The real McCoy', says the narrator of a hustling story in Phil Andros's *$tud* (1969), 'A real sexy stud and they can all smell it, every one. It scares half of 'em to death and makes the other half so dry in the mouth they can't talk. You been just with girls before this, huh?'[80] Those attracted to the masculine-presented hustlers were quite clear about their appeal. Painter summarized his preferences in a letter in 1944: 'I have a psychotic admiration for virility... I like the forceful, devil-may care bravado and abandon, the uninhibited freedom of strong, independent youth... The physical manifestation of this is admiration of the strong, muscular virile body... the tough, rough, careless, uninhibited, freedom-loving boy of the lower classes, especially seamen and tramps.'[81] He interpreted his desires in terms of a mix of the masculine and feminine, craved contrasts that existed within as well as between bodies, but where (unlike the fairy prostitute) the masculine prevailed. Painter was sensitive to the combinations of hardness and vulnerability in his objects of desire: the psychological softness inhabiting a brutal body; the muscularity beneath a silky skin.[82] What these men had in common, apart from their availability, was their ostensible masculinity and youth. Rechy's invented prose – 'youngmanoutofajob', 'youngmanlostinthebigcity' – reveals more than it intends; the hustler as 'youngman' was pivotal to his appeal.[83] The perfect combination of youth and masculinity was to be found in the bodies of the hustlers and others of that milieu. Kenneth Anger's biker consuming the cigarette with 'youth' written along it had a certain symbolism (see Figure 51).

There is a moment in the novel *Midnight Cowboy* when Joe Buck first arrives in New York, planning to live by his body. He grasps his crotch, and, though the text is no respecter of such silences, mutters under his breath: 'I'm gonna take hold of this thing and I'm gonna swing it like a lasso and I'm gonna rope in this whole fuckin' island.'[84] The hustler's identity rested with his bodily appeal. He was a sexual object.

The hustler's objectification – until the end of the film he is referred to as 'it' rather than by name – is represented perfectly in the form of *My Hustler*'s Paul America, 'that blond maniac, beautiful god'. Watching permeates the whole film. We watch the desirers watching Paul, and watch him ourselves as he preens and strokes his body on the beach and, later, in front of the bathroom mirror. For his client Ed and his neighbour Genevieve the hustler is in the distance (the camera reminds us of their emotional detachment), but for us he is close up. In the bathroom scene, Paul and Joe (an older, experienced hustler) talk about their teeth and dentists, sports, and eventually hustling, in a prolonged, though modest, display of male bodies. They shower, shave, urinate, deodorize, dowse with cologne, clean their ears, brush their teeth. 'You have a very nice body.' 'Do you work out?' Joe admires Paul while Paul admires himself. The whole scene takes place in front of the bathroom mirror, enabling the camera to consume the hustler's body back and front. 'You've got a beautiful body, you know that!' The veteran advises the novice while at the same time trying to hustle him. Joe strokes the younger hustler's back and massages him while discussing the rewards of being paid for sex.[85] (See Figure 52.) The hustling seems to have been operating at more than

52. Paul America (reflected in the mirror) in *My Hustler* (1965).

one level. Paul America claimed that he had been on LSD for the one-day shoot, had no idea what the film was about, and 'thought I was just going through some practice motions'.[86] The critic Parker Tyler observed that the film could have been called *The Hustler Hustled*.[87] Paul America may have had the last laugh. The gossip was that, hustler-like, he had stolen from the art collection of the New York art curator and associate of Warhol, Henry Geldzahler.[88]

The camera in Morrissey's *Flesh* likewise focuses on a hustler's body, that of the 1960s icon Joe Dallesandro. With Dallesandro, writes David James, 'the distance between himself and his body, isolated as an object of visual consumption and of promised though always deferred physical consumption for the audience and the john, produces the extreme passiveness of both his role as a stud and his style as an actor'.[89] Morrissey's film, a product of Andy Warhol's Factory, was a ninety-minute lingering over the hustler's body as he went about his daily way of providing a living for his wife and child. Indeed the film opens with a side close-up of Dallesandro's sleeping face, and then his naked body from the rear, pausing either on his face or his body for over three minutes. The camera is nearly always on Joe, whether it is his cock, torso, legs, face, nipple, armpit, or tattoo. It cruises him on the street, scanning upwards: lingering briefly on his blue-jeaned crotch, belt, black T-shirt, open light-blue shirt, and red bandana. Joe poses naked as a Greek statue. He is fellated by a topless dancer, Geri Miller, who later dangles her breasts in his eyes. He is cuddled, admired and then visually devoured by a transvestite, the brilliant Jackie Curtis. (See Figure 53.) Curtis's visual attention upstages Miller's oral ministrations, though typically we never actually see the latter. Joe is caressed ('We're not queers') and then blown by a Korean War veteran. And, finally, he is undressed, admired ('there it is... do you like it, Patti?'), and stroked yet again by his wife and her girlfriend after he returns home after a day of hustling.[90] As Jennifer Doyle has observed, 'Often it appears as if most of the energy expended in the film goes into consuming Joe Dallesandro.'[91] Critics have argued that the audience is placed in the position of the john, paying to watch the hustler – and that Warhol and Morrissey were, in effect, pimping Dallesandro.[92]

This favoured masculinity was presented both clothed and naked. Hustlers certainly paraded their looks on the street. New York hustlers in the 1930s were said to be of two types: the 'roughly dressed' and the 'smooth', clad, respectively, in jeans and suits. Painter's unpublished history of the prewar period contains a very early reference to the specialist tastes referred to in *Midnight Cowboy* (cited earlier) and familiar

53. Jackie Curtis visually consumes Joe Dallesandro in Paul Morrissey's *Flesh* (1968).

in the homosexual representations of the 1960s and 1970s: clothing suggesting 'the virile occupations of seamen, truck driver, cowboy, cyclist, soldier, sailor, laborer, etc'. This was the masculine garb of dungarees, blue jeans, short-sleeved summer polo shirts, caps, studded belts, and boots. It was, as we have seen, the clothing of trade.[93]

The other look was that of the suited 'smooth' hustler found in bars and on the street. Painter warned of a 'cheap and flashy' look, of the way in which a man's shoes were a test of his 'economic status', and how suede footwear on hustlers usually indicated a gift from a homosexual john! And yet the suited look portrayed a hard masculinity, clear from the photographs in Painter's archive, even if he did not bother to analyse it. (See Figure 54.) The 1930s representations in the photographs earlier in this book proclaim a gangster look of hard masculinity equal to the appeal of any working man's attire. Both the 'rough' and the 'smooth' hustler transmitted a masculinity that appealed to those interested in same-sex encounters: 'those who wish to dominate masculinity and those who wish to be dominated by it'.[94]

Dotson Rader's hustlers, we will see, wore 'tight whites and levis,

54. New York hustler, 1945. From the Thomas Painter Collection. Reproduced by permission of The Kinsey Institute for Research in Sex, Gender, and Reproduction, Inc. Author's note: the man, who was a former New Jersey gangster and heroin addict, lived with Painter in the 1930s.

laundry packed bulking around the meat'.[95] It was said that some hustlers of the 1930s tailored their jeans tight to outline the buttocks, thighs and genitals.[96] Others wrapped a handkerchief around their penis or used a water-filled condom or a banana down their pants to indicate hidden masculine promise.[97] This part of the male anatomy is certainly outlined in William Gedney's 1960s photographs of the young New York hustler, lounging, open shirted, in tight white trousers, much as described by Rader.[98] (See Figure 55.) But the young men in some of the surviving photographs from the 1950s and 1960s proclaimed a less obviously phallic masculinity. As we saw, while it is true that these photographs of hustlers show young men with their torsos exposed through transparent or opened clothing, the important point is that theirs was the clothing of working-class youth.

The visibility of the fairy and the transvestite resided in their paraded male femininity. One might say that their queerness was apparent to queer and straight alike. But the proclaimed masculinity of trade was less obvious. Their revealed flesh might be a mercenary homosexual lure or it could represent the courtship preening of a young man seeking female sex. The masculine attire could indicate pandering to a fetish or it may merely be occupational dress. Painter's 1940s history had been hesitant when it came to the hustler's 'recognition factors'. They were better looking than most young men. They tended to extremes of prettiness and virility, and were young (late teens or twenties). Their clothing was identifiable but, as intimated, it was also the garb of large sections of the male population. The hustler loitered as if not waiting for anything in particular, but then so did many other non-hustlers. In a sense, the confusion did not matter, given that many 'normal' working-class men were equally approachable for casual sex. (Ultimately, it was the gaze that was the main determiner of availability: 'the hustler's eyes'. The hustler returned the gaze.)[99]

Hustlers also displayed their looks more nakedly in the photographs that were often taken as mementos and passed around. (See Figures 56 and 57.) The 'Professor' in Rechy's *City of Night*, based on an unnamed 'very well-known figure' and friend of Gore Vidal and Truman Capote, likewise had an album of photographs of 'several sailors, servicemen, various youngmen in trunks: all staring at the world with a look strangely in common: a look which at first I thought was a coldness behind the smile and then realized must be a kind of muted despair, a franticness to get what the world had offered others and not extended readily to them'.[100] Melcarth, Painter, and Henry Faulkner all had extensive hustler and trade photographic collections, drawn on in this book.

New York hustlers

55. Male hustler, 1967. William Gedney Photographs: New York. Duke University Rare Book, Manuscript, and Special Collections Library.

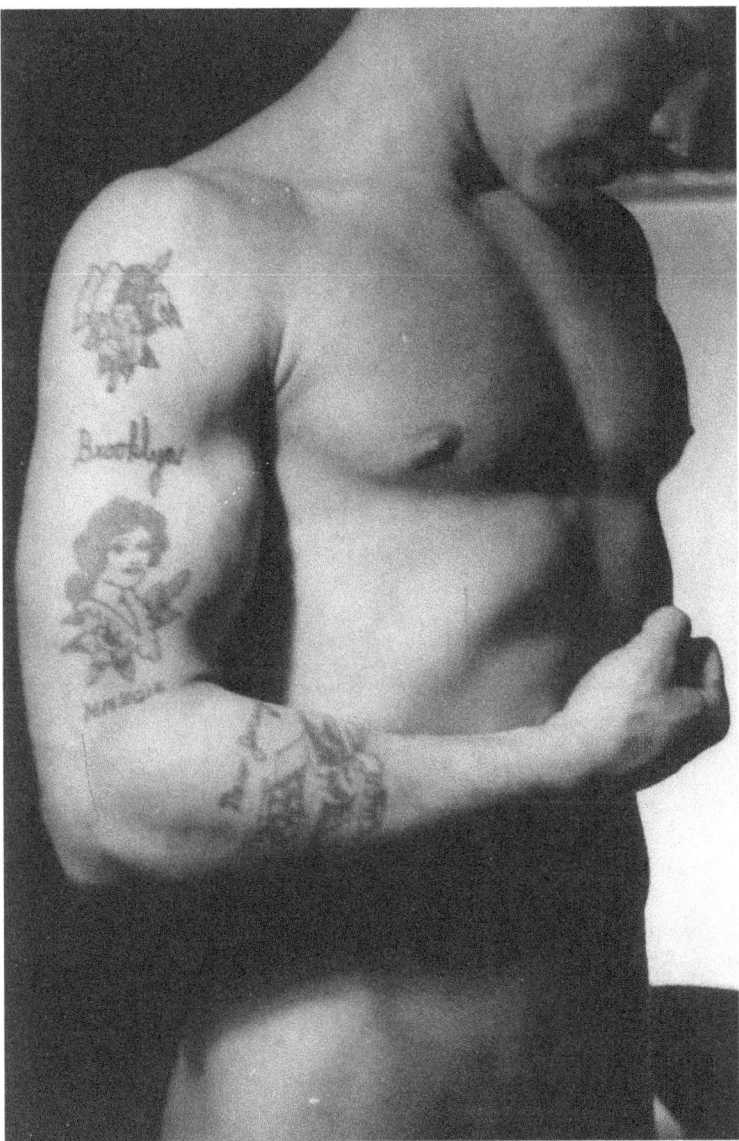

56. Hustler masculinity, 1953. From the Thomas Painter Collection. Reproduced by permission of The Kinsey Institute for Research in Sex, Gender, and Reproduction, Inc.

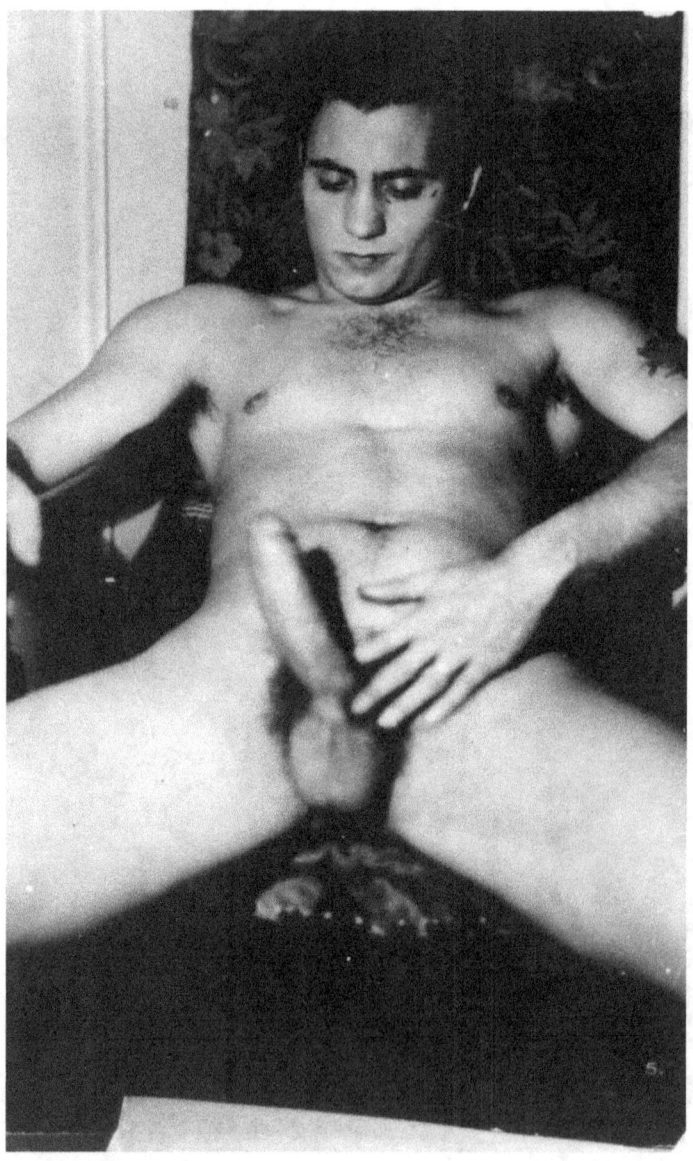

57. Pornographic pose of hustler, circa 1940s. From the Thomas Painter Collection. Reproduced by permission of The Kinsey Institute for Research in Sex, Gender, and Reproduction, Inc. Author's note: the man lived with Painter in the 1930s but Painter did not take this picture which circulated as pornographic material.

So it is significant that the hustler and his like featured in Warhol's pornography collection – *Buck, Butch,* and *Trade* – and in muscle magazines.[101] (See Figure 58.) Dallesandro was photographed for *Physique Pictorial* and *MANual,* for example.[102] For the visual trope of trade was an important element in the erotic mix of what was, in essence, homosexual pornography.[103] Thomas Waugh has clearly established the material range of such imagery in drawings as well as photography and film.[104] The hustler's physicality informed such pictures; as we have seen, his world overlapped with the worlds of the gym, body-building, and the muscle magazine. In 1973, *Physique Pictorial* admitted that many of its models were hustlers, 'young men who aggressively offer their sexual services for a sum of money'.[105]

As their clients knew, narcissism was a strong motivator – what Rechy called 'obsessive ravenous narcissism craving attention', 'that devouring narcissism'.[106] Rechy referred to a one-way desire, that of the score or john or client, but the desire was two-way in the sense that the hustler craved attention. 'To reciprocate in any way for the money would have violated the craving for the manifestation of desire toward me.'[107] When asked by a literary interviewer why he still hustled when he earned money by writing, Rechy replied 'Hustling is linked to narcissism, and being paid is proof that one is very strongly desired and desirable'.[108] Charles Henri Ford wrote of one paid encounter: 'Stamos is in love with himself, I'm a mirror for him. "I love you – I love you", he said last night, whilst taking all sorts of "strength and health" poses, looking at, and slapping, his own prick. Who was he talking to?'[109]

There is a scene in John Cheever's novel *Falconer* (1975) where a hustler catches a glimpse of himself in a bathroom mirror: 'One look at himself naked in the mirror and he couldn't get away. He couldn't get enough of it. He couldn't tear himself away . . . He didn't notice me, he didn't see anything but himself. So there he was, fondling his balls in the mirror'.[110] Tennessee Williams, who would have known all too well from his own encounters, refers in *The Roman Spring of Mrs. Stone* (1950) to 'young men with languid graces and a measure of beauty who only looked at mirrors', and has the hustler/gigolo Paolo rest his hands on his suited thighs 'as though infatuated by the feel of his own body'.[111] He sits

> with his legs dropping wide apart and with one hand laid on the centre of his being, which was his groin. That hand laid there was like an electric wire plugged into a socket for the purpose of giving power and light to the

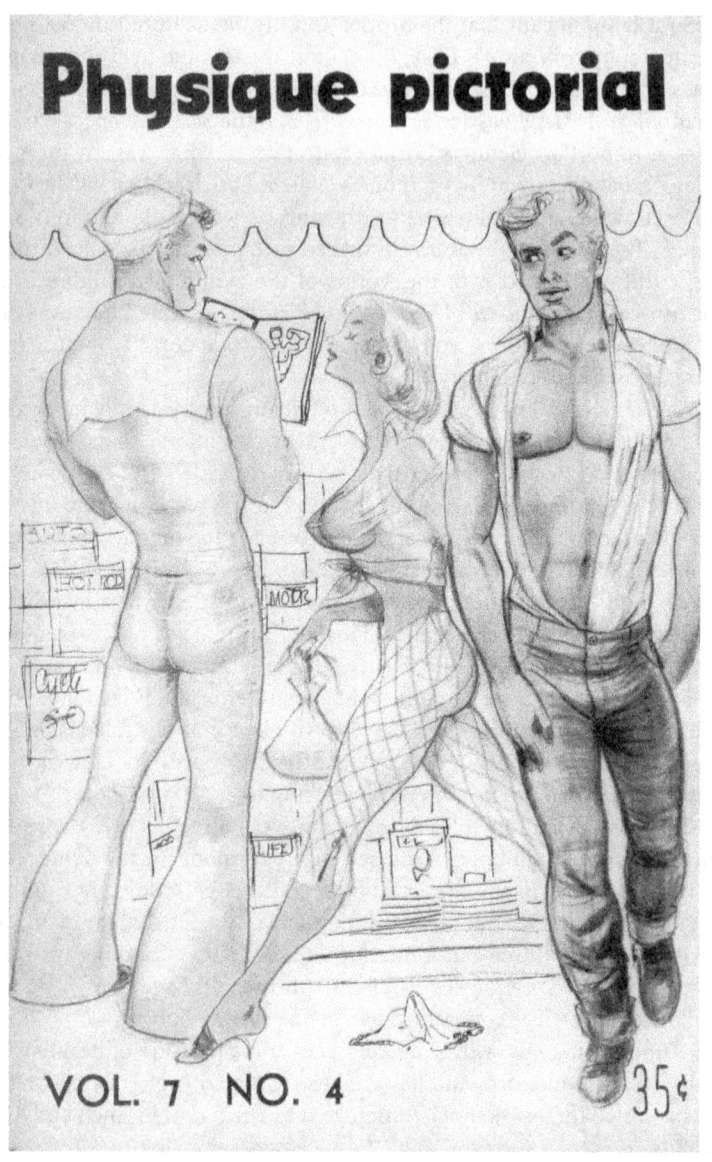

58. 'Flirtation' by Art-Bob, the cover art for the magazine, *Physique Pictorial* (1957). Author's note: this illustration is an example of the sailor and hustler as homoerotic fantasy figures and also suggests the triangulation of desire discussed elsewhere in this book.

59. Joe Dallesandro in a mirror with his tattoo. Photographed by Jack Robinson, circa 1971. © Condé Nast Archive/CORBIS.

invariable subject of discussion which was the sexual experience by which and for which the young Conte Paolo existed.[112]

Painter recalled models who, although they might not accept, were insulted if he did not make a sexual approach.[113] As much as economic need, the desire for admiration explained the success of Painter and other recreational photographers in enticing a constant parade of subjects. The progression from amateur subject to physique magazine model to film career was logical, if rare. The narcissism of film captured the narcissism of hustling in the hustlers playing hustler in *My Hustler* and *Flesh*.[114] It is represented by Paul America's mirror in *My Hustler* and Joe Dallesandro's self-referential tattoo 'Joe' in *Flesh*.

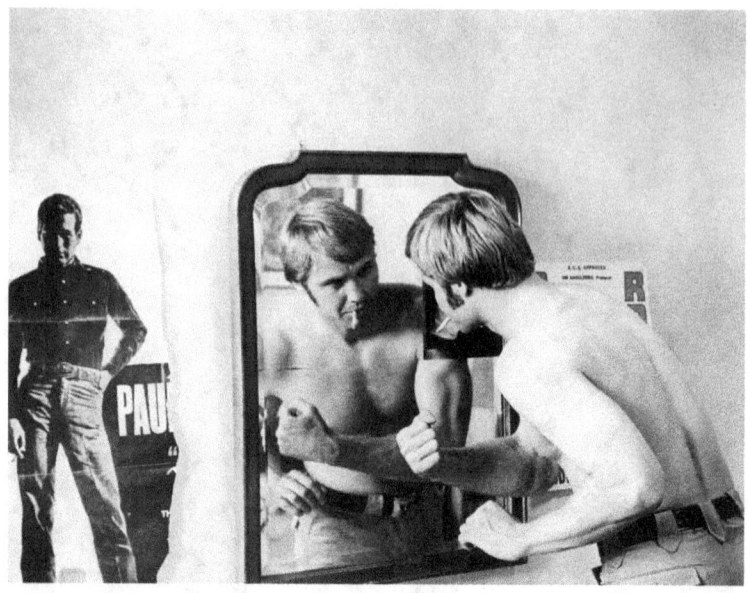

60. Jon Voight in *Midnight Cowboy* (1969). © John Springer Collection/CORBIS.

When John Schlesinger placed Jon Voight in front of the mirror in *Midnight Cowboy*, he knew exactly what he was doing.[115] (See Figures 59 and 60.)

However, the best example of narcissism reductio ad absurdum is Samuel Steward's work of textual hustling, *Understanding the Male Hustler* (1991), a self-interview, where, under one of his many pseudonyms, the hustler interviews – and lusts after – himself: 'Oh, that black black hair, that smile, those lips . . .'[116] There is self-loving within the self-loving, with the hustlers who could only ejaculate in front of a mirror or who favoured a client with prism spectacles because he could see himself while receiving oral sex.[117]

'The trouble with me is', reflects a character in William Burroughs's *Queer*, 'I like the type that robs me.'[118] As we have seen, hustlers and their like were also violent. Dotson Rader's hustler thought that 'When you hustle, the john has an intensity about him, but what is operative in his excitement is not only the sexuality of the encounter – which, I sometimes think, is a minor factor – but the potential for violence.' 'Violence',

61. Paul America on the beach in *My Hustler* (1965).

he continued, 'and the hint of the possibility of sudden death, animate the eroticism in that situation.'[119] Rechy wrote of the potential brutality in every interaction with a hustler and of his growing realization that for some men 'this is one of the proclaimed appeals – that steady hint of violence'.[120] The psycho-sexual link between aggression and sex that was such an important part of the appeal of such men was also a feature of hustler/trade representation. Significantly, when the actor Ramon Novarro, a client of New York male prostitutes in the 1940s, was killed by hustlers in his Hollywood Hills home in 1969, a nude photograph of his killer appeared in a physique magazine.[121] A 1983 issue of *Physique Pictorial* included earlier nude photographs of three models or hustlers who were serving time for killing their respective clients: the ultimate machismo.[122]

Tennessee Williams's male prostitute in his short story 'One arm' is dangerous as well as beautiful: he had killed a client. The minister who becomes attracted to him while visiting him on death row is drawn by this very combination – as was, no doubt, the story's author. The violence is even more pronounced in an earlier, more sexually explicit, unpublished

62. Hustler/hoodlum, circa 1950s. From the Thomas Painter Collection. Reproduced by permission of The Kinsey Institute for Research in Sex, Gender, and Reproduction, Inc.

version of the story, written in Manhattan in 1942. The disgusted hustler kills the john while the man is giving him oral sex.[123] In Israel Gerber's tale of homosexual self-loathing, *Man on a Pendulum* (1955), a hustler appears as an avenging angel, scourging the troubled subject: 'My face was horribly disfigured. I broke out into uncontrollable and hysterical laughter. I felt good about being disfigured. I felt cleansed.'[124] Herlihy's literary hustler is involved in an act of sado-masochistic violence and his client orgasms while being beaten by the enraged Buck. The incident was controversial because of the portrayal of the homosexual, but one of Herlihy's aims must surely have been to convey the mix of sex and danger involved in such transactions.[125]

Of course being beaten was not the intent – it was an unfortunate consequence of the sociology of the desired – but part of the hustler's sexual appeal was his menace as well as his masculinity. Hence the blond hustler's incongruous knife in *My Hustler*. Whittling with a large blade is not normal sunbathing activity but it reminds the viewer of the underlying danger behind the beauty of the male prostitute. (See Figure 61.) The knife intrudes into the narcissism of the bathroom as a similar warning.[126]

Both Painter and Melcarth dwelt on the theme of violence in their photographs of hustlers and trade. Sometimes it was a menacing look, combined with a scribbled caption (or memory) of the subject's character: the hustler in Figure 62 was a gangster and 'notorious mugger of queers', who died of a heroin overdose. The bodies portrayed are muscular, potentially violent, often tattooed, sometimes scarred. The lighting frequently highlights the menace but can also add a terrible beauty to the portrait. (See Figures 63 and 64.) Painter and Melcarth's preoccupation with addicts and gangs was linked to their sexual attraction to unpredictable violence and, presumably, to their own heightened masculinity when sexually involved with such figures. Photographs were frequently of past or future sexual contacts. Richard Taddei has said that Melcarth's form was to photograph his pick-ups the morning after. Painter sometimes explained that such and such a model had been photographed just after sexual contact: the semi-erections indicating as much.

The classical associations of trade were early recognized by Claude McKay, the Jamaican-American poet and writer, a figure central to the Harlem Renaissance. In an unpublished poem, 'Boy Prostitute', probably from the 1930s, McKay invoked an earlier Renaissance:

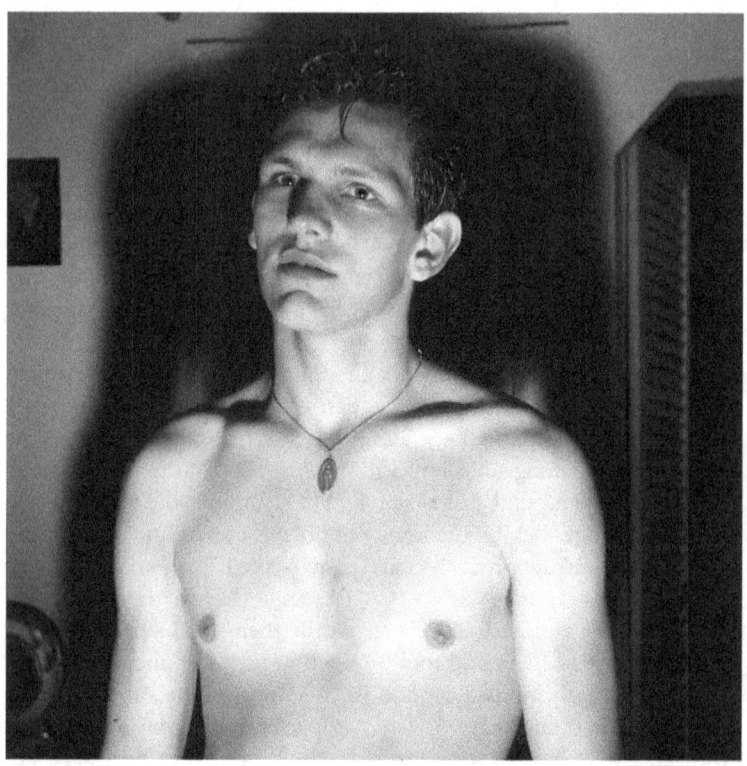

63. Hustler, 1950s. Collection of Richard Taddei, New York. The photograph was taken by Edward Melcarth.

> Oh, had he lived in high Renaissance days
> He might have stirred the mighty Angelo,
> And Raphael might have put angelic rays
> Around his golden head, and made it glow
> With beauty everlasting like a star.
> His figure could adorn an altar place,
> And mortals feeling beauty at the bar,
> Kneeling to God, would turn toward his face . . .[127]

A beauty that might have been celebrated in a previous era, McKay continues, is in this modern age sold in competition 'for a wage'. But while beauty was celebrated, there was a sting at the end of McKay's poem. The inevitable result of such commerce was the boy 'gains his first sensation of disease'.[128]

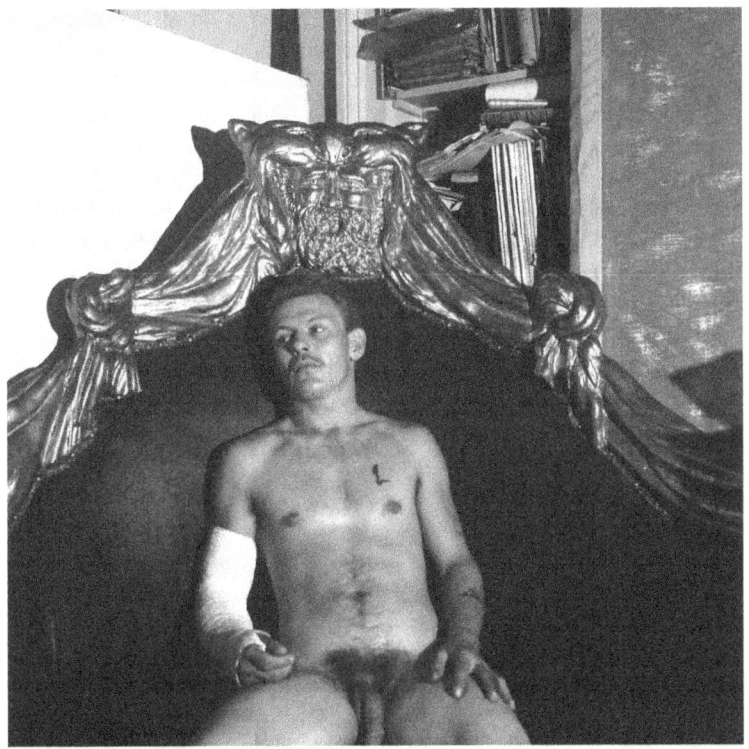

64. Wounded hustler, 1950s. Collection of Richard Taddei, New York. Author's note: the chair, a Melcarth creation, was later housed in the gay bar The Anvil. The photograph was taken by Edward Melcarth.

Melcarth, we have seen, was preoccupied with the classical potential in the visual beauty of trade.[129] His heroic heads are the heads of hustlers. His large painting *Last Supper* (1962) has hustlers and trade as Christ and the Apostles (Figure 47). The table on which this supper is served is the bar or counter at a diner or cafeteria (a hustler hang-out?) and Judas is a busboy or waiter. There are no dark and light sides in this imagery and it is by no means clear which of the young men is the Christ, presumably an intentional ambiguity. It could certainly not be said of Melcarth's Christ (whichever figure he is) that 'everything in the picture strains towards him' as has been claimed of Leonardo's Christ.[130] Is he the man with the cap askew? If so, John has his back to him and Peter's arm and hand interrupts our line of vision to the Christ. Melcarth followed the early painters of the *Last Supper* rather than Leonardo in positioning

Judas on the viewer's side of the table (or rather counter). My colleague Erin Griffey thinks that the source for Melcarth's *Last Supper* was Paolo Veronese's *Feast in the House of Levi* (1573) which he would have seen in Venice. Veronese intended it as a rendition of the *Last Supper* but changed the name after appearing before the Inquisition: 'Melcarth's appropriation of a painting that subverted traditional iconography is very fitting.'[131] Though the critic for the *New York Times* approved of what he saw as an attempt to 'transform the banalities of modern life through the rhythms and colors and compositions of the Renaissance' and liked the richness of the painter's colours, he was not impressed with what he took to be a direct borrowing of the imagery of Leonardo's masterpiece. Melcarth's was, he proclaimed, a 'magnificent act of innocence'. But the critic had not quite grasped the intended message, for he thought that *Last Supper* was a painting of a group of construction workers eating.[132] It was the reviewer who was the innocent.

The man from the *New York Times* would have been even more horrified by one of Melcarth's photographs had he ever seen it. It is a photograph of a young Times Square hustler as Adam and the photographer as God – in homage to Michelangelo's sixteenth-century Sistine Chapel masterpiece. (See Figure 65.)

A comparable tendency is at work in Paul Cadmus's painting,

65. Hustler as Michelangelo's Adam and Melcarth as God (his hand), 1950. From the Thomas Painter Collection. Reproduced by permission of The Kinsey Institute for Research in Sex, Gender, and Reproduction, Inc.

Playground (1949). (See Figure 66.) (We examined the artist's sailor trilogy in Chapter 2.) The ethereal young trade in a New York inner-city playground, lounging, partially disrobed, engaging in affectionate male-to-male bodily contact as well as (on the margins) opposite-sex

66. Paul Cadmus, *Playground*, 1948. Egg yolk tempera on hardboard panel, 23½ × 17½ in. Georgia Museum of Art, The University of Georgia, Athens, Georgia. © The Paul Cadmus Estate.

interaction, offered precisely the attractions that we have been discussing. One man has a baseball bat held, suggestively, between his legs. Another, the central figure, what the critic Lincoln Kirstein called a 'gilt-haired earthling', has his trouser front partially loosened and has his hands inside his trousers at the back, clasping the top of his buttocks. A dark-haired man in profile, with his shirt down to expose his shoulder and breast, has his hand in his pocket clasping what appears to be an erection. The man climbing the wire fence appears as one of Rechy's street angels or a Capeman before the Capeman. Thomas Painter told Alfred Kinsey of his strong attraction to Cadmus's painting when he saw it exhibited in 1949. Painter said – in a curious artistic endorsement – that he had masturbated several times to the exhibition catalogue reproduction. Cadmus's show 'is the most flagrantly homosexual thing I have seen in many – well, I have *ever* seen, as a serious art exhibit'.[133] While Kirstein's commentary does not mention homosexuality, he does recognize the 'hoodlum' element in the painting. He notes a discrepancy between the 'beauty' of the central figure and 'any hope to make use of his potential through thought or skill'. Perhaps Kirstein had hustling in mind as one of the ingredients of the 'delinquency' that he thought was these young men's inevitable fate.[134]

A passage from Dotson Rader's *Gov't Inspected Meat and Other Fun Summer Things* (1971) captures the idealization and objectification of masculinity in the imagery of hustlers and trade that we have been examining:

> The hustlers in tight whites and levis, laundry packed bulking around the meat, inside their mannered pose the marooned silence, under the ass of Almighty America, them, our countrymen, victims keeping it stiff, the lips, that is. They were the butchest, the most rugged, the most tried and losing, roughly beautiful creatures on the street; like a pack of Plains dogs, eyes sealed open and alert to score. The life, friend, the life.[135]

Though I am far from pitting an argument for the sordid reality of sex work against notions of rarefied representation, it is necessary to make it perfectly clear that a certain amount of romanticizing was involved in this image work. It was not just the pose of the hustlers that was 'mannered'. If the beauty of these 'roughly beautiful creatures' was exaggerated, so too was the nature of 'the life'.

As in Rader's 'under the ass of Almighty America', the nation was not infrequently invoked in discussions of the hustler. The hustler represented various elements of what was good or bad about modern America: the aptly named Paul America, the hustler in Warhol's *My*

Hustler, was emblematic. In the most optimistic scenario, the hustler quite literally lives the American Dream:

> Male prostitution is one of the last remnants of *laissez-faire*. Each hustler is on his own. He is subject to no regulation other than his own conscience, which is rarely developed to any great extent. There is little fear of police interference. The young man is his own boss, working when he wants to, loafing, eating, and sleeping the rest of the time. He is living out the American dream of the rugged individualist – to be in business for himself. Unlike the female prostitute, he is not dependent upon pimps, procurers, or other intermediaries.[136]

Presumably there is more than a smattering of ironic intent. However, there is no sense here of any economic imperative, no mention of the Depression-era hustlers, or of the waves of migration supplying paid and unpaid sex. (And, though we could scarcely expect otherwise, obviously no hint of the impact of crack cocaine and AIDS that was to follow.)

There was, then, a darker side. Rechy's *City of Night* is America. Its opening lines are: 'Later I would think of America as one vast City of Night stretching gaudily from Times Square to Hollywood Boulevard – jukebox-winking, rock-n-roll-moaning: America at night fusing its dark cities into the unmistakable shape of loneliness.'[137] The chronicles of the drug-ravaged Beat writer and hustler Herbert Huncke certainly puncture comforting images of the American dream:

> It was in 1948 – January – during a siege of severe New York winter weather. It had snowed for several days – stopped – clearing up – growing milder – the snow melting into dirty slush – then becoming intensely cold – snowing again . . . At night the city streets became even more deserted with only a few to be seen on Forty-second Street – probably one of the busiest streets of any city in the world – a few like myself living in cafeterias – sleeping in the all-night movies – staying away from the cops on their beats – who were angry to be out . . . walking through the underground tunnels down toward Penn Station – through the station into the rest rooms – sitting on the toilets sleeping – sometimes writing – looking to pick up someone who had money and wanted sex – and was willing to pay for it – anxious only for a place to sleep – take a bath – shave – obtain clean clothing – even food. Maybe steal a suitcase – roll a stray drunk – meet a friend – talk – make it until the morning and a cheap movie. I had been living in this manner since shortly after the beginning of the New Year. I was broke – hungry most of the time – poorly clad for contesting the rage of the elements – staying awake using Benzedrine inhalers – occasionally smoking pot – somehow maintaining a junk habit – just managing to keep straight enough not to

collapse completely – stealing – ready to make a dollar at anything – always looking for a good take – something big enough to allow me a chance for a bed of my own – a place to live or at least die in out of the cold – not to be found crouched – a corpse in the doorway. I wanted to die and I felt I was dying – could observe death feeding on me – see it in the pallor of my skin – the patches of oozing sores on my chin and face – the tiny red flecks in the whites of my eyes – in the way my skull showed through my skin at the temples – and I could smell it from my dirt-coated bleeding feet – from my crotch – from my clothing.[138]

Here, in breathlessly powerful prose, Huncke manages to combine the poetry of life in the city with a most unromantic view of hustling life.

Or we could turn, outside our period of focus, to the even more wrenching memories and road stories of the artist David Wojnarowicz. There is nothing romantic about his posthumous *The Waterfront Journals* (1996), these 'dispatches from that region of dissolute grace', his chronicles of hustlers, addicts, ex-convicts, runaways, and drifters, with their graphic accounts of escapes from death, transvestite misunderstandings, amputee sex, rape, cuttings, sexual assaults, run-ins with the police, and beatings.[139]

My argument in this chapter has been for the ubiquity of the imagery of the hustler and trade in the American visual arts and literature. Andy Warhol, Paul Morrissey, John Schlesinger, William Friedkin, James Leo Herlihy, Charles Wright, Paul Goodman, Irving Rosenthal, John Rechy, Samuel Steward, Lanford Wilson, Mart Crowley, Lou Reed, Gore Vidal, Tennessee Williams, Dotson Rader, Edward Melcarth, William Gedney, Charles Henri Ford, John Cheever, William Burroughs, Claude McKay, Herbert Huncke, and David Wojnarowicz have included hustlers in their work; Rechy, Rader, Huncke, and Wojnarowicz were themselves one-time hustlers. Arthur Miller, William Inge, Kenneth Anger, Truman Capote, Richard Avedon, and Paul Cadmus can all be said to have used the trade aesthetic in their work.

It was not some hidden representation or discourse. While the persona of the hustler was certainly central to the more avant-garde sectors of American culture and society, it also figured in more mainstream cultural discourse. Where the to-be-looked-at aspect of hustling was stressed, the trade aesthetic was relatively commonplace: from a Melcarth sculpture and Cadmus painting to a Brando poster, Avedon photograph, or Academy Award-winning Hollywood film. Warhol himself acknowledged this when he recorded his jealousy of the film *Midnight Cowboy*'s appropriation of the hustler. 'I realized that with both Hollywood and the underground making films about male hustlers – even though the two treatments couldn't have been more different – it took away a real drawing card from the underground, because people would rather go see the treatment that *looked* better. It was much less threatening.'[140] Critics like to use the term 'outlaw' when they refer to the role of the hustler in US culture in the 1960s. If it refers to representation of the hustler as a means of critiquing aspects of American society (Wojnarowicz's shadow of the American dream) or to engagement in activities punishable at law (Rechy's outlaw sex), then there is some validity to this characterization. But in terms of the sheer presence of the imagery of these men and their kind, their look, it was in-law rather than outlaw.

Notes

1 R. Barthes, *Incidents*, translated by R. Howard (Berkeley and Los Angeles, 1992), p. 59. This incident occurred in 1979.
2 M. W. Turner, *Backward Glances: Cruising the Queer Streets of New York and London* (London, 2003), pp. 60–1. See also R. B. Brasell, '*My Hustler*: gay spectatorship as cruising', *Wide Angle*, 14: 2 (1992), 54–64; H. Bech, *When Men Meet: Homosexuality and Modernity* (Cambridge, 1997), pp. 104–8: 'The gaze'.
3 T. Waugh, 'Cockteaser', in J. Doyle, J. Flatley, and J. E. Muñoz (eds), *Pop Out: Queer Warhol* (Durham, NC, 1996), p. 54.
4 J. Doyle, *Sex Objects: Art and the Dialectics of Desire* (Minneapolis, MN, 2006), p. 87.
5 M. Moon, 'Outlaw sex and the "search for America": representing male prostitution and perverse desire in sixties film (*My Hustler* and *Midnight Cowboy*)', in his *A Small Boy and Others: Imitation and Initiation in American Culture from Henry James to Andy Warhol* (Durham, NC, 1998), ch. 5. This essay appeared originally in 1993.
6 For La Tourneaux, see D. Ragan, 'The party's over', *New York Times*, 21 November 1993; C. Kaiser, *The Gay Metropolis 1940–1996* (New York, 1997), p. 191.
7 J. L. Herlihy, *Midnight Cowboy* (New York, 1965).
8 C. Wright, *The Messenger* (New York, 1963).
9 It should be noted that the lesson occurs after many pages of descriptions of male-to-male sex: K. B. Raul, *Naked to the Night* (New York, 1964).
10 W. Miller, *The Cool World* (London, 1957), p. 180.
11 P. Goodman, *Making Do* (New York, 1963).
12 J. Barr, *The Occasional Man* (New York, 1966), pp. 9, 27.
13 I. Rosenthal, *Sheeper* (New York, 1968), p. 9. First published in 1967.

14 J. Rechy, *The Sexual Outlaw: A Documentary* (New York, 1977), p. 21.
15 L. Wilson, *Collected Plays 1965–1970* (Lyme, NH, 1996), pp. 5–7.
16 M. Crowley, *The Boys in the Band* (Harmondsworth, 1970), pp. 42, 43, 47, 52–3, 56, 57, 60. First published in New York in 1968.
17 M. Guslow, 'Theater: a slice of East Village life', *New York Times*, 9 September 1969; T. Shales, 'The Rapists: heavy hands', *The Washington Post*, 9 November 1972.
18 Lou Reed, lyrics to his song 'Walk on the wild side' (1972).
19 J. Shearer, *The Male Hustler* (Cleveland, OH, 1966), cover, and p. 8. See also J. O'Day, *Confessions of a Male Prostitute* (Los Angeles, 1964); J. Garcin, *The Stud Hustler* (Cleveland, OH, 1969); J. W. Wells, *The Male Hustler* (New York, 1971).
20 C. Gorham, *McCaffery* (New York, 1961, 1970).
21 J. Caruso, *Queer Hustler* (Las Vegas, 1965). Nor does his cover portrait indicate especially 'rough' trade!
22 S. Steward, *Understanding the Male Hustler* (Binghamton, NY, 1991), pp. 19–21. The examples given here – *$tud* (Washington, DC, 1966); *My Brother, the Hustler* (n.p., 1971); *San Francisco Hustler* (n.p., 1971); and *Renegade Hustler* (San Diego, CA, 1972) – were Steward's own hustler fiction under the name of Phil Andros.
23 G. Vidal, 'Three stratagems', in his *A Thirsty Evil: Seven Short Stories* (New York, 1956), p. 12. Written in 1950.
24 Ibid., p. 10.
25 For Magrem, see Vidal's story 'Pages from an abandoned journal', in ibid., pp. 105–32. Written in 1956.
26 Ibid., p. 11.
27 T. Williams, *The Roman Spring of Mrs. Stone* (London, 1957), p. 48.
28 T. Williams, *Plays 1957–1980* (New York, 2000), pp. 856, 995; T. Williams, *The Theatre of Tennessee Williams: Volume 5* (New York, 1976), p. 235; T. Williams, *Collected Stories* (New York, 1985), pp. 301, 343, 488, 570; M. Paller, *Gentlemen Callers: Tennessee Williams, Homosexuality, and Mid-twentieth-century Drama* (New York, 2005), pp. 171–3; T. Williams, '*And Tell Sad Stories of the Deaths of Queens . . .*', in E. Mann and D. Roessel (eds), *Political Stages: Plays That Shaped a Century* (New York, 2002), p. 405; J. Francis, 'Camping out: sexuality as aesthetic value in Tennessee Williams's *And Tell Sad Stories of the Deaths of Queens . . .*', *Tennessee Williams Annual Review*, 9 (2007): www.tennesseewilliamsstudies.org/archives/2007/09francis.htm.
29 University of Delaware Library, Newark, Delaware, Tennessee Williams Collection, Box 1, Series 1. 10, F27: T. Williams, 'Kirche, Kutchen und Kinder (an outrage for the stage): First Draft' (1979), p. 1; H. Russ, '*Kirche, Kutchen und Kinder* by Tennessee Williams', *Psychoanalytic Review*, 67 (1980), 277–81.

30 T. Williams, *One Arm and Other Stories* (New York, 1954), p. 7. First published in 1948.
31 Williams, *Plays 1957–1980*, p. 656.
32 T. Williams, *Plays 1937–1955* (New York, 2000), p. 481.
33 For example, J. M. Clum, *Still Acting Gay: Male Homosexuality in Modern Drama* (New York, 2000), p. 122.
34 Williams, *Plays 1957–1980*, pp. 44, 157–8, 181.
35 For example, R. Barrios, *Screening Out: Playing Gay in Hollywood from Edison to Stonewall* (New York, 2003), p. 262.
36 John Clum's tendency. See Clum, *Still Acting Gay*, pp. 122, 135–6, 140–1. Although he almost breaks out of this particular conceptual straitjacket in J. M. Clum, 'The sacrificial stud and the fugitive female in *Suddenly Last Summer, Orpheus Descending*, and *Sweet Bird of Youth*', in M. C. Roudané (ed.), *The Cambridge Companion to Tennessee Williams* (Cambridge, 1999), p. 141
37 A point made by David Savran, though for a slightly different reason: D. Savran, *Communists, Cowboys, and Queers: The Politics of Masculinity in the Work of Arthur Miller and Tennessee Williams* (Minneapolis, MN, 1992), p. 82.
38 R. B. Vowles, 'Tennessee Williams: the world of his imagery', *The Tulane Drama Review*, 3: 2 (1958), 54.
39 For an important start, see J. E. Muñoz, 'Rough boy trade: queer desire/straight identity in the photography of Larry Clark', in D. Bright (ed.), *The Passionate Camera: Photography and Bodies of Desire* (London, 1998), pp. 167–77; J. Doyle, 'Tricks of the trade: Pop Art/pop sex', in Doyle, Flatley, and Muñoz (eds), *Pop Out*, pp. 191–209; R. Montez, '"Trade" marks: LA2, Keith Haring, and a queer economy of collaboration', *GLQ*, 12 (2006), 425–40.
40 The Kinsey Institute for Research in Sex, Gender, and Reproduction, University of Indiana, Bloomington (hereafter, KI), The Thomas Painter Collection (hereafter, Painter), Box 1, Series 2, c. 1, Vol. 6: Painter Letters: 27 February, 8 August, and 19 November 1949; Box 1, Series 2, c. 1, Vol. 7: 19 February 1950.
41 Painter, Box 1, Series 2, c. 1, Vol. 6: 5 March 1949; Box 1, Series 2, c. 1, Vol. 10: 5 July 1953.
42 Copies of the sunglasses are still being manufactured and are available online from the Guggenheim Museum Store: www.guggenheimstore.org/pegusu.html.
43 Painter, Box 1, Series 2, c. 1, Vol. 6: 27 February 1949.
44 For the two types, see J. A. Suárez, *Bike Boys, Drag Queens, and Superstars: Avant-Garde, Mass Culture, and Gay Identities in the 1960s Underground Cinema* (Bloomington and Indianapolis, 1996), p. 157.
45 For Thomson, see A. Hughes, 'In Virgil Thomson's rooms', *The New York*

Times, 16 April 1972. For the outing, see M. Signorile, 'The other side of Malcolm', *OutWeek*, 18 March 1990; C. Winans, *Malcolm Forbes: The Man Who Had Everything* (New York, 1990).

46 For information about the purchases, see Archives of American Art, Smithsonian Institution, Washington, DC, Edward Melcarth Papers, Box 1 of 4: Folder of Photographs of Paintings – Melcarth 1; Folder of Photographs of Paintings – Melcarth 2; Folder of Photographs of Paintings – Melcarth 3.

47 E. Kinetz, 'Those who serve, those who are served', *New York Times*, 30 November 2003.

48 See C. Angell, *Andy Warhol Screen Tests: The Films of Andy Warhol Catalogue Raisonné* (New York, 2006), Vol. 1, pp. 27 (Paul America, 1965), 30–2 (Archie, 1966), 72–3, 216–41 (Philip Fagan, 1964–65).

49 W. Koestenbaum, *Andy Warhol* (New York, 2001), pp. 82–5.

50 D. Crimp, 'Face value', in N. Baume and others (ed.), *About Face: Andy Warhol Portraits* (Hartford, CN, 1999), p. 115.

51 Ibid., pp. 119–22.

52 Koestenbaum, *Andy Warhol*, pp. 47, 65–6, 85–9.

53 Angell, *Andy Warhol Screen Tests*, p. 217.

54 R. Meyer, 'Warhol's clones', in M. Dorenkamp and R. Henke (eds), *Negotiating Lesbian and Gay Subjects* (New York, 1995), p. 101, for the 'connotation' comment. See also R. Meyer, 'Most wanted men: homoeroticism and the secret of censorship in early Warhol', in his *Outlaw Representation: Censorship and Homosexuality in Twentieth-century American Art* (Boston, 2002), p. 128.

55 For the spectacle of Holden's masculinity, see S. Cohan, 'Masquerading as the American male in the fifties: *Picnic*, William Holden and the spectacle of masculinity in Hollywood film', *Camera Obscura*, 25–26 (1991), 42–72.

56 W. Inge, *Four Plays* (New York, 1990), pp. 75–6.

57 Ibid., pp. 92–3.

58 W. Inge, *Eleven Short Plays* (New York, 1990), pp. 20, 71, 85, 94, 112, 125, 126.

59 M. De Angelis, *Gay Fandom and Crossover Stardom: James Dean, Mel Gibson, and Keanu Reeves* (Durham, NC, 2001), pp. 8, 12.

60 S. Kashner, Dangerous talents', in G. Carter (ed.), *Vanity Fair's Tales of Hollywood* (New York, 2008), p. 64.

61 F. Negrón-Muntaner, 'Feeling pretty: *West Side Story* and Puerto Rican identity discourses', *Social Text*, 18: 2 (2000), 98.

62 Ibid., 98.

63 Suárez, *Bike Boys*, p. 155.

64 Ibid., ch. 4.

65 Ibid., pp. 162–3.

66 The photographs appeared in *Life*, 7 January 1966. I would have liked to

include them in this book but the Avedon Foundation refused permission for reproduction. They can be viewed online at the Fraenkel Gallery www.fraenkelgallery.com/index.php#s=23&p=0&a=3&mi=4&pt=1&pi=10000&at=1.

67 New York Public Library Manuscripts and Archives Division, Truman Capote Papers, circa 1924–1984 (hereafter, Capote Papers), Box 7, Folder 10, *In Cold Blood* Research Notes.
68 Ibid., Box 7, Folders 9 and 14.
69 Ibid., Box 7, Folder 10.
70 Ibid., Box 7, Folder 9.
71 T. Capote, *In Cold Blood* (London, 1981), pp. 129–30. First published in 1966.
72 Capote Papers, Box 7, Folder 10.
73 Capote, *In Cold Blood*, pp. 133–4.
74 G. Plimpton, *Truman Capote* (New York, 1997), p. 215.
75 D. Rader, *Blood Dues* (New York, 1973), p. 57.
76 Ibid., p. 34.
77 Ibid., p. 120.
78 Ibid., p. 203.
79 Ibid., pp. 28, 31.
80 P. Andros, *$tud* (Boston, 1982), pp. 183–4.
81 Painter, Box 1, Series 2, c. 1, Vol. 2: 26 June 1944.
82 Ibid.
83 J. Rechy, *City of Night* (New York, 1984), p. 32. First published in 1963.
84 Herlihy, *Midnight Cowboy*, p. 103.
85 *My Hustler* (1965: Andy Warhol).
86 G. Flatley, 'How to become a superstar – and get paid, too', *New York Times*, 31 December 1967.
87 P. Tyler, *Screening the Sexes: Homosexuality in the Movies* (New York, 1993), p. 56. First published in 1972.
88 G. Butt, *Between You and Me: Queer Disclosures in the New York Art World, 1948–1963* (Durham, NC, 2005), p. 2.
89 D. E. James, *Allegories of Cinema: American Film in the Sixties* (Princeton, 1989), p. 78.
90 *Flesh* (1968: Paul Morrissey).
91 Doyle, 'Tricks of the trade', p. 199.
92 James, *Allegories of Cinema*, p. 79; N. de Villiers, 'How much does it cost for cinema to tell the truth of sex? Cinéma vérité and sexography', *Sexualities*, 10 (2007), 355.
93 KI, Thomas Painter, 'Male Homosexuals and Their Prostitutes in Contemporary America' (New York, 1941), Vol. 2: 'The Prostitute', p. 87.
94 Ibid.

95 D. Rader, *Gov't Inspected Meat and Other Fun Summer Things* (New York, 1971), p. 3.
96 Painter, 'Male Homosexuals', Vol. 2, p. 87.
97 KI, Thomas Painter, 'Male Homosexuals and Their Prostitutes in Contemporary America' (New York, 1941), Vol. 1: 'American Homosexuals', p. 223.
98 Rare Book, Manuscript, and Special Collections Library, Duke University, William Gedney Photographs: New York, 1954-1984: NY0055: 'Male hustler standing on a street corner', 1967; NY0541: 'Male hustler standing on street corner and lighting cigarette', 1967; NY0719: 'Brooklyn', 1969 (although the images dated 1967 are on this contact sheet).
99 Painter, 'Male Homosexuals', Vol. 2, pp. 87-8.
100 Rechy, *City of Night*, pp. 77-8; C. Casillo, *Outlaw: The Lives and Careers of John Rechy* (Los Angeles, 2002), p. 119.
101 A. Warhol, *Andy Warhol, 365 Takes: The Andy Warhol Museum Collection* (New York, 2004), Take 100.
102 See, for example, *Physique Pictorial*, September 1967, January 1969 (the first issue to reveal the uncovered penis) and July 1975; *MANual*, June 1967.
103 The best quick guide to the dominance of the trade aesthetic in one popular physique magazine is Taschen Publishing's *Complete Reprint of Physique Pictorial, 1951-1990*, 3 vols (Berlin, 1997).
104 T. Waugh, *Hard to Imagine: Gay Male Eroticism in Photography and Film from Their Beginnings to Stonewall* (New York, 1996); T. Waugh, *Out/Lines: Underground Gay Graphics from Before Stonewall* (Vancouver, 2002); T. Waugh and W. Walker, *Lust Unearthed: Vintage Gay Graphics from the DuBeck Collection* (Vancouver, 2004).
105 *Physique Pictorial*, April 1973.
106 Rechy, *City of Night*, pp. 21, 54.
107 Ibid., p. 54.
108 Rechy, *Sexual Outlaw*, p. 46. This book is itself an extended exercise in narcissism, as is his recent memoir, J. Rechy, *About My Life and the Kept Woman* (New York, 2008).
109 Harry Ransom Center, University of Texas, Austin, Charles Henri Ford Papers, Box 21, Folder 2: 'Flesh and Marble: A Street Diary', p. 59 (diary of a trip to Greece in March 1962).
110 J. Cheever, *Falconer* (London, 1977), p. 113.
111 Williams, *Roman Spring*, pp. 30-1.
112 Ibid., p. 28.
113 Painter, Box 1, Series 2, c. 1, Vol. 10: 20 September 1953.
114 This is discussed most usefully in S. Koch, *Stargazer: Andy Warhol's World and His Films* (New York, 1974), pp. 79-85, 114-31.
115 *Midnight Cowboy* (John Schlesinger: 1969).
116 Steward, *Understanding the Male Hustler*, p. 4.

117 Ibid., p. 33.
118 W. S. Burroughs, *Queer* (New York, 1987), p. 33. *Queer* was written in the 1950s.
119 Rader, *Gov't Inspected Meat*, p. 191.
120 Rechy, *City of Night*, p. 32.
121 M. Friedman, *Strapped for Cash: A History of American Hustler Culture* (Los Angeles, 2003), pp. 38, 163–6.
122 *Physique Pictorial*, November 1983. It has a sailor model on the front and back covers.
123 'One arm' is in Williams, *One Arm and Other Stories*, pp. 7–29. It is said to be based on a hustler the author had encountered in Canal Street in New Orleans in the late 1930s. The unpublished 1942 version is in Harry Ransom Center, University of Texas, Austin, Tennessee Williams Collection, Box 31, Folder 13 (dated 1942, Manhattan).
124 I. Gerber, *Man on a Pendulum: A Case History of an Invert* (New York, 1955), p. 137.
125 Herlihy, *Midnight Cowboy*, pp. 232–3.
126 *My Hustler* (1965: Andy Warhol).
127 Manuscript Division, Moorland Spingarn Research Center, Howard University, Washington, DC: Alain Locke Papers, Box 164–186, Folder 29, Claude McKay, 'Boy Prostitute'.
128 Ibid.
129 For twentieth-century homosexuality's use of classical Greek and Roman imagery, see A. Richlin, 'Eros underground: Greece and Rome in gay print culture, 1953–65', *Journal of Homosexuality*, 49 (2005), 421–61.
130 For Leonardo's *Last Supper* (1495–8), see L. Steinberg, *Leonardo's Incessant Last Supper* (New York, 2001). The quote comes from ibid., p. 38.
131 Erin Griffey, personal communication.
132 B. O'Doherty, 'Art: Edward Melcarth work echoes Renaissance', *New York Times*, 31 March 1962.
133 Painter, Box 1, Series 2, c. 1, Vol. 6: 10 December 1949.
134 L. Kirstein, *Paul Cadmus* (New York, 1984), p. 74.
135 Rader, *Gov't Inspected Meat*, pp. 3–4.
136 D. W. Cory and J. P. LeRoy, *The Homosexual and His Society: A View from Within* (New York, 1963), p. 97.
137 Rechy, *City of Night*, p. 9.
138 H. Huncke, *The Herbert Huncke Reader*, ed. B. G. Schafer (New York, 1997), pp. 116–17.
139 D. Wojnarowicz, *The Waterfront Journals* (New York, 1996), esp. pp. 21–3, 26–9, 35–7, 60–1, 69–71, 114–27. The quote comes from the back cover: it is from a *Time Out New York* review.
140 A. Warhol and P. Hackett, *POPism: The Warhol '60s* (New York, 1980), p. 280.

7

Conclusion

I brood on the lack of universality in our sexual appetites. A loves his wife and no one but her. B loves young men, and when these are scarce he makes out with men who impersonate youth. C likes all comely women between the ages of twelve and fifty, including all races. D likes himself, and jacks off frequently. He also likes men who resemble him sufficiently to make the orgasm narcissistic. E likes both men and women, depending on his moods, and I don't know whether he is the most tragic or the most natural of the group. None of them share, at any discernible level, the desires of the others. They share customs, diets, habits of dress, laws, and governments, but naked and randy they seem to be men from different planets. (John Cheever, 1968)[1]

The New York writer Gore Vidal, an inhabitant and cartographer of that city's sexual environment in the period before the late 1960s, was consistent in his scepticism about dividing it into gay and straight. He cited Alfred Kinsey approvingly in 1970 as revealing how things actually were: 'Everyone is potentially bisexual. In actual practice a minority never commits a homosexual act, others experiment with their own sex but settle for heterosexuality, still others swing back and forth to a greater or lesser degree, while another minority never gets around to performing the penis–vagina act.'[2] Homosexual and heterosexual, he said in 1974, resisting the sexual ideology of his interviewers, described acts rather than identities; they were adjectives and not nouns. In the 1980s, he repeated his belief that there was 'no such thing as a homosexual or a heterosexual person' but rather heterosexual or homosexual acts. 'Most people are a mixture of impulses if not practices.'[3]

Yet this belief in sexual indeterminacy was increasingly at odds with the worldview of those who were quite clear that there were only two nations. 'Gay liberation killed sex with straight men' was one man's summary of the change.[4] An excruciating demonstration of this disjuncture occurred in Vidal's interview with the gay playwright and activist Larry Kramer in 1992, where a refusal to categorize ('I don't categorize ... There is no such thing as a homosexual person. There are homosexual *acts*') confronted a sexual politics where identity was everything ('I think that, for some time, there's been a very strong desire to be categorized as homosexual, to be proud of being gay'). The generational divide was such that Kramer could scarcely hide his incredulity: 'But, Gore, you *are* gay. You've lived with a man for forty years or something, and everyone who knows you personally knows you're gay. And I think *you* think of yourself as gay.'[5] Vidal had an identity even if he did not know it!

Kerwin Kaye has called this historical moment 'valorizing the homosexual prostitute, even against his will' – a nice description.[6] As early as 1963, experts on homosexuality were interpreting hustler heterosexuality as pretence and their contempt for their clients as 'projected self-hatred'.[7] During the 1970s, it was increasingly difficult to acknowledge the heterosexuality of the hustler, even for those with an intimate knowledge. Laud Humphreys wrote in 1971 that, while hustlers 'share a heterosexual self-image', the money that they received was motivated less by economic than by moral imperatives. 'For them the amount of money received holds little importance, a pack of cigarettes or a handful of change sufficing to justify their involvement in the forbidden behavior, *which is what they really wanted*.'[8] In an interview in 1973, the ex-hustler John Rechy referred to the 'heterosexuality' of the 1950s hustler as a sham. 'Hustlers used to be "strictly straight". We weren't, of course. That was bullshit, but bullshit we were doing ourselves. But that's what was expected of us ... Gay liberation has changed that on both sides: that of the hustler and that of the client.'[9] A recent biographer goes even further. The early Rechy used prostitution to deny 'his homosexual feelings'. Hustling was the first phase of 'his coming out'.[10] However, the real point is that gay liberation (and Rechy's personal preferences) coloured his assessment.

A similar tendency occurs in C. A. Tripp's influential 1970s study of homosexuality, *The Homosexual Matrix* (1975), when he discusses homosexual self-denial. The first of his 'basic denial-umbrellas' is the gender-role justification, where the man who assumes the dominant role in homosexual intercourse (the inserter in anal sex, the fellated in oral sex, the non-penetrated) reasons that what he is doing 'is not really homosexual'.[11] Tripp described it as an odd notion but one with a long history and widespread influence: 'it is astonishing that so many observers have been taken in by these posturings, and are willing to believe that male homosexuality requires inversion, that it only applies to the passive partner'. 'With this rationalization', he continued, 'a great many males in more than a few societies have been able to satisfy their homosexual requirements with equanimity.'[12] Tripp's attitude is reflected in the word 'posturings'. Such activity was 'patently homosexual' for both partners; it appears in his book in the chapter on the social forms of homosexuality.[13]

Even our informant Thomas Painter was to become influenced by binarism. In 1968, he began to question his own categorization of the hustlers as heterosexual. 'Now I don't know *what* to call them.'[14]

While this book has focused on New York, there are suggestions that we are dealing with a wider American phenomenon with a long past. We should recall Kinsey's claim that almost 40 per cent of the total male population had experienced 'some overt homosexual experience to the point of orgasm'.[15] The homosexual Donald Webster Cory observed in 1951 that, despite the impact of Kinsey, 'America has little realization of the widespread nature of bisexual activities, and it continues to classify people in the public mind as homosexual or heterosexual. Few people outside of the gay world realize how many of these homosexually-inclined bisexuals marry, and how much homosexuality is practiced or desired among married men.' Cory was not really challenging categories – his bisexuals were essentially homosexual – but at least he allowed for trade across the lines of the usual sexual demarcation and for the prevalence of bisexuality.[16]

Town and country interacted. As Colin Johnson has argued, they were not hermetically sealed entities in terms of their sexual histories. The codes around so-called active and passive sex, penetrator and penetrated, masculine and feminine, discussed in earlier chapters, recurred in prison populations throughout the nation and were shared by itinerant workers, tramps, and hoboes as well as by soldiers, sailors, and seamen. Johnson has noted the difficulty of unravelling the origins of the sexual protocols of the 1920s and 1930s that were found in city, country town, and logging camp as well as in the fields and on the road.[17]

In the 1940s, Painter met young men in Dayton, Ohio, who allowed themselves to be fellated without payment – 'usually gives it away'. 'There is no prostitution of heterosexuals to homosexuals as we know it in Times Square.' The men would simply engage in sex with another man if approached. One such man said 'He *likes* to be fellated. Says it is about

Conclusion

the *same* degree of pleasure as derived from heterosexual coitus.' 'This, I should gather, is the hustler before he hits Times Square or Michigan Boulevard or Hollywood and Vine or Market Street. This also is the youth who makes life tolerable for thousands of small city homosexuals over the country – because thousands of him never go to New York or San Francisco, but live in the Daytons and pass on to the rising generation their knowledge of Queers.' Painter thought that these boys were not homosexual but could not really be called heterosexual either: 'a male who likes that much to be fellated is not "normal"'.[18] Curiously enough, Arno Karlen visited Dayton – self-advertised as 'THE CLEANEST CITY IN AMERICA' – to interview people for his 1971 study *Sexuality and Homosexuality*, choosing it, he said, because it had the reputation as 'one of those cities whose name represents the sticks to dwellers in capital cities'. A high-school teacher told him that he knew of star athletes in one school who 'got spending money hustling fags' and of a recent police bust of a group of 'kids' who hustled by making contacts through a ham radio network. A reporter said that hustling was commonplace at the bus station and various 'rough' bars.[19]

This kind of instrumental, unreflective sex was said to have been a national characteristic of both rural and urban working-class males during our period of interest. The so-called boys of Boise, alleged victims of an Idaho homosexual vice ring in 1955, were in fact hustlers, some of them gang members, who were often paid for sex according to a predictable code. As one of them told John Gerassi ten years later, 'I was the one getting blown. I never did it to the queer. Sometimes I masturbated him, but I never blew him. I didn't think it was evil . . . all the other guys said they did it.'[20] Samuel Steward, who should certainly have known given his claimed five thousand sexual contacts, said that such males just wanted sex and it did not matter whether the recipient was male or female. 'A man enjoyed a good blow job just as much as he did a good screw.'[21]

We may be reminded of Edmund White's T-shirted Kentucky farm boys of the 1950s, discussed in Chapter 1, available but with a somewhat limited sexual repertoire.[22] Gore Vidal has told the story about a young Wyoming cowhand with whom a friend had casual sex in the 1960s: 'my friend was, as usual, guilt-ridden; so much so that the boy finally turned to his seducer and with a certain wonder said, "You know, you guys from the East do this because you're sick and we do it because we're horny".'[23] John Loughery quotes a source who said that in Tulsa in the 1940s and 1950s the police were known to demand 'certain oral intimacies' from homosexual men.[24]

John Howard's history of the queer South in the period 1945–85 located men who had homosexual sex but who did not consider themselves homosexual. One of his informants said that the men he had sex with had sex rather than talking about it: 'We did not sit around and have intellectual discussions about being gay . . . You just did it, and didn't do too much speculating.'[25] A Chicago interviewee in a 1971 study confirmed Howard's claim. 'Working-class homosexuals are prostitutes or have polymorphous behavior and don't consider themselves homosexuals', the man told Arno Karlen. 'A lot of southern boys are like that, and lots of them are available.'[26]

Painter kept Kinsey informed with anecdotes about the sexual availability of rural youth in the late 1940s and early 1950s. Niagara Falls farm boys could be fellated for a pack of cigarettes.[27] Vermont farmers fucked one another; queers were said to take their holidays there because of the farm youth who frequented the local bars.[28] Indianapolis was known by one of Painter's friends as 'Tradeapolis' because of its soldier hustlers and generally available trade.[29] One of the contributors to an oral history of gay lives in the rural Midwest recalled that young straight men in Rochester, Minnesota, would come to the homosexuals for blowjobs when they failed to pick up women in the local bars.[30]

The Kinsey team's sexual histories provide statistical support. In 1948 they estimated that 30 per cent of US males had been brought to climax by male oral sex, and 14 per cent had 'brought other males to climax by the same techniques'.[31] They also observed that the 'highest frequencies' of homosexual sex that they had encountered were in individual rural communities:

> there is a fair amount of sexual contact among the older males in Western rural areas. It is a type of homosexuality which was probably common among pioneers and outdoor men in general. Today it is found among ranchmen, cattle men, prospectors, lumbermen, and farming groups in general – among groups that are virile, physically active. These are men who have faced the rigors of nature in the wild. They live on realities and on a minimum of theory. Such a background breeds the attitude that sex is sex, irrespective of the nature of the partner with whom the relation is had. Sexual relations are had with women when they are available, or with other males when outdoor routines bring men together into exclusively male groups. Such a pattern is not at all uncommon among pre-adolescent and early adolescent males in such rural areas, and it continues in a number of histories into the adult years and through marriage . . . Such a group of hard-riding, hard-hitting, assertive males would not tolerate the

Conclusion

affectations of some city groups that are involved in the homosexual; but this, as far as they can see, has little to do with the question of having sexual relations with other men. This type of rural homosexuality contradicts the theory that homosexuality in itself is an urban product.[32]

Homosexuals, as Painter once put it, 'fellate, pedicate, frictate, actively and passively, masturbate and mutually masturbate – and sometimes make combinations of these acts' – but often did so with a person who did not consider himself to be homosexual.[33] Looking back from the 1960s, he recalled, 'I spent a lot of time & energy fighting off, so to speak, the homosexual advances of these heterosexuals'.[34] Earlier, he had claimed that few pedicators were homosexual; insertive anal sex was far more likely to be practiced by 'normal males'.[35] We can also recall the sexual partners of Henry Faulkner, the fellator 'par excellence', who astonished his friends not so much by his number of contacts ('a steady stream of his trade coming up to be fellated') but with his success rate, 'the ease and speed with which he propositions anyone he sees – and gets affirmative results'. 'It is a revelation to me', wrote Painter, 'a definite broadening of the homosexual horizon to seemingly anyone (in the age group 15–23 which he likes) as a willing fellatee.'[36]

> Think he so straight prob'ly take it up the ass. I deal with straight guys they all take it up the ass. Then they go back to the wife and the girlfriend and talk about queers! They climb on toppa some cunt and sweat and shake. They can't come they say, Honey, put your finger up my ass please honey pop my ass. I pop your ass you bozo. I put my dick up your straight pussy so many times your old lady die laughin she see you with your buns in the air!
> *(Pause.)*
> I see him his buddies cruisin B-way every goddamn night. Lookin for cunt so weird – you know that come from nowhere look with the plaid shirts and the lettermen jackets they don't know it but they look like faggots. I cut one outa the pack – he so lame he say, Hey man know where I can get me some warm pussy? You know you gonna end up on toppa his butt grindin in to him he squeak and moan like a doll you squeeze it! Then he go back to Utica throw out his little brother the little queer can't live with such a real fuckin man and his real fuckin wife and real fuckin brats – just one big fuckin t.v. show. Little brother too pretty too sexy for such a big bullshit stud.[37]

This monologue by a young hustler called Blow in Alan Bowne's 1981 play *Forty Deuce* – and again in Paul Morrissey's 1982 film of the same name – conveys some of the themes of this book. The conflicted and asserted masculinities and the hetero–homo sex should hold no surprises. Despite its ludicrous plot, *Forty Deuce* is a grittier portrait of Times Square hustling than the Oscar-winning *Midnight Cowboy*, Kevin Bacon's teenage Ricky a more believable hustler than Jon Voight's cowboy.[38] Whether suppressed or more overt, Bowne's hustler–john violence ('She just scratch me so I would beat the fuck outa her') meshes with earlier discussions of this dialectic of desire.[39]

Forty Deuce appeared right on the cusp of the early impact of AIDS so is uncomplicated by that issue, yet we are essentially in a different universe to the hustling era of the 1950s and 1960s. Some of the hustlers of *Forty Deuce* are far younger than those we have been dealing with. They are like the *very* young hustlers photographed in Larry Clark's *Teenage Lust* (1983) at much the same time.[40] This corresponds to another moment in the history of representations of the hustler, what Kaye has termed the 'new social category' of the runaway.[41] We are referring here to the 'boy prostitute' of Robin Lloyd's best-selling 1970s expose of 'chickens' and 'chickenhawks': the claimed half-a-million runaway boys 'peddling their bodies'; 'Boy prostitutes in Times Square outnumber female hookers five to one' was the claim on Lloyd's cover.[42] There are no twelve-year-old hustlers, alive or dead, in our book.

While not exactly absent from the earlier scene, drugs are even more of a feature in this environment. (The name of the prostitute 'Blow' captures the duality of sex and drugs: 'I sell dick, I sell dope. I come, I go.')[43] There is a scene in the film where the hustlers are lined up, offering amphetamines and cocaine as well as their bodies: 'Coke, speed, cock?'[44] (See Figure 67.) The plot of the play and film, such as it is, hinges on the fact that the hustlers are trying to raise money for a drug-selling venture. And, apart from the referenced 'straightness' of their clients, heterosexuality does not much feature in this hustling: the indicated desires and interactions are all homosexual. ('Let social historians note', wrote one wit, 'that "Forty-Deuce" may be the first play to simulate even an unintentional act of homosexual-sadomasochistic-pedophilic necrophilia.')[45] There are no wives or girlfriends benefiting from these hustlers' sexual labour. The only 'pussy' referred to is male; the only girlfriends are male buddies; the only she's are he's. There are no females in the play, and, apart from a john's escort glimpsed during the opening credits, the only woman in the film is a dyke, an African-American drug dealer. So there is both continuity and change between the periods before and after the late 1960s, but essentially we are dealing with different sexual environments.

David Wojnarowicz's mesmerizing work of autobiographical fiction,

Conclusion

67. 'Coke, speed, cock?' *Forty Deuce* (1982: Paul Morrissey).

The Waterfront Journals (1996), drew on street stories collected in the 1970s and 1980s, many of them involving hustlers.[46] The young artist worked briefly as a teenage hustler in Times Square in the 1960s so he drew on personal experience.[47] His unpublished journal for 1978 records a chance meeting with a man whom he had hustled with in Times Square when he was only eleven. The man was still a hustler. They reminisced about the Mafia boss who sent one of his minions to approach them. They were taken in a limo to a place somewhere in the East 70s. A man and women had watched them as they got into the waiting car: 'I remember the girls eyes – she looked at me in a mixture of understanding and sadness; not quite pity but as if she would offer alternatives were there any on this whole wide country and there were none.' Their john told them about the Mafia, showing off his gun and its bullets. 'He wanted to get it on with the two of us at once but we said: no – we were still new to hustling together and to have sex in front of each other would confirm what we were doing in each others minds – it would make concrete the act of selling ones body.' The man took David's companion into the bedroom. He later returned and said that the man wanted David as well and would pay $25 extra each. David pushed him off. He could still see the Mafioso's 'huge bloated belly hospital white body like a huge codfish'. It turned out that his friend had lied about the money. He had been 'forcibly fucked' by the man and wanted the same to happen to David so that he did not lose face. They were paid and went back to Times Square to watch a horror movie.[48]

The prevailing theme of the stories in *The Waterfront Journals* and Wojnarowicz's *Close to the Knives* (1991) is male same-sex interaction. They are recognizably modern homosexual stories. When he wrote of the hustlers on 42nd Street, the 'occasional John who'd picked me up for some cash and wild times', and being 'in a midtown bathroom, fucking some businessman in a quiet toilet stall for twenty dollars', he was writing as 'a homosexual in America'.[49] This premise is continued effectively in the film based on Wojnarowicz's writings, Steve McLean's *Post Cards from America* (1994).[50]

The John Rechy of the 1960s versus the John Rechy of the 1970s perfectly illustrates this homosexualization of the hustler. The hustlers of *City of Night* (1963) were not considered 'queer'. If they lived with fairies (treated as women) and were paid for sex with men, their status as 'trade' was secure.[51] 'With Chuck', Rechy wrote of one hustler, 'and I knew this instinctively and without a doubt – there was nothing ulterior in his making it with males. It was merely easier in the world in which he found himself. That sexually he liked only girls, I never doubted.'[52] *The Sexual Outlaw* (1977), however, is a choreographed celebration of homosexuality on the eve of AIDS, a homage to gay masculinity that could only have come from the 1970s. The sexual outlaw of the book's title is unambiguously homosexual: 'The promiscuous homosexual is a sexual revolutionary. Each moment of his outlaw existence he confronts repressive laws, repressive "morality". Parks, alleys, subway tunnels, garages, streets – these are the battlefields.'[53] 'When gay people suck and fuck in the streets, that . . . is a revolutionary act.'[54] These outlaws, fucking and sucking for sexual freedom, include hustlers. The hustler is now homosexual – cruising for excitement as well as money. When the latter, 'he will most often pretend to be "straight" – uncomfortably rationalizing the subterfuge by reminding himself that those attracted to him will usually – though certainly not always – want him to be that, like the others of his breed'.[55] Getting paid for sex is no longer the *heterosexual* hustler's alibi: instead, it is a means of heightening his *homosexual* longing. 'There is a terrific, terrible excitement in getting paid by another man for sex.'[56]

Granted, there is an argument for a degree of ambivalence in the sexuality of the hustlers in Gus Van Sant's *My Own Private Idaho* (1991).[57] And the character Scott, played by Keanu Reeves, goes off with a female.[58] However, he was never a convincing hustler (not merely because of Reeves's acting inability), and the more believable Mike, played by River Phoenix, who is in love with Scott, seems more homo

68. River Phoenix as Mike Waters and Keanu Reeves as Scott Favor, hustlers in Gus Van Sant's *My Own Private Idaho* (1991). Fine Line/Photofest.

than hetero.[59] (See Figure 68.) The young Mexican immigrants in Van Sant's earlier film, *Mala Noche* (1985), based on the 1970s memoirs of the Portland poet Walt Curtis, are more attuned to the sexuality of the hustlers that we have focused on.[60] They like girls but will take advantage of a *puto* (faggot), trading their bodies, or the promise of their bodies, for cash, car rides, bed for the night, alcohol, and drugs. They may fuck but will not be fucked; can be sucked but will not suck. Homosexual sex, for them, is something that they will later abandon.[61]

With one or two exceptions, then, the 1980s and early 1990s fictional hustlers are different creatures. The young Kansas hustler Neil McCormick in Scott Heim's moving novel *Mysterious Skin* (1995) is attracted to males from an early age, thumbing through his mother's *Playgirl*, daydreaming about its pictures of rugged masculinity, watching his mother and her boyfriend having sex and imagining himself 'in Mum's position'.[62] When he hustles in New York he has to deal not only with the long-established threat of violence (he is raped by a john) but also with AIDS: 'I was locked here, in this new place where KS no longer meant the abbreviation for Kansas.'[63] (See Figure 69.)

The sex in Bruce LaBruce and Rick Castro's *Hustler White* (1996) – a range of explicit interaction set in and around Santa Monica

69. Joseph Gordon-Levitt as Neil McCormick, the young gay hustler in Gregg Araki's film version of *Mysterious Skin* (2004). Desperate Pictures/Tartan USA/Photofest.

Boulevard in Los Angeles – is unequivocally gay. There is not a woman in sight. Even the baby is male. Like the earlier films *Flesh* and *My Hustler*, the camera lingers on the hustler's body. Yet the imagery is gay rather than straight: from the writer character, played by LaBruce ('To the boy his glazed, fixed stare has just passed over the searching gaze of any one of a thousand potential tricks of the day'), to the self-presentation of the hustler (see Figure 70). The only references to heterosexuality are the voice-over – 'Are you gay or straight?' – and the information that the hustler, Monty Ward, started hustling when his girlfriend left him with their baby.[64] (Ironically, however, off-screen, the lead actor, the model Tony Ward who is married with children and formerly dated Madonna, refuses to identify as gay or straight: 'I don't define myself.')[65]

Studies of hustlers in the 1980s and 1990s are preoccupied with their role as transmitters of HIV and their link with drug culture. Thus in an AIDS-related study of over two hundred male prostitutes in Atlanta, Georgia, 1988–91, most were drug users, especially of cocaine and crack-cocaine. Drugs have far more of presence in this cohort than they had for the hustlers that we have dealt with.[66] We have been covering a pre-AIDS era, whereas half of homosexual hustlers, nearly a fifth of heterosexual

70. Tony Ward as the hustler Monty Ward in Bruce LaBruce and Rick Castro's *Hustler White* (1996). © Bruce LaBruce and Rick Castro.

hustlers, and over a third of bisexual hustlers in the Atlanta study were HIV-positive.[67]

The heterosexual hustler by no means disappears. Nearly half (46 per cent) of the hustlers in the Atlanta study self-identified as heterosexual ('straight'); researchers noted the presence of men who wore tight jeans, had tattoos, and 'exhibited overt displays of stereotyped masculine traits through their stance, dress, and mannerisms'. (Such display intensified when potential customers were nearby.)[68] 'All these men specifically mentioned having girlfriends or sexual relations with women. They showed the field team pictures of their girlfriends and recounted stories about their sexual conquests.'[69] The old trope about active/passive resurfaces. 'These prostitutes reported that they most often dominated the sexual situation with their paying partners, noting that those men who choose hypermasculine-appearing men (trade) wish to be dominated. They generally limited their sexual activity . . . to masturbation and oral sex . . . They almost always were fellated and most vociferously denied engaging in receptive anal sex.'[70] The sociologists who coordinated the study concluded that the 'sexual identity' of the heterosexual hustler 'was validated by the hypermasculine persona which they projected; their girlfriends, real or imagined; and their refusal to engage in anal sex, particularly passive anal sex'.[71] Their denial of all forms of anal sex is not exactly born out by the evidence, for the article also records that while only one in twenty admitted to practicing receptive anal sex, over half had admitted to engaging in using a condom in insertive anal intercourse.[72]

The lure of trade continued in the homosexual imaginary. We can see it in the artist Keith Haring's obsession with young Hispanic men, including the heterosexual LA2 (Angel Ortiz) and Gil Vazquez ('He's ... straight and has a girlfriend').[73] One of his closest friends complained that Haring surrounded himself with Puerto Rican hustlers.[74] Not unsurprisingly the trade aesthetic features in the art and photography of Edward Melcarth's former student Richard Taddei.[75] (See Figures 71–73.)

We can see trade too in Larry Clark's photographs of rough white teens – whatever authorial intent. These portraits of teenage trade depend upon a sexualized female presence and heterosexual sex. His very young hustlers pick up a drugged teen and have group sex with her, and when one of his subjects is quoted it is to distinguish himself from the 'faggot' who came on to him – 'I say no I'm straight I'm straight I'm straight'.[76] The photography of Philip-Lorca diCorcia deliberately plays with the 'fantasy of trade', men on Hollywood's Santa Monica Boulevard who are not necessarily hustlers but who may well be, are photographed in frames reminiscent of trade imagery – including a mirror shot – and captioned with a dollar amount, $50, $30, $25, indicating the fee paid for their posing but which clearly holds open the possibility that it could be their sexual price.[77]

The heterosexuality in Clark's work may be more fragile than I am intimating; José Esteban Muñoz is perceptive in his claims for the way in which 'queerness continues to hum in the background' of such photographs and how the female is used to anchor them in heterosexuality.[78] Indeed the mix of hetero and homo, so featured in the sexual regime that we have been covering in this book, and arguably present in Clark's teens, where naked male flesh and homoerotic interaction predominates, continues in the 1980s New York described by Juan Rivera, one of the artist Keith Haring's Puerto Rican lovers. Haring would pick up boys at Coney Island: 'They were gay ... they were straight.' And Haring and his friend the pop icon Madonna would compete for the Puerto Rican trade – 'Street-looking Latino boys ... 'Cause they both liked the *same* boys' – what Frances Negrón-Muntaner has referred to as Madonna's 'queer Latin hunger'.[79]

However, the homosexual hustler has increased visibility in this

Conclusion

71. New York hustler, 1980s. Collection of Richard Taddei, New York.

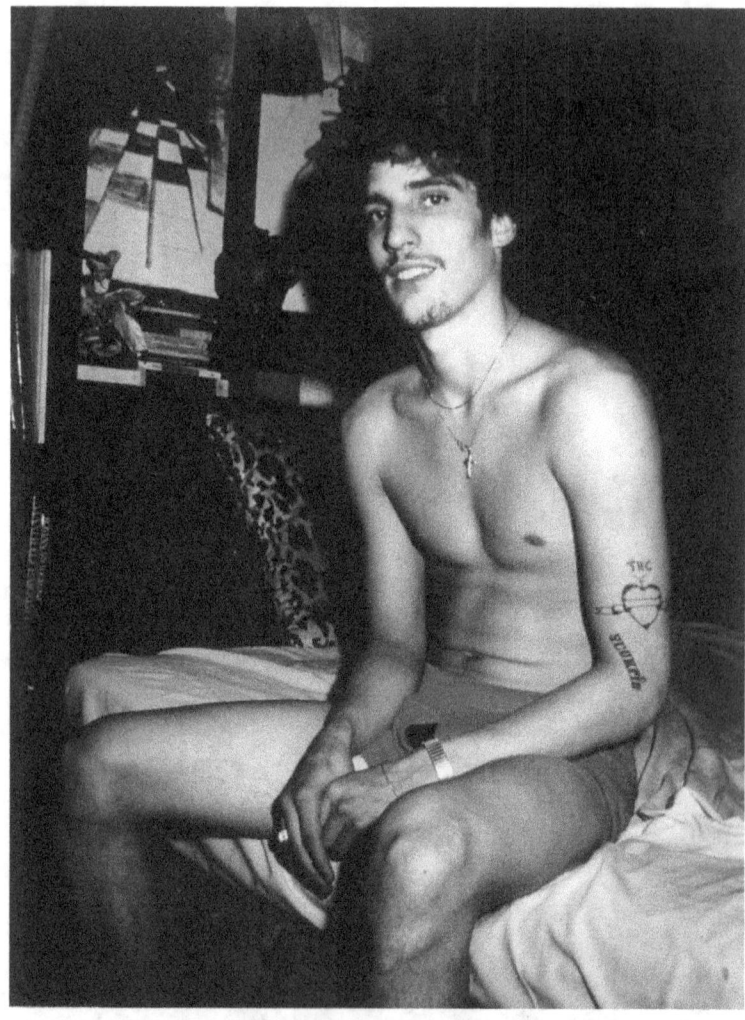

72. New York hustler, 1980s. Collection of Richard Taddei, New York.

period. Muñoz argues that Clark's heterosexuality becomes stretched in the last section of *Teenage Lust*, with the pictures of young Puerto Rican hustlers.[80] Indeed, Clark's text says as much:

> the main thing about 42nd Street, I mean about all those pictures, the main thing is just about one or two pictures of the kids' eyes, the way a kid looks at a man, and the way when he's looking at the camera, he's actually looking

Conclusion

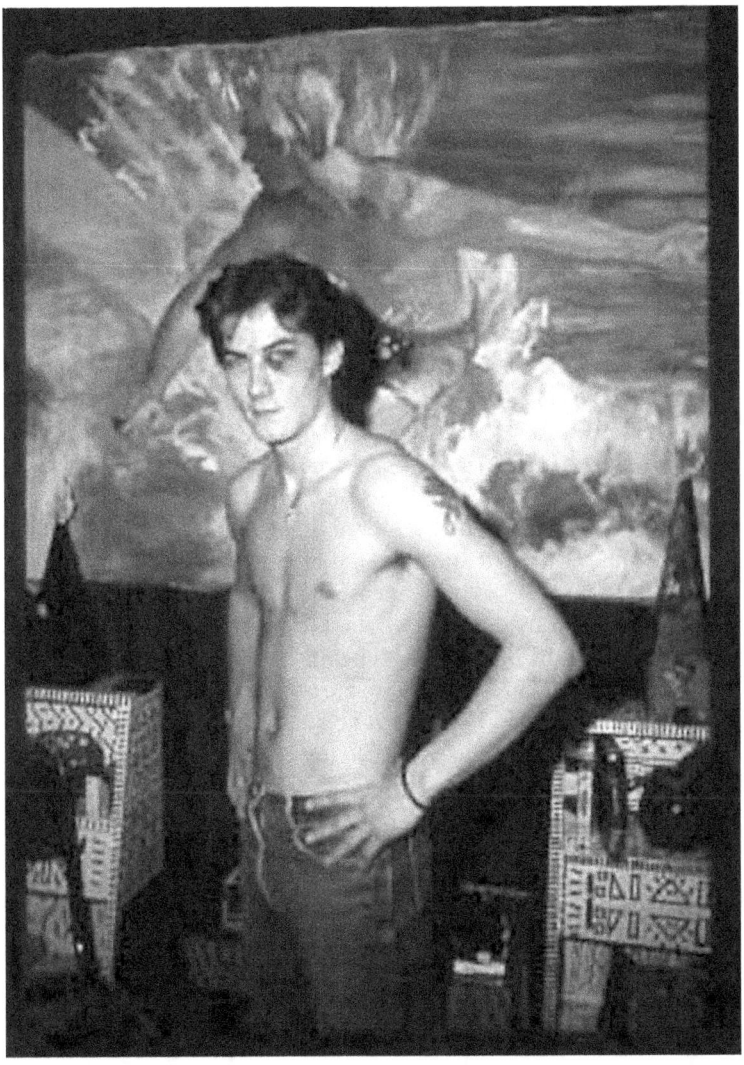

73. New York hustler, 1980s. Collection of Richard Taddei, New York.

at a man . . . The picture is of what the kid is offering. The kid is offering himself.[81]

Rivera worked as a 42nd Street hustler in the late 1970s when he arrived in New York. He was gay – 'I knew I was gonna be a faggot 'cause I liked boys' – and was briefly 'married' to another hustler, but rapidly became aware that johns wanted their prostitutes straight.[82] His partner told him, 'You don't blow johns. You don't get fucked. You just strip and serv'em dick.'[83] Even though customers knew it was pretence, it was what they expected. 'The money kept my face straight; gave me a straight *macho* face.'[84]

A study of Boston hustlers during the 1970s possibly indicated a shift in the sexual terrain when it assessed its subjects at a mean of 3.3 in the Kinsey scale, indicating a slight favouring of the homosexual in the previously discussed heterosexual/homosexual sexual rating. Street hustlers and part-time male prostitutes were closer to a 4 in the 0–6 scale where 6 indicated exclusive homosexuality.[85] (Our hustlers, we may recall, were a 1–2.) When the researchers in Atlanta asked their subjects 'Aside from hustling, are you gay, straight or bisexual?' nearly a fifth (18 per cent) identified as homosexual ('gay').[86] The percentage was even higher in a study of fifty New York male prostitutes in the late 1980s: 50 per cent were classified as homosexual.[87] Indeed the report's authors specifically discussed other studies that had 'found increasing proportions of male prostitutes to be bisexual and homosexual'.[88] In his account of Times Square hustlers in the early 1990s, another research project prompted by AIDS and featuring the impact of crack-cocaine, Robert McNamara classified 66 per cent of his Times Square hustlers as heterosexual, 23 per cent as homosexual, and 11 per cent as bisexual – though he noted that in 1992 Times Square was a heterosexual hustler haunt, with the homosexual hustlers favouring Greenwich Village.[89] A recent study of Canadian male sex workers, including street hustlers, even included a special group, the liberationists, 'young homosexuals . . . for whom prostitution is a way of living out fantasies, exploring new experiences and partners, and profiting from these discoveries'.[90] The writer and former hustler Rick Whitaker, who combined paid sex with a serious drug intake when he moved to New York in the late 1980s, could easily be placed in this category. He was certainly a gay hustler.[91]

By contrasting the sexual milieu of the 1950s and 1960s with that of the 1970s and 1980s and arguing for the homosexualization of the hustler, I am not claiming that the heterosexual hustler was impossible after the late 1960s or that his world is now unrecognizable. Indeed that rather nebulous recent phenomenon of DL or 'On the Down Low', the name given to the behavior of African-American men who although ostensibly straight will have sex with other men while proclaiming that they are not gay, seems hauntingly familiar.[92] There is a sense in which the sexual flexibility of the 1990s onwards, of what has been called the queer generation, is more in keeping with the subject matter of this book; Henry Abelove has noted that his queer students are more at ease with pre-liberationist than post-liberationist material, more attuned to the 1950s and 1960s than the immediate period after Stonewall.[93] The hustlers in Amos Badertscher's *Baltimore Portraits* (1999), his photographic study of Baltimore street life from the 1970s onwards, certainly convey the sexual indeterminacy that I have been keen to convey for my earlier period. His textually framed photographic archives of fragmentary, drug-addicted lives, often ended by AIDS, include both 'she' and 'he', the sexually androgynous and unambiguously feminine as well as rough trade.[94] There are hustlers who have girlfriends but seek out men for survival and the supply of drugs. 'Like all boys of his class he is "straight" but has been hustling men since 14.'[95] 'Having sex with men is about a lot of things – authority, abuse, thrills, aspirations, boredom, survival – but it isn't necessarily about identity.'[96]

In order to discuss Mexican sexuality in the 1990s, Héctor Carrillo juxtaposed two templates of sexual identity. One was what he termed the 'traditional system' or the sex/gender model, where, much as we saw of George Chauncey's analysis of sex in early twentieth-century New York, gender was the determiner of sexual identity. For a man what was important was his demeanour rather than the sex of the person with whom he had sexual relations. Male 'normality' was governed by declared masculinity – direct eye contact, dominant behaviour – and by an assumption that normal men were sexual penetrators or inserters. Male abnormality was reflected in effeminacy and woman-like demeanour (effeminate men did not make direct eye contact and were to receive rather than initiate any sexual attention) and by their passivity: they were assumed to be receptive rather than insertive in anal sex. Thus when *hombres* or *hombres normales* (normal men) had sex with *maricones* (effeminate men) their masculinity was reinforced rather than undermined and they were not classified as homosexual. 'Absent from this model', explains Carrillo, 'is the notion of "bisexuality" as a separate category, because individuals considered *normal* are given some latitude to transgress and have sex with members of their own sex without losing their status, as well as to continue engaging in sexual interaction with members of the opposite sex.'[97] The masculine homosexual is invisible in this gender-based sexual model. The other model of sexual identity is the 'modern' model based on sexual object choice, with the identities that readers will be familiar with: heterosexual, homosexual, and bisexual. What governed normality was the sex of a person's sexual partner, not their effeminacy or masculinity. *Hombres heterosexuales* were 'normal' masculine men attracted to women. *Homosexuales* were men attracted to other men 'regardless of whether they or their partners are masculine or feminine in demeanor'.[98] Men no longer had to be effeminate to be homosexual. Those formerly of the normal group who had sex with both men and women were now *bisexuales* or bisexual.

However, the most important point about these two models is that Carrillo's subjects did not always conform to a single regime and he refers rather to 'amalgams and convolutions', to a hybrid sexual culture, where, for example, male homosexuality was still conceived in terms of effeminacy and where it was possible to have normal homosexuals (because they exhibited an accepted masculinity) and (by a similar logic) heterosexuals who preferred sex with men.[99] Carrillo has categories such as normal but also heterosexual, heterosexuals with a homosexual interest, normal men who have sex with homosexuals, and '*hombres normales* who have sex with *hombres normales*'.[100] That Carrillo's work has more than passing interest for those interested in the history of sexualities in New York is clear from a recent study of the sexual attitudes and practices of Dominican and Puerto Rican men in this very city in the early twenty-first century. Though Miguel A. Muñoz-Laboy describes his subjects as bisexual, their desires and practices are very similar to Carrillo's informants. In this New York ethnography there is 'lifetime homoerotic desire and casual sex with women', 'lifetime heteroerotic desire, but commercial sex with men', 'lifetime heteroerotic/transgender desire', and 'lifetime sexual desire for women and men'.[101]

Carrillo's world (and that of Muñoz-Laboy) is not unlike the one that we have been exploring in this book; indeed at one point he invokes the 'multiple systems' of Chauncey's New York from the 1930s to the 1950s as a comparable sexual mix.[102] The difference between Carrillo and Chauncey, however, is that the latter is certain of a transition from one sexual regime to another where a separation between homosexual and heterosexual is both inevitable and complete. Carrillo, however, even for the 1990s, resists such certainties, preferring to think of adaptation, reinterpretation, and personal negotiation. It is, moreover, a dynamic, ongoing process: 'A map of these hybrid interpretations would depict the categories as static and frozen in one time period and would not represent the flexibility that hybridity generates.'[103] My book deals with the 'multiple systems' of sex that Chauncey recognized, but did not sufficiently explore – in terms of either their range and complexity in the 1930s and 1940s or their sustained role in the sexual history of the 1950s and 1960s.

It should be clear to the reader that I am resisting gay identity as a heuristic guide to the period before the late 1960s. Another Vidal-like moment occurred when the gay historian Eric Garber interviewed the writer and artist Richard Bruce Nugent, a survivor of the Harlem Renaissance, about what Garber called 'gay' culture in Harlem in the 1920s and 1930s. There was a clear gap in perception when they talked about a particular speakeasy:

E. Was it predominantly gay there or just partially gay?
B. Well you know that very few places were predominantly . . . I don't know what you mean by predominant 'gay'. What do you mean by 'gay'?
E. Were most of the people there . . .
B. Most of the people there would go to bed with one another if that's what you mean . . .
E. I do.
B. O. K. Then everyone was gay . . . There were the men, there were the dames. What they did in bed I don't know. I guess they did in bed what they wanted to do.

It was clear from this interview and Nugent's follow-up conversations and correspondence that although he might identify as gay in the 1980s he was at a loss to describe the earlier period in such terms. He went on to talk about the attraction of 'trade' and of sex, even love, involving men who might have to be paid for their affection or who disparaged 'queers' while sexually involved with them.[104] He wrote to Garber that a person's 'sexual preferences were not a matter of any group concern – but the business of individuals who made their preferences known to other individuals one met or socialized with in the ordinary course of daily living'.[105] (Nugent, it should be noted, was the author of the 1926 prose poem 'Smoke, Lillies, and Jade', with a protagonist who has sex with both men and women without feeling the need to name his desires, a text used by the literary critic Scott Herring as an example of 1920s sexual illegibility.)[106] In another interview (for Jeff Kisseloff's oral history of Manhattan) Nugent observed of Harlem in the 1920s, 'People did what they wanted to do with whom they wanted to do it. You didn't get on the rooftops and shout, "I fucked my wife last night." So why would you get on the roof and say, "I loved prick." You didn't. You just did what you wanted to do. Nobody was in the closet. There wasn't any closet.'[107]

He was even more succinct in the documentary *Before Stonewall* (1985), remarking, somewhat against the grain of the film's teleology, 'We didn't call it, we did it.'[108]

The post-Stonewall shadow, like all shadows, obscures rather than reveals and casts its pall over the most sensitive of analyses. Thus Chad Heap's meticulous history of Chicago and New York in the 1920s and 1930s uses the term 'gay' though he knows (indeed states) that it is anachronistic, and continually invokes the 'now-hegemonic hetero/homo sexual binary' when it is never actually demonstrated and in fact flies in the face of the very material that he has so skilfully retrieved. Thus his history has a clear end point in place by 1940: 'the refashioning of sexual normalcy and difference from a gendered system of marginalized fairies and mannish women to a cultural dyad that privileged heterosexual object choice'.[109] In Heap's history, the 'gendered framework of sexuality' is perpetually yielding to 'the now dominant binary of heterosexuality and homosexuality'.[110] Margot Canaday's otherwise ground-breaking history of sexuality and citizenship is firmly anchored in a paradigm that it never questions. It is a history of the state's role in the inscription of a 'homosexual-heterosexual binary' in place by the 1950s.[111]

Sexual history's assumed shift in sexual configurations from acts to identities (homosexual and heterosexual), supposedly in place by the mid-twentieth century, finds little support in the world of the hustler revealed in the pages above. And this was in 'Gay New York', theoretically the most sophisticated site for developing modern sexualities. The configurations of active and passive were part of a more complex reconfiguration of these simple divisions, with rules of engagement that were frequently breached in a genuine sexual multiplicity. The hustler was neither homosexual nor heterosexual, and was involved in a range of acts that did not proclaim the sexual identity demanded by modernity. He did not, as I hope I have demonstrated, operate in some kind of historical vacuum. The sexual and cultural context of male prostitution is far more significant than the prostitutes themselves.

'Acts do not translate, one-for-one, into identities', Janet Halley has wisely observed. 'Once that equation is gone, it becomes difficult to maintain the corollary assumptions that the world properly provides two and only two sexual orientation identities, and that heterosexuality is pure of sodomitic practice and homoerotic impulse.'[112] The world of trade and the hustler certainly illustrates her axiom. Commenting on a study of Los Angeles homosexuality in the 1960s involving sailor sex, Halley argues that its languages of situational sex, susceptibility, and passivity, imply an uncomplicated sailor heterosexuality that may have not existed: alternatively, we should not assume such men's unequivocal homosexuality.[113] Trade, as Chris Cagle has observed, seems to fall 'in between the very mappings of identity and behavior'.[114]

'You straight?' is the rhetorical question posed by the hustler Joe Dallesandro in *Flesh* (1968). 'Nobody's straight; what's straight? It's not a thing of being straight or being not straight, you just do whatever you have to do.' And then later he adds: 'It's only going to suck your peter, man!'[115] It is interesting that, although the whole tone of the film is homoerotic, the only engaged sex that we actually see is with women (his wife and his girlfriend). Sexual interactions with males are off-camera or detached, a perpetual deferral that Thomas Waugh has called cockteasing.[116]

Ironically, that most sensitive of 1990s cultural commentators, Michael Moon, while reclaiming the varied sexualities of the film *Midnight Cowboy*, seemed unable to apply the same analysis to *My Hustler*. Paul America 'poses' as trade. Such men *pretend* to be straight. Moon refers to 'this ragged pretense', with the enactment of 'a particularly complex kind of epistemology of the closet' when the hustler and john 'imaginarily reclothe themselves in the fantasmatic bodies of two straight guys'.[117] Yet I would argue that, like *Flesh*, the film *My Hustler* (1965) is interesting for its sexual indeterminacy. It is true that there are assumptions of sexual selfhood, that hustlers engaged in homosexual sex will become homosexual themselves like the experienced hustler Joe, 'the Sugar Plum Fairy', played by Joe Campbell, who, in the 1950s and early 1960s, was Harvey Milk's New York lover before he went to San Francisco. Thus Joe's amusing speech about olives: 'when you first start out, I mean, you know you think a john is a john . . . it's just so much sex, but after a while, you know, it's like olives, you get accustomed to it'. But the film also allows for resistance to this proposition. 'Not everyone gets accustomed to olives', the younger hustler Paul retorts. 'Not that you don't like girls or anything', continues Joe, accommodating a hetero/homo mix, 'but you actually . . . sort of enjoy making it with a younger guy once in a while.'[118] One of the lures that the homosexual Ed offers the hustler Paul at the film's end is access to beautiful women. At least one contemporary critic recognized the polymorphous sexuality of Warhol and Morrissey's films.[119]

The world of trade and the New York hustler, then, has implications for the way in which we view the sexual history of America after 1940. Not only was the sexual fluidity of the 1920s and 1930s (discussed in this book's early chapters) remade and retained in the 1940s, 1950s and 1960s, but the association of homosexuality with effeminacy – still powerful during these later decades – meant that many of those engaging in what might clearly seem homosexual acts did not consider themselves to be homosexual. Many men who were homosexual distinguished between their masculine same-sex desires and personae and those of the effeminate faggot. In 1963, Donald Webster Cory and John P. LeRoy, authors of *The Homosexual and His Society: A View from Within*, were noting the emergence of what they saw as a new homosexual type, the muscle-builder, whose very fashioned masculinity was a protection from admitting a homosexuality firmly associated with effeminacy. 'One may see himself as anything, but not as a "queer"'![120]

'I just can't explain it, I reckon. But there's something about a man's body that haunts you and makes you do things that you wouldn't think of doing before. Like I said, I ain't queer, but honest ... I think a man's body is purtier than a woman's.' The hyper-masculine marine and the hustler in Carl Corley's *Trick of the Trade* (1968), who really did go off together into the sunset, said that nothing was more powerful than 'two real he men in bed coming on with each other'.[121] The homosexuality described in my book – with its tensions between perceived masculinity and effeminacy – is a long way from the influential notions of gay 'collectivity' or 'peoplehood'.[122]

We have been traversing confusing sexual terrain where current concepts are not always the most helpful guide to what the writer John Cheever (in this chapter's epigraph) called 'the lack of universality in our sexual appetites'. But it is an important mental journey. Writing of his ongoing project on the sexual cultures of 1960s New York, including Warhol's oeuvre and milieu, Douglas Crimp has stressed the significance of such work. 'Without knowledge of the insurgent disruptive force expressed in early queer alternative cultures, we are left with a bland narrative of progressive normalization'.[123] If this book helps to chart an earlier history, a history that destabilizes rather than merely confirms sexual identities, it will have been worth writing.

Notes

1 J. Cheever, *The Journals of John Cheever*, ed. R. Gottlieb (New York, 2008), pp. 245–6.
2 G. Vidal, *Sexually Speaking: Collected Sex Writings* (San Francisco, 1999), p. 53.

3 Ibid., pp. 138, 195.
4 An interview from the early 1990s, quoted by J. Loughery, *The Other Side of Silence: Men's Lives and Gay Identities: A Twentieth-century History* (New York, 1998), p. 347.
5 Vidal, *Sexually Speaking*, pp. 254, 257, 258. Emphasis in original.
6 K. Kaye, 'Male prostitution in the twentieth century: pseudohomosexuals, hoodlum homosexuals, and exploited teens', *Journal of Homosexuality*, 46 (2003), 1–77 (31 for quote).
7 D. W. Cory and J. P. LeRoy, *The Homosexual and His Society: A View from Within* (New York, 1963), pp. 99, 100.
8 L. Humphreys, 'New styles in homosexual manliness', in J. A. McCaffrey (ed.), *The Homosexual Dialectic* (Englewood Cliffs, NJ, 1972), p. 75. My emphasis.
9 W. Leyland (ed.), *Gay Sunshine Interviews: Volume 1* (San Francisco, 1978), p. 260.
10 C. Casillo, *Outlaw: The Lives and Careers of John Rechy* (Los Angeles, 2002), pp. 75–6.
11 C. A. Tripp, *The Homosexual Matrix* (New York, 1987), pp. 125–6. First published in 1975.
12 Ibid., pp. 126, 127.
13 Ibid., p. 127.
14 The Kinsey Institute for Research in Sex, Gender, and Reproduction, University of Indiana, Bloomington (hereafter, KI), The Thomas Painter Collection (hereafter, Painter), Box 1, Series 2, c. 1, Vol. 25 and 26a: Painter Letters: 5 August 1968. Emphasis in original.
15 A. C. Kinsey, W. B. Pomeroy, and C. E. Martin, *Sexual Behavior in the Human Male* (Philadelphia, 1948), p. 650.
16 D. W. Cory, *The Homosexual in America: A Subjective Approach* (New York, 1951), p. 205.
17 C. R. Johnson, 'Columbia's Orient: Gender, Geography, and the Invention of Sexuality in Rural America' (PhD Thesis, University of Michigan, 2003), pp. 157–60. See also C. R. Johnson, 'Casual sex: towards a "prehistory" of gay life in bohemian America', *Interventions*, 10 (2008), 303–20.
18 Painter, Box 1, Series 2, c. 1, Vol. 2: 29 July 1945.
19 A. Karlen, *Sexuality and Homosexuality: A New View* (New York, 1971), pp. 63–4.
20 J. Gerassi, *The Boys of Boise: Furor, Vice, and Folly in an American City* (Seattle, 2001) p. 32. First published in 1966.
21 T. Kissack (ed.), 'Alfred Kinsey and homosexuality in the '50s: the recollections of Samuel Morris Steward as told to Len Evans', *Journal of the History of Sexuality*, 9 (2000), 487.
22 E. White, *My Lives* (London, 2005), p. 115.
23 Vidal, *Sexually Speaking*, pp. 53–4. The essay originally appeared in 1970.

24 Loughery, *Other Side of Silence*, p. 180.
25 J. Howard, *Men Like That: A Southern Queer History* (Chicago, 1999), p. 123.
26 Karlen, *Sexuality and Homosexuality*, p. 43.
27 Painter, Box 1, Series 2, c. 1, Vol. 6: 16 July 1949.
28 Painter, Box 1, Series 2, c. 1, Vol. 7: 26 March 1950.
29 Painter, Box 1, Series 2, c. 1, Vol. 8: 30 September 1951.
30 W. Fellows, *Farm Boys: Lives of Gay Men from the Rural Midwest* (Madison, WI, 1996), p. 63.
31 Kinsey, Pomeroy, and Martin, *Sexual Behavior in the Human Male*, p. 373.
32 Ibid., p. 457, 459.
33 Painter, Box 1, Series 2, c. 1, Vol. 6: 21 May 1949.
34 Painter, Box 1, Series 2, c. 1, Vol. 25 and 26a: 5 August 1968.
35 KI, Thomas Painter, 'Male Homosexuals and Their Prostitutes in Contemporary America' (New York, 1941), Vol. 1: 'American Homosexuals', p. 231.
36 Painter, Box 1, Series 2, c. 1, Vol. 7: 26 March and 20 April 1950. Faulkner's biographer seems unaware of his links with Painter, is curiously silent about his subject's time in New York, and rather naive about his friendships (described as mostly 'platonic'): C. House, *The Outrageous Life of Henry Faulkner: Portrait of an Appalachian Artist* (Knoxville, TN, 1988), p. 90.
37 A. Bowne, *Forty Deuce: A Play* (New York, 1983), pp. 39–40. First performed in 1981. *Forty Deuce* (1982: Paul Morrissey).
38 Bacon played Ricky in both play and film.
39 Bowne, *Forty Deuce*, p. 70.
40 L. Clark, *Teenage Lust* (New York, 1983): '42nd street series'.
41 Kaye, 'Male prostitution in the twentieth century', 39.
42 R. Lloyd, *For Money or Love: Boy Prostitution in America* (New York, 1976).
43 Quoted in M. Yacowar, *The Films of Paul Morrissey* (Cambridge, 1993), p. 97.
44 *Forty Deuce* (1982: Paul Morrissey).
45 F. Rich, 'Theater: "Forty-Deuce", street hustlers' story', *New York Times*, 25 March 1981.
46 D. Wojnarowicz, *The Waterfront Journals* (New York, 1996).
47 D. Wojnarowicz, *In the Shadow of the American Dream: The Diaries of David Wojnarowicz*, ed. A. Scholder (New York, 1999), pp. 47, 59.
48 Fales Library Special Collections, Elmer Holmes Bobst Library, New York University, MS 092, The David Wojnarowicz Papers, ca. 1954–1992, Box 1, Folder 6: New York Journal, 'Human Head III', 24 April 1978.
49 D. Wojnarowicz, *Close to the Knives: A Memoir of Disintegration* (New York, 1991), pp. 170–1.
50 *Post Cards from America* (1994: Steve McLean).

51 J. Rechy, *City of Night* (New York, 1984), p. 97. First published in 1963.
52 Ibid., p. 129.
53 J. Rechy, *The Sexual Outlaw: A Documentary* (New York, 1977), p. 28.
54 Ibid., p. 71.
55 Ibid., p. 39.
56 Ibid., p. 153.
57 For this ambivalence, see R. Lang, 'My Own Private Idaho and the new queer road movies', in his *Masculine Interests: Homoerotics in Hollywood Film* (New York, 2002), pp. 249–53.
58 M. De Angelis has discussed this actor's pansexual screen image: M. De Angelis, *Gay Fandom and Crossover Stardom: James Dean, Mel Gibson, and Keanu Reeves* (Durham, NC, 2001), ch. 4.
59 *My Own Private Idaho* (1991: Gus Van Sant).
60 *Mala Noche* (1985: Gus Van Sant).
61 W. Curtis, *Mala Noche* (Portland, OR, 1997). First published in 1977.
62 S. Heim, *Mysterious Skin* (New York, 2005), p. 26. He is also molested by his basketball coach.
63 Ibid., p. 235.
64 *Hustler White* (1996: Bruce Labruce and Rick Castro).
65 See http://tony-ward.com/_private/2009IDmag.htm.
66 J. Boles and K.W. Elifson, 'Sexual identity and HIV: the male prostitute', *The Journal of Sex Research*, 31 (1994), 39–46.
67 Ibid.
68 Ibid., 42.
69 Ibid., 43.
70 Ibid.
71 Ibid.
72 Ibid., 42, 43.
73 R. Montez, '"Trade" marks: LA2, Keith Haring, and a queer economy of collaboration', *GLQ*, 12 (2006), 425–40; J. Gruen, *Keith Haring: The Authorized Biography* (New York, 1992), p. 215.
74 Gruen, *Keith Haring*, p. 140.
75 See his website at www.richardtaddei.com/Index.html.
76 Clark, *Teenage Lust*, no pagination.
77 Montez, '"Trade" marks', 428; P. Galassi and P. L. diCorcia, *Philip-Lorca diCorcia* (New York, 2000), pp. 12–13, 50–73 (p. 66 for the mirror shot).
78 J. E. Muñoz, 'Rough boy trade: queer desire/straight identity in the photography of Larry Clark', in D. Bright (ed.), *The Passionate Camera: Photography and Bodies of Desire* (London, 1998), p. 173.
79 A. Cruz-Malavé, *Queer Latino Testimonio, Keith Haring, and Juanito Xtravaganza: Hard Tails* (New York, 2007), pp. 39, 41, 43; F. Negrón-Muntaner, *Boricua Pop: Puerto Ricans and the Latinization of American Culture* (New York, 2004), p. 147.

80 Muñoz, 'Rough boy trade'.
81 Clark, *Teenage Lust*, no pagination. He wrote this in 1981.
82 Cruz-Malavé, *Queer Latino Testimonio*, pp. 15, 22.
83 Ibid., p. 22.
84 Ibid., p. 23.
85 D. M. Allen, 'Young male prostitutes: a psychosocial study', *Archives of Sexual Behavior*, 9 (1980), 413.
86 Boles and Elifson, 'Sexual identity and HIV', 40. Data from transvestite hustlers had been gathered but was not included in the study: ibid., 41.
87 R. R. Pleak and H. F. L. Meyer-Bahlburg, 'Sexual behavior and AIDS knowledge of young male prostitutes in Manhattan', *The Journal of Sex Research*, 27 (1990), 557–87.
88 Ibid., 577.
89 R. P. McNamara, *The Times Square Hustler: Male Prostitution in New York City* (Westport, CT, 1994), p. 38.
90 M. Dorais, *Rent: The World of Male Sex Workers* (Montreal and Kingston, 2005), p. 41.
91 R. Whitaker, *Assuming the Position: A Memoir of Hustling* (New York, 1999).
92 J. L. King, *On the Down Low* (New York, 2005), by a practitioner, does not really throw a great deal of light on the subject. More useful is S. Herring, *Queering the Underworld: Slumming, Literature, and the Undoing of Lesbian and Gay History* (Chicago, 2007), pp. 196–209.
93 H. Abelove, *Deep Gossip* (Minneapolis, MN, 2003), pp. 53, 94–5.
94 A. Badertscher, *Baltimore Portraits* (Durham, NC, 1999).
95 Ibid., Portrait of Walt MacNew.
96 T. Curtain, 'A Baltimore essay: photography, sexuality, community', in ibid., p. 2.
97 H. Carrillo, *The Night Is Young: Sexuality in Mexico in the Time of AIDS* (Chicago, 2002), p. 39.
98 Ibid., p. 62.
99 Ibid., p. 79: the title of the chapter.
100 Ibid., p. 93.
101 M. A. Muñoz-Laboy, 'Beyond "MSM": sexual desire among bisexually-active Latino men in New York City', *Sexualities*, 7 (2004), 55–80.
102 Carrillo, *The Night Is Young*, pp. 79–80.
103 Ibid., p. 96.
104 GLBT Historical Society Archives, San Francisco, Eric Garber Papers, Box 1: R. Bruce Nugent File, Interview Transcripts 1981–82.
105 Ibid., Letter from Bruce Nugent to Eric Garber, 18 September 1981.
106 Herring, *Queering the Underworld*, pp. 139–44.
107 J. Kisseloff, *You Must Remember This: An Oral History of Manhattan from*

the 1890s to World War II (Baltimore, 1999), pp. 288–9. First published in 1989.
108 *Before Stonewall* (1985: Greta Schiller and Robert Rosenburg).
109 C. Heap, *Slumming: Sexual and Racial Encounters in American Nightlife, 1885–1940* (Chicago, 2009), pp. 10, 11, 12.
110 Ibid., pp. 83, 96, 139, 156, 231, 233, 240, 241, 250, 252, 263.
111 M. Canaday, *The Straight State: Sexuality and Citizenship in Twentieth-century America* (Princeton, 2009), pp. 3, 4, 11, 176–7, 215, 216.
112 J. E. Halley, 'Reasoning about sodomy: act and identity in and after Bowers v. Hardwick', *Virginia Law Review*, 79 (1993), 1738.
113 Ibid.
114 C. Cagle, 'Rough trade: sexual taxonomy in postwar America', in D. E. Hall and M. Pramaggiore (eds), *RePresenting Bisexualities: Subjects and Cultures of Fluid Desire* (New York, 1996), p. 248.
115 *Flesh* (1968: Paul Morrissey).
116 T. Waugh, 'Cockteaser', in J. Doyle, J. Flatley, and J. E. Muñoz (eds), *Pop Out: Queer Warhol* (Durham, NC, 1996), pp. 51–77.
117 M. Moon, 'Outlaw sex and the "search for America": representing male prostitution and perverse desire in sixties film (*My Hustler* and *Midnight Cowboy*)', in his *A Small Boy and Others: Imitation and Initiation in American Culture from Henry James to Andy Warhol* (Durham, NC, 1998), pp. 121–2.
118 *My Hustler* (1965: Andy Warhol).
119 G. Youngblood, *Expanded Cinema* (London, 1970), pp. 117–19.
120 Cory and LeRoy, *The Homosexual and His Society*, p. 85.
121 C. Corley, *Trick of the Trade* (New York, 1968), p. 28.
122 C. Nealon, *Foundlings: Lesbian and Gay Historical Emotion Before Stonewall* (Durham, NC, 2001), p. 2.
123 D. Crimp, 'Getting the Warhol we deserve', *Social Text*, 59 (1999), 64.

Epilogue

'I noticed that all my homosexual patients manifested strong unconscious heterosex trends and all my hetero patients unconscious homosexual trends. Makes the brain reel, don't it?'
  'And what do you conclude from that?'
  'Conclude? Nothing whatever. Just a passing observation.' (William Burroughs, 1959)[1]

In his brilliant *Cain's Book* (1960), his story of life as a junkie in New York in the 1950s, the Beat writer Alexander Trocchi referred, almost in passing, to a same-sex sexual encounter: 'I felt the warmth of his ear against mine and his hand. Belt, thighs, knees, chest, cheek.'[2] Though it took up few pages in Trocchi's novel, it was intellectually (his word) important to the experience of the protagonist: 'I had broken another limit and found that I could love a man with the same sure passion that moved me to women generally.'[3] The man with whom the protagonist had sex was Puerto Rican and said that his name was Manuelo. It was anonymous sex in that the men did not know one another and could not really communicate. Neither spoke the other's language. 'There were no common memories between us; we shared our male sex only, our humanity, and our lust.'[4]

The central character of the novel (Trocchi) is clear in his sexual preference for women – it is obvious, unstated, in all his interactions – yet is also unembarrassed about this sex with a man.

> It was not the first time I had had sexual experience with a man, but it was the first time it was not in one way or another abortive, it was the first time I had encountered a man who knew how to take all that was given without a trace either of embarrassment or of that shrill crustacean humour dedicated homosexuals sometimes adopt, and my body afterwards was heavy with the kind of satisfaction I have often envied women.[5]

He declares the sexual satisfaction derived from homosexual sex, even hinting at a certain feminization in the experience, while making it clear that he is not of the 'shrill' tribe of 'dedicated homosexuals'. The incident had no special importance in what was to follow; the remaining sexual interactions were with women. It is, in our terminology, heterosexual homosexual sex. Hopefully, this book, the one you have in front of you now, will have made it a little clearer why this might happen in New York in the 1950s to reputedly one of the most heterosexual of avant-garde writers. We would say that Trocchi's textual experience is by no means a cultural oddity.

We began the Prologue of this book with a long quotation that included allusion to the hustler Herbert Huncke, the very man who provided a rather laconic précis of life as a hustler in the epigraph to Chapter 3, and who, at the start of Chapter 4, claimed to have astonished Alfred Kinsey with his claim that he had homosexual sex without thinking himself homosexual. In Chapter 6, Huncke was used to prick the romanticism of hustler imagery. So he has had something of a spectral presence in this book and it is worth returning to him at its finish. He is the hustler whose main claim to cultural fame is that he is accredited with putting the beat in Beats; he is said to have coined the term in the 1940s.[6] We can now see what Huncke looks like in two photographs of him at different stages of his life. One was taken in a Times Square photo booth around 1940, when the hustler was in his mid-twenties; he seems drugged, with cigarette in mouth and slumped down in his chair (half the image consists of the booth's backcloth). (See Figure 74.) The other was taken later, in 1953, in a Manhattan hotel room, when Huncke was in his late thirties. (See Figure 75.) The photographer was his friend the poet Allen Ginsberg.

Huncke's apparitionality is not confined to this book. The character Albert Ancke in John Clellon Holmes's Beat novel *Go* (1952), as central to Beat literature as Jack Kerouac's *On the Road* (1957), is indeed our real-life hustler. For the Beats, the hustler functioned as a synecdoche for wider bohemian life. *Go* recalled a fascination with Times Square and its possibilities: 'Undifferentiated reality. That is, life lived moment to moment as it unfolds . . . the Times Square world was a gigantic ante-room, off which myriad other worlds opened – hustlers, thieves, whores, pimps, lost kids, musicians, etc.'[7] Huncke is mentioned early in *Go*, as a 'phantom', someone whom the main character Paul Hobbes (Holmes) has never actually met but whom everyone is talking about, 'one of those

74. Herbert Huncke, circa 1940. © Allen Ginsberg/CORBIS.

shadowy figures that he always associated with the glaring nighttime confusion of Times Square, its unruly bars, teeming cafeterias and all-night movies'.[8] We always seem to be waiting or looking for Huncke, sometimes because he is away in prison. Half-way through *Go*, they are still seeking Ancke (Huncke), 'for when on the Square they always searched him out, believing him, night and day, (some watchful Ariel of hipsters),

Epilogue

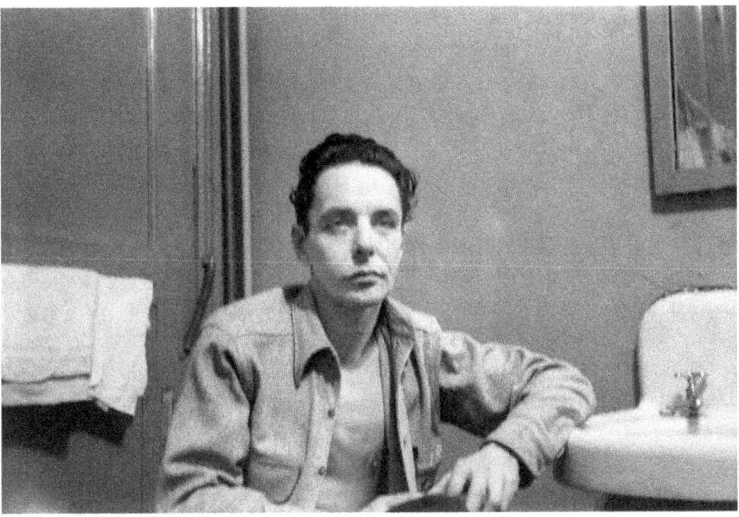

75. Herbert Huncke, 1953. Photograph by Allen Ginsberg. © Allen Ginsberg/CORBIS.

always elusively there among the lights and hurry'.⁹ When Hobbes – we – finally meet Huncke, in a club, we do not even know that it is him (we are told later); he and a tall languorous woman are unsuccessfully trying to interest a 'cool' man. The cool man in the club represents the ennui of postwar America: 'You see, it's really the end of feeling, through feeling too much. Look, he's not even interested in the girl . . . or in anything! Even sex is a drag because he's gone to the end of it. He's gone to the end of everything!'¹⁰ And when we do know that the hustler is Huncke and hear something of his life – 'and the restless, continually circulating fraternity to which he belonged' – he falls asleep.¹¹ For the remainder of the novel, as in real life, he dominates David Stofsky's (Allen Ginsberg's) domestic life and helps it spin out of control, but still spends much of his time sleeping: 'His waking hours were only intermissions.'¹²

Huncke is also a junky – a weird rhyming confirmation of his status – that possibly explains why he is such an asexual hustler. He is withered and crumpled; with its sunken chest and wasted legs, Huncke's body is a long way from Painter's idealized hustler bodies.¹³ He is dishonest and unreliable. Indeed Huncke is literally Junkey in Jack Kerouac's debut novel, *The Town and the City* (1950), the man who sat in a 42nd Street cafeteria for eighteen hours a day, sometimes for twenty-four when there was nowhere else to go, 'his expression always weary, indifferent, yet somehow astonished too, aware of everything. He had the look of a man who is sincerely miserable in the world.'[14]

So although Huncke is a minor character, he plays an important role as the Beat writers' link to the world with which they are fascinated but to which they do not really belong. Through the hustler Huncke they have vicarious contact – in Allen Ginsberg's case actual acquaintance – with 'all the passers, connections, addicts, homosexual prostitutes, petty crooks and musicians who made up the underground of drugs, crime and craziness which he frequented'.[15] As early as the late 1940s, Ginsberg had recorded his tortured relationship with the hustler, the man whom everyone warned him about (they could never understand the young poet's forbearance), who took over his apartment and bed (Ginsberg resorted to the couch), who used his room to store the proceeds of various robberies and to entertain hoodlums, and who systematically stole from him to feed his drug habit.[16] 'I had begun to notice that the bookshelves were barer than before, that my radio, typewriter, winter clothes, and an oriental statuette were not there anymore.'[17] Yet he – as was Kerouac – was clearly fascinated by Huncke, the man who had experienced everything, and who was, by his early thirties, already an old man, bored, or rather wearied, with life. 'Of how much he was guilty, only he knew. I had hints and explanations of days, of weeks, of whole seasons of robbery and violence and corruption – a whole lifetime of innocent evil.'[18] Ginsberg readily admitted that he and Kerouac mythologized the man, 'a literary trick' – perhaps he was a modern saint or an angel – though his journals make clear what lay behind the façade.[19] This formative encounter with Huncke resulted in the arrest of both Huncke and Ginsberg in 1949 and the latter's brief incarceration in a mental institution. Still, Huncke makes flitting appearances in Ginsberg's early poetry, and later, with his 'shoes full of blood', in the magnificent poem *Howl* (1956).[20]

Huncke is Herman in William Burroughs's *Junky* or *Junkie* (1953). The narrator – Burroughs – gets to know him in the Angle Bar on Eighth Avenue, 'a meeting place for 42nd Street hustlers'. 'Herman did not have a habit at this time. In fact, he seldom got a habit unless someone else paid for it. But he was always high on something – weed, Benzedrine, or knocked out of his mind on "goof balls".'[21] The Herman of *Junky* is very like the Albert of *Go*. He pushes marijuana with the narrator and moves into his apartment: 'He had lived in other people's apartments all his life.'[22]

And he is there, or not there, in the unedited version of Kerouac's *On the Road* (1951): 'Where was Hunkey? I dug the Square [Times Square] for Hunkey; he wasn't there . . .'[23] The edited version of 1957, appropriately, changes Huncke's name to Hassel![24] Huncke is there too in Kerouac's journals and private correspondence: 'Hunkey scares me', he wrote in his journal in 1948, 'because he has been the most *miserable* of men, jailed & beaten and cheated and starved and sickened and homeless, and still he knows there's such a thing as love'.[25] 'Tell me of Huncke. Man of enigma-knowledge and despair of aggression.' 'By the way, where *is* Huncke?'[26] He thought Huncke 'the greatest storyteller I know, an actual genius at it'.[27] 'Incidentally', he wrote to Ginsberg in early 1948, 'Huncke is brooding again, and it seems that Huncke is never so great as when he's beat down and brooding and bitter. I really believe this cruel fact. I see him all the time.'[28]

When he published *Lonesome Traveller* in 1960, Kerouac has Huncke as but a ghost inhabiting Bickford's Cafeteria in Times Square, along with the spirits of long-dead gangsters and the Beat poets. 'There's a whole floating population around Times Square that has always made Bickford's their headquarters day and night. In the old days of the beat generation some poets used to go in there to meet the famous character "Hunckey".'[29]

Huncke has a chapter devoted to him in Irving Rosenthal's strange and compelling *Sheeper* (1967). 'Huncke says', it begins, 'I used to be the youngest in the group I ran around with. Now I'm the oldest. Well that's life.'[30] Huncke talks about sex 'as something joyful but no longer indulged in'. He has beautiful boys in tow that he 'is unable to make'.[31] He is the once desirable young man who has lost his looks and now complains about his scabies and haemorrhoids.[32] His possessions are few, just the occasional items from the cars that he robs: manicure sets, silk pyjamas, and 'big bottles of fairy cologne'.[33] He does not need much because he is constantly in prison. He embroils his friends in the 'tragedy and disaster' that perpetually shadows him.[34] 'Why bother with him at all?' poses the narrator. 'Because he is a Beauty Trap and the finest storyteller my spirit has ever lifted to.'[35]

Huncke even makes an appearance in the 1977 journals of one of the next generation, the artist (and former teenage hustler) David Wojnarowicz. 'Woke up early with a phone call from Herbert Huncke. He was calling me to ask me to please meet him at the courthouse on 100 Center Street.'[36] Huncke had been arrested for drug possession yet again. This was in the published selection from the artist's notebooks, but references to Huncke continue in the original manuscripts at the New York University Library. Huncke tells the story of how he found $4,000

Canadian in the front seat of a car that he was robbing.[37] Huncke shows up looking 'extremely weary – nothing that sleep could or would take care of – a bone/body weariness – that comes with hard living – I wonder for him what he thinks about moving like a slight vagabond thruout this city'.[38] Huncke (confirming *Sheeper*) has lost the urge for sex:

> Really I have had no desire for sex for the last 10 years. Up til 10 years ago I'd want to get into bed a lot – I'd always see some young cat with a good body that I wanted to have sex with ... or some girl with a beautiful figure I wanted to put my hands around but then suddenly at one point I just decided I was tired of waking up and feeling ... oh I don't know ... you know sex is a head thing ... I mean you use a lot of thoughts in sex like what makes this person excited ... what turns that person on ... It just suddenly made me very tired and so it just dropped from my life.[39]

When he had recently been approached by a good-looking man in the building where he was apartment-sitting, Huncke said to him 'I'm really sorry man ... but I just can't ... If I got to bed with you I'll just get you all excited and myself half excited and it just wouldn't work ...'[40]

Huncke has left us his own writings, including *Guilty of Everything* (1990), that chronologically indistinct memoir with the wonderful title.[41] There is a 1948 testament of self-disgust in Ginsberg's papers: 'I've grown to dislike my name ... its mere utterance creates an almost weary and loathsome feeling in me.'[42] But there are also flashes of insight into the life of a 42nd Street hustler as experienced and observed by one of their number. He writes of a 'stranger cold and tired and lost and afraid and filled with sorrow', the fatigue from being on one's feet all day, the young men 'frightened of sex but curious and rather in awe', and of the comradeship, even love, between those earning their living on the streets.[43] He knew 'hardcore Forty-second Street hustlers – who were sharp dressers and reputed to go out occasionally on jobs – maybe a stickup or burglary. I had seen one of them knock a man flat in one well-aimed blow.'[44] 'I learned much about sex and about the vast number of people who make up the so-called less desirable element in our American way of life', he wrote in a disturbing account of sex in a park. 'Haunted people – lonely people – misfits – outcasts – wanderers – those on the skids – drunkards – deviates of all kinds – hustlers of every description – male and female – old people and young people – and they come from every section of the country.'[45] But he keeps returning to the friendships forged: 'Huncke – you may never win a race but you're still my horse.'[46]

His journals and miscellaneous manuscripts, some ultimately published, some not, survive in Stanford University Library, nurtured and preserved by his friend Irving Rosenthal. 'Junk and existing day to day occupies me. Junk is absorbent', Huncke wrote in a 1963 journal. 'The last few days have been hectic and contained much violence. Hanging around a restaurant on the corner of . . . the Bowery I have participated in adventures one might expect of scenes from a Hollywood movie. Hoodlums and shady characters – Drug addicts, prostitutes, pimps, nickel and dime hustlers, Brooklyn mobsters, goof-ball addicts, odd types and Bowery bums.'[47] A journal for 1967 describes a life crumbling like the apartment in which he was then living: 'Plaster constantly sifts down in all the rooms of the place . . . I feel cold inside as I think of the next tomorrow'. He steals art books and meat (a strange combination but there were markets for both) to sell to feed a bag-a-day heroin habit and a taste for injected amphetamine, acquired, he hints, through an earlier association with the aforementioned Trocchi. Huncke records 'the same needs – the same sense of bewilderment and the same lack of knowing which way to turn or what to do'.[48]

Huncke was interviewed by Rosenthal in 1961:

> Huncke was sharing an apartment on East Sixth Street. The occupants and habitues of that apartment were shooting amphetamine on an hour-by-hour basis and had been doing so for six weeks, with disastrous effects. Not only were they dropping like mallards into the jails and looney bins of Manhattan, but Beauty was besmirched, and even Huncke was becoming a nervous wreck.[49]

He was interviewed again in the late 1970s for an oral biography of Kerouac. He talked more of others than he did of Kerouac, describing Burroughs's method of shooting up and his own recruitment by Kinsey to procure subjects for his research on sex – 'I became a pimp for Kinsey'. (Typically, there is a returned letter from Kinsey to Huncke in the Kinsey archives: Huncke had provided his sexual history and then moved on, address unknown.)[50] Like Burroughs, Huncke talked about the Angle Bar (with one door on Eighth Avenue and the other on 43rd Street), where Kinsey and the Beats rubbed shoulders with the young hustlers of 42nd Street. 'They let you hang around the bar if you had enough to buy yourself a drink. You could stand at the bar, and before long, somebody would approach you, or maybe you had a john for the night or for the evening.'[51]

We also have some of his letters. The Huncke–Ginsberg correspondence is littered with evidence of Huncke in extremis. '(Favorite word of mine – difficult.)'[52] He contemplates suicide but it requires too much effort. 'I had hoped I would drop dead' he wrote to Ginsberg's friend Peter Orlovsky, probably in 1960, 'it seems I can't make the effort to commit suicide'.[53] He is lying low because someone is after him with a pistol, he explained in a rushed, undated New York note.[54] 'No end of people are on my tail', he complained in 1967.[55] The identifiable prison notepaper stretches from the 1940s to the 1960s. The requests for monetary assistance are unrelenting: from short missives asking for the bearer to be given money for drugs because its author is too drug-sick to move, to more detailed outlines of the support needed (rent, food, clothing) upon release from incarceration.[56] 'Welfare is entirely out of the question. I'll explain why when I see you.'[57] To call them begging letters would be wholly inappropriate for it fails to capture the sense of entitlement forged by years of dependency on friends. 'What gives – man', he wrote to Ginsberg from Riker's Island in 1966, 'already two letters to you and not so much as a – go to hell – for reply ... I've run the story often enough to you – for you to know exactly how difficult the situation is or can become in prison – when one is without funds'. 'Anyway', he concluded in a manner that would have tried the patience of the closest companion, 'I'll expect an immediate reply to this.'[58] It must not have been easy knowing Huncke; his requests for current contact details were invariably met with resistance, for the would-be provider was fully aware that an importuning letter would follow, or, worse still, the importuner himself would be at the door looking for temporary accommodation. Ginsberg must have dreaded the words, 'Allen – I suppose the present predicament I find myself in was inevitable ...'[59] Allen was one of Huncke's most constant providers – though by no means the only one. Other support networks have probably vanished with the archives of their owners. Kerouac sent him a cheque in 1959; he had asked for $25, 'a huge sum, I'm not Frank Sinatra'.[60] The artist and musician Bill Heine gave Huncke money.[61] Rosenthal was also subjected to missives from Rikers: 'Irving – Have half been expecting a letter.'[62] But his patience did not equal Ginsberg's: 'Your entire relationship with me has boiled down to my waiting for the "touch": How much will Huncke ask for? ... Fuck you Huncke.' Huncke was just 'like a horrible spider', Rosenthal told the spider himself, 'with a soft come-on waiting to pierce you just before he flees'.[63]

There is a 1967 Huncke suicide note – typically complete with PS and PPS as if the writing of the letter was an act of procrastination.

Epilogue

> Dear Allen –
> By the time you receive this I hope I should be dead. I'm simply too tired and confused to feel capable of making it any longer . . . and my shame at my lack of self control – so that I have stolen from everyone – lied and broken trust and lack the temerity to seek out friends or make new friends – since it is always with a certain calculation or premeditative eye as to what possible help . . . they offer.[64]

Explaining that he stole only from friends so that they would not press charges and consequently found himself broke, without a bed, and 'no friend foolish enough to trust me in their home or pad', he informed the long-suffering Ginsberg that the situation was so desperate that suicide was the only answer.[65] Huncke favoured a drug overdose – although his lack of funds must have precluded that option. Perhaps it was the ultimate importuning letter, merely another 'touch'. Anyway, Huncke lived until 1996, long enough, as we have seen, to be interviewed in a documentary about Alfred Kinsey.

Herbert Huncke conveys better than anyone – for that was his life – the intersecting spheres of petty criminality, drug addiction, commercial sex, and the inevitable life in prison. It was, as we have seen, a violent life too, though Huncke was a thief rather than a gangster. ('Never was a criminal more petty and unsuccessful'.)[66] The brutality of some of Painter's sexual contacts is alien to what we know of Huncke's character.

It may be tempting for the reader to read Huncke as a stand-in for the subject of this book. He could certainly wax eloquently on urban life: 'Bryant Park – long a favorite haunt of mine – 42nd Street – I find one of the most fascinating spots . . . For sheer beauty – don't miss the breaking of dawn across the east river – or a full moon – bathing Avenue C in magic light at two or three in the morning', he wrote to a friend in 1961.[67] Granted, he is a strange doppelgänger – given his puny physique, hinted effeminacy, and supposed asexuality. Yet the New York hustler is sometimes as elusive as Huncke and we meet him through the interventions, the writings of others. It might also be claimed that the writer of this book – and you, the reader – are, like the Beats, complicit in comparable, vicarious contact with 'crime and craziness'.

Notes

1 W. S. Burroughs, *Naked Lunch: The Restored Text*, ed. J. Grauerholz and B. Miles (New York, 2001), p. 32.

2. A. Trocchi, *Cain's Book* (New York, 1961), p. 53.
3. Ibid., p. 66.
4. Ibid., p. 65.
5. Ibid., pp. 65–6.
6. See, for example, R. Weinreich, 'The Beat generation is now about everything', in J. G. Hendin (ed.), *A Concise Companion to Postwar American Literature and Culture* (Oxford, 2004), p. 74.
7. A. Charters, 'Go in 1952', in J. C. Holmes, *Go* (New York, 1997), p. 316. *Go* was first published in 1952 and deals with New York in the period 1948–49.
8. Holmes, *Go*, p. 7.
9. Ibid., p. 147.
10. Ibid., pp. 210–11, 236.
11. Ibid., p. 237.
12. Ibid., p. 257.
13. Ibid., pp. 209, 235–6.
14. J. Kerouac, *The Town and the City* (New York, 1970). First published in 1950.
15. Holmes, *Go*, p. 237.
16. See A. Ginsberg, *The Book of Martyrdom and Artifice: First Journals and Poems, 1937–1952*, ed. J. Lieberman-Plimpton and B. Morgan (Cambridge, MA, 2006), pp. 262–314. The relationship can also be traced in B. Morgan, *I Celebrate Myself: The Somewhat Private Life of Allen Ginsberg* (New York, 2006).
17. Ginsberg, *Book of Martyrdom and Artifice*, p. 267.
18. Ibid., p. 271.
19. Ibid., p. 282.
20. Ibid., pp. 263, 423, 483.
21. W. S. Burroughs, *Junky: The Definitive Text of 'Junk'*, ed. O. Harris (New York, 2003), pp. 2, 9.
22. Ibid., p. 17.
23. J. Kerouac, *On the Road: The Original Scroll* (New York, 2007), p. 211. See also, pp. 219, 231, 349.
24. J. Kerouac, *On the Road*, 50th Anniversary Edition (New York, 2007), p. 131.
25. J. Kerouac, *Windblown World: The Journals of Jack Kerouac 1947–1954*, ed. D. Brinkley (New York, 2004), p. 100. Emphasis in original.
26. J. Kerouac, *Selected Letters, 1940–1956*, ed. A. Charters (New York, 1995), pp. 147, 355.
27. Ibid., p. 127.
28. Ibid., p. 140.
29. J. Kerouac, *Lonesome Traveller* (New York, 1968), p. 109. First published in 1960.

30 I. Rosenthal, *Sheeper* (New York, 1968), p. 105. First published in 1967, but drawing on earlier experiences.
31 Ibid., pp. 106, 110.
32 Ibid., pp. 106, 108.
33 Ibid., p. 108.
34 Ibid., p. 110.
35 Ibid., p. 112.
36 D. Wojnarowicz, *In the Shadow of the American Dream: The Diaries of David Wojnarowicz*, ed. A. Scholder (New York, 1999), pp. 25–8.
37 Fales Library Special Collections, Elmer Holmes Bobst Library, New York University, MS 092, The David Wojnarowicz Papers, ca. 1954–1992 (hereafter, Wojnarowicz Papers), Box 1, Folder 4: New York Journal, 'Human Head II', 15 September 1977.
38 Ibid., 8 September 1977.
39 Wojnarowicz Papers, Box 1, Folder 3: New York Journal, 'Human Head I', 29 July 1977. Ellipses in the original. A version of this, without Hunke being identified, appears as 'Man drinking coffee in Thirty-third Street pizzeria, New York City', in D. Wojnarowicz, *The Waterfront Journals* (New York, 1996), pp. 81–2.
40 Ibid.
41 H. Huncke, *Guilty of Everything: The Autobiography of Herbert Huncke* (New York, 1990).
42 Ginsberg, *Book of Martyrdom and Artifice*, p. 242.
43 H. Huncke, *The Herbert Huncke Reader*, ed. B. G. Schafer (New York, 1997), pp. 20–1.
44 Ibid., p. 101.
45 Ibid., p. 60.
46 Ibid., p. 327.
47 Department of Special Collections, Stanford University Libraries (hereafter, Stanford), Stanford, California, Irving Rosenthal Papers (hereafter, Rosenthal Papers), Box 13, Folder 3: Typescript of Herbert Huncke's 1963 Journal.
48 Rosenthal Papers, Box 13, Folder 1: Huncke's Journal, 28 October 1967.
49 Rosenthal Papers, Box 12, Folder 5: Huncke–Rosenthal Correspondence 1961–1962: Transcript of an Interview in 1961.
50 The Kinsey Institute for Research in Sex, Gender, and Reproduction, University of Indiana, Bloomington, Kinsey Correspondence Collection: Herbert Huncke, 26 January 1943.
51 B. Gifford and L. Lee, *Jack's Book: An Oral Biography of Jack Kerouac* (New York, 1994), pp. 53–4. First published in 1978.
52 Stanford, Allen Ginsberg Papers (hereafter, Ginsberg), Subseries 1.1. Correspondence 1940–1949, Box 1, Folder 33: Huncke to Ginsberg, 23 March 1946.

53 Ginsberg, Subseries 1.3. Correspondence 1960–1969, Box 32, Folder 29: Huncke to Orlovsky, no date [1960?].
54 Ibid., Folder 27: Huncke to Ginsberg, no date [1968?].
55 Ibid., Folder 26: Huncke to Ginsberg, 16 April 1967.
56 Ibid., Folder 23: Huncke to Ginsberg, 29 November 1964; Folder 25: Huncke to Ginsberg, 12 December 1966.
57 Ibid., Folder 25: Huncke to Ginsberg, 4 December 1966.
58 Ibid., Folder 24: Huncke to Ginsberg, 19 September 1966.
59 Ibid., Huncke to Ginsberg, 31 August 1966.
60 J. Kerouac, *Selected Letters, 1957–1969*, ed. A. Charters (New York, 1999), p. 222.
61 Rosenthal Papers, Box 12, Folder 5: Huncke–Rosenthal Correspondence 1961–1962: Letter from Huncke to Rosenthal, 21 February 1962.
62 Ibid., Letter from Huncke to Rosenthal, 12 January 1962.
63 Rosenthal Papers, Box 12, Folder 6: Huncke–Rosenthal Correspondence 1965–1968: Letter from Rosenthal to Huncke, early February 1966.
64 Ginsberg, Subseries 1.3. Correspondence 1960–1969, Box 32, Folder 26: Huncke to Ginsberg, 28 October 1967.
65 Ibid.
66 Rosenthal, *Sheeper*, p. 112.
67 Rosenthal Papers, Box 12, Folder 5: Huncke–Rosenthal Correspondence 1961–1962: Letter from Huncke to Stan Persky, 20 December 1961.

Index

Note: 'n.' after a page reference indicates the number of a note on that page. Individual works of literature or art are not indexed but are referenced instead by the author or artist.

Abbott, Jack 134, 135
Abelove, Henry 251
Agron, Salvador 90–1, 133
AIDS 17, 225, 240, 242–4, 250–1
America, Paul 189, 205–6, 215, 217, 224, 255
Anderson, Nels 103–4
Andros, Phil *see* Steward, Samuel
Anger, Kenneth 9, 95, 201–2, 204, 226
art and hustlers/trade 9, 11, 20, 55, 57–8, 82–3, 87, 96, 98, 119, 123, 130, 132, 175, 188–9, 194–6, 198, 202, 206, 221–4, 226, 241, 246, 253, 270
Auden, W. H. 11, 122
Avedon, Richard 202–3, 226, 230–1n.66

Badertscher, Amos 251
Barr, James 102, 119, 189–90
Barrios, Richard 151
bars 1–9, 12–13, 22–3, 34, 55–6, 61, 67, 77, 79, 82, 84–5, 89, 92, 94, 97, 101, 117, 119, 138, 170, 172–4, 176, 190, 221, 237–8, 264, 266, 269

Barthes, Roland 188
Beats 1, 4, 130–2, 166–7, 171, 177, 190, 207, 225–6, 262–71
Benjamin, H. and Masters, R. E. L. 87, 125, 128
Benny, Jack 154, 161
Berg, Louis 156–7
Blake, James 135–7, 181n.53
Boone, Joseph 39, 41
Bowne, Alan 239–40
Brando, Marlon 9, 82, 193–4, 198, 202–3, 226
Brown, Ricardo 174
Bruce, Earle 65–6
Bruce, Kennilworth 40–1, 55, 65, 149
Burroughs, William 79, 92, 131, 171–2, 176, 216, 226, 262, 266, 269

cab drivers 9, 104, 148, 199–200
Cadmus, Paul 11, 55, 57–8, 196, 222–4, 226
Cagle, Chris 255
Campbell, Joe 255
Canaday, Margot 35, 70n.2, 104, 170–1, 254

275

Index

Capote, Truman 97–8, 174, 202–3, 209, 226
Carillo, Héctor 251–2
Cassady, Neal 1–2, 131–2, 177
Castro, Rick 243–5
charity girls 105
Chauncey, George 13, 14, 17, 31n.95, 35–7, 42–3, 45, 68–9, 148, 251–3
Cheever, John 7, 178, 213, 226, 234, 256
Clark, Larry 240, 246, 248–9
Clement, Elizabeth 105
Cocks, H. G. 15
Cohan, Steven 154
Cohn, Roy 7, 178
Coney Island 18, 49, 89–90, 196, 246
Corber, Robert J. 174, 186n.172
Corley, Carl 173, 176, 256
Cory, Donald Webster 82, 123, 160–1, 175, 236, 256
Crimp, Douglas 197–8, 256
Crowley, Mart 101–2, 165, 173, 190, 226
Curtin, Kaier 161
Curtis, Jackie 206–7

Dallesandro, Joe 177–8, 189–90, 206–7, 213, 215, 255
De Angelis, Michael 200
Dean, James 200–2
Delany, Samuel 7, 79, 86, 132–3
Demuth, Charles 11
DiCorcia, Philip-Lorca 246
Doan, Laura 15
Doherty, Thomas 151
Doyle, Jennifer 189, 206
Duberman, Martin 12, 175
Dyer, Richard 171

effeminacy 5, 23–6, 39, 45–8, 55–9, 63–9, 147–78, 251–2, 256

Faulkner, Henry 96, 209, 239, 258n.36
film and hustlers/trade 5, 9, 78, 81–2, 87, 95, 177–8, 189, 191, 193–4, 196–202, 204–7, 213, 215–19, 226–7, 239–45, 255
Fishman, Joseph F. 155–7
Forbes, Malcolm 57–8, 195–6
Ford, Charles Henri 9, 34, 39–40, 92–3, 129–30, 213, 226
Foucault, Michel 13, 15
Friedkin, William 166, 189, 226

gangs/gangsters 22, 40–1, 51, 59–60, 67, 89–92, 112, 114–18, 121–2, 133, 189, 198, 201, 207–8, 218–19, 237, 267
Garber, Eric 253
Gedney, William 84, 209, 219, 226
Gerassi, John 237
Gerber, Israel 219
Ginsberg, Allen 1, 2, 11, 79, 131, 171, 263, 265–8, 270–1
Goodman, Paul 189, 226
Gorman, Cliff 166
Griffey, Erin 222
Gross, Alfred 49–51, 58, 122

Haines, William 151, 154
Halley, Janet 15, 254–5
Halperin, David 14–15
Haring, Keith 246
Hartley, Marsden 11
Heap, Chad 40–2, 45, 254
Heim, Scott 243
Henry, George 5, 12, 17, 47–51, 58–64, 69, 122, 158–9,
Herlihy, James Leo 78–9, 189, 204, 206, 219, 226
Herring, Scott 42, 253
Hickock, Richard 202–3
Holmes, John Clellon 171, 263–5
Houlbrook, Matt 14, 16
Howard, John 14, 238,

Humphreys, Laud 80, 129, 169, 235
Huncke, Herbert 1–2, 4, 23, 77, 82, 111, 112, 130–1, 225–6, 263–71

Inge, William 199–200, 226
itinerants 44–5, 60, 103–4, 155, 236

Jackson, Charles 160
Jacoby, Richard 133
James, David 206
Johnson, Colin 104, 236
Johnson, David 148
Johnson, Edwin 135

Kahn, Samuel 42, 157–8
Kallman, Chester 11, 122
Karlen, Arno 237–8
Kaye, Kerwin 235, 240
Kerouac, Jack 1–2, 4, 131–2, 147, 171, 177, 263–70
Kinsey, Alfred 1, 2, 4, 17–18, 20–3, 25–6, 89, 111–15, 119–20, 132, 137–40, 173, 234, 236, 238–9, 250, 224, 263, 269, 271
Kirstein, Lincoln 10–11, 175, 224
Koestenbaum, Wayne 198
Kramer, Larry 235
Krim, Seymour 166–7
Kulick, Don 116, 118
Kunzel, Regina 31n.96, 133, 137

LaBruce, Bruce 243–5
La Tourneaux, Robert 189–90
Legman, Gershon 125, 177
Lerman, Leo 11, 56
Lindner, Robert 161
literature and hustlers/trade 189–94
Lloyd, Robin 240
Loftin, Craig 172, 176

Loughery, John 32n.107, 169, 237
Lugowski, David 151

McKay, Claude 45, 47, 219–20, 226
McNamara, Robert 92, 250
marines 7–8, 10, 16, 21, 37, 79, 111, 114, 119, 149, 173, 175–6, 198, 203, 256
Martin, Eddie Owens 55–6
Mattachine Society 172–3
Maugham, Somerset 40
Maynard, Steven 103
Meeker, Martin 164–5, 172–3
Meeker, Ralph 194, 199
Melcarth, Edward 87, 90, 95–8, 101, 118–19, 124, 194–8, 202, 209, 219, 221–2, 226, 246
Meyer, Richard 55, 198
military 35, 67, 79, 96–7, 160, 173
see also servicemen
Miller, Arthur 163, 199, 226
Miller, Warren 189
Minton, Henry 31n.99, 63, 114, 146n.137, 185n.163
Mizer, Bob 82
Moon, Michael 255
Morrissey, Paul 177–8, 189, 206–7, 215, 226, 239–41, 244, 255
movie houses 18–19, 86–7, 132–3, 150, 190, 264
Muñoz, José Esteban 246, 248
Muñoz-Laboy, Miguel A. 252

Negrón-Muntaner, Frances 201, 246
newspaper boys 104–5
Niles, Blair 65, 148, 150–1
Novarro, Ramon 217
Nugent, Richard Bruce 10, 42, 253–4

O'Hara, Frank 11, 132

Index

Painter, Thomas 2, 13, 17–23, 25–6, 31–2n.99, 43–4, 46, 48–9, 51, 55–60, 63, 67, 77–90, 92, 94–100, 102–3, 111–20, 123–6, 128, 138–40, 172–4, 176, 189, 194, 202, 204, 206–9, 212, 215, 219, 224, 236–9, 265, 271
Patterson, Haywood 135, 156, 157
peg houses (male brothels) 16, 20, 40, 46, 53, 56, 59, 61, 79, 82–4, 89
Phoenix, River 242–3
physique culture 82, 87–8, 213–15, 217, 232n.102
Polsky, Ned 132
Pomeroy, Wardell 21–2, 111, 114
pornography 78, 132–3, 212–13
prisons 89, 98, 103, 112, 118, 131, 133–7, 155–8, 202–3, 236, 264, 267, 270–1
Puerto Ricans 9, 20, 22, 58–9, 89–93, 102–3, 112, 114–18, 133, 176–7, 189, 201, 246, 248–50, 252, 262

Rader, Dotson 10, 85, 96, 171, 203–4, 207, 209, 216–17, 224, 226, 240
Rapoport, I. C. 25, 26, 84
Raul, K. B. 189
Read, Kenneth 13
Rechy, John 5, 7, 16, 79–81, 85–7, 101, 118–19, 170, 173, 176, 190, 204, 209, 213, 217, 224–7, 235, 242
Reed, Lou 190
Reeves, Keanu 242–3
Reiss, Albert 121–3, 176
Rivera, Juan 246, 249–50
Rivers, Larry 11, 132
Roberts, Whitey 167–8
Rorem, Ned 11, 123, 178, 203
Rosenthal, Irving 131, 190, 226–7, 269–70
Russell, Jamie 176

sailors 7–11, 16, 20, 35–40, 51, 53, 55–6, 58, 60–2, 64–5, 67, 79–80, 82–3, 94–7, 118, 122, 130, 149, 152, 191–2, 194–5, 199, 201–2, 207, 209, 214, 233n.122, 236, 254–5
 see also marines
Schlesinger, John 78, 87, 189, 192, 216, 226, 240, 255
Schneider, Eric 92
Schwarz, A. B. Christa 47
Scully, Robert 148–9
Sedgwick, Eve Kosofsky 14, 15
Selby, Hubert 25, 67–8, 163
servicemen 7, 18, 35–9, 41, 51, 55–6, 67, 94–7, 168, 209
 see also marines; military; sailors
Shearer, Johnny 190–1
Sinfield, Alan 15, 170
Smith, Perry 202–3
Stearn, Jess 164, 173
Steward, Samuel 9, 16, 78, 107n.54, 130, 191, 204, 216, 226, 228n.22, 237
Stimpson, Catherine 171
Suárez, Juan 41, 201–2

Taddei, Richard 98, 218, 246–8
Tchelitchew, Pavel 9, 130
Tellier, Andre 65, 148, 150
Terry, Jennifer 63–4, 75n.175, 158
Thomson, Virgil 11, 195
trade aesthetic 188–227, 232n.103, 246
transvestites 7, 23, 24, 40, 45, 59–60, 148, 156, 198, 206, 209, 226, 260n.86
Tripp, C. A. 168–9, 235–6
Trocchi, Alexander 262–3, 269
Tyler, Parker 11, 34, 39–40, 149

Van Sant, Gus 242–3
Van Vechten, Karl 7, 10, 39–40, 42, 130

Index

Vidal, Gore 7, 8, 9–10, 103, 169, 174, 177, 191, 194, 209, 226, 234–5, 237
Vining, Donald 8, 94, 122–3, 174–5
violence 51, 89, 92, 97–101, 134, 201–4, 216–21, 240, 266, 269
Voight, Jon 78, 189, 216, 240

Ward, Tony 244–5
Warhol, Andy 7, 130, 175, 189, 196–200, 205–6, 213, 219, 224–7, 255–6
Watson, Steven 39
Waugh, Thomas 189, 213, 255
Wescott, Glenway 8, 42
West, Mae 148

Whitaker, Rick 250
White, Edmund 12–13, 98, 169–170, 237
White, Kevin 34, 50
Williams, Tennessee 8–10, 16, 86–7, 93–4, 96–7, 175, 191–4, 199–200, 203, 213, 217–18, 226
Wilson, Lanford 79, 190, 226
Windham, Donald 10, 97–8
Wojnarowicz, David 226–7, 240–2, 267–8
Woodlawn, Holly 7, 23
Worby, John 104, 155
Wright, Charles 189

YMCA 10, 16, 37, 87

EU authorised representative for GPSR:
Easy Access System Europe, Mustamäe tee 50,
10621 Tallinn, Estonia
gpsr.requests@easproject.com

www.ingramcontent.com/pod-product-compliance
Lightning Source LLC
Chambersburg PA
CBHW050209240426
43671CB00013B/2271